Paul Stump contribute
popular culture to *The*
Harpers & Queen, The
Statesman. The Music's
book. He is currently wri
of Roxy Music.

....al al biography

THE
MUSIC'S *ALL* THAT MATTERS
PAUL STUMP A HISTORY OF
PROGRESSIVE ROCK
QUARTET BOOKS

First published in Great Britain by
Quartet Books Limited in 1997
A member of the Namara Group
27 Goodge Street
London W1P 2LD

A catalogue record for this book is available from the
British Library

ISBN 0 7043 8036 6

Printed and bound in Finland by WSOY

CONTENTS

THE
MUSIC'S ALL THAT MATTERS

PREFACE: AUTHOR 'NOT MAD' SHOCK

More than a few of the various people who subjected themselves to interview for this book observed (gratifyingly) that I seemed 'far too young' to write about Progressive rock. Plenty of others observed (less gratifyingly) that I seemed 'far too sane' to do so.

Neither is strictly true. I was just about old enough to catch the end of the genre's glory days when it was still dithering under a parodistic gaggle of fatuous rubrics: Progressive rock, techno-rock, flash-rock, art-rock, pomp-rock, (almost all of them flawed). I was fourteen; my family was living in Newport in South Wales. Perhaps I needed an escape route. The reason that my father brought home a cassette copy of Genesis's 1978 album *And Then There were Three* was, I suspect, as much to listen to it himself on headphones while visiting the dentist as for my own delectation.

The record was about a year old; as with many defining

records, its status has since shrunk from staple to shelf-filler in my collection, its gelatinous textures and toothsomely sweet melodies far from what I'd now term classically Progressive. But I loved it then; for a musical devotee whose favourites included Tchaikovsky and the Sex Pistols, this was something very *different*; it was musically and emotionally broader in scope than anything in the charts, apart from maybe 'Oliver's Army' by Elvis Costello.

But hold hard! Why was this music so roundly abominated by the men who knew (*sic*), the rock press? Sure, Special AKA, the Mekons and the Fall were great – but so was this. I went on to discover similar music; Yes, ELP, Steve Hackett, The Enid – only to encounter not simply the same attitude, but a venomous intensification of it.

I was witnessing the start of the cultural exile of all such music, which would be conveniently abandoned in the categorized ghetto of Progressive rock. The quibbling about generic titles in the 1970s now gave way to a blanket condemnation of all the music that, to me, seemed to occupy just as important a position as the music of John Cooper Clarke.

So began a long and painful engagement with the vagaries of the UK's musical cognoscenti; to this day I still haven't discovered exactly what, intrinsically, is so wrong with Progressive rock as a genre. True, it seethes with ordure, groans with junk, but it also contains some of rock and pop's most glittering inspirations. More than in any other part of rock's galaxy, there is extraordinary fecundity in its music. As the Progressive bassist Cliff Orsi asserted in an excellent article for the Classic Rock Appreciation Society, Progressive, for all its faults, was one of the few genres of rock in which almost every proponent sounded original, different and individual. This did not guarantee quality, but it at least kindled interest. Yet Progressive remains bedevilled by criticisms far more obsolete than the music itself. In 1979, these criticisms were excusable; now, they are not. Progressive rock deserves putting into context, it deserves reappraisal, it deserves a fair trial. Its obsolescence, its cultural illegitimacy, is now taken for granted; during this book's assembly, the (otherwise excellent) BBC–TV history of rock and roll, *Dancing in the Street,* dismissed Progressive as a mere footnote, in which unless songs were at least twenty minutes long they weren't thought worth their salt. Is there any other realm of the arts and entertainments where such a breathtakingly cavalier judgement at such a prestigious level of historical evaluation – television – could be allowed to go unchallenged? It is difficult to imagine a TV programme writing off the marginalized currents of other artistic spheres so casually. Would they dismiss Wyndham Lewis and the Vorticists as 'fascist oafs', Fauvists as 'primary-colour daubers' or Beat poets as 'illiterates' in a similarly philistine vein? Hardly.

I realize that this book will only partly redeem this situation. I realize also that many readers will, at some point of dismissal, hurl this book across the room in pique. The subject, broad enough as it is, has assumed an extra cultic dimension and encouraged greater specialization through the marginalizing tendencies of the modern (and postmodern) cultural drift. I have, therefore, steeled myself for furious reproaches from fans of Caravan, Camel, Renaissance and others; ditto the whinges of completists and of musicians whose already tinder-dry egos have been rendered yet more volatile by years of neglect (justified or otherwise). Pleasing everyone is impossible. I have also made every effort to ensure accuracy, but I'm sure someone in Trowbridge or Steeple Bumpstead – with every single Strawbs/Curved Air/Greenslade LP under his bed – will be able to locate errors. I also apologize (this time unreservedly) to non-British readers. I realize that each country tackled the Progressive project in its own way (even Chile did, but that's another story). To Americans, Germans, French and especially Italians, I'm sorry. But as I hope will become clear, Progressive rock, more than any other genre in the rock canon, fed on quintessentially British cultural formations.

As I outline further on, I want this book to perform three functions: to address the topic critically (a first, to my knowledge) with the hindsight and experience that twenty years or so gives us; to allow those old enough a nostalgic chuckle or two; and to encourage others to investigate and reappraise Progressive – or indeed any kind of rock music – with an ear for the *music* as well as an eye for the social conditions surrounding its production. The book was written between January and autumn 1996. It coincided with the final year of a four-year honours degree course at the University of East London, and I would like to thank the staffs of the European Studies and French Departments for their indulgence. The interviewees for this book should have been far more numerous; most regrettably, circumstances beyond my control led to my cancelling an interview opportunity with Robert Fripp of King Crimson in March. While unwilling to talk about this music, Fripp intended to talk about the music industry in the UK in the 1970s. No rescheduling opportunity arose, but I am none the less grateful to him for his kindness and patience in our dealings on the telephone, and for his supplying me with a dossier detailing his ongoing legal proceedings with EG Records. Similar clashes led to the cancellation of an interview with Fish of Marillion, who also must be thanked for his understanding and interest in the project.

Sincere thanks to those who were interviewed, particularly to Bill Bruford, whose own contributions, professionalism and goodwill are to be commended; Anthony Phillips, for the meal in the caff; Steve Hackett, for the minicassettes – some of the interview didn't come out, I'm afraid, but the section on Genesis would have been impossible without him – John Peel, for the hospitality and wine; Dave Stewart, for encouragement; Chris Cutler, for intellectual inspiration; Tom Newman, for being a great interviewee, and for the addresses; Mike Stobbie; Cliff Orsi; Paddy of Moria Falls; Pete Sinfield, for a terrific afternoon; Robert Wyatt and Alfreda, for everything. Thanks also to Glenn Sweeney, Paul Schütze, Roger Dean and Robert John Godfrey for their interviews and sundry kindnesses.

Also thanks to Rob Ayling and the extraordinary Voiceprint undertaking; Mark Sinker; Paul Higgs; Una Clarke; Leah, Nick and Bob Price; Julie Rudge; Tony Herrington, Rob Young and Mike Barnes at *The Wire*; John Bland and Andy Aliffe for services above and beyond the call of sanity; Rowan, Nicki and Emma

Stump (family credits); Ian Pegington, Wieke van der Graaf; Alan and Steve Freeman at Ultima Thule; Bernard Gueffier; Francis Grosse and Alain Robert at Muséa; Rupert Christiansen; John Preston; Marina Benjamin; Michäel Schneider; Isabelle Durand; Pete Gray, Phil Howitt; Geir Hasnes; Simon Bullivant; Ged Parsons; Alistair McGowan and Ronnie Ancona; Paul Evans; and for their kindness, patience and warmth, the Chaigné family of Luisant, France (Yolande, Michel, Céline and, particularly, Christelle, to whom I dedicate this book).

INTRODUCTION

Contrary to received opinion, Progressive rock's main trouble isn't self-indulgence. It isn't critical ignorance or illiteracy. It isn't even pretentiousness (an epithet the music's progenitors so often bear with patient stoicism). Oh no. Progressive's problem is its name.

Progressive rock is maybe the most self-consciously 'adjectival' genre in all rock; its very name implies intrinsic properties. This is rock which, evidently, 'progresses'. Already we are head down in the brambles with our legs in the air ... apart from the nature of the progression itself, can rock be said to progress?

Such questions aren't directly this book's concerns.

This book is concerned with first defining and then examining the phenomenon of Progressive rock. Most, if not all, of the people I've interviewed have asked me how I define Progressive; not a few have been suspicious of being classified under its rubric. With the press Progressive has had, I don't blame them. But perhaps that's the trouble: the music's reputation. Progressive rock is a vague and pejorative term, a kind of virtual category, most commonly associated with the ambitious rock experiment-alism of the 1970s, when popular music's three-minute parameters split asunder, and the music suddenly found itself stretched in all directions, aspiring after artistic significance one minute, political relevance the next. Progressive rock was the soundtrack to the counter-cultural upheavals of the late 1960s, and the period's gallant pipedream of thoroughgoing societal and cultural transformation.

Rock was seen as part of a 'progressive' culture, and all forms of the music were deemed 'progressive' that appeared to defy commercial precedents. In time, however, the term was reserved for a diffuse collection of musics characterized by high degrees of instrumental and compositional complexity. Commonplace rock trappings – beat and melody – were withheld in favour of executive musical expertise as a criterion of absolute value; composition and construction were deemed equally valid means of 'expression' as spontaneous creativity; cultural/social relevance was sought through cross-pollination from other musics such as folk, classical and jazz.

Since the demise of this extended and often overblown form in the late 1970s along with the commensurate rise of its antipode, the ultra-fundamentalist and blue-collar-basic Punk, critical opinion has begun to concretize the term 'Progressive' as representing *any form of rock music which foregrounds musical expression as a discrete and sovereign means of communication*; whereby the performance strives, or appears to strive, to extend popular music beyond the confines of the run-of-the-mill pop song and conventional song structures; where the music tries to attain a cultural 'otherness' distinct from rock or pop conventions.

But hasn't Rave culture effectively condemned the three-minute rule to the ashcan of history? Don't the Residents and Pere Ubu and other US and European avant-garde outfits play similar games with rock? Answer: yes, they do. But they do so without the specific heritage of music-making that makes true Progressive unique.

In a way the title of this book is a lie. The music is *not* all that matters. The ideology – the Progressive ideology – of artistic idealism in British pop music trails a continuous *cultural* thread back to the 1940s. The art-school tradition with its championing of individual creativity, genius and Romantic personal adventurism in the arts, informed many strands of British popular music, but a specific coincidence of cultural, social and economic conditions in the mid- and late 1960s facilitated the making of music for music's sake. It is the heritage of this phenomenon that I have attempted to trace.

Most of my interviewees deny the existence of 'Progressive rock' as an entity, accepting it merely as a convenient label invented by journalists after the event. I share their cynicism, but also think the application of the term 'Progressive' to the likes of Peter Gabriel, the 1990s incarnation of King Crimson, and even to free improvisers such as Chris Cutler is accurate. What unites all these musicians is a shared Progressive ideology of rock utterance; that hankering after a rock-derived 'sublime' which forms the core of Progressive rock music.

Progressive musicians, if their A&R staff were to be believed, weren't just rock musicians. They were – in the 1970s, anyway – 'artists', driven by high Romantic notions of personal expression and originality, individual authenticity, honesty and similar praiseworthy universals. Theirs was a music (those same publicists assured us) that never stood still, scorned convention, was in a state of permanent evolution – in contrast to the mercenary, stereotypical contemporary pop against which it was marketed. Indeed a vocal minority of Progressive musicians adopted genuinely radical revolutionary artistic and political viewpoints and splinted their musical experimentation with rigorous theoretical radicalism. These men and women represented a different facet of Progressive rock to that popularly and fatuously paraded as the genre's ideal-type (show-off stadium rockers) and their contributions – the Rock In Opposition heritage of Henry Cow, the Art Bears and Recommended Records, as well as selected others – occupy a central place in this book alongside more traditional exponents of the genre such as Genesis and Yes. All in all, they combined to create the most distinctively English and compositionally controversial of all rock and pop forms (which is why I concentrate almost entirely on the British Isles in my study).

My aim is to expose the complexities and contradictions of a brand of music and rock inspiration all too often dismissed as a hopelessly effete, excessive musical movement rightly swept aside after Punk's timely invasion of British rock in 1976–7. As a logical extension of this argument, I wish to explain the decline in Progressive's fortunes thereafter, and more seriously, examine the critical and commercial limbo to which it has since succumbed.

I do not believe that Punk (which, in Logan and Woffinden's words in *The NME Encyclopedia of Rock*, sought 'to make rock and roll angry once more ... to restore its relevance to the street'[1]) was solely responsible for the demise of Progressive rock. Progressive's Baroque and recondite agendas had already distanced it from cultural consumers in the cash-strapped 1970s, and its pricey preoccupation with ambition in terms of music-making alienated record companies.

Subsequent discourse on Progressive has unblinkingly portrayed it as a kind of monstrous historical aberration, a musical Third Reich, that seemed to have no cultural remit even for existing in the first place. But blanket and unreasoning demonologies never help understanding, and it is this attitude that I wish to challenge. No matter what one's opinion of it, Progressive should be judged in its historical context and musically reassessed with this in mind.

It's too easy to maintain about Progressive rock, as routine rock discourse has it, that it died out, as the comedian Alexei Sayle once said of music hall, 'because it was crap'. If nothing else, this presupposes its supplanting by something new and better. Heavy Metal, one-time 1960s sibling of Progressive and its eventual replacement in the hearts and minds of Progressive's predominantly white bourgeois adolescent male commercial constituency, could hardly be said to have 'improved' on Progressive; Progressive's chief crimes against good taste, its excess and bombast, are wildly magnified in Heavy Metal. A low-key Heavy Metal band is simply an oxymoronic proposition. That style's reliance on musical virtuosity and camp clichés of the spectacular recalls progressive, but its exaggeration of them to comic-book stature should, ideally, guarantee that it is seen as even more redundant than its ill-fated sister genre. But Heavy Metal continues to flourish worldwide.

Postmodernity has seen to it that relativism in cultural discourse has enabled Heavy Metal to take its place in the critical pantheon of rock. Postmodernity relativistic emphasis on the impossibility of assigning absolute value to artistic endeavour, the absence of any superiority of one cultural commodity over another, has ensured the critical re-evaluation of Heavy Metal, as it has done with Country and Western. Once derided as little more than a sentimental, spangled sewer of proto-Confederate cack, it has now been substantially reappraised, not just through the sacrament of new blood from the likes of Nanci Griffith and Dwight Yoakam, but as a genre *per se*. Importantly, the reappraisals of such musics have not been simply ironic, satirical gestures from smartass rock critics; Heavy Metal crucifixes and leathers and hillbilly laments for dead dogs and vanished lovers are no longer just kitsch toys. The rock press has responded to the renewed market clout of such things by allotting them some measure of reasoned coverage. Not so with Progressive. Unknown because unloved, unloved because unknown, it has not even attained respectability at the time of writing, even in a decade obsessed with 1970s revivalism.

As rock's self-inflationary tendencies grow ever greater (step forward, U2 and your *Zoo TV* beano), can the charge of over-ambitiousness still be realistically levelled at Progressive? The latter half of the 1980s, in the wake of Live Aid's (and MTV's) successful globalization of rock corporatism (excess, self-indulgence and unreconstructed old-codgerism) have seen the establishment of a culture in rock that makes the big guns of Progressive rock's pomp seem like ascetic and virtuous Stakhanovites by comparison.

Not that this bothers the media, specifically the rock press. Their continued taboo on discussion of Progressive as anything but a stain on rock history needs to be suspended if any kind of reappraisal of Progressive is to occur.

One problem with Progressive's critical reception has revolved around the question of the music itself. The complexity of Progressive's discourse – the esoteric nature of its practice – has been a cause of much critical disquiet. Technical ability is anathema to rock criticism to a degree found in no other cultural sphere. The saloon-bar reaction to this in the musicians' community is that such critiques emanate from frustrated musicians; I would suggest that the predication of Progressive on the content *and* form of music has opened up this abyss between itself and criticism.

That is why this book concentrates primarily on *music*. Simon Frith, who once claimed that Disco was musically more 'interesting' than Progressive rock, can nevertheless state just as blithely his 'ignorance' of the technique of musical composition.[2] While one could cite Dr Johnson's celebrated rejoinder that 'I may not know how to make a chair, but I know a good chair when I see one', it is also worth considering the words of musicologist Allan Moore:

> The problem is that a commentary that does not have a sound theoretical underpinning is likely to be of uncertain quality at best. Certainly no sociologist would attempt to explain ... the role of the record companies in the changing business of popular music without having an acceptable framework of cultural theory on which to base it ...[3]

I am not a musicologist. Neither, I am sure, are many of my readers. Neither, I am even more sure, are many musicians reading this. But as Moore states, musicology is 'an interdisciplinary' affair.[4] That is why I believe that the Progressive phenomenon must be examined not only musically, but also in terms of the ideological and cultural ephemera that both bore and emerged from the creation of that music. It must therefore be explained in terms of contemporary developments in cultural affairs generally, even in politics, economics, and contemporary attitudes to sex and race. Moreover, as Moore puts it, rock must be understood on its own terms, not on the terms of concert music or indeed ethnic or any other music. As he rightly states, 'the norms of this [critical] tradition leave untouched those very factors where rock can be at its most interesting (and complex and profound): timbre, texture, sound manipulation, performance practice etc'.[5] But to that end, the social conditions of its production must also be taken into account. This must also embrace a study of how Progressive relates to postmodernism, a curiously overlooked kinship raising many interesting points which, I hope, will enable us to look again at the place of Progressive in rock history.

The inaugural nature of this study will doubtless render it flawed; but as I have stressed, it is not opinions I wish to reinforce in this book but discussion that I want to inspire. And aren't stories about ELP's carpeted stages and Yes's cardboard cows a bloody good laugh, too?

I wish to avoid overt over-intellectualization – precisely the accusation most frequently levelled at Progressive. Additionally, I am aware that my approach may alienate many Progressive followers who have waited too long for a study of this sometimes inspired, sometimes repugnant but always fascinating music. To them I would say: stick at it. The mythos of Progressive rock, both that which it has itself nurtured and that of popular critical discourse, are my chief targets. Much rewriting is being done here. Intellect, however, for better or worse, was a Progressive selling-point.

One Progressive musician told me: 'Progressive rock was typically British. Inspired amateurism – like Churchill and his brick wall, like the Beatles.' Now this is hardly accepted wisdom, is it? This doesn't equate with the accepted wisdom of the music as middle-class head-trip, does it, the hyper-professional rock-as-athletics, rock-as-spectacle monster of the Progressive of legend? Yet this musician was *there, closer than most to the action*. What *can* he mean?

I believe that such an approach is essential for just the reason that people *have* waited a long time. After such an unjustified delay their music deserves a dignified and thorough hearing. One of Progressive's proudest boasts was that it was 'thinking' music.

This was often far from true; Progressive's personnel, on both sides of the stage or studio glass, were often too engrossed in the consumption and production of a spectacle to think about music beyond swallowing record-company bromides about it coming straight from the heart and the head. This book tries to make up for this intellectual gap. If Progressive followers really *do* think about their music more than pop fans do, this is their chance to prove it.

My opinion is that Progressive has produced some of the finest of all rock and pop music. Its achievements, past and present, real or imagined, deserve a more reasoned reaction than knee-jerk dismissal or cheap hagiography. Bearing that in mind, it needs, therefore, to be repeated that the main reason for writing this book is that it's high time someone did.

1 DUFFEL COATS FROM OUTER SPACE
(BOHEMIA, ART SCHOOLS AND POP)

FROM ART SCHOOL TO HEAVEN

In 1991 the writer and director Hanif Kureishi wrote: 'Throughout the second half of the 1960s, the Beatles functioned as that rare but necessary and important channel, popularizers of esoteric ideas ... [they were] the only mere pop group you could remove from history and suggest that, culturally, things would have been significantly different.'[1]

Kureishi's thesis was simple: not only did the Beatles change music beyond recognition in the 1960s, they also changed society; or, at the very least, the changes that took place in 1960s Britain would have been unthinkable without them.

'When the mode of the music changes, the walls of the city

shake.' So went the 1960s axiom. Period fantasy? Kureishi's claims, provocatively fanciful and superficially unrelated to this book, do however make an ideal starting point for it. Progressive, creature of the 1970s, could not have been created without those aspects of the 1960s that might never have reached mainstream cultural awareness had the Beatles not existed.

One of the most substantial of the Beatles' achievements was their transformation of the popular song. Originating in Liverpool in the late 1950s, their initial passion for no-holds-barred rock'n'roll knew no bounds. 'What a lot of fucking shit you play,' John Lennon told the Liverpool College of Art music club, referring to their predilection for Miles Davis and the MJQ. 'Why don't you play something proper – like Chuck Berry?'[2] Lennon retained a lifelong passion for rock'n'roll, but quite apart from Lennon's crude defence of his musical loves, most critics agree, that the music that made the Beatles famous owed its success to its Englishness, or at least its dilution of Americanness. The Beatles were still castigated by the British left for being surrogate agents of US cultural imperialism, but what is perhaps most remarkable about the Beatles' music is its *difference* from the American-derived rock argot of the day. It used blues and R&B voicings, yet in wholly new ways redolent of whistleable British street-corner song ('She Loves You'). Not that this was a process beyond Americans – throughout the 1960s, Brian Wilson of the Beach Boys collaged traditional harmonies of all kinds, from bluegrass to blues to Baroque. But as producer Joe Boyd claims: 'In a way, the best groups ... the ones who did best in America, were the ones who were quite unafraid to be English.'[3] The Beatles defined themselves irreversibly as English musicians by redefining English music. It is perhaps facile to date this stylistic divergence so precisely, but George Harrison's use of sitar on *Revolver*'s 'Norwegian Wood' is perhaps a start.

Sitar playing may not be an English bifurcation, but it sure as hell isn't American either. Such ethnic influences that informed American popular music were derived from territories over which America enjoyed post-war hegemony: Hawaiian steel guitars, mariachi bands, echoing in the minds of posted GI or package holidaymaker. The sitar in 'Norwegian Wood' was quite different; few Britons felt any cultural ties with the Indian subcontinent beyond those roused by handing fares to Bengali bus conductors, consulting Sikh doctors and evading eye contact with both. Additionally, and crucially, the degree of compositional autonomy which the Beatles publicly flaunted – hey, these boys can write as well as sing! – lent them the air of precocious schoolkids. Until then, ethnicity in music had been as much the property of mood-music studio technocrats such as Martin Denny or big-band maestri like Perez Prado, industry-approved arbiters of taste who effortlessly manipulated the mass-musical tastebuds of the Western world. The novelty of the Beatles' own initiative in this field underlined the fact that the Beatles were Different. Pop was supposed to be loud, noisy, irresponsible. And now these uppity yobs had overturned every stereotype in the book. The Beatles made cultural divergence a *mass* cultural property. The brought the horizon closer for an entire nation.

True, Jeff Beck's raga-derived 'drone' effect on the Yardbirds' 'Still I'm Sad' (1965) predated 'Norwegian Wood'. And the modern jazzers (John Coltrane, Miles Davis, Horace Silver) so influential to the art-school cadre of young rock musicians had long since been inducting Third World harmonic and melodic inflections into their output. But when the Beatles did it, people sat up and took notice. As Derek Taylor, the Beatles' PR genius, noted: 'They had the capacity of very attractive children for getting away with it.'[4] There was experimentation at the very forefront of popular culture. Suddenly the unthinkable was not only thinkable but attainable as well.

The ambition that drove the Beatles had surfaced elsewhere: Stan Kenton's revolutionizing of the big-band sound with 'symphonic' jazz, the cross-cultural experiments of Gil Evans and Miles Davis, and the sweeping strings introduced into the conventional jazz big band by the likes of Gordon Jenkins and Nelson Riddle had lent a new sophistication and ambition to popular arranging. Leonard Bernstein's *West Side Story* had revitalized a moribund Broadway with lyrical, musical and scenic grit; the works of Stephen Sondheim and the likes of *On a Clear Day You Can See Forever* also introduced a new breadth of dramaturgy to feel-good musical theatre. The bursting of the rock 'n' roll bubble had not occurred, with the genre attractively made over by moguls; the kids were obviously not willing to discard rock'n'roll, and with even their parents taking an interest as the early excesses of rock became the anodyne Bobby-era sounds of Vee, Vinton *et al.*, in the early 1960s, the wilier majors began investing in its production to appeal to kids and elders alike. How else would Phil Spector have been expected to produce the staggering euphony of his mid-1960s epic singles? With material input and precocious genius from Spector and Brian Wilson, the pop single swiftly shed its three-minute straightjacket. Pop songwriters began writing with the possibilities of the new medium in mind. Bert Bacharach and Hal David grew into pop songwriters knowing there would be sizeable forces there to write for, which may explain their subtly nuanced harmonies.

Music was a growing industry. EMI's profits rose 80 per cent in 1963–4 alone (Beatles-driven, but graphs were rising industry-wide). The audience was expanding and diversifying daily – with living standards sprinting ahead in the Western developed economies, hi-fi equipment sold like there was no tomorrow.

And that market had to be catered to; critical theory is unanimous concerning the fact of the low production values of much pop music in the 1950s and early 1960s being attributable to many session musicians believing what they were playing was rubbish and performing accordingly. The music was produced not for reproduction on expensive radiograms, but for small portable machines. Why waste a large orchestra on a 7″ single for a kid in his or her bedroom? But the growth of record reproduction technology (from Liberty's 'Visual Sound Stereo' to Columbia's '360-degree Sound'), driven by competition between rival manufacturers for the custom of an increasingly affluent middle class, not unnaturally led to an improvement in the production values of the records played on this technology. Pursuing the same logic, why have a stereo wonder if there weren't the musical textures there to show off its capabilities? The wonders of the Hollywood Bowl Symphony Orchestra and the 101 Strings could be exploited in the pop marketplace as well as in the MOR marketplace. In short, popular music wised up to the explosion in record-player ownership and the consequent possibilities of reproduction technology in the 1950s and 1960s (which in turn drove down prices and increased further their availability). Technology fed ambition, which fed technology, a deterministic phenomenon we shall return to in the 1970s. This expansion assumed its own dynamic – so pervasive had popular music become, and so rapid its development by the early 1960s, that it must have been difficult to escape the notion of perpetual change but also, to attentive ears, the swift development of harmony and melody.

But in the 1960s these were still experiments. Other musics were forming and re-forming their own constituencies of taste away from the bourgeois arena of pop. Jazz listenership was not exclusively non-bourgeois in the 1950s and 1960s – far from it. Indeed the jazz, input into easy-listening music was considerable, and jazz having been a part of the American subconscious for decades already, elided with the world of showbusiness (Louis Armstrong, Mel Tormé) with considerably greater ease than the parvenu rock'n'rollers, were who welcomed into the showbiz establishment only when suitably groomed.

Nevertheless, a jazz audience existed that was primarily young, questioned bourgeois standards, and was increasingly deracialized (popular music was racially polarized even in the 1950s. Nat 'King' Cole, Johnny Mathis and Lena Horne struck pop crossover gold, but few white stars entertained black audiences. 'Color music' was still a term bandied around rock'n'roll into the 1960s in the USA.) 'Cool' and West Coast jazz, itself a product of a bohemian interracial milieu on both eastern and western American seaboards, enticed through its defiance of accepted popular culture. Kerouac's iconographization of jazz helped set in amber its rebel mythology. Presley's co-option by mainstream society excluded him as a symbol of resistance for those who felt out of kilter with the barbaric consumerism and rigid morals of the 1950s. Too many Beats had read too much Marx for them to embrace anyone associated with mass consumption and, by extension, massive profit-making. Jazz, on the other hand, was nay-saying; it flaunted blackness in colour-barred Western society. 'The great thing about the jazz world,' wrote Colin MacInnes in *Absolute Beginners*, 'is that no one, not a soul, cares what your class is, or what your race is.'[5]

British bandleader Humphrey Lyttelton was motivated to play jazz in his evenings off from art school in the late 1940s; but his rejection of the norms of 1930s dance hall jazz, of stylized band uniforms and an embrace of early black US influences seemed to claim jazz for a new audience, one which turned its back on the popular music of their parents. The harmonic and formal explorations of be-bop, West Coast and 'cool' jazz helped concretize the attitude towards the music among young people of the 1950s: it was seen as radical and unconventional, the soundtrack to art-school life in Britain in that decade.

In Frith's words, 'jazz was art school music on both counts: as a form of emotional and physical expression subversive of polite concert hall tradition and as something more complex, truthful ... than the Light Programme and the High Street hit parade.'[6] These elitist implications were mirrored by the practices of jazz fans: the obsessive collection of recordings, discussion, criticism. Purist jazz's distance from crass/mass commercial concerns foregrounded the cult of Romantic creativity: 'to the Romantic and Expressionist artist, particularly, the element of improvisation, of spontaneous creation and swift, almost intuitive interpretation of a theme which is present in jazz of all periods, seems an echo of the extempore nature of much of his own work.'[7]

The popularity of jazz among students (predominantly – though not exclusively – of art colleges) made inevitable its elision with contemporary art chic (surrealism, abstract expressionism, Beat literature, existentialism). To a lesser degree it also provided a soundtrack to the frivolous surrealism of arts balls, which would provide the young Beatles, the Temperance Seven and giggle-rock anarchists the Bonzo Dog Band with early public platforms.

Indeed jazz's two-fingered image became a vital plank on the platforms for disruption upon which 1960s alternative culture matured; CND's Aldermaston marches, for instance, were full of jazz fans. Writer Jeff Nuttall says: 'On the march you got pacifists ... Quakers ... and you had the beatniks who suddenly emerged ... nobody had known about them outside ... Soho coffee bars and jazz clubs.'[8] Jazz's blackness lured; underground impresario Barry Miles recalls: 'Black people were the only ones who knew about jazz ... They also smoked rather good dope.'[9]

The cocktail of forbidden music, forbidden substances and forbidden company kindled a West London counter-culture mirrored in other British cities with black presences; for the first time middle-class white youth was in contact with working-class black culture and through it discerned a means to defy a perceived   middle- upper-class Establishment. The cut-up culture of Andy Warhol and Allen Ginsberg was, like that of Jackson Pollock and Roy Lichtenstein, another slap in the face for cultural normalcy (the Beat Hotel in Paris was a also cultural nerve-centre for the avant-garde of Europe in the early 1960s, with William Burroughs in permanent residence and Ginsberg, Gregory Corso and Laurence Ferlinghetti in attendance).

The Beat Hotel was also patronized by Australian beatnik Daevid Allen, an experimental poet who'd hung around the Paris scene and played a little jazz in 1961 before meeting Robert Wyatt, a comfortably-off if academically under-qualified jazz fanatic, in London. Wyatt was himself something of a Europhile, and during summer holidays patronized the Beat-exile hotbed of Deya in Majorca, befriending the jazz-loving English novelist Robert Graves there. Wyatt and Allen formed a jazz trio which debuted at London's _über_-chic Establishment Club in 1963, with a friend of Wyatt's, Hugh Hopper, asked to provide experimental tape loops for Allen's increasingly ambitious poetry readings.

Certainly the influences of this trio were the suitably iconoclastic: Cecil Taylor, Ornette Coleman and John Coltrane. Allen left for Paris shortly afterwards; keyboardist Mike Ratledge, who had jammed with the trio, then helped Wyatt and Hopper form the Wilde Flowers, who began gigging actively in and around Canterbury in Kent. Wyatt remembers:

> We just played covers that we could play – we collected Don Covay and Solomon Burke records, and the simpler jazz things of the time – Cannonball Adderley doing soul tunes. There was some soul. You take Booker T and the MGs: it's very easy to move from that to Jimmy Smith and on into jazz. It wasn't that we even particularly played like that but that was our education.
>
> The paradox was that the English scene was very black, much more so than the American, and the Scottish scene was even blacker than that, with your Average White Bands and Jack Bruces – steeped in soul. As far as we were concerned, there was already something called progressive rock – which was jazz.[10]

(One record company executive later told Wyatt: 'I don't know if you're our worst-selling pop act or our biggest-selling jazz act.')[11] Despite the preponderance of standards, of Chuck Berry and Ray Charles numbers, bassist Hopper told the local press that the band were aiming for an 'Indian influence' which, given the material available from the period, seems a trifle disingenuous.[12] But – as Hopper later maintained – it's undeniable that 'He's Bad for You' does indeed combine 'Elvin Jones and John Coltrane and has a special atmosphere which is very representative of quite a lot of the early Wilde Flowers sounds – combining jazz, Eastern influences etc.'[13]

Wyatt had dreams:

> One of the characteristics of pop music that I didn't like is the fact that it was based on guitar. I wanted to work with instruments that could give you uninterrupted sounds, totally sustained. I wanted to work with a keyboard player, except all the keyboard players at this time were some bad imitation of Jimmy Smith or Booker T. But that wasn't the case with Mike [Ratledge]. He was using his knowledge as a keyboard player,

who were generally speaking more technically competent than the guitar players of the time.[14]

In an article written for the *Kent Observer* in 1966 Wyatt also writes warmly of the effects of microphones and tape recorders in modern jazz.[15]

By this time the Wilde Flowers had changed their name to the considerably more resonant and contemporary-sounding Soft Machine, named after Burroughs's novel (with an eye on their audience?) although long-time Softs member Jimmy Hastings claims: 'I never even read it.'[16]

FREAK ALERT

Between 1961 and 1964 the London underground took shape around this loose coalescence of jazz, Beat poetry and avant-garde art. Barry Miles organized a poetry reading featuring Ginsberg, Ferlinghetti and Corso in the Albert Hall in June 1965 (an ironic prefiguring of the gigantism to which Progressive would later fall victim?); disruptive 'happenings', inspired by avant-garde currents (specifically surrealism and Dada), were more frequent – the artistic *zeitgeist* with shock tactics.

Musical anti-commercialists also found a refuge in folk, and found themselves bitterly divided over their hero Bob Dylan's 1965 adoption of 'electric instruments' – a heresy in folk, for the intervention of electricity effectively placed the expression of the individual performer in the mediating and meddling hands of promoters and hucksters. But the desire for expressions of non-commercial 'authenticity' in music-making also, paradoxically, brought adherents flocking to the electric blues boom of the early 1960s in the UK – the music of Cyril Davies, Alexis Korner and the Rolling Stones.

The Stones' 1965 visit to San Francisco is quoted as perhaps *the* seminal event in the coupling of rock and avant-garde art, suggesting that commercial credentials and authenticity of expression could apparently coexist. They were English, but playing black American music. Their ideological purity could not be doubted but they also sold thousands of records. Frith quotes

Ron Nagle, a ceramics graduate from San Francisco State College, who was inspired by the event to form a band, which was '... an excuse to get up there and act weird. It was the art-school mentality. A lot of English groups had come out of art schools just like us and the only guys around the city who had long hair then were artists too.'[17] To this party came the aid of the Happening, a multimedia, polysensory riot of experimentation which in the case of the Charlatans, San Francisco's first major-league psychedelic band, used light projected through liquid pigments, long a staple of Californian avant-garde performance.

In 1964, Drs Timothy Leary, Ralph Metzner and Richard Alpert endorsed freak culture with the publication of their *The Psychedelic Experience*, which took the hallucinogenic panaceas of Huxley's *The Doors of Perception* out of their author's original ultra-elitist context (i.e. LSD as the visionary enlightenment for the initiate and genius few) and encouraged the *masses* to 'turn on, tune in and drop out'.

The art-school preoccupation with art's sacred stature, the primacy of individual expression, had been filtered through jazz to young British musicians who now saw the Beatles pointing a guitar-led route to riches. In addition, with Dylan's apparent harnessing of 'authentic' musical forms (irrespective of folk-purist whinges) to high avant-garde poetic art, which garnered some highbrow interest in popular culture, the scene was set – Romantic ideology among musicians and a receptive audience for the ideology – for a new mode of expression in British rock.

For the underground, jazz was still the crucial music of resistance, particularly as its cutting-edge proponents, Ornette Coleman, John Coltrane and Archie Shepp, seemed to be diving headlong into the sort of abstractions visible elsewhere in the arts, but as John Dunbar perceptively notes, when the Beatles headed Londonwards in 1965, rock and roll suddenly became fashionable too.[18]

TURNING ON
Rock writer Nicholas Schaffner proclaims – unarguably – that the 'house orchestra' of this community was the Pink Floyd.[19]

Formed by Regent Street Polytechnic architecture student (and amateur bassist) Roger Waters in 1965 with school-buddy guitarist Syd Barrett (a student at Camberwell art college), fellow architecture student and drummer Nick Mason and Rick Wright (an ex-Poly student) on keyboards, the bank had originated in a ramshackle combo called the Abdabs. Barrett and fellow guitarist Brian Close had joined Mason, Waters and Wright's Sigma 3, which became the T-Set, the Screaming Abdabs and then the Abdabs, utilizing the voice of Juliette Gale (later Mrs Rick Wright). After her (and Close's) departure, the subsequent line-up, named Pink Floyd by Barrett through the simple conflation of the names of two Louisiana bluesmen, Pink Anderson and Floyd Council, proposed something entirely new within a classic Beat band formula.

'During the solo instrumental bits, I couldn't work out if the guitar or the keyboards were playing, recalled Peter Jenner.[20] Sonic extremity, added to the *outré* nature of Barrett's lyrics, lent a whimsical grandeur to the early Floyd that infatuated the underground, along with pick-up avant-garde orchestra AMM, for whom 'all noise [was] music'.[21] AMM's was an aleatory, improvised act complete with white coats, lab effects, hand-crafted instruments and wall-to-wall free extemporization at Spontaneous Underground Sunday-afternoon happenings. John Hopkins made a John Cage comparison: '*sounds* were being played'.[22]

By 1966, posters were proclaiming the Floyd as 'London's farthest out group'. Nobody else was doing what the Floyd were doing, not only musically but also in imagistic terms. Whereas AMM were of recognizably avant-garde jazz/classical descent, Pink Floyd were, when all was said and done, run-of-the-mill pop musicians who happened to be in the right place at the right time to let heart and head run wild. Their lightshows were handled by art students, notably by a slide/oil system developed at Hornsey by 'destruction' artist Mark Boyle, who declared: 'The most complete change an individual can effect on his environment, short of destroying it, is to change the attitudes towards it.'[23]

Clearly what was at stake here was no longer simply music, but the entire artistic realm, a striving towards *Gesamtkunstwerk* that the modernist pioneer and archangel of Romanticism, Richard Wagner, would have recognized; music, once again, sat at the centre of a multi-artistic endeavour. As one 1960s survivor said: 'There was always cash floating about in the music business – it was the engine room of the underground.'[24]

The first notable public manifestation of this 'avant-garde Beat', as it was tentatively labelled, was at the October 1966 launch of *International Times*. This was to be celebrated with an 'All Night Rave' at the Roundhouse, a disused building in north London which had once housed the equipment used to winch early steam trains up the gradient from Euston Station in the 1830s. 'We developed some really ludicrous polaroid effects, with a polarizer and analyser in the projector, stretching polythene and latex rubber,'[25] one Roundhouse stalwart later claimed.

Soft Machine were present, and also provided services as house band alongside Pink Floyd at the newly-opened UFO Club in London's Tottenham Court Road in December 1966. Early suggestions of Progressive aesthetics crystallize yet further with Wyatt's memories of the predominantly seated audience at the UFO. 'It's impossible if you've got a room full of beer-swigging people standing up waiting for action, it's very hard starting with a drone. But they'd wait half an hour sitting down for the first tune – it was an influence on what the musicians played.'[26] As, presumably, was the reaction of audiences elsewhere. The Softs had segued numbers so that outraged crowds, there to dance, would have no chance to boo. Wyatt asserts that this necessity mothered the band's penchant for long tracks – it also cut the band off from its audience: 'I never had a clue what (people) *really* thought of us.'[27]

While Pink Floyd were cleaning up in London, Soft Machine retained their European links. Having toyed with a variety of names (including the Four Skins), the band had been 'discovered' by US pop entrepreneur Kim Fowley, who produced their first single, 'Love Makes Sweet Music'. It flopped ignominiously, so the Softs retreated once more to the safer terrain of the Continent, met up with Daevid Allen and played in a multimedia production of Pablo Picasso's play *Désir Attrappé par la Queue* ('Desire Caught by the Tail') at the Festival of Free Theatre at Cogolin, which was roughly broken up by the local gendarmerie. On their return to England, Allen was turned back by immigration officials and ended up imprisoned in France. The band's avant-garde credentials were also enhanced by their collaboration in an Edinburgh Festival fringe performance by the Traverse Company of Alfred Jarry's experimental theatre piece *Ubu Roi*.

In terms of the avant-garde, however, everybody was by now trying to out-avant everyone else. John Lennon met Yoko Ono through Barry Miles and McCartney attended lectures on Italian serialist composer Luciano Berio. The Beatles as an entity, fresh from the extraordinary 'Strawberry Fields'/*Revolver* strike out into uncharted waters, planned to go one better with *Sergeant Pepper's Lonely Hearts Club Band*, which would take the language of pop, its melodic and harmonic syntax and, while endeavouring to keep it intact, would subject it to all manner of new calisthenics. While the Floyds and the Softs sought to dismantle that syntax and rebuild it in their own images, the Beatles preserved it, even if the swirling sound turbines of 'Being for the Benefit of Mr Kite' and 'A Day in the Life'.

Pink Floyd and Soft Machine were head honchos on the UFO Club stage, but it soon became apparent that the underground's increasingly visible public profile in the previous months had brought other freaks out of the woodwork. The Move were a kind of prototypical paraffin-powered supergroup, a Brumbeat summit uniting guitarist Roy Wood from Mike Sheridan and the Nightriders, fellow guitarist Trevor Burton from Danny King and the Mayfair Set, exuberant, telly-trashing vocalist Carl Wayne, bass player Ace Kefford and durable drummer Bev Bevan, the backbone of Carl Wayne and the Vikings. Kings of Birmingham's Cedar Club, the Move were lured to a residency at London's Marquee in late 1966. Their debut single, 'Night of Fear', took London's clubland eclecticism on to *Top of the Pops* in an agreeably lite version, Wood politely lifting a line from Tchaikovsky's '1812 Overture'. On stage at least, the Move, recalls Joe Boyd, were 'in a way rather more advanced than Floyd.'[28]

Expatriate Indian tabla player Sam Gopal found himself onstage with his own psychedelic combo, the Sam Gopal Dream, a curious crew which counted among others in its ranks keyboardist Andy Clark from mid-1960s pop no-hopers the Fenmen. Tomorrow, fellow UFO regulars, were a comparable London act; aspirant, acid-additive R'n'Bers, with a pre-Yes Steve Howe 'playing some amazing feedback stuff'.[29] UFO enjoyed immediate success, not least because of its lightshow directed by Mark Boyle. Within three weeks of the UFO opening, 120 light shows had started up within London alone.

'There *was* a visual side to it,' declares Boyle. 'In none of the other music revolutions had there been this visual side.'[30] The ill-fated colouristic experiments of Alexander Scriabin notwithstanding,[31] this was correct; which leads one to the inescapable conclusion that what was under construction here was not just a musical community but an entire leisure *commodity*, one which immediately began generating its own signs and signifiers: dislocation, sensory autonomy, pluralism. The discourse, the Romantic individualism consecrated by the Beats in the 1950s, was beginning to assume its own concrete identity.

Then, inevitably, came the recording industry. By 1967 a measure of a consumerist vinyl culture was already in place, with shops like Musicland, One Stop and Town Records the Meccas for *outré* records. John Peel:

Distribution was basically crap, and outlets were few and far between. But it was good, it *felt* good like that. It lent the whole thing an aura of exclusivity, queuing up waiting for the latest imports from America. But distribution was appalling, especially for radio. In my capacity as 'groovy DJ' that was incredibly frustrating. Record companies knew bugger-all about what they were doing. You'd phone up and ask for a record by someone like Marsupilami, obscure but signed to a major, and they'd know nothing about it. Unless you made contact with the company hippie – obligatory then – you hadn't a hope. Half of the stuff you had to buy. Lots of people still depended on mail-order.[32]

But showbiz was already reconnoitring the underground; as early as 1966, pop entrepreneur Mickie Most approached Soft Machine promising them big-time chart fame – provided they agreed to his artistic terms. The band refused. If nothing else, hitting the Hit Parade might have played in their minds as a possibly retrograde financial step, let alone one of artistic sacrilege; they might have alienated more people than they pleased, and they were already visualizing an audience for an explicitly anti-commercial, anti-singles market, which Led Zeppelin would later so profitably exploit.

Polydor capitalized on both the blues boom and the underground by forming the supergroup Cream from guitar god Eric Clapton and jazz vets Jack Bruce and Ginger Baker. This aggregation swiftly became the embodiment of the new ideology of rock. Simon Frith comments: 'The commitment to musical truth informed an "anti-commercialism" which turned out to have a remarkable selling-power.'[33] Cream's emphasis on solo improvisation within a blues context, their off-the-wall lyrics (courtesy of poet/musician Pete Brown) and psychedelic splurges masquerading as album covers were the first example of the record industry co-opting the Romantic idea of the individual genius to lucrative effect. Polydor also showed interest in Pink Floyd; they were wooed by Joe Boyd, who persuaded them to take on the band with a £1,500 advance. But Polydor vacillated and EMI snapped up the band, characterizing the group as 'representatives of a new movement which involves experimentation in all the arts'.[34]

Pete Jenner asserts, however: 'There was no circuit then for "good" rock music: very few college gigs, hardly any concerts – it was easier to work in Holland or France.'[35] In Bedfordshire, pints were poured on the Floyd from the balcony as they refused to pander to audience demands for danceable renditions of their two hits, 'Arnold Layne' and 'See Emily Play'. Bassist Waters could stomach that, as long as 'there was one freak who turned up who liked us so the audience spent the whole evening beating the shit out of him'.[36] By now the underground's chic seemed to have outgrown its radicalism. There was Susie Gorler-Wright, the psychedelic debutante; Floyd handyman Peter Wynne-Willson's uncle was the Bishop of Bath and Wells. Ferlinghetti was living with TV folkie Julie Felix. Paul Channon, Jonathan Aitken and Norman St John Stevas, all later ministerial appointees of Margaret Thatcher, argued publicly for the decriminalization of drugs. The Establishment were poking inquisitive tentacles into the possibilities of popular culture; individually, by way of personal adventure, and then to a more institutional extent, as in William Rees-Mogg's 'Who Breaks a Butterfly on a Wheel?' reaction to the Rolling Stones' drug busts in *The Times* in 1967.

It became apparent that quite apart from the traditional showbiz slog the new music was finding itself invited into more exalted venues. In 1967 Pink Floyd played the Queen Elizabeth Hall on London's South Bank (they had also been involved in a debate with musicologist Hans Keller on BBC TV as to the validity of their music). The posters read: 'Games for May, space age relaxation for the coming of spring – electronic compositions, colour and image projection, girls, *and the Pink Floyd*'.[38]

'Anthony King [the promoter] was no idiot,' remembers Susie Wynne-Willson. 'He was into the idea of marketing it as Art.'[39] The press release ran:

> The Floyd intend this concert to be a musical and visual exploration – not only for themselves, but for the audience too. New music has been written and will be given for the first time, including some specially prepared four-way stereo tapes. Visually, the lights men of the group have prepared an entirely bigger than ever before show.[40]

The grandiosity of the preamble masked some residual iconoclasm, nevertheless: Waters hurled potatoes at a gong, Mason sawed wood, eggs were fried onstage.

TUNING IN

The Piper at the Gates of Dawn, the band's first long-player, was recorded in Studio 3 at EMI Abbey Road – while the Beatles worked next door in Studio 2 piecing together *Sergeant Pepper*.

But while this new musical vehicle might have appeared shinily and forbiddingly futuristic, its chassis was of tried and tested material. The intimidating instrumental 'Pow R. Toc H.' alternates chaotic noise with expressive blues piano. 'Lucifer Sam' sports a soul bassline. 'Candy and a Currant Bun' (originally christened 'Let's Roll Another One' before a tut-tutting BBC got it hurriedly altered) for example, which does not appear on the album but backed the Floyd's first single, 'Arnold Layne', derives . from Howlin' Wolf's 'Smokestack Lightnin'. Pop ate itself again on 'Flaming', with Barrett's vocal lines and the metres of the music playing hide-and-seek, while Wright's harpsichord clatters happily; on 'The Gnome', his arabesques on electric piano are similarly inventive. The Hank Marvin influence on the guitar in 'Astronomy Dominé' is insultingly obvious, but the track, listened to even with hindsight, is of awesome chordal disarray and adventure. The band typically utilized jazz structure, whereby (a 'head') theme, usually short, sharp and fragmentary, would be played, and then give way to improvisation based on its chord sequence – 'thirty minutes of electronic noise – because these people just wanted to see what it was like if they rubbed the strings on a mikestand, or in Townshend's case, smashed it into an amp – and they thought it was interesting,' commented Chris Cutler later.[41] Then the song would reprise the theme; the result would be an experience like 'Interstellar Overdrive'. Barrett rolled ball-bearings down his fretboard and banged it with a hairbrush. In Cutler's words, 'It somehow chimed with the *musique concrète* he'd heard in Stockhausen. And it was still kids getting onstage and making a noise and being excited about it.'[42] The sound created could not have – in its own time – assumed many other connotations than those of space; as Allan Moore maintains, the impression of instrumental soloists independent from one another, and from the beat, evoked a solipsism akin to that generated by the loneliness of interplanetary travel.[43] In addition, the pop-cultural analogy of technically advanced, avant-garde music with science fiction (and fact) via the trusty mediations of B-film soundtracks (themselves copied from electronic composers who'd influenced Barrett) helped establish the Floyd's image as troubadours of a new age.

If the Floyd's album was a masterpiece of measured, disinterested contemplation of a fast-approaching future, that the first Soft Machine album was a headlong dash for that future. It didn't actually appear in the UK until after 1969, having been recorded while the band were on tour in the USA with Jimi Hendrix. Both sides of the record played continuously, with the sectioning of songs purposely haphazard. Riffs and melodies again frame free-blowing sections, and for now Mike Ratledge's coruscating organ solos are still rooted in pop-blues patois; despite their sheets-of-sound profligacy, one couldn't imagine Coltrane transposing them for saxophone (the apocryphal intelligence is that Ratledge cranked up the distortion to such a level that if the player removed his fingers from the keyboard it would start feeding back, hence the unquenchable torrent of notes).

Wyatt's vocals lead the melody, and a psychedelic fancy such as 'Joy' takes off the Monkees and underground-musician culture – 'most of all I like to talk about me'. Solos tend to take off and land on 'wrong' beats, prefiguring much of what was to come in bands like Henry Cow and Egg. Dave Brubeck had blazed a trail in the popularizing of what were to pop musicians, unusual metres, but whereas in the early 1960s the 5/4, 3/4 and 9/4 of 'Time Out' had been a novelty, in the feverish experimentalism of 1967, 11/8 was thought to be *de rigueur*. Terry Riley's own arrhythmical experiments of the period (*A Rainbow in Curved Air*) were also exercising enough bohemian interest to have surely been at least a subconscious influence on Soft Machine's career. But in the excruciating minimalism of Kevin Ayers' 'We Did It Again', parodic pop is brought to bear on jazz-rock tempi. In the 1980s this process was reversed by Progressive musicians such as It Bites, who reversed the process by bringing jazz-rock to the aid of pop. Technology is well in evidence; the production blurs tonal and timbral distinctions between instruments as on early Floydian experiments, and instruments 'become' themselves to the ear only as *solo* instruments. Layered vocal phrases are superimposed over each other in rhythmically irregular sequence, giving rise to mouth-musical echoes.

The approach was duplicated on *Second* (1969; the winner of a prestigious French *Meilleur Disque* award) and radically distilled on *Third* (1970); unanimously acclaimed as the band's zenith; Ayers had left by the second album, mentally and physically broken by a US tour (then as now often an experience of debilitating and disorienting excess for callow rock musicians) and the prodigal Hugh Hopper, from the band's formative Wilde Flowers days in Kent, replaced him on bass. For a short period Andy Summers, once of Dantalion's Chariot and later of the Police, depped on guitar. Maniacally segued pop, hard-bop soloing and surrealism: the bracing, Beatles-ish piano riffs heralding the lyrically absurdist 'Pataphysical Introduction Part 1' and the chromatic monody of 'A Concise English Alphabet'; the celestial, shimmering West Coast vocal harmonies ('Hello Der'), the whole gallimaufry has a hilariously unstable harmonic centre and sacrifices verse–chorus structure to the monstrous sprawl of the side-long sequential compositions.

The melodies contain wider and wider leaps around the octave as time proceeds. Disruption is sharpened up; 'These Foolish Things' is quoted in 'Have You Ever Been Green' and, through the agency of furious improvisation and multi-tracking, the smartly-titled 'Out of Tunes' is a textbook freakout. Floydish sound manipulation was present (the delay systems used here and there on Wyatt's drums, for example, prefigure treatments evident on Pink Floyd's *Ummagumma* (1969). By 1970, however, the extreme variation of style and mood had been decanted into a less volatile brew, with the post-bop influence rising to the surface. The succession of tune and improvisation, peripheral before, moves centre stage. While the seemingly random digressions of the first two albums are absent, there is a focused intensity developing the music over much longer paragraphs, alternating free improvisation with lengthy vamps in unorthodox metres to backdrop solo extemporization – usually richly indebted to Coltrane. Even the brass and woodwind additions echo Coltrane's modalities; as Moore points out, the improvisations frequently utilize registers or notes only superficially related to or independent of stated themes or melodies.[44]

Music was becoming an experience for the head, not the feet. The celebrated underground poet Lady June put it best:

The more acid one takes, in one's minds the music sounds tremendous – but outwardly it sounds like a heap of shit. People who aren't taking the same stuff as you aren't hearing the same thing you're hearing in your head. That's when all the bones of contention came, because it wasn't working as a whole. That's when it all started to fragment.[45]

And fragment it did, although only to remake itself in another image – Progressive rock.

DROPPING OUT

The Covent Garden-based Middle Earth club's usurpation of the Roundhouse's role in London's club culture in October 1967 further extended contemporary rock's forays into English Romanticism, which would also flower with Gandalf's Garden. It didn't last long; according to one source, the police, unable successfully to legally bust the Middle Earth, informed Covent Garden market traders that the clientele were crucifying children and the righteously outraged mob tore the place apart.[46] The Now gatecrashed the Future's party; a gang of quasi-musical hangers-on known as 'The Pink Fairies Drinking Club' smashed up King Crimson's second gig at Oxford Circus's Speakeasy, a club whose very existence was seen by some as an affront to the underground. Robert Wyatt, for instance, saw it as a tragic betrayal of the ideals of the underground that rock groups were now playing in 'expensive clubs that were difficult to get into'.[47] In the words of the IT journalist and putative White Panther boho activist Mick Farren, in the winter of 1967–8 the hippies 'either died or went home [and] ... gangs of skinheads started to invade'.[48]

The fundraising Fourteen Hour Technicolor Dream of the summer of 1967 is seen by some as the symbolic death of the underground as a distinctive entity. Soft Machine and Pink Floyd topped the bill at Alexandra Palace in north London, but the heady days of subversive experiment in 1966 already seemed far away. It also marked the highpoint of Farren's Deviants, formed after an encounter with a twenty-one-year-old millionaire, who put up £700 for their first album. This effort, *Ptoof!*, described by one associate as 'the worst record in the history of man',[49] appeared to fulfil the dislocating credentials of the underground, with churning grunge-garage punk played at maximum speed with minimal ability, as did the music of the Flies, an act who literally pissed on their audience. But to both these acts had accrued a harshness and hardness, whether acquired by accident or design. These were people clearly out for a good time, no matter who got hurt. The Flies were to be heard yelling 'sell-out' during Pink Floyd's set. It was to be the last Syd Barrett played live with the band. Chris Rowley remembers: 'There was definite fall-out after the Fourteen Hour Dream ... there was a big shake-out in the underground press because a lot of the entrepreneurial types made off with the money.'[50]

In the USA, the summer of love turned into the murderous rampage of the Weathermen; the student uprising in Paris was left to flounder by the unions; Dubček was crushed in Prague; and on the streets of London the underground staged its own toytown Alamo at the American Embassy in Grosvenor Square. Bottles may have been thrown with vigour, but as one eye-witness remembers, 'We all got home in time for the evening news.'[51] The underground had, in effect, been seduced by its own publicity, co-opted into the Society of the Spectacle. Of the college sit-ins that year, Mick Farren said, 'The colleges, which were our financial bread and butter, started having sit-ins, which meant we [the bands] didn't get paid any more. Which upset us.'[52] Was this what idealism had come to?

It's endlessly debatable as to whether the souring of the underground dream was or was not inevitable. The question need not concern us here. What does concern us is the significance of the Fourteen Hour Technicolor Dream in the genesis of Progressive rock and ideology. Behold a host of watersheds; it marked Barrett's dissociation from the underground's premier band, Pink Floyd, and their subsequent shift of aesthetic direction, with its huge effect on Progressive in the 1970s. It produce a schism in the musical language of the underground, underlined by the Floyd's emphasis on composition and leaning towards more formally classical, more *bourgeois* musical expression. Against them were ranked the likes of the (Social) Deviants, disciples of dirty-fingernailed guitar-led rock, and the still-evolving Soft Machine. All would sire sub-genres: the Floyd laid the foundations for symphonic rock with its associated big-business potential, the Deviants blazed a trail for a blue-collar Heavy Metal audience to arise from those alienated by the bourgeois elitism of the art school. Heavy Metal would coexist with Progressive under the same marketing banner for a time, as a kind of working-class beer tent fringing the counter-culture party before becoming seduced by the black American blues tradition and being reincorporated into the Western popular mainstream. And from this schism came a third way, which eschewed the studied formality of symphonic rock and the rawness of hard rock: the improvisational and avant-garde purists had coalesced around Soft Machine, and these men and women would carry the inviolable flame of jazz into the 1970s at the heart of the musical movement its notes and its ideology had helped create.

2 BEAT BOYS IN THE APOLLO AGE
(THE MUSICAL LIBERATION OF MIDDLE ENGLAND 1967–69)

LOVE IS ALL YOU NEED

Billions of words have been expended on the 1960s; to attempt to analyze the decade's historical impact here would be superfluous. Specific aspects of the 1960s cannot be ignored, however. They were germane to the subsequent narrative of Progressive. Economically, the West was in good shape; consumer spending and standards of living rose unabated. Sexual and racial liberalization proceeded apace; internationally, independence for many erstwhile colonies fuelled Third World nationalism and provoked worldwide castigation of US interference overseas. Simultaneously this aided the rediscovery of radical politics in a form distinct from that of the established Left's Stalinist communism. Emphasis was now laid on decentralization (specifically in anti-imperialist discourse against superpower intervention in Vietnam and Czechoslovakia) and on the liberty of the human subject; the message was that socialist salvation could come about through the liberation not only of the collective whole but also of individuals. Scientifically, the development of military and space technologies lent the post-war boom an almost irresistible vitesse. Could it ever stop? When Gagarin went into space in 1961 and Armstrong walked on the moon in 1969 it seemed to many that utopia, however wrought, might be within sight. And the Beatles would be there to throw open the gates of the New Jerusalem.

The Beatles' extraordinary social and musical progress through the late 1960s beggars description. John Lennon claimed that he and his buddies were bigger than Jesus; the placid indifference of middle England (if not, admittedly, of the US religious right) to the comment suggested that these were indeed charmed men. Musically, they hit the top of the charts with the lyrically ambiguous 'Day Tripper' and then George Harrison's 'Within You Without You' took the sitar backing of 'Norwegian Wood' a stage further, employing an entire arsenal of north Indian instruments. Nobody batted an eyelid; they just bought the record. George Martin's extraordinary string quartet arrangement on 'Eleanor Rigby' crowned perhaps the most adventurous mainstream pop song ever; 'Strawberry Fields Forever' experimented with vari-speed and backward-playing tapes and still got to No. 2; and most importantly, the release of *Sergeant Pepper's Lonely Hearts Club Band* in June 1967 was the most definitive statement to date of pop's aspirations to art. This was a 'concept album' writ large, a collection of songs as a continuous entity, the first mainstream example of its kind (a disputable but convenient contention) which, in Allan Moore's words, represented 'an early endeavour for rock to build a unity greater than that of the individual, self-contained utterance', achieving its lofty ambitions not just through simple modulating bridge passages but through motivic recurrence.[1]

Honoured guests of any and every party going in London, the four Beatles' whims were serviced by the younger members of an artistic establishment falling over themselves to grab a slice of reflected glory (e.g. Peter Blake's *Sergeant Pepper* cover). Pop stars no longer aspired to respectability; respectable artists aspired to be pop stars.

Cultural liberation was surely at hand. If the 'total revolutionaries' of the day were to be believed, the proselytizers of an artistic catalyst for revolutionary thinking, then social reorganization must inevitably follow.

But more implicit by far in the counter-cultural project was the liberation of the subjective individual. The liberation of the Beatles as individual songwriters had been a start; writing their own material nullified mediation between performer and production process, a luxury unavailable to most popular entertainers outside the jazz world. And as Lennon said: 'I started thinking about my own emotions – I don't know exactly when it started, like "I'm a 'Loser" or "Hide Your Love Away".'[2] Lennon, inspired by the apparent importance of his own utterance, had been granted the confidence to assume this quintessentially Romantic outlook and his record label became convinced of the profitability of letting him exercise it. It was an infectious notion; the Who looked to Pete Townshend to write their own 'originals': '... me being at art school, being able to say long words like "perspicacity", which I heard on a Spike Milligan album, I was elected to do the job.'[3]

THE ZEN ETERNAL
Liberation of self, materially or otherwise, became the Grail. The first Soft Machine gig was at a house bought by the Sufi Idris Shah (a friend of Robert Wyatt's chum Robert Graves) from J. G. Bennett and disciples of G. I. Gurdjieff. The latter's esoteric take on Indian philosophy, along with *Siddhartha* and other works of enlightenment by Hermann Hesse (not to mention the *Tibetan Book of the Dead* which had so impressed Leary), inspired a generation to 'open up a window on the Zen Eternal',[4] in Jeff Nuttall's memorable phrase. Rock, the soul of the future in sound, became synonymous with the natural, the organic, anything unharmed by human hand. The mystique of passing over and out of either the physical world or one's immediate

physical surroundings was intrinsic to the rock agenda – either through the agency of hallucinogenic drugs or by taking the trail to precisely those wellsprings of philosophy the Gurdjieffs of this world repropagated: the Golden Road of Western mythology had been diverted from Samarkand to Katmandu (or further for those with stronger stomachs). It attracted a caravan of VW-van-driving, foot-blistered or brain-blasted drop-outs throughout the 1960s.

Ken Kesey and the Merry Pranksters kicked off a rolling road campaign of surrealistic street demonstrations to 'zap' America, echoed in the 1969 cult road movie, *Easy Rider*. With the advent of pop festivals, kids could trek into the countryside to hear the music, because, well, it was more 'natural' there, wasn't it? The Man hadn't got his hands on the countryside, had he? Rock wanted the wind in its hair and the sun on its back.

English composer, historian and theosophist Cyril Scott, who wholeheartedly personified the symbolist, occult, Art Nouveau and Oriental cosmology beloved of the hippies, predicted in the 1930s that 'a new species of violin' would pour forth 'floods of melody from the higher planes, to be translated into earthly sound by composers sensitive enough to apprehend them,'[5] itself a succinct paraphrase of Scriabin's gnostic predictions of the 1910s. By the late 1960s, his predictions were unconsciously adopted by hippydom; the guitar was the magic carpet to the transcendent. Scott (who, interestingly, lived to see this development) also idolized the 'natural' and the outdoors. His reflections on late 1960s rock culture are, regrettably not recorded.

By 1969, the first British pop festivals (notwithstanding the stalwart jazz and blues festivals at Richmond and Bath) were featuring both rock bills and a rapidly self-transforming rock audience (the Bath Festival became in 1969 the Bath Blues and Progressive Music Festival). The agent of transformation was a peculiarly middlebrow English pastoralism reflecting the English/Anglo-Saxon/European nature of much of the music's aesthetic motivation.

The urge to the countryside, writ large in the mass migrations of youth to the back of beyond when festivals got big, could trace its roots back into the 1960s; *The Piper at the Gates of Dawn*, the title of Pink Floyd's first album is, of course, the title of a chapter from Kenneth Grahame's *The Wind in The Willows*, a literary classic of wide-eyed Romantic mysticism and pastoralism. Tellingly, perhaps, the chapter in question is a mesmerizing farrago of pantheism and nature-worship.

Even pop hopped aboard the flower-powered ruralist bandwaggon; drippy Dylan clone Donovan brought in harp and woodwind section for his fey 'Jennifer Juniper', Honeybus tootled oboes for 'I Can't Let Maggie Go' and as late as 1969 the idyllic could still sell records, as evidenced by Manfred Mann's lyrical references to morning sun, golden hair, fields of corn and rivers in 'Fox on the Run'.

Then there was the ultimate horizon, outer space. Stanley Kubrick's 1968 cinematic masterpiece, *2001 A Space Odyssey* combined a technocrat's escapism, with its staggering gadgetry, a Romantic's escapism with its vistas of limitless emptiness, and a hip psychedelic's escapism with its celebrated 'star gate' sequence in which Keir Dullea makes his oft-deconstructed journey through hyperspace. The metallically glinting obelisk which dominates the film embodies cultures of unimaginable past and unimaginable future, a dichotomy which would underpin much of Progressive ideology.

Popular culture tapped cultural representations from the *fin-de-siècle* whereby the soul and the psyche became viable artistic commodities. Beardsley prints became popular; club names like the Perfumed Garden recalled Rabindranath Tagore and Stefan George; graphic art's swirling monstrosities resembled an orgy of influences from Sidney Sime to Gustav Klimt. (Indeed one third-eleven psychedelic band called themselves the Art Nouveaux and issued a single 'Extra Terrestrial Visitations' in 1967 – like, totally *out there*.) Rediscovered authors included the aforementioned Hermann Hesse (specifically *Siddhartha* and *The Journey to the East*) and J. R. R. Tolkien, whose characters and settings lent themselves to all manner of psychedelic and Progressive flim-flam (although few musical representations of his work actually exist in the British Progressive canon). Even the maverick Mervyn Peake suddenly merited a fresh look, with Dawn Records

Progressive band Titus Groan taking their name from his Gormenghast trilogy. The common thread linking all these disparate figures was an obsession with the interior being and its troubled relationship to an idealized other transfigured by beauty but mediated by bourgeois convention. The revolution itself had therefore to take on an all-embracing character – spiritual, cultural, political – it had to be *lived*. It was to be the precursor of 'revolution as lifestyle', which would shape the attitudes to marketing the trappings of that revolution in the years to come.

PLUGGING IN THE PROVINCES I – THE MUSICIANS

Britain's provincial middle classes, and especially the provincial middle and lower middle classes, for all London's patronizing bohemian ostracism of them, had a revolutionary role to play.

Here the incalculable scope of the Beatles' influence tells most plainly. With unprecedented opportunities for travel, education and for entertainment (exemplified by the phenomena behind the emergent university rock-concert circuit), and newly equipped with both reproduction and recording hardware, provincial middle-class youth were able to participate in this revolution, and did so in enormous numbers. The Beatles' success produced a money-grabbing reaction in showbusiness that immediately offered them a wide variety of outlets – both live and in the studio – to strut their stuff.

In other words the roads of Britain (now usefully linked by motorways) teemed with a motley class cross-section of musicians who, in the wake of the Beatles' relocation to London and the subsequent national media focus on the underground they patronized, headed for the capital, beguiled by its promise.

What was remarkable about this new corps of musicians was the fact that art school had often passed them by and the Underground had been only a secondary source of artistic inspiration. While not components of the scene, they had been drawn, moth-like, to its radiance. From Southend in Essex came Procol Harum, where pianist/vocalist Gary Brooker had played in pop band the Paramounts. When the Paramounts (famously, the Rolling Stones' favourite British R&B act) split in 1966,

Brooker met lyricist Keith Reid, advertised in *Melody Maker* for a band, and within a year 'A Whiter Shade of Pale', buoyed aloft on Matthew Fisher's tumultuous Hammond organ and its stately pageant of Bach's 'Sheep May Safely Graze' chords, made Procol Harum into international stars.

The Moody Blues were more frazzled R&B leftovers who'd emerged blinking from the same Birmingham cellars as the Move in the mid-1960s when London's loot beckoned. Stripped of vocal focal point Denny Laine and in freefall from the heady heights of their hit 'Go Now', they recruited bassist John Lodge, while vocal duties went to the winsome-faced and winsomer-voiced Justin Hayward. This mellow marriage produced a concept album *avant la lettre*, *Days of Future Passed*, which revolved (leadenly) around times of the day. Recorded with the London Festival Orchestra, the original hubristic intention had been a recording for group and orchestra of Dvořák's New World symphony.

The band's ambition didn't wane on their follow-up, *In Search of the Lost Chord*, where they played all thirty-three listed instruments themselves, including an obligatory smattering of Oriental ones. But by now another staple of the band's sound was the Mellotron. A curious forerunner of sampling technology, it was a rudimentary tape-frame of string and choral sounds which could be manipulated by two small keyboards. Its compact orchestral and vocal effects were to prove not only a must for all Progressive artists (as will be seen later), it also saved the Moodies a few bob in the studio and on stage when an orchestra wasn't to hand. The album's vintage whimsies, 'Voices in the Sky' and 'Ride My See-saw', sported melodies couching beguiling lyrics of open-air wistfulness.

By now the band were accruing the kind of wealth that befitted the bourgeois imagery of their lyrics and the orchestral gauzes that hung around their music. They decamped to Cobham in Surrey in 1969, setting up their own record label, Threshold Records, with plans for a string of record shops. The rest of their story is largely superfluous to this book: an odyssey of supertax and superstardom, a musical mothership on a stately course from sold-out stadium to sold-out stadium, with very slight adjustments to the smooth-running musical machine set in motion by *Days of Future Passed*. Rather, the legacy of the Moodies to Progressive is that sole album, with its use of orchestra. Not that its musical role is that innovatory – its role is essentially that of a texturally sweetening adjunct – but rather it became important because of the prestige lent to the hitherto-sniffed-at 'pop' by the apparent willingness of classical musicians to collaborate with long-hairs. As Bill Bruford put it, 'Once one band had an orchestra, everyone wanted one.'[6]

The Nice arose from itinerant beat-blues outfit Gary Farr and the T-Bone. Organist Keith Emerson and bassist Lee Jackson had hawked themselves around the speakeasy circuit before teaming up with guitarist Davy O'List and drummer Brian 'Blinky' Davison in R'n'B diva P. P. Arnold's backing band, and their guest slot in the first half of the show playing originals and outrageously customized standards caused such a sensation that suddenly they found themselves with an album contract with Immediate Records in 1967 and half the underground groupies in London wanting to sleep with them. According to a probably apocryphal story, the band (still with Arnold guesting on vocals) had stormed that summer's Windsor Festival by letting off smoke bombs outside the tent in which they played to a dismayingly tiny audience of just five people; alarmed onlookers arrived to find the Hammond-organ-humping Emerson twirling a whip, Arnold leaping around the tiny stage and the guitar and bass churning out the group standard 'Flower King of Flies'. The crowd liked what they heard and stayedThe Nice were on their way.

Jethro Tull traced its roots to Blackpool in 1963 when Edinburgh-born Ian Anderson formed a group called the Blades with schoolfriends Jeffrey Hammond-Hammond (on bass) and drummer John Evan, who switched to keyboards when Barriemore Barlow from Birmingham joined. Toying with names like John Evan Smash, this down-at-heel blues brigade moved to London in December 1967 to cash in on what they imagined was a still nascent blues scene, but post-psychedelic disillusion left Anderson stranded alone in London with just new bassist Glenn

Cornick for company. With guitarist Mick Abrahams and drummer Clive Bunker, and a name borrowed by Anderson from an eighteenth-century English agriculturalist, the band signed with MGM and were promptly credited as Jethro Toe on their first single. A Marquee residency, a Floyd-supporting Hyde Park gig and success at the Sunbury Jazz and Blues Festival in August, however, led to Island Records signing them.

King Crimson originated in Dorset, from the ashes of a whimsical psychedelic comedy outfit called Brain, which transmuted into Giles, Giles and Fripp – Mike Giles (drums) and Peter Giles (bass) had trodden the traditional beat route in Trendsetters Ltd and guitarist Robert Fripp had been in a soul band, the League of Gentlemen. When Peter Giles quit in 1968, fellow Bournemouth refugees Greg Lake (bass) and Ian McDonald (woodwind) joined, the musicians took up a short residency in an Italian restaurant in Jermyn Street backing a Latinate crooner, and a legend took shape.

Pete Sinfield, the band's celebrated lyricist and general dramaturg, who handled lights, Mellotron and VCS3 synthesizer as well as undertaking basic gofering, was in computers:

> I was so stoned most of the time that I couldn't work beyond two or three hours a day. They were primitive things, IBM 360s with wheels going round like in Bond movies. We'd screw up the programme by putting in a loop and just get on with our poker game because we were all wannabe artists anyway. I thought, 'I must do something that goes along with what my boho friends are doing.' So I formed a band, modestly called the Creation. I wanted to be a cross between Donovan and The Who. I met Ian McDonald, who had played clarinet in an army band. He said,' I think someone ought to tell you – you're really a hopeless musician. But would you like to write some lyrics?'
>
> Ian was a guitarist who wanted to be a saxophonist. He teamed up with Mike Giles and his brother, they advertised for an organist and one day Robert turned up. He couldn't play organ, but he could play guitar. Judy Dyble, who went on to sing in Fairport Convention, she was Ian McDonald's

girlfriend – she was around for a bit. But when these guys played I was in awe. I liked jazz, but I was in heaven here. Nobody could sing, so they got Greg in – bit of a pop star, another Bournemouth boy, from the Gods. One of the songs I'd written for my band was 'In the Court of the Crimson King', which started off as a kind of Country and Western song. I hung around and became the roadie – the roadie that wrote lyrics. I'd seen an early Floyd gig, so I built some lights and by this time I was doing the sound and lights and the roadying. We were still Giles, Giles and Fripp. We had to do a gig in Newcastle. They thought they were getting King Curtis; they got us. The MC stood up and said, 'Ladies and gentlemen, I present for your entertainment Giles, Giles and Fripp who have – unaccountably – changed their name to King Crimson. Who, at the end of their act, will perform a *freak-out* for you.' And we did, because we didn't have much material.[7]

Throughout the late 1960s the degree of social mix among the personnel rolling into London to staff the coming rock colonization was more than apparent. Yes, for example, sported ex-Accrington milkman and jobbing trucker Jon Anderson, who had already endured years on the UK and the German USAF base circuit as a pop singer (as Hans Christian, no less; the early manifestation of the high-pitched skirl which would vocalize so distinctively on innumerable Yes recordings was likened by one friend to Cilla Black). But alongside him in the formative Yes lineups were ex-Haberdashers Aske schoolboy and reformed acidhead Chris Squire, playing bass, and, on drums, an alumnus of Tonbridge School, one Bill Bruford.

Bruford remembers that social diversity was a key factor of the scene.

It could lead to tension, though. When Yes started, we got our wages before every gig. Being the middle-class one, I ventured the suggestion we should put it in bank accounts. Or even – horrors – a *band* bank account, just to be careful; they went bananas. You had working-class guys in that band who were naturally suspicious of having their money taken out of their hands – especially if they happened to have worked in the music business already. You'd get conflicts like that.[8]

Progressive's 'bourgeois' origins are the stuff of myth; few of its practitioners remember anything but a bewildering social polyocracy united by what had in effect been the revelation of music in the 1960s, and ease of access to it as consumer and artist.

When Bill Bruford told his father of his desire to be a musician, he said,

'What's that?' My musical education was very broad, though, thanks to my mother, who was very musical: showtunes, Sinatra, American pop, twelve-bar blues, Connie Francis, Scotty Moore's guitar solo on 'Hound Dog'. I also remember Sonny Stitt and Art Blakey on *Jazz 625* on BBC 2.[9]

Bruford's testimony revealingly indicates that jazz as 'other' was not simply a bohemian fixation – it represented an alternative at public school, indeed almost an alternative to an alternative, as it offered a listening experience of anti-Establishment authenticity even beyond that of pop.

We liked the Beatles and the Stones, but not as much as jazz and R&B, where we could hear people really playing their hearts out. One guy took me to see Graham Bond in Hildenborough. John McLaughlin was playing guitar with him, Jack Bruce I think, and Ginger Baker. Amazing. They looked like they were all exhausted – and they were playing material from Ray Charles's LP *Genius + Soul = Jazz*.[10]

Anthony Phillips, one of the founder members of Genesis during the band's formative years at Charterhouse, tells a picaresque tale of how pop even integrated itself into the milieu of upper-middle-class youth to the extent of the threat of near-violence;

At Charterhouse there was a blues camp and a soul camp. Peter Gabriel was a soul freak, I followed John Mayall. The school weren't keen on us; pop bands were regarded as anarchists. There was a music teacher called Jeffrey Ford – a bit precious, but he let us do this unofficial concert – a beat concert, in the main hall! Not the official end-of-winter-term school concert. 'Only one condition,' he told us, 'no announcements. Like a classical thing!' In the second half this Genesis precursor band called the Anon went onstage and one of the leads blew. Embarrassing silence ... so Richard McPhail [later a Genesis roadie], who was singing, said, 'Sorry, ladies and gents, it's all part of the act – and now, we'd like to do one of our own songs.' And there was a Vesuvian Jeffrey Ford in the wings, going, 'Right, last number – off.' And he stopped the concert. He stopped the concert, and there was nearly a riot.

Charterhouse was like Colditz; just going up to Carnaby Street was exciting. When we signed with Jonathan King's publishing company in 1968, all our dads had to come up and sign for us because we were under-age.[11]

But these incomers, whether youngsters like Bruford and Phillips or older hands like Andersons (Jon and Ian) or Emerson, were detached from the political and social idealism of the original counter-culture.

One cannot of course claim that original 'underground' acts boasted a greater counter-cultural 'purity' than their provincial imitators; many of the provincials (with the notable exception of Robert Fripp) would end up figuring as major players in 'Establishment' rock culture. Few musicians of any origin actually had an agenda bar that of their own survival. 'Psychedelia?' (says Bruford.) 'I couldn't have given a monkey's about it. I'm sure I went to Kensington Market and bought my purple flared trousers but all I was interested in was being Elvin Jones, like Mitch Mitchell was. I wanted to be Elvin Jones with Yes.'[12]

The club names said it all – the Middle Earth, Gandalf's Garden, the Perfumed Garden – so long as it sounded exotic and looked preposterous, a scene could coalesce around it in London in 1968. But as yet the music played was not Progressive in the ideology and form it would later assume. It was merely 'progressive' in the sense that the sounds these musicians made seemed to shake up, superficially, existing popular-music expression and urge it vaguely towards modernist/Romantic art music a beseeching of – or a defiant gesture towards – a parental generation that had explicitly belittled the idea that their children's music could ever attain artistic credibility. The cultural centrality of the modernist concept of 'progress' still unassailed, the relative adventurism of these young men and their revisionist disrespect towards fixed ideas of popular music seemed, ideally to warrant the term 'progressive'. It was, however, a musical adventure still rooted in the black American vernacular. While Pink Floyd and Soft Machine members had cut their teeth on black music, their exposure to both avant-garde jazz and classical influences in the formative years of the underground had lent them a radicalism of utterance as yet unbestowed on the influx of musicians from the provinces who, beyond a few brave private hearings of Boulez or Stockhausen, still possessed voices heavily burred with the time-honoured harmonic and melodic textures of R&B/jazz/soul/MOR-based popular music. But this didn't mean they couldn't have fun with the form and do so without recourse either to melodic genius or studio dexterity.

PLUGGING IN THE PROVINCES II – THE RECORDS

Jethro Tull
Who exactly was having fun with the form? An examination of *Stand Up* (Jethro Tull's second album), Yes's first two albums, the recorded output of the Nice and two key Procol Harum LPs tell us all we need to know.

Tull's penchant for quirky melodies, was still couched in the blues that had dominated their first 1968 album *This Was,* but the racy abandon of the uneven rhythmic metres that would characterize their later output suggests a lively imagination aiming at bigger things. There is timbral dissension from accepted praxis: Anderson's declamatory, folkish vocal rasp, his sandblasting flute playing derived from the US jazzman Rahsaan Roland Kirk, the spacious yet intimate and modestly disciplined arrangement of tidy songs such as 'Jeffrey Goes to Leicester Square' with its mandolin, organ, hand drum and flute introduction.

A Bach bourrée is bluesed up with Glenn Cornick's filthy backstreet bassline as centrepiece; this tailoring of material to the talents of individual members is most obvious in the adherence of melodic shape to Anderson's own vocal inflections as in 'Back to the Family'; he seems to lead the melody, rather than merely sing along to it. The meteoric success of the album was the launchpad to international superstardom, and with the highly visible success of singles like 'Living in the Past' (from *Stand Up*), with Anderson playing his Shagrat the Vagrant mac-twigs-and-stubble persona for all it was worth on 'Top of the Pops', it seemed that the UK had a major popular music force on its hands, adulated in equal measure by press and fans. The third album, *Benefit* (1970), maintained the invention (and sales) of its predecessor, once again teasing unexpected emotional reflexes from time-honoured voicings and rhythms to signpost something that, if it was not a wholly new kind of pop song, at least offered the listener new bearings in his or her search. Anderson's incongruous appearance in teenybopper magazines, divested of filthy raincoat and stage leer but still captive to a Piltdown hirsuteness, seemed to suggest pop really was undergoing change. Concision was the key word; Tull's gifts were in the small, in the hidden things, in the nostalgic intervals between Anderson's voice and the chords and melodies of the pieces, in the agreeably different impulses behind them offered by Cornick and Bunker, in the friendly and uncluttered soundstage whose combinations of instruments sound simultaneously timeless and brand-new.

King Crimson

Perhaps King Crimson's impact was, retrospectively, the most influential in Progressive rock. Recovering from the Speakeasy débâcle with the Pink Fairies, Robert Fripp and his band kept polishing their music in a Fulham basement. Their reputation was less harmed than their pride, and in July 1969 they astonished the half-million-strong crowd at the Rolling Stones' Hyde Park free concert with music of hitherto unheard-of sophistication and bite for a mere support act.

The recording of that music was just as arresting as its performance; housed in a sleeve of stunning shock-value, the scarlet orifices and numbed eyes of the unfortunate subject on the cover of *In the Court of the Crimson King* have gone down in rock iconography. Released in October 1969, it was hailed as a masterpiece among the press, and by performers (the embryonic Genesis were so impressed they pinned the cover to the wall in their communal home as a reminder of what they wanted to be) and public alike.

If Progressive rock as a discrete genre can be said to have had a starting point, *In the Court of the Crimson King* is probably it. All the elements that characterize Progressive's maturity are in place: jazz and blues influences are subservient to intense compositional rigour characterized by Mellotron-induced Western classical symphonic arrangements (a riot of heavy-duty string, plaintive flute and icy choral effects). Individual and collective passages of arresting virtuosity and a rhythmic discontinuity bordering on the perverse are also components of an essentially tonal, approachable whole inoffensive to any classical or pop listener. Rococo, Romantic imagery saturates Sinfield's lyrical input: 'The seeds of time were sown/and watered by the deeds of those/who know and are known' ('Epitaph').

A likeable, loquacious and warmly self-depreciating man from comfortable origins in an uncomfortable area – Fulham – Sinfield recalls that his prep-school teacher

> instilled the sounds of Shakespeare in me. As for lyrical influences, they went perhaps, beyond Dylan and went back to Rimbaud and Verlaine and people like that. Having a shout and trying to be sexy at the same time. I wasn't much influenced by Ferlinghetti and that crowd – I was more interested in Kerouac, I suppose, but who wasn't? I thought most of it was nonsense – I thought, 'Anyone can do that.'[13]

Sinfield's favourite lyric, 'Talk to the Wind', does at least, in the words of its author, 'still work from an outsider's point of view'. Was he writing it to be sung by singers or for the poetic hell of it?

I wrote it with Ian – it was really written for this soft side of King Crimson. It was sort of influenced by Joni Mitchell.

The name King Crimson was mine – I wanted something like Led Zeppelin, something with a bit of power to it. Anything better than Giles, Giles and Fripp. King Crimson had arrogance to it. As for the cover ... I asked a friend of mine, Barry Godber – who was one of the artists I hung out with in my computer days. It's his face, in a mirror. He died, very sadly – he was only twenty-six, wonderful chap. But his face is there for ever, so it's a small mercy.

Sinfield also had a limited instrumental role, manipulating the new VCS3 synthesizer.

The thing is about the VCS3 is that you could only just about play melodies. I'd been in computers, but I knew a little bit about synthesized noises and I always liked *musique concrète*. Morton Subotnick, Tod Dockstader, Terry Riley. I got this thing very early on and found you could process drums through it. It had a ring modulator and I used to feed in the drums as a trigger and play around with the oscillators. We could do a bit with voices and guitars, too. I was always fascinated by the barriers between noise and sound.[14]

Crimson's emphasis, despite their avant-garde affinity, spoke a rocker's tongue from the start; the blowtorch riffs of '21st Century Schizoid Man' and the acidity of Fripp's guitar tone throughout are proof enough. But the band score through the subtlety of their arrangements which suffer only due to the imitations they spawned, for instance, the dainty interplay of instruments on the verses and serene instrumental interludes of the title track (Mike Giles's flute arabesques, Fripp's lazily wistful blues-inflected guitar and the exquisite precision ornamentation of Ian McDonald's percussion). 'Schizoid Man', on the other hand, showcases rhythmic ensemble expertise in discordant and often autonomous syncopated group riffs spinning off the metre of the up-tempo middle section. This album underlines more than perhaps any other Crimson album a residue of classical dynamics and phrasing, of a range of atmospheres expressed in a range of (harmonically quite conventional) ways, easily recognizable in the acceptable taxonomy of Western musical illustrative syntax (the usage of soft sonorities of woodwind and acoustic instruments for introspective passages etc.). But Fripp would later explore harsher territory, rephrasing rock dynamics and textures and through a fascinating harmonic schema that would allow individual performers to abandon tonality altogether.

The first lineup of King Crimson disintegrated in America in December 1969 when Mike Giles and Ian McDonald quit the band, citing the 'plasticity of rock and/or the US' as factors.[15] Greg Lake would leave during the recording of *In the Wake of Poseidon* (1970) to invent Emerson, Lake and Palmer.

Poseidon marked a decisive shift away from the Baroque pictorialism of *Court*; as Tamm has observed, Fripp assumed more production duties and took it upon himself to distil the band's sound, introducing a raw, airless edge of asperity to it he would later gloss as '*audio vérité*'.[16] The berserk boleros, atonality and dissonant progressions of the side-long 'Devil's Triangle' suite was 'Schizoid Man' cubed; while 'Cat Food' is, again in the words of Tamm, 'like Bartok scoring a Garfield movie'.[17] It would provide the band's only appearance on 'Top of the Pops'.

Musicians came and went; Elton John was booked to sing on *Poseidon* before Fripp had second thoughts; Bryan Ferry auditioned and failed; Jon Anderson of Yes guested on *Lizard* (1970) and Steeleye Span bassist Rick Kemp joined for all of a week before the ever unconventional Fripp settled the bass problem by signing an unknown singer, Boz Burrell, and teaching him to play the instrument.

Fripp continued to confound; *Lizard* saw a return to tunes, albeit in an acrid minor-key vernacular Fripp would make his own. But Fripp's nervous energy, adept at layering atmospheres in filmic, twentieth-century classical mode as on 'Big Top' from *Lizard* (whereby layers of music of ambiguous tonal relations contrast moods as well as notes within the same bars) do no favours to Holst's 'Mars'.

Fripp would soon disband Crimson for a second time. When he reconvened the band later that same year, it would be with a lineup that radically shifted his own music and that of the band not out of the commercial Progressive sector, but towards the boundaries of commercialism and pose questions as to just how unconventional a mainstream attraction of the mid-1970s could be. Fripp wanted to push his luck, and he wanted to push the minds of his listeners and the patience of his paymasters like nobody before him.

Yes/Procol Harum/The Nice

Yes debuted in 1968–9 with an eponymous album that also attempted a makeover of popular-song forms. This time, however, the emphasis was more on pop; whereas Tull mediated the blues, Yes *mediated already-mediated* blues, and brought to its aid a plethora of other musical voicings, creating a hybrid of similar vitality but greater idiosyncrasy.

Yes's debut opens with a stabbing, chiming 'Pictures of Matchstick Men'-type freakbeat guitar ostinato, while the pyramid harmonies later to become integral to the band sound are a straight lift from the Association, which on 'I See You' with its frisky, featherweight jazz vamp, nods to the Johnny Mann Singers. 'Day Tripper' is quoted by the bass during the band's epic (and somewhat derivative) cover of Lennon/McCartney's 'Every Little Thing'. Pop chords are resettled rather than revised, with an emphasis on light and shade in their texture rather than a reorganization of their constituent parts. Arrangements were also of accomplished novelty, with an early fondness for lightweight melodies to pilot themselves between punctuations of knuckle-duster ensemble chords ('Looking Around'). *Time and a Word* (1970) was less successful, notably because of the dismal orchestral accompaniment that swamped the songs. From the opening pastiche of Elmer Bernstein's 'Big Country' strings which heralds a version of Richie Havens's 'No Opportunity Needed, No Experience Necessary' this is circus-band adumbration. Engineer Eddie Offord played up Chris Squire's buccaneering bass to add at least a dash of sophistication to the lumpen mess. The chordal language is similar to that of the first album, although (no thanks to the strings) there is evidence of a greater vertical complexity, with much use made of the entire range of all the instruments available to the musicians, an approach greatly extended later in Yes's career.

Procol Harum's *Shine on Brightly* (1968) and *A Salty Dog* (1969), given the arduous task of bettering the blockbuster success of 'A Whiter Shade of Pale', inevitably dimmed commercially but enraptured critics. The blues still saturates the music of *Shine on Brightly*, but the Baroque chordal developments (cf. 'Pale') of Matthew Fisher's Hammond open the music's perspectives out thrillingly without lending an ounce too much grandiloquence. Outstanding too is the extravagant but not unnecessarily decorative nature of Robin Trower's insistent guitar. The vast 'In Held 'Twas in I' from *Shine On*, in eight sections totalling seventeen minutes, was at the time probably the most ambitious continuous single composition by an English rock band. From Brooker's cringingly dopey opening monologue (all zonked Himalayan epiphanies and bedsitter self-pity), a career down through the octaves takes the music through desultory impressionistic piano and in the two songful episodes that follow the development of the music is both logical and skilful. After Trower's falling, chromatic guitar scales scribble messily all over a dissonant organ pedal note, a four-square march (interestingly harmonized) introduced pioneering – if sometimes naïve – recapitulations, instrumental in the creation of new sections. The inflated coda, with its heavy-handed choir and pealing guitar, is forgivable after such effort. *A Salty Dog* tames such ambition but, as with Yes, the poppiness of the music comes not from emulation of current chart trends but from reinventing pop's repertoire of tensions and releases. Trower's bellicose guitar and Keith Reid's ever more elliptical lyrics (once, legend attests, the lyrics of 'A Salty Dog' alone provided an American English Literature student with a subject for an entire MA thesis) lent the band extra kudos.

The Nice's claim to fame, somewhat unfairly, is as the band who gave the world Keith Emerson. But when was rock history ever fair? Emerson's imprint was on the music from the start – how could a virtuoso Hammond organ player whose stagecraft included wrestling, raping and generally beating up on his instrument be otherwise? Emerson was pure music-hall, a honky Hendrix whose very real sonic adventurism – such as his celebrated and ear-bending trick of ramming knives down between the organ keys – was ignored by the addled attitudes of gullible audiences and writers who merely wanted grandstanding gimmicks. Emerson, unfortunately, either pandered more to mob expectations than Hendrix, or was coerced thereto. Here, auto-destructive art became mere spectacle; certainly Emerson never conducted aural experiments for as long as Hendrix, and the Progressive story might have been healthier if he had. His musicianship was prodigious and allied intellect to stamina – for instance, his adaptation of Bernstein's 'America' deftly employed a figure from Dvořák's *New World* symphony. This cheekily skilful obtrusion didn't cut much ice with Bernstein himself, who prevented The Nice from releasing the song in the US after they had set light to the Stars an Stripes during a performance of it at the Royal Albert Hall.

Texturally, Emerson was also a special talent. Compare and contrast his syrupy Reg Dixon tone on 'Little Arabella' (1967) with the outrageous sounds emanating from the organ on the band's *pièce de résistance*, 'Rondo' (1967). These were sounds of a kind which Emerson claimed the instrument's inventor 'never knew existed'.[18] This wasn't strictly true, but a worthwhile enough statement. Only the avant-garde likes of Stockhausen (whose *Mikrophonie II* experiments predated the Nice by several years) had taken the Hammond this far and returned safely. Dave Brubeck's 'Blue Rondo à la Turk', which had also used the same Mozart material as The Nice emptied into 'Rondo'; was never like this. Emerson's glissandi sound like great sheets of steel being torn from their moorings and flying through a wind tunnel; Emerson's distribution of the beat and emphasis was more conventional than Brubeck's but odd enough. The suite 'Ars Longa Vita Brevis' from the album of the same name (1968) is farcically overlong, but also contains much invention, although *The Nice*, a live album from 1969, is only patchy.

This helped define the band, and ultimately, in the post-Progressive backlash, condemn it. Emerson became more and more devoted to 'overhauling', 'damaging' or 'pissing all over' classical music (according to preference). It is absurd to suggest, as some have, that these were 'improvements', perhaps betraying a memory only of the half-baked claims made for Emerson both by press and publicity blurbs. Emerson was far too much of a rock'n'roll showman to believe that his versions of Sibelius, Bernstein, Bach or anyone else were 'improvements'. What Emerson did was improve on what was around him in 1967.

The Nice indubitably wrote some of the most memorable psychedelic pop songs of the period, vacillating teasingly between the West Coast and MOR, notably the refrain of 'The Thoughts of Emerlist Davjack' which echoes the Association and Marmalade, the bizarre epic-pop heyday when aching post-Romantic harmonies and bubblegum bounce became indissoluble. The final two pieces of *Five Bridges* (1970) are, respectively, a beautifully clever crocheting-together of Dylan's 'Country Pie' and Bach's chords from the sixth Brandenburg Concerto, with 'One of Those People'. This latter, a berserk miscarriage of a pop song, perhaps illustrates the Nice's real gift: to reduce pop forms to their constituent parts, alter their horizontal profile by cutting down paragraphs and overturning expected progressions of chords and rhythm, which gives Emerson just as much of a chance to display his considerable technique without recourse to braggadocio. In the Nice's attempts at 'classical' pieces, Emerson's teeth are blunted; he merely seems content to make sensational gestures as opposed to radical statements, to be integrated into a performance with professionalism and precision much as he might integrate snatches of Tchaikovsky or Beethoven into a solo just for the hell of it.

Soft Machine had, in the space of two albums, taken pop harmony by the scruff of the neck and recast it; from being simply an element of emotional reflex, conventionally situated in the recognizable context of the song, sunny pop harmony fuelled a much more febrile musical unit; in doing so, it became, like serialism, free improvisation *et al.*, a wild card, a random element. Yes, Procol Harum and the Nice subjected it to similarly exacting exercises, but maintained it as a normal part of harmonic relations in recognizable musical structures; extending it vertically and horizontally, but retaining the emotional syntax and merely adding others – those of jazz and classical music.

LOOKING BOTH WAYS – THE PAST *VS.* THE FUTURE IN PROGRESSIVE IDEOLOGY

What cultural critic Stuart Hall called the 'American moment',[19] launched by the hippies in the mid-1960s, and since expanded into an international counter-culture, was turning bitter at the core by 1970. The breadheads, demons of West Coast fundamentalism, were suddenly at large; Jeff Dexter blamed the festivals: 'They destroyed the underground – everyone tried to make a buck.'[20] Subsequent events and analysis thereof seem to prove him right.

Underground folk darlings the Incredible String Band switched to prima-donna mode and refused to perform at the Royal Albert Hall unless Joe Boyd ensured they had the requisite 'lucky' carpet bussed in for them to perform on. The Move and Arthur Brown started to charge huge amounts of money to play gigs.

There was also growing popular resistance to the Underground that media investigation had turned up and illuminated: a tribe of tabloids dismissed Baroness Wooton's report on drugs in 1968 as a 'junkie's charter'.[21] In poet/bandleader Pete Brown's words, 'In those days it was still a family audience – with parental control over what their children purchased ... The Beatles – working-class boys writing lovely songs. Everyone got into it. Mums, Dads, everyone. But the minute that, say, Lennon got busted, there was a complete cooling ... '[22] The pastoral hippy idyll was jolted by Brian Jones's death at the quintessential English rural dreamscape, A. A. Milne's House at Pooh Corner. Moguls and hucksters sniffed around rock, cashing in like there was no tomorrow; Jonathan King suggested that Genesis (then officially unnamed) record *From Genesis to Revelation* – 'It was terribly pretentious – the history of Man's evolution in ten simple pop songs,' winced Peter Gabriel a decade later.[23]

Endorsement from on high had also deserted popular music. Sir Harold Wilson abandoned his youth credentials by condemning student 'agitators' for 'anti-British' behaviour.[24] The Britishness debate was fuelled by Enoch Powell, whose notorious 'rivers of blood' speech found a growing army of footsoldier supporters in the skinhead movement. If hippyism stood for breaking down barriers, for exploration and travel within and without, skinheads stood for erecting them.

But there were also the first flowerings of the Anglicization of rock discourse that would characterize mature Progressive. On a crude surface level, songs covered at rock clubs nationwide were increasingly those of British artists, demonstrating a pride in British pop music inconceivable only a year or two earlier. Songs like Spectrum's 'Portobello Road' and Donovan's 'Sunny Goodge Street' (not to mention the Kinks' 'Waterloo Sunset' and Pink Floyd's 'Grantchester Meadows') were an indication that there was now a prestige, abstracted consciously or subconsciously, in the folk roots of both modern and pre-modern Britain that gave indirect strength to musical expression. But there was also a subtler shift of emphasis going on. Critics talk of Barrett 'transforming the slide guitar into a feature of the Floyd's English dreamscapes' on recordings as early as those on *The Piper at the Gates of Dawn*.[25] We have already investigated, of course, the pastoral Kenneth Grahame references of titular explicitness; there is no evidence or ironic intent, the work contained on the album was in direct conflict with its nomenclature.

One of the most salient features of the emergent pastoral nature of the fledgling Progressive movement was the phenomenon of the now all-but-forgotten Incredible String Band. Formed by Clive Palmer (vocals, guitar, bass) and Robin

Williamson (vocals, guitar, various) as an Edinburgh-based jug band before Mike Heron (vocals, guitar, various) joined, their first eponymous album (1966) was undemonstratively winsome folk in the cautiously experimental van of Dylan's electric trials. Their second effort, however, was of extraordinary audaciousness. *The 5000 Spirits or the Layers of the Onion* (1967) in Allan Moore's words, 'seemed to concern qualities of gentleness and otherness,'[26] and in critic Robin Denselow's opinion, 'showed a mystical, pantheist involvement in a very live universe'.[27] The ISB cultural trawl-net extended even further than any 'rock act', not least their spiritual mentor, Bob Dylan, had so far been prepared to explore, using Egyptian rebec, Indian gimbri, Arabic tamboura and various whistles. Titles like 'Gently Tender' and 'Painting Box' appear to bear out Moore's prognosis. Their ecstatic reception at the Newport Folk Festival in 1968 and the No. 5 placing in the British charts of their third album, *The Hangman's Beautiful Daughter* (1968), which added harpsichord, kazoo and Hammond organ, was indication enough of how deeply rooted the musical pluralism of the Underground had become in popular consciousness. According to Chris Cutler: 'They were one of the most important bands of the era, and they are almost completely neglected now. Instead of AABABA etc, their developments would go linearly, A-B-C-D-E-F-G-H-I-J-K-L-M and beyond; no one else *thought* that way ever ... [28]

The feminine element of the ISB, illustrated in the title of their third album (and indeed eventually reflected in the unusually democratic lineup – two women, two men), reflected an equation of the feminine with the 'natural', with that 'other' side of human nature that conventional society was supposed to have suppressed, best expressed by the changing face of female iconography as glutinously expressed in *Elvira Madigan's* demurely fresh-faced, golden-tressed heroine standing like a flower in a bourgeois wasteland (another echo of past bourgeois European aesthetic and cultural ideals and preoccupations).

In the wake of the US group the Band's well-publicized 'back-to-the-roots' Big Pink experiment, their communal attempt to reintroduce themselves to the American folk heritage by actually living in the wilds, a horde of bands imitated them. What happened was a practical extension of pastoralism; now rock musicians, while not exactly retreading the footsteps of Cecil Sharp or Ralph Vaughan Williams in tapping the countryside for musical input, adopted an emphatically Romantic attitude that affirmed that inspiration derived from subjective experience of non-urban places. The social milieu may have been different, but the aesthetic which drove these musicians into the countryside was the same: a romanticized retreat from expanding industrial society. Not only was 'nature' their aim; the Beatles' 'communal' house (in *Help*) also inspired. Yes went to South Molton in Devon. Genesis hid out in Dorking and Crowborough, safely within the Home Counties public-school belt. Gentle Giant rented a farm at Southwick, near their Portsmouth base (a location featuring in the impossibly fey story – in Gothic script, of course – about how 'six dedicated musicians in a house far from the centre of town' was enough to captivate a friendly, 'gentle' giant). These leanings would remain a tacit part of Progressive ideology always, but would also surface explicitly in the text of Progressive folk artists in the early 1970s.

The tension in Progressive between the technical and the pastoral, the future and the past, was interesting. Technology meant newer, better music the argument ran. But that also compromised the diehard pastoralism of grassroots hippyism and the marketable eco-idylls by now assuming centrality in the genre's visual identity. In terms of recording technology, the industry kept pace with musicians' ambitions and vice versa. Sixteen-track recording debuted at the end of the 1960s; given the prevalent format of the LP, wider vertical complexity (more choice of tracks) could complement longer horizontal developments.

Music papers routinely rhapsodized over electronic experiments: King Crimson's embrace of the VCS3 synthesizer and the well-publicized meeting of Robert Moog and Keith Emerson at the time of ELP's celebrated debuts in live and studio performance (much space was given to the fact that Emerson's Moog cost a then unheard-of £4,000). The Apollo moon landings in 1969 had been seen as the ultimate triumph of technology and of the post-war economic miracle, and while the Apollo hardware embodied the American military–industrial complex so mistrusted by the counter-culture, the counter-culture's prime mode of entertainment (rock) was intractably wedded to the electronics industry just as surely as space travel was. 'We never had any sort of PA until we played Hyde Park,' says Glenn Sweeney ruefully of early Third Ear Band days. 'Simply because you had to, we went up to 4,000 watts, although if you're dealing with 250,000 people even that's not enough.'[29]

For Pink Floyd, however, technology dictated the metamorphosis of rock musician into rock auteur. Nick Mason takes up the story:

> All the things that interested us in a studio were not the things that were involved with improvisation. Very quickly we found that what we were aiming for was to try and perfect things and then build them up, particularly in the early days when we were working with four and eight tracks. There was a hell of a lot of layering that went on, where things had to be sort of set in stone ... so you became more and more conscious of trying to get something absolutely right ... because once you started layering things ... any little glitsch ... got worse and worse.[30]

The beneficiary of this technical advancement was the Floyd's first post-Barrett effort, *A Saucerful of Secrets*. Initial reaction to the band's preference for arrangement over (at least perceived) spontaneity was unfavourable. 'Little new here,' charged Miles in the *IT*. 'Too long, too boring, and totally uninventive,' he said of the title track, making a not-irrelevant comparison with the 1957 composition 'Metamorphosis' by the Soviet émigré Ussachevsky. 'In the same way that bad sitar music is initially attractive, electronic music always turns people on at first – then as one hears more the listener demands that something be made and done with all these "new" sounds, something more than "psychedelic mood music".'[31] The piece does have its moments of epigonism – the 'celestial voices' section ending the work is simply too pat an imitation of the Ligeti choral pieces used in Kubrick's *2001* the year before, although Wright's eerie organ chords, halfway between F. W. Murnau and Scooby Doo, resolve satisfyingly into the blissful coda. But despite a fearless plundering of sound from all registers of all instruments used, there is more of a concentration on the passive mood-painting that Miles cautions the band against than on the edgier *Piper*.

While the band could be found rapping with radical-chicster conductor-composer Leonard Bernstein about their music, further Establishment recognition was forthcoming when the band contributed material to a BBC satire on the Apollo 11 moon landing, *What If It's Just Green Cheese?* The Floyd were still regarded as radical; in their 'More Furious Madness from the Massed Gadgets of Auximenes' show in April 1969 rhythmic hammering and sawing gave way to the performance being given over to a transistor radio while the 'workmen' sat down for tea. Found sounds, then eye-poppingly futuristic, featured heavily in Floyd's music. Waters recorded at home in a toolshed in his garden. There was talk of Floyd earnings being spent on rows of houses to be let to the deserving poor.

There is a tendency towards greater organization in the music, but never at the absolute expense of free-form improvised atmospherics. The contrast of the punchy introduction section and the initial verses of 'Let There Be More Light' which opens the album is the music of an ensemble thinking, musically, in long-term paragraphs, and of pitting sections of music one against another. The hypnotic incantation of electronics returns from *Piper* in the hair-raising drone 'Set the Controls for the Heart of the Sun', puffed by Waters as being about 'an unknown person who, while piloting a mighty flying saucer, is overcome with solar suicidal tendencies and sets controls for the heart of the sun'.[32] The title, Karl Dallas later noted, is derived, purposely or otherwise, from William Burroughs. Dallas also perceptively states that with the eclipse of the now definitively acid-damaged Barrett (who apparently sat outside the studio at EMI with his guitar for days waiting to be asked to play and would shortly be expelled from the band) Gilmour's chunkier, fatter timbre strengthened the band's sound.[33] The style would later go on to become the height of boilerplate rock cliché, but in this context sounds exciting. Gilmour later bitched: 'I used an echo box *years* before Syd. I also used slide. I also *taught* Syd quite a lot about guitar. I was a couple of streets ahead of him at the time and was teaching him to play Stones riffs every lunchtime for a year at technical college.'[34] Barrett, nevertheless, on his one appearance on the album, steals the show with his brainwave invitation of a Salvation Army band into the studio to play 'anything they wanted'[35] for the final track, 'Jugband Blues', whereby the treated caterwauling of the brass is faded in and out of Barrett and Gilmour's harsh guitar accents while verses accelerate and decelerate as they meander tipsily towards the chorus. This would be Barrett's final contribution to the Floyd canon he had done so much to consecrate; a slave to acid, the disintegration of his personality and playing and his eventual ousting from a band personally concerned and professionally hampered by his behaviour has been told too often elsewhere (particularly in Nicholas Schaffner's eloquent *A Saucerful of Secrets*) to be worth repeating here. An episode of harrowing sordidness, it contained such tragicomic spectacles as adolescent female fans screaming adoration at what they fondly imagined to be Syd while on tour, when in fact it was David O'List, guitarist of support band the Nice, who had been recruited in desperation as an impromptu stand-in.

Barrett was gone by 1968, and the music, already piloted by the other Floyds on *A Saucerful of Secrets* away from the kookier excesses of Barrett's unique genius, became more and more calculated and leant less toward haphazard innovation of new forms and voices than tentative experimentation with well-tried ones.

The next album, the double *Ummagumma* (1969), offered fans two live sides of often involvingly spiritual live improvisation and also two sides of frequently risible solo experimentation. Rick Wright's three-part 'Sysyphus' is appropriately if unintentionally laboured, lurching from toneless elbow-pounding (not unlike an excitable two-year-old let loose on the bass end of a piano keyboard) to queasy Mellotron chords vying for supremacy with deranged guitar. It's the result, apparently, of Wright 'wanting to make *real* music'.[36] Really? Waters used the band for one song, the shimmering idyll 'Grantchester Meadows', whose sampled birdsong and bees (swatted mercilessly to end the song) mirrors the song 'Cirrus Minor', recorded as part of the soundtrack to the 1968 Barbet Schroeder film *More* (evidence that the pastoral–industrial duality was operative even within the music of the technocratic Floyd universe itself). Waters was also responsible for a knockabout piece of studio-derived onomato-poeia, 'Several Species of Small Furry Creatures Gathered Together in a Cave and Grooving with a Pict'. It sounded uncannily literal, but Waters deflated the mystique of this oft-quoted piece of fascinating *musique concrète*: 'It's a very light-hearted and easy exercise. It's really just slowing down and speeding up tape.'[37] Playing the record at 16 r.p.m. transforms the high-pitched vocalist into Dave Gilmour, while Waters can be heard saying, 'That was pretty avant-garde, wasn't it?' At 45 r.p.m., Waters is tapelooped, imploring, 'Bring back my guitar.' The song's McGonagallesque poem, emoted in Lochnagar accents, was improvised in the studio. Gilmour's 'Narrow Way' was a tripartite suite, pleasantly contrasted although clumsily riff-based and unyieldingly thick in its rock-band textures and plodding, four-square rhythms, although the adventurous, if tasteful exploration of the range and potential of a stack of different acoustic and electric guitars in a short space of time is diverting. Mason's percussion extravaganza, 'The Grand Vizier's Tea Party' is partly redeemed by the editing and splicing techniques used, which offer new dimensions to simple rolls on timpani, snare, shakers and cymbals.

Atom Heart Mother (1970), with its orchestra-and-chorus-accompanied twenty-three-minute title track, sealed the band in the big league, and helped establish (some might say 'preserve in aspic') the elements of the Floyd sound. The theme to 'Atom Heart Mother', of Gilmourian provenance, sounded, to Waters, 'like the theme from some awful Western ... [it] had that heroic, plodding quality'.[38] The orchestration, completed with the help of accredited musical eccentric and electronic experimenter Ron Geesin, was serviceable if not exemplary. Motivically, the work is simple enough – there is caution here, with nobody overstepping his abilities. The band were not afraid to use solo orchestral instruments for statements, such as the mournful cello that intones the first main theme early on. Wright's insistence on repeated triplets as chordal accompaniment wears thin, however. Critics have harped tiresomely on the excellence of the stereo imagining on the piece; while the viscous, enveloping quality of Wright's organ swimming between channels is undeniably impressive, this, and apparently motiveless pieces of sampled sound (e.g. an accelerating motorbike), seem once again to emphasize the primacy not of composition but of engineering music. This would be admirable if the engineering did not appear to serve a purely expedient purpose, that is once again to underline not a radical view of the world through sound, but a fairly conventional one. These criteria apply also to the record's other breakthrough Floyd piece, 'Alan's Psychedelic Breakfast'.

In legend a tribute to EMI soundman and band buddy Alan Parsons, it's a flawed exercise utilizing both music and noise. But the snaps, crackles and pops of Parsons moving around his flat at sun-up are arranged, it would seem, in linear time. What we are hearing is nothing more than a reportage of events, and their integration into the piece's musical language is somewhat meaningless. The frying of eggs, assuming the properties of monsoon rain on a roof, is one interesting divergence into the realm of pure noise as an end in itself.

It's a very uncharitable view, perhaps, and one that can only be taken with hindsight, but the work of Subotnick, Cage and Stockhausen, exploring the character of noise as music, had been there long before. Not that the relationship of music and found sound did not ask interesting questions about the ambient nature of music, especially the simple piano/guitar chords and the developments thereof that the Floyd lazily wove in and around the soundscape.

In 1973 Gilmour told Chris Welch that the development of the Azimuth (a primitive device for projecting sound 360 degrees around an auditorum), as early as 1967, had been 'purely down to setting moods and creating an atmosphere'.[39] Ditto the quadraphonic tapes the band used at concerts. 'In 1967, no one realized that sound could get better. There was just noise, and that's how rock and roll was. As soon as you educate people to something better, then they want it better. Permanently. PAs were terrible in those days – but we've got an amazing one now.'[40] The Floyd's use of futuristic technology, while laudably dedicated, and in the context of its time highly inspired, rarely strayed beyond means-ends rationality of creating not art but commodity. The Middle Earth Club was daily beginning to seem just as distant as Middle Earth itself.

(NO) MESS OF BLUES

Chief among the side-effects of these cultural sea-changes was less a tangible anti-Americanism than an unspoken disengagement with learned American methods of popular-cultural expression, which brings us to one of Progressive's central tenets: the semi-conscious neutralization of the influence of African–American music. Progressive ideology's ruralism had freely drawn on European culture. The music was of similar cultural provenance, i.e. predominantly white parentage. Even the Floyd's steely cutting-edge sound rendered blues voicings as meek subordinates to Western avant-garde or classical timbres.

Many of the interviewees for this book – and those whose words have been lifted from elsewhere – openly admit their admiration for mid-1960s soul yet also claim that by the end of the 1960s the only interesting music was being made by predominantly white album artists.

That this represented a decision to exclude black music is a red herring; Hendrix's guitar playing was still the key to most musicians' thinking in the late 1960s, as were the crossover experiments of Miles Davis. But the discoveries of Anglo-Saxon/European mythologies upon which to base an emergent rock aesthetic necessarily involved the subordination of the urban American milieu from which much black music sprang. The work of Keith Emerson, who rendered black boogie-woogie and blues pianism as a merely servile illustrative component of his music alongside the music of the Western symphonic tradition, is an example. 'Black musicians are now implicitly regarded as precursors who, having taught the white men all they know, must gradually recede into the distance, as white progressive music, the simple lessons mastered, advances irresistibly into the future,' wrote Dave Morse of the era.[41] Roger Waters's formative album buys may have been of Leadbelly and Bessie Smith but Rick Wright (his card-carrying Stockhausen listenership was widely publicized) told the *NME* that his ambition was to 'hear his own symphony performed at the Royal Festival Hall'.[42] The only blues influences – indeed the American ones – were now strictly second-hand. As Pete Jenner later confessed; 'There was this spirit, this idea that there should be some sort of linkage with America ... America was much more exciting than it is now because you couldn't get there easily.' But he admitted that the Underground remained 'very, very English. While we read our *Naked Lunch* and our Jack Kerouac ... almost nobody actually *went*.'[43]

3 SAMPLERS, SUBSIDIARIES, SHOWMEN
(PROGRESSIVE ROCK AND IDEOLOGY CONSECRATED 1969–73)

FUTURE ROCK?

Jonathan Eisen, one of the first American rock journalists to elevate the music into a religion and its practitioners to a priesthood, was a Believer: 'Born of a hybrid of blues and country-western ... [rock] is now a full-throated school that incorporates everything from blues to Indian classical raga, from Bach to Stockhausen.'[1]

This was the gospel of rockism circa 1970; it was the music of the future, the new classical music. If this was indeed a new dawn, the news hadn't reached those responsible for it. In the UK, Progressive musicians, the big, bad, bold boys of an artistic *bouleversement*, were, materially at least, prophets without honour. Or clothes or food, in some cases. Take just four examples of life in what latterday critical opinion has termed a hedonistic sloth-fest.

One story relates how the Nice, major stars at the time, bussed all the way across Ireland with support acts Yes and the Bonzo Dog Doo-Dah Band on a nationwide tour to a gig which did not officially exist. The probably apocryphal account of Keith Emerson passing time in a pub playing upright-piano accompaniment to the Bonzos' Vivian Stanshall's rendition of bawdy Irish ballads is a memorable one.

Peter Wynne-Willson told Pink Floyd's biographer Nicholas Schaffner of contemporary promotional agencies: '[They] paid no regard to the routes that we would take. It would get to the stage that the roadie would *have* to get some sleep – but we still had to get to the next place ... he would jam his foot on the accelerator and go to sleep. And whoever was sitting next to him ... would actually steer.'[2]

To Genesis, 'going up north [visiting Buxton in an old and windowless bread van] was like visiting another planet'.[3] John Peel gets nostalgic:

> I remember going to gigs with the Edgar Broughton Band. They were these revolutionaries, kill-the-pig guys, and the two Broughton brothers had their Mum and Dad roadying for them, so on the way to gigs we'd have to stop in lay-bys so their mum could cook some soup.
>
> We had to drive ourselves. I did gigs with my own gear. You had to do that to make ends meet. And if you'd meet anyone anywhere, you'd meet them at the Blue Boar on the M1 at four o'clock in the morning. People didn't get paid then – no riders, no vegetarian meals or three bottles of Blue Nun. And at festivals, always the prospect of not getting paid.'[4]

The Blue Boar, a service station on the arterial M1 motorway near the Midlands town of Daventry, was a lodestone of English rock in the early stages of its mobility; bands great and small heading homewards from the multiplicity of venues the beat and rock booms had opened would meet there. In the words of Rick Wakeman, a man meant to be a pampered, hip demigod of narcotized rock indulgence, 'It would only serve food on paper plates with plastic knives and forks ... nobody would go near it who wasn't either in a band, a Hell's Angel or escaped from prison.' Wakeman's own worst memory of the place was having the entire canteen staff adoringly surrounding his then-employers, the Strawbs, before finding out they'd in fact mistaken them for Jethro Tull.[5]

Bill Bruford recalls of the late 1960s rock 'boom':

> Yes lived like a fire brigade – all packed into this one place, in a constant state of readiness. Nobody could go anywhere in case we got a call to say we'd got a gig in Skelmersdale. I can see Jon Anderson now on the staircase in Munster Road screaming down the phone, pouring invective on agents, managers, promoters, demanding more money, for the petrol, whatever. 'How dare you charge me such-and-such ... ?!' Anything to keep his fledgling band alive ... and God bless him, he did keep it alive.[6]

PROPHETS, SEERS, SAGES ... AND A&R MEN

How and why? The eruption in the number of bands in the 1960s led to a commensurate expansion in stage space; pop had to be exploited, and the country was suddenly awash with venues. Rock proved a different kettle of fish; several interviewees hint darkly at early reluctance at backward British venues to entertain the performances of long-hairs. But any slack was taken up by the university and polytechnic circuit. Heftily subsidized and enjoying booming student numbers, British universities also proved fertile ground for anti-Establishment attitudes. Housing a generation freed of domestic responsibilities in a well-stocked academic climate titillating both the sensory palates and the pockets of youth, student-union social secretaries began answering the demand for live music with acts to match the aberrant aspirations of students. Anything that appeared to insult the tastes of the preceding generation from whom many students were now (at least putatively, and perhaps temporarily) free, was courted and welcomed.'The university circuit,' remembers Glenn Sweeney of the Third Ear Band, 'was brilliant. No hassles, or at least not as many as at ordinary gigs.'[7]

Musician and producer Tom Newman recollects:

> What happened was that you had big student numbers, subscriptions of £10 a year or seven-and-six on the night to get in to see bands they were suddenly hearing about on the grapevine or in the papers. They got everyone, often by word of mouth. Led Zeppelin ... Yes ... it's odd, really, that there's so little of that nowadays. Back then, student unions always signed up people who weren't on the telly. Now, you get them clamouring for people who *are* on the telly.'[8]

Most student unions were expected to make a £500-per-year loss on their bookings, with only Essex and Kent universities expecting a profit. British bands who reaped success in America came back with their loon-pant pockets sizeably enhanced and expecting them to be filled commensurately – by 1970 the Who were already demanding £1,000 a night – but redbrick colleges practically kept Progressive alive, and helped create an audience for Progressive as a lifestyle, as a separate culture, a signifier for a newly-defined 'other'.

Rock album sales had overtaken pop single sales for the first time in 1969 and the industry reacted accordingly. Sixties proto-lad Pete Shertser read the signs: 'We had a go [at setting up an independent record label] and it was crazy: grands! We were getting these pound notes flying in every direction.'[9] Major labels set up their own 'progressive' subsidiaries (EMI's Harvest, Philips's Vertigo, RCA's Neon, Decca's Deram Nova), as well as taking on distribution duties for small independent labels like Island and Charisma. Some majors plunged willy-nilly into the market, with Atlantic's signing of Led Zeppelin a prime example. The big boys were careful to assure the kids that they were all on the same side: 'The revolutionaries are on CBS' and 'The man can't bust our music,' bellowed Columbia's publicity. In such a fervid seller's-market atmosphere, it is hardly surprising that an extraordinary cross-section of acts emerged from the woodwork for industry inspection.

'Guitarist/writer seeks receptive musicians determined to strive beyond existing stagnant music forms' – small ads of this kind multiplied virally in the crepuscular murk of the back end of the *Melody Maker* (for the record, this one attracted Genesis to guitarist Steve Hackett).[10] The 'scene' was super-fluid. If it was remotely connected with the counter-culture, with *anything* termed 'progressive', it was signed. Progressive folk, child of hippy eco-mania, swiftly acquired a uniquely contemporary character. It is unlikely such music could have been made at any other period in musical history, so much was it a shotgun-wedding of various flavours of the month.

From 1968 ubiquitous rent-a-hippy Marc Bolan had led the way with Tyrannosaurus Rex. Mod and ace Face about Town (retired), Marc Feld changed his surname to Bolan, strapped on a creaky guitar, finagled his way into the underground with unimpeachable chutzpah and picked up bongo player and sometime Pink Fairy Steve Took. Indiscriminately studded with second-hand Donovanisms, Bolan's early albums were rococo pearls of hippy indulgence which now do little but beg the question as to how long Bolan expected anyone to buy his pose. Done dirt cheap and sounding cheaper (his debut cost just £400 to record) *My Children Were Fair And Had Sky In Their Hair ... But Now They're Content To Wear Stars On Their Brows, Prophets, Seers and Sages, the Angels of the Ages, Unicorn* and *A Beard of Stars* were rag-and-bone fantasy, a gallimaufry of occult images purloined from unnumbered second-rate poets and drawled over a back-to-the-earth minimalism of guitar and bongos. *Unicorn* reached No. 12 in the album charts in 1969. John Peel was a tireless patron.

Time has not been kind to Bolan's reputation – standard sneers of barefaced exploitation of the *zeitgeist* are all too common – and once the fey star-child (accused widely also of shamelessly plagiarizing his hero Syd Barrett) had found a more commercial, electrified and contemporary niche than warbling warmed-up legends, he rode a white swan into the sunset and chart superstardom with T. Rex.

Folk's relationship to Progressive is of a complexity which warrants further investigation later. But by the end of the 1960s, the feelers between genres were (profitably) out. There were a clump of such bands, Tudor Lodge, Trader Horne, Trees and Mellow Candle, signed while the signing was good by anyone who thought long hair might make a buck. The hook was (usually) a female vocalist such as Trees' entrancing Celia Humphries, her contribution to *The Garden of Jane Delawney* (1970) offering possibly the Ur-text of Progressive folk.

Others preferred a rootsier approach. Progressive folk was all right for the chicks, but what about the boys? It was too much to expect the dominant soul, blues and jazz influences which had driven so many musicians to emulation in the 1960s simply to be hegemonized by non-American musical currents. And so the market was ripe enough for those who wanted to maintain the clubby sweat of the city as the prime mover of popular music, who wanted to retain music's relationship with the body as well as keep it connected to the head. Mick Abrahams and Blodwyn Pig manhandled jazz and blues into the rock van, as did Bakerloo and Scotland's lusty Mogul Thrash. You couldn't get manlier than these fearless fusioneers of the earthiest musics of the lot; heroic hod-carriers of the coming rockist millennium, their day soon passed. But for the time being promoters were trawl-netting the country for any sign of Progressive, anywhere, from rock operas at Watford Town Hall to song cycles wafting through the Devizes Poperama. Gigs could be inspired or downright awful. Nobody cared. Rock – specifically Progressive – had found its audience. Yes's Chris Squire played a *twenty-minute* bass solo over the Young Rascals' 'Good Loving', and according to Bill Bruford: 'It was the same with the guitar solo. The rest of us would leave the stage and Peter [Banks] would go on, and on, and on.'[11] Banks himself recalls: '... for five, ten, fifteen minutes, and I can imagine what everybody must have been thinking: Jesus Christ, when's he going to stop?'[12]

Not that audiences, or record companies, minded. They trekked to Scotland to sign String Driven Thing, to Wales to sign

Love Sculpture. From Ireland came, among others, Andwella's Dream, who still excite Progressive obsessives today with their haunting and unusually full-blooded blend of folk and psychedelia. Tom Newman, then of cult psychedelic-Progressive outfit July, recalls: 'Nobody went around actually *calling* themselves progressive. The press did, the industry did.'[13]

John Peel:

> There were promotions like RCA's Groupquake – there was one by a band called Auto Salvage which was quite good, but the rest were just shite. In a way, the subsidiaries were great. Now either the major labels buy indie labels or they use the indie labels to overfish the talent. But in those days the labels seemed to know they had a responsibility beyond straight-forward commerce. They'd set these things up as dormitories, knowing they might make a loss, but knowing they might find something profitable[14]

INDEPENDENTS' DAY

Faced with the boom in the market but often stymied by the unwillingness of established major record companies to exploit it, many set up record labels on their own to cater on a small scale to a new, product-hungry audience. Island Records was one such enterprise, and in their then-manager Dave Betteridge's words: 'There was a new intelligent rock – there was a college circuit being built and a new audience was emerging. And we were running in tandem, supplying their needs.'[15]

John Peel set up on his own, founding Dandelion Records with Clive Selwood, *wunderkind* of then-hip Elektra Records. Peel remembers:

> He had the Doors, MC5, you name it – and trading on that, we persuaded CBS to fund Dandelion. We had a friend, Bridget St John, who we wanted to record. Nobody else did, so we thought 'bugger it', and used CBS's money. CBS got tired of us, we went to Warners', they got tired of us – they saw things in terms of hit records – and we ended up with Polydor.

We did have a small hit with Medicine Head in 1972. But we only wanted to cover costs.

I never felt any affinity with the industry – an awful lot of selfish, priggish, pompous, self-important people. Tony Stratton-Smith of Charisma I liked – but he obviously relished the fight of the industry. And, I'll admit, there were lots of strange gentlemen who got involved with the industry in a dislocated way who came up accidentally with some rather good stuff.[16]

Ex-soccer journalist Stratton-Smith was a Falstaffian *bon viveur* personified. Gravitating to the Nice from managing flower-power flops like the Koobas and Creation, he watched in dismay as his band's record label, Immediate, folded under them like an old deckchair in 1967, inspiring him to set up his own independent, Charisma. He opened up the Lyceum to rock concerts and featured in *Rolling Stone*, as one of the genre's most aggressive young movers and shakers.

Charisma was among the first to pioneer one of Progressive's first marketing ploys, a label 'package tour' of acts, with Lindisfarne, Van der Graaf Generator and Genesis touring large venues and colleges in the UK, with prices pegged at six shillings (30p) to maximize audience potential.

The Charisma package was the wheeze of one Tony Smith, a small, furiously energetic man, son of the indefatigable John Smith, who'd coped heroically with the first British Beatles tour. Smith thought beyond his stature and his years, using both his own oft-lauded skills and the cachet of the Smith name to hustle the Who on at Sadlers Wells and get Emerson, Lake and Palmer a Christmas gig at the Odeon in Piccadilly.

'This [package touring] was a great idea,' says Dave Stewart, then organist with various Progressive lineups, most notably Egg.

Several labels did that. It was good that they were prepared to get stuck in supporting bands and their music at *live gigs*, whereas you sometimes signed to a label who would give you x thousands of pounds to go out on the road and 'promote your album'. The only guys who got any money out of that bloody arrangement were the promoters. There were loads of musicians going round thinking the world owed them a living. You know, sign to CBS and get them to subsidize your touring arrangements. Great, but it makes you a CBS employee.[17]

Stratton-Smith also helped pioneer the 'sampler album', whereby Progressive bands from specific labels were showcased on LP, most famously on Vertigo's *Vertigo Annual* or on Harvest's *Picnic* double-albums (both 1970) which sought, often clumsily, to define the new market's profile.

Sleevenotes were corny enough; Egg were particularly culpable, stating baldly on the back of their first album that theirs was serious music which was 'not for dancing to'.[18] As if dubbing one track thereon 'Symphony No. 2' wasn't 'highbrow' enough, their second album, *The Polite Force*, enumerated the music's funny time-signatures on the sleeve – just to show how 'progressive' these boys were (underlined, in case you'd missed the point, in a written endorsement by producer Neil Slavin).

On a larger scale, the design company Hipgnosis had already moved the gnostic, allusive aspects of prototype Progressive imagery into the big league by erecting forty-foot cardboard cows on Sunset Boulevard in Los Angeles to promote Pink Floyd's 1970's album *Atom Heart Mother* (whose cover is an enigmatically unremarkable photograph of a dairy cow).

Progressive, notably in the case of the subsidiary labels, traded on mystique and marque. As with Sun and Riverside Records, which had so animated young musicians in the 1950s and 1960s, these were enterprises that would trade on the cachet of an *independent* name at a time when independence was a Good Thing, knowing their clientele would purchase anything on these labels as a badge of artistic integrity.

Charisma's roster was never radical; Audience, Graeme Bell's Bell and Arc, Rare Bird and especially Capability Brown were undemonstrative and undemanding purveyors of plangent hooks, herbily flavourful folkish harmonies, necessarily ethereal Hammond organ and growling fuzz bass. Archetypal were String

Driven Thing, who ditched their West Coast psychedelic pop for Progressive folk, signed to Charisma in 1972 and, with violin and banjo prominent (hence the name), released songs like 'It's a Game' (later covered by the Bay City Rollers). That said, the 'Famous' Charisma label, as it satirically billed itself, also offered a home for Monty Python and erstwhile Floyd collaborator and electronic prankster Ron Geesin. In short, a microcosm of Progressive Englishness, amplified eccentricity for the catastrophic 1960s hangover of early-1970s Britain, with its strikes and teeth-brushing in the power-cut dark.

Vertigo, home of acts as diverse as Black Sabbath and Rod Stewart, is perhaps the most enduring indication of the plurality of the term 'Progressive' circa 1970. 'Rock' or 'heavy music', as it was then generically termed, were still bound for little reason beyond the fact that the music wasn't pop, and that Radio 1 DJ and knowing rock philistine Tony Blackburn would make provoking periodic sallies against it. But the majority of Vertigo artists told another story, of the increasing specialization and individual codification of a conscious Progressive ideology. Cressida's debut album earned plaudits then as now, but its kaleidoscopic cross-fertilization of styles underlines a somewhat creaky and cack-handed eclecticism as opposed to serious comparison and contrast of musical language. Its sticky-back plastic soundstage sounds dated too (a *Daily Sketch* 'LP of the Week' honour seems to confer upon it veritable antique status) but it remains an essential purchase for all those interested in the genesis of the Progressive aesthetic. Similarly, Gracious's single album with its dauntingly portentous track listing ('Introduction' – 'Heaven' 'Hell' – 'Fugue in D Minor' – 'The Dream') and the axiomatic arrangements (the painfully predictable use of harpsichord on 'Fugue' for example) smack of trainee surgery – clearly these were committed yet inexperienced young men with knowledge of classical, jazz, blues and rock music limited enough to enable them to create no more than a stitched-together Frankenstein's monster.

Vertigo also boasted Manfred Mann's Chapter Three and Ian Carr's Nucleus, both able emulators of the free-jazz/rock bandwaggon set rolling by Soft Machine and being given a definitive shove in the US by Miles Davis's ground-breaking *Bitches Brew* album, but which would prosper in the UK under the banner of Colosseum, whose *Valentyne Suite* still agitates Progressive completists as the first album issued on the Vertigo label in March 1970.

Vertigo survived the waning of Progressive music's popularity in the early 1970s, even unearthing new talent. One such was the improbable Ramases, a remarkable man who had graduated from martial-arts instruction in the RAF to selling central heating at enormous profit in Scotland. After a 'visitation' by the spirit of the ancient Egyptian king Rameses in his car one day, he turned to music, as artist Roger Dean recalls, as the means of 'telling people about the meaning of the universe.

So he called himself Ramases, got himself a leopard and a recording contract and did just that.'[19] Accompanied by his wife Sel, Ramases signed to Vertigo in 1970; four musicians who would later form the quasi-Progressive pop group 10cc, covertly undertook his earthly duties by performing most of the music of his first album, *Space Hymns*, in 1971. Astonishingly, a follow-up, *Glass Top Coffin*, appeared in 1975.

Dr Z had relatively workaday origins by Ramases's standards, although being the pet project of a north Wales professor and keyboard player called Keith Keyes might not conform with many commentators' ideals of the traditional gestation of rock creativity. *Three Parts to My Soul* (three part ... trio lineup ... obviously boffins) was basically the work of a harpsichord–bass–drums outfit who sang, among other things, of the tripartite split in human nature. Amidst the hokey agonizing over enlightenment, the album was passable enough if, in the ambivalent phrase of discographer Vernon Joynson, the listener doesn't mind 'being showered with philosophical content whilst listening to rock'.[20]

Vertigo's Affinity featured in an early TV attempt to tap into the underbelly of the rock boom, when cameras went on the road with the band and preserved for posterity a litany of haplessness and helplessness; battered by ill-fortune, bankrupted by the industry, Affinity's TV outing was fifteen minutes of shame, at its most poignant when the keyboard player's fragile health rendered him unfit to tour further. Beggars Opera, a Glaswegian three-piece, a kind of Easterhouse ELP, racked up three albums, the ostentatiously performed but melodically challenged *Act 1*, (1970), followed by 1971's *Waters of Change*, which was preceded by a left-field European hit with the non-album track 'Sarabande'. *Pathfinder* (1972) over-eggs the already indigestible pudding of 'MacArthur Park' and by 1974, *Get Your Dog Off Me* signed the band's death warrant.

Alongside Heavy Metal icons Black Sabbath, Uriah Heep proved to be Vertigo's cash cow. *Very 'eavy, Very 'umble* (1970) seems notable now only for the hyperbole of one American critic: 'If this band makes it, I'll have to commit suicide.'[21] Formed, like so many contemporary rock acts, from the hapless remnants of beached beat boys, the brawny rock of the band's debut always craved a little feminine touch, but when it came it resembled little more than the amateurish *maquillage* of a novice transvestite. At least the organ effects, operatic vocals, brass and woodwind on *Salisbury's* (1971) sixteen-minute title track *sounded* brave. Perhaps it wasn't a gimmick – although that might not hold for 1972's *Look at Yourself*, which sported an easy-stain mirror cover enabling the buyer to – hey – do just that! *July Morning* featured Moog synthesizer, members of Afro-rock band Osibisa and Manfred Mann, but it proved to be not so much a beginning of interesting things as a definitive end, as Heep lumbered off into terminal Heavy Metal fatigue.

Of the rest of the Progressive subsidiaries, Dawn (Pye) vanished without trace in the mid-1970s just before the ignoble implosion of their parent company. Their stable succoured acts from Vincent Crane's galumphing Hammond-led Heavy Metal trio Atomic Rooster through the Be Bop Preservation Society (led by *Play Away* bassist Spike Heatley) to the cheerless but intriguing soundscapes of folk-inflected hippies Comus, whose *First Utterance* matched lyrics of Heavy Metal-like physical degradation with flimsily engaging acoustic music through which a solo violin intermittently shines.

Poor relation among the Progressive labels was RCA's Neon,

which in retrospect boasted only two acts of note, the ludicrously over-populated if entertaining free-jazz orchestra Centipede, whose personnel (Ian Carr, Karl Jenkins, Keith Tippett, Robert Wyatt, Roy Babbington, Elton Dean, Roy Marshall, Alan Skidmore) reads like a Burke's Peerage of modern UK jazz; and the over-rated Spring. Probably noted now only for the inclusion of latterday Dire Straits drummer Pick Withers, Spring nevertheless retain some cachet among Progressive cognoscenti for the merits of their one-off self-titled album. Indeed its spacious and supple musical explorations into relatively sedate artistic territory (undemonstratively poppish motifs, textbook rock solo developments) possess an emotional punch lent by the tasteful use of Mellotron, showcasing one of the most notable deployments of the instrument anywhere on record.

Buoyed by Pink Floyd's sales, EMI's subsidiary Harvest tried to sell Babe Ruth, Bakerloo, Pete Brown's Piblokto! and the Panama Ltd Jug Band. Decca signed Progressive acts to their own marque and to Deram Nova, including (guitarless) Aardvark, Mellow Candle and others; their bankers, however, were the Moody Blues, whose infatuation with the symphony orchestra had, as Bill Bruford suggested it might, ignited a fad for orchestral sonorities and the cultural prestige attached thereto, throughout the rock community.

CLASSICALLY GASSED
What followed was symptomatic both of the era's burgeoning confidence and of its sapling aesthetic sensibilities. Most importantly, it indicated the opening up of daylight between two Progressive agendas. On the one hand, listener-friendly, Beatles-derived Progressive music, in its shotgun marriage with that ultimate symbol of Western bourgeois art music – the symphony orchestra – distanced itself from the other flank of Progressive. These were musicians – notably of the Canterbury and Notting Hill constellations (dealt with further in Chapter 4) – who were unwilling to divorce their music from the anti-bourgeois cultural discourses of the Underground which had kick-started their musical inspiration in the first place.

After – but not simply because of – the orchestral experiments and the flirtation with classical music, the flirts – Keith Emerson, Yes, Pink Floyd – found a less demanding and more homophonic path to tread while those who ignored the blandishments of art music (Soft Machine and its little universe, Hawkwind *et al.*) continued to occupy a commercially inferior position and maintain affiliations with the non-bourgeois currents that helped inspire and finance them. The split symbolized the ceremonial installation of a rock aristocracy and the centrality of Progressive music and mores in that ceremony.

'If Wagner were alive today, he'd work with King Crimson,'[22] frothed *Melody Maker's* Richard Williams over one of the band's weaker efforts, *In the Wake of Poseidon* (1970). But this was par for the course.

Popular music's flirtation with the classics had either been on the classical world's terms – composers like Ellington were 'permitted' to enter the concert hall through the indulgence of white musicians cognisant of genius – or had been coquettish couplings which would call classical's more hummable moments to the service of a pop hit – from Andre Kostelanetz's symphonic renderings of pop tunes in the 1930s to B. Bumble and the Stingers' rehash of Tchaikovsky's *Nutcracker*. In Walter Benjamin's age of art's mechanical reproduction, could such plunder be prevented? Now, a white artistic community, raised on parental radio renditions of Addinsell's *Warsaw Concerto* and Melachrino's cascading strings, hankered after artistic kudos through the means of commercial gimmickry, outright pretension or simply an accidental adjunct to the blurring of artistic distinctions in the social fluidity of the mid-1960s. It could be argued that the Nice's theatrical takes on 'Rondo' and Sibelius's *Karelia* were little more than the B. Bumble mentality writ large.

One such group had been Love Sculpture, whose penchant for covers extended from Willie Dixon's 'Wang Dang Doodle' through Bizet's 'Farandole' to, most famously, Khachaturian's 'Sabre Dance' which enjoyed massive sales in 1968. It is a classic of its kind; Khachaturian's folksy Armenian oompah-oompah rhythm enables rasping blues guitar to conjure a hard-blowing heavy rock band and retain the rhythmic shape of the piece without the joins being visible; the original's purposeful simplicity has enabled countless reorchestrations for forces ranging from penny-whistle orchestras to musical kettles, which renders accusations of bad taste superfluous. The space for guitarist Dave Edmunds to fill with tricksy solo lines locates it brilliantly in its timeframe, both as novelty classic, aspirant rock arrangement and *en vogue* virtuoso showcase.

Says John Peel,

> That arose from a session for the BBC. In its raw form it was fantastic. I broke regulations by playing it twice on 'Top Gear'. Great show-off piece — I've always been a sucker for a bit of rousing vulgarity [an interesting postulation in terms of Peel's later professed antipathy to ELP] and of course there was a precedent for it in the 1960s; the Cougars' 'Saturday Night at the Duckpond' and 'Swan Lake', twangy guitars doing golden classics.[23]

Vanilla Fudge, an American band, had also been part of this sub-genre, responsible for the hair-raising and organ-heavy retread of the Supremes' 'You Keep Me Hangin' on' that stormed American charts in 1967. And with record companies lacquering ever shinier layers of strings on ever-longer pop epics such as Richard Harris's 'MacArthur Park' and Barry Ryan's 'Eloise', well, ambition was just the done thing, wasn't it?

The look-mum trickery of pop musicians meeting the pretensions of the Moodies and their musical directors generated scarcely controllable aspiration. There would be more to come; the Who's *Tommy* started off merely as a concept album, and composer Pete Townshend hotly disowned claims that he'd described it as a 'rock opera'. But in the swell-headed atmosphere of late-1960s rock, for which any mountain was scalable, such assumed cultural respectability just came naturally. Rock aspiring to 'opera'? Why not? Never mind the fact that Townshend's drama was even more unstageable than Wagner's *Ring*. 'Rock opera' became, overnight, a patented term. Townshend may not have thought of *Tommy* as an opera but too many in the business thought it was unprofitable not to have the public, hungry for louder, longer rock music, believe the illusion. A semi-staged version hit London and New York in 1970 (the latter at the Metropolitan Opera House).

Pop musicians setting their sights on classical respectability had a flipside; classical musicians edged into pop. 'It's exaggerated,' says then Genesis guitarist Anthony Phillips.

> There weren't all that many music graduates in rock. I only recall a couple. Rare Bird [early protégés of Charisma Records] had two keyboard players who were supposedly Royal College people. There honestly weren't that many who came over, because a lot of people who might have wanted to come over couldn't, because they were so overtrained that when they tried to improvise it didn't work. There *was* Rick Wakeman, and Francis Monkman of Curved Air, who started off as a guitarist but was a fabulous keyboard player, teaching at one of the colleges. There was that input anyway, those rolling Bach-like chords you'd get with Matthew Fisher in Procol Harum, and he wasn't formally trained.[24]

There were starred piano students like Robert John Godfrey, sometime of Barclay James Harvest, later of The Enid (see below), and composition stars like David Bedford, tutored by Luigi Nono and possessed of a generally more thoughtful musical approach, evading the gestures of nineteenth-century Romantic Western European music – shop-soiled by populist overuse – which Progressive's petit-bourgeois graduates were already eagerly copping.

It was all very well souping up 'Sheep May Safely Graze' or wallpapering everything with Bachian triplets – but where was the fun in that? Pulses were still predominantly rocky, still using the rhythmic surge with which Elvis had come out fighting twelve years before.

But did things have to end there? Whether rock musicians seriously believed that they could write viable classical works is endlessly debatable. In 1969, the slaughter of so many other sacred cows aside, Ned Rorem, the American classical composer, was on record as saying that the Beatles matched Schumann in terms of songwriting; rock gigs had been taking place at London's Royal Albert Hall and Festival Hall for some years. The Nice – under the auspices of a commission from the Newcastle Arts Festival – cut *Five Bridges,* which attempted to 'bridge' (ho hum) rock and classical – with orchestra in now-obligatory attendance. And Deep Purple, an unremarkable psychedelic combo led by keyboardist Jon Lord and guitarist Richie Blackmore lending all manner of rowdy ornamentation to standard tunes, also got serious. But it was only when rockers attempted to fuse their music with the multifarious timbres of a classical orchestra that their compositional inexperience became obvious.

Deep Purple's 'Concerto for Group and Orchestra', premiered at the Albert Hall in 1970 under the baton of no less than Sir Malcolm Arnold, attracted mixed notices at the time. One critic thought its structure clumsy, its instrumentation banal, its invention feeble, and its claim to serious composition derisory.[25] Music broadsheets were more favourable, but none the less cautious, cowed by the thought of making too arbitrary a judgement on 'classical' music. After all, the reasoning would go, that was what Lord *meant* it to be, wasn't it? The fact that Lord was probably not much better qualified to write classical music than they were to write about it never entered most journalists' heads. The US was less restrained in its scepticism; but *Rolling Stone*'s opinion that classical rock was like 'mating a sabre-toothed tiger with a stallion and expecting to come up with anything besides bullshit'[26] didn't stop the US producing acts like Walter Carlos and his Bach Moog synthesizer adaptations, or the 'Switched-on Symphony', an extravaganza of almost comedic bad taste on the West Coast in 1970 featuring the Nice, Santana and the Los Angeles Philharmonic Orchestra conducted by Zubin Mehta.

'"Concerto" was, quite simply, spectacularly awful,' says Peel now, 'and the worst thing is, I thought it was crap then, too. People say, "Oh, you used to play a lot of Purple on 'Top Gear'," which I did, but when they brought in an orchestra I bailed out.[27]

Such aberrations must be contextualized with regard to the intoxicating *zeitgeist*; listening to the album today, the passable musicianship of the band aside, there is still a scarcely credible gulf between their playing and the orchestra's. As Rick Wright would point out after Pink Floyd's own uneven dalliance with orchestral textures, *Atom Heart Mother*, Lord goofed; he attempted not to integrate the band's sound with that of the orchestra but to contrast it, which magnified not only (unintentional) textural discord but also highlighted his inexperience in using orchestral scoring techniques.

Keith Emerson of the Nice possessed some 'serious' aspirations – the band's adherence to the dynamics of Sibelius's '*Karelia* (Intermezzo)' (1968) betray them – but the funkily athletic insert to the piece, whereby the chords are retained and neatly soloed over, also indicates a rocker's mind at work as well as a rocker's heart. Only later did the spectre of portentousness darken the horizon, with the ill-conceived *Five Bridges* album, which featured a five-movement work for band and orchestra, diminishing both symphonic and rock input. The suite is lopsided, with two initial orchestral movements and three band ones; the orchestra is used with a fresh, prentice naïveté, laden with acknowledgements to others, in this case Bernstein, Copland (especially the fondness for stabbing ensemble strings lines), Bartók and Stravinsky, but with an ear for genuine harmonic pedigree. The finale contrasts band with orchestral paragraphs in one of Emerson's most gripping melodic inspirations, but some perfunctory exchanges of motif aside, there's really not much point in the band playing with the orchestra or vice versa. Their work is pleasing individually, but doesn't hang together. The revamp of 'Karelia' seems equally schizoid, its back broken by Emerson's mandatory assault on his Hammond. The furious barrage of noise seems simply silly here, although it would wow punters long into his ELP days. *Five Bridges* also contains one of the most horrendous, bloodiest barneys between classical and rock; the highly sluggish performance by a second-division orchestra (the Sinfonia of

London) of the third movement of Tchaikovsky's Sixth exposes the limitations even of the stylish Emerson's playing and the relative yobbishness of rock syntax next to the lacework of Tchaikovsky's multiple lines. This is neither good classical nor rock music; its only redemption lies in its sheer vulgarity, in the bluesy scales Emerson plays over the original's chords. The textures of neither genre are properly utilized; it is like listening to two transistor radios simultaneously playing, one tuned to Radio 3, one to Radio 1. Rock doesn't expand its vocabulary; classical merely sees its vocabulary contracted.

Bands could learn, however; Procol Harum's *With the Edmonton Symphony Orchestra* (1972) is probably the best example of rock–classical orchestration and is a strangely neglected rock artefact of some value. As *Rolling Stone*'s Richard Cromelin noted, the unostentatious if weighty orchestrations were used to add a remarkably fresh range of tone-colours, with surprising good taste, to earlier, starker numbers and to emphasize dynamic variations, as on the juggernaut 'Conquistador'.[28] Certainly Pink Floyd's use of orchestra and choir on *Atom Heart Mother* hangs together a little better than Deep Purple's Barnum-and-Bailey spectacular. Constructing their orchestra group dynamic through hours in the studio, the Floyd matched the contours of electric instruments with those of acoustic ones with more finesse than Deep Purple even aspired to in the unforgiving glare of a live setting.

Experiments by the now long-forgotten New York Rock Ensemble, Ars Nova and Symphonic Metamorphoses (comprising jobbing players from the Detroit Symphony Orchestra) attempted to marry rock and blues with the classics with the technical and musical know-how of the late 1960s but, as session musicians grounded ineradicably in funk, soul and R&B traditions, the vernacular of American popular music is never far away. Chicago Transit Authority (later Chicago), phenomenally influential on any number of British musicians for about a fortnight in 1970 (long enough in those days) at least had the cultural dignity to employ brass and reed sections in homage to their blue-note antecedents, as did the comparable Blood Sweat and Tears, in spite of interesting Bartók and Prokofiev references in their 'Forty Thousand Headmen' (1970).

The orchestral angle was, however, taken to extremes by Barclay James Harvest from Oldham, Lancashire. Patronized by local breadhead John Crowther and housed by him in an eighteenth-century farmhouse on Saddleworth Moor, they were paired with piano virtuoso Robert John Godfrey, who set up the Barclay James Harvest Orchestra from Royal College of Music alumni for the band's heavily touted first (eponymous) album. 'This orchestra is no fuddy–duddy set-up with old men in tall hats,' Godfrey told *Melody Maker*. 'Most of them have long hair and are very groovy.'[29] Shame about the music, which was fuddy-duddy in the extreme, a ponderous alliance of second-division pop hooks crippled by laboured development; not even Godfrey's refined arrangements can save most of Barclay James Harvest material from the dustbin of history to which critical disfavour has (for once) accurately consigned them.

The cultural respectability which rock music seemed to crave continued to give groups airs. Electronic avant-gardist and BBC employee Tim Souster secured Soft Machine a slot at the Proms on 13 August 1970, where they performed to bewilderingly mixed reactions. *Musical Quarterly* reported that: 'with this concert the Proms have now returned to their Victorian beginnings of something for everybody, and have admitted that pop music is worthy of recognition.'[30] *Music Review*, however, sniffed: 'I should like to know on what premise I am expected to take seriously a small group of musicians whose range of tone does not exist and whose scale of dynamics is no more than an unvarying [triple-forte].'[31]

The Ballet Trust sent scouts to watch bands such as Caravan, desperate to secure their services for scores (projects almost always aborted with dispatch). Pink Floyd, too, were approached by Roland Pettit to score a ballet after Proust's *A la Recherche du Temps Perdu* for Rudolf Nureyev (the project never came properly to fruition, but did appear in a severely compromised incarnation in 1972). They also played at the Montreux Classical Festival in 1971. The distinguished musicologist Richard

Middleton endorsed not only the Floyd but the entire Progressive rock ideology in 1972; of *A Saucerful of Secrets* (1968), he wrote,

> It is comparable to no other music except 'serious' electronic music, particularly the use of live electronics by some avant-garde composers. Here, then, pop and modern art display their fundamental similarity of developmental direction most clearly ... pop, generally culturally behind avant-garde art, takes the unusual step of travelling as far away from the traditions of Western culture as the most extreme ... avant garde ... the modern artist and the adolescent meet ... [32]

The relationship between high and low culture was not as cordial as might be imagined, however. In 'We Got an Arts Council Grant', Robert Wyatt sings caustically of André Previn and George Hosking 'making sure the loser wins' and preferring pop music that's 'not so loud'.

States Wyatt,

> That song was about the battle for the Roundhouse and the use thereof. It had already been used by the likes of us, cultural gypsies, but there was always the threat that proper people were going to come along and take it off us. But there was this sense of utter contempt for anybody who seemed to have pretensions beyond pop music. There's a Disraelian view of culture here – the poor had their merry little japes but we're the sensitive ones and we do proper things and what a wonderful dual community we are. It was less of a glass ceiling than a reinforced concrete ceiling.[33]

Didn't the likes of Wyatt's band Matching Mole get gigs at the Queen Elizabeth Hall, however? And what about Soft Machine at the Albert Hall? How did Wyatt see himself fitting into that beneficial scheme of things?

Truthfully, I don't know. We got offered gigs and did them. I don't remember any engineering of things. We'd go where we'd got to go. There were a few individuals though who would really try and get things like this, like Tim Souster. There were people on our side who were very open to what was going on. They weren't posh but were at the posh end of things – people like Michael Nyman. I attended a few Greater London Arts meetings – it's so mysterious how these things are sorted out with these shady committees and suchlike.[34]

When questioned by an Italian writer in 1976 on the cultural significance of Soft Machine, keyboardist Mike Ratledge confessed:

> In a way we never pretended to have any. To me, a cultural message is a decal job from the outside. Sure, our early tunes were about Dadaism and 'Pataphysics – things we were, as individuals, really into – but actually, there weren't any links with the music, save the ones people want to find in it.[35]

AIRS ON A SHOESTRING

'The most important thing anyone has to remember about the industry then was how amateur it all was,' declares Bill Bruford.[36] But amateur or not, money-making wheels were turning. The Underground press, desperate to milk the most plural of pluralities in their coverage of changing times, had neglected music, at least in relative terms: 'There was nothing in [the *International Times*] about music,' recalled Mick Farren.[37] The first self-declared Progressive music paper, *Sounds*, appeared in October 1970 (motto: 'Music is the Message'), taking its cue from US pioneers *Rolling Stone* (which had had a brief and acrimonious run on the English market just prior to *Sounds* and whose rump production team began publishing the criminally badly distributed *Friends*). *Sounds* initially ran a 'Campus' column, detailing bands on the university circuit, profiling individual social secs and running stories about the availability and costs of bands.

Journalists like Nick Kent and Charles Shaar Murray, doyens of rock coverage in the Underground press, formed the vanguard of professional rock critics, but in doing so wedded themselves to the promotional machinery of the record industry and undermined any pretensions, no matter how well-intentioned, to independence. First *Melody Maker* and then the *NME* went 'Progressive' in 1968 and 1972 respectively, assembling their own wet-dream teams of journalistic talent from student and Underground presses. The *NME* adopted a self-consciously comic angle on rock, lining up gags with serious analysis. Features on the consumer durables of rock – hifi, instruments – burgeoned.

Radio had catered to the market in fits and starts with 'Top Gear', a Radio 1 compromise to lure disillusioned pirate listeners, that employed John Peel's Radio London format (perfected on the West Coast of the USA in 1966–7) of playing album tracks. Peel claims: 'It doesn't sound radical now, but at the time, people just didn't do it. One talks about the university circuit doing a lot for Progressive rock, but the BBC did a lot too – in the sense of an eighteenth-century patron of the arts.'[38] Robert Wyatt also acknowledges radio's importance: 'Without people like John and his producer, John Walters, and later on Alexis Korner's radio show, a lot of us wouldn't have been able to earn a living.'[39] Radio 3 dipped a demure toe into troubled waters by inviting rockers on to the airwaves, to a howl of protest. Peel adds: 'A lot of the most popular things were the sessions. You know, unique things, things you couldn't buy, performances you – everyone – could be at, for nothing.'[40]

Then TV got in on the act, with 'The Old Grey Whistle Test' debuting in 1970. Decca, who were supplementing their classical earnings with crossover collections for stereo snobs such as *The World of Strauss*, released in 1970 (presumably to cash in on the Progressive sampler craze) *Wowie Zowie – The World of Progressive Music* featuring such heroes [*sic*] of the genre as John Mayall, the Moody Blues and William Strickland (although Genesis, albeit with a track from their poppiest album, *From Genesis to Revelation*, are also dutifully in attendance).

The audience ballooned. No longer were 'progressive' sounds limited to consumption by an elite few in London and on university campuses.

Simon Frith's 1972 study of youth culture in Keighley, West Yorkshire, investigates contemporary teenage musical mores, and is essential reading for anyone interested in the development of consumer attitudes to rock. It indicates just how deeply the cultural terms of the Progressive project had been assimilated by record buyers. Frith distinguishes between buyers of singles (predominantly working-class, more women than men) and buyers of albums (top-streamers, middle-class and with the automatic pilot set for university and careers). Loyalties were robust; one Progressive fan dismissed pop as 'commercial trash which gets in your head and you can't escape and it does nothing for you except make you puke'.[41] Another album buyer told Frith: 'Rock music, progressive and heavy are fantastic. If they were not there life would not be worth living. They are the backbone behind music as a whole – showing us what it should really be like.'[42]

Frith shows that while Progressive fans actively rejected 'an image', or identification with a collectivity, an image *was* in the making.

A fiction was invented that rock production somehow promoted 'serious' aspirations, artistic struggle etc, over and above the tackiness, frippery and materialism of pop. But even then, Progressive was nevertheless establishing its *own* strain of commercial gimmickry, one which paradoxically strove to underline the genre's essential and inviolable distance and difference from pop. The (non-Progressive) Small Faces' pre-emptive venture into marketing vacuity, the round sleeve of their 1969 *Ogden's Nut Gone Flake* album, was merely a curtain-raiser for such silliness as Curved Air's 1970 debut, *Air Conditioning*, sporting a transparent vinyl disc and a transparent sleeve. This was followed by such pitiably facile efforts as Uriah Heep's aforementioned *Look at Yourself* mirror-sleeve . The rock LP sleeve was, of course, in the process of becoming an artefact of considerable cultural sophistication, but the emphasis – particularly with Progressive – was squarely upon *art*, or at least a popular misconception of same.

One figure who would go on to become forever associated

with the manufacture of the Progressive *imago* was Roger Dean, a graduate of both the Royal and Canterbury Colleges of Art – 'where, incidentally, Robert Wyatt was modelling for us'.[43] He had shared a house with members of Pink Floyd in the late 1960s and roomed with Syd Barrett, which got him the commission to design a logo for EMI's Progressive offshoot Harvest. From there Dean also received the lucrative commission to design the seating at Ronnie Scott's club in London. He was told that his work would look well on an album cover, and that it would be a 'great mechanism for displaying your work to a wide public'.

> So I did an album cover for Gun in 1968. The next few were all jazz, because of the Ronnie Scott connection. One day I got talking to David Howells, an A&R man at CBS who'd moved to MCA. He gave me the chance to design covers for Osibisa, and then Phil Carson at Atlantic offered me either Yes or Led Zeppelin – I chose Yes.[44]

Of the explosion in rock's visual terms of reference, which John Peel likes to relate to 'childhood; Arthur Rackham and stuff',[45] Dean ponders:

> The thing that changed was that it went from the hands of the record companies who, if they were professional, were professional in the sense of record promotion only. And so the process of designing the sleeves was taken over by artists, either by photographic artists like Storm [Thorgerson] at Hipgnosis or graphic artists like Rick Griffin in the USA. And what's happened since is that it's been taken over by professional graphic design companies. The busiest year I ever had I designed just four covers. A big company can do fifty a week. It's a question of keeping pace with releases. People now buy an album a week – there's more product around. At one stage I bought one album in an entire year – *Aoxomoxoa* by the Grateful Dead – and then only for Rick Griffin's cover. I didn't have a record player, so I never listened to it.[46]

Thorgerson and friend Aubrey 'Po' Powell (one-time flatmates of a fast-deteriorating Syd Barrett) had been approached to design the sleeve for Pink Floyd's second album, *A Saucerful of Secrets* (1968). Thus was born Hipgnosis (punning on both 'hip' and 'gnosis', pointed out Thorgerson, implying both the chic and exclusive), who with Dean would practically set in stone the runic imagery of Progressive's necessarily allusive, elusive visual ciphering. Henceforward record art became a genre in itself – gatefold sleeves, once reserved for double-albums, were now essential to maximize the visual impact of the 'work'.

The promotional machinery of the rock industry still ground exceeding slow, but a broader base of distribution for money-spinning merchandise both within the industry – promotional discs, stickers, gewgaws etc – was mirrored by an explosion of consumer interest in rock accessories from beyond the industry. 'Group posters, rock posters of any sort, became popular,' says Roger Dean. 'That all really evolved through Californian concert posters – Family Dog etc. – and you already had pin-ups of artists. But with Progressive guys you had to have them in concert, working, creating. Then along came the fantasy posters.'[47] There seemed a neat enough line traceable between the stomach-turning Art Nouveau bastardizations of West Coast rock-poster art and the fragile refinement of Dean's own *fin-de-siècle* aestheticism. Dean cites no overt influences, merely 'appreciating the input' of a constellation of artists ancient and modern whose plutocracy of origin and stylized, ethereal execution mirrored Progressive's own ideology and would serve Yes, Dean's chief patrons, very well, although not nearly as well as it served Dean himself. 'The posters actually outsold the records. There was no real competition. The competition for me was other posters, not record-sleeve designs. *Close to the Edge* (1972) in particular sold really really well.'[48] By 1971 the newborn *Sounds* magazine was placing a category for 'best album sleeve' in its annual readers' poll.

Bands were actively depersonalized. Even on landmark albums such as *Pet Sounds*, *Sergeant Pepper* and *Abbey Road*, the artistes were used as the album's visual selling point. From the Moody

Blues' *Days of Future Passed* onwards, however, this was a custom that began to wither. Even the original release of the Floyd's *Piper* was accompanied by a (suitably psychedelicized) group shot. Having said that, their individual talents were (paradoxically) marketed as promotional tools for instruments (less of a problem for record buyers with Progressive aesthetics to maintain – after all, instruments were the means to the end of the musical revolution, and surely no more than that).

This marked a transition in rock industry practice. From simply selling artists to consumers by image (the Dave Clark Five, the Kinks, the Beatles as besuited pranksters), they sold rock merchandise through artists whose commercial marketing in terms of record promotion would have been unprofitable ('Alan White of Yes plays Ludwig drums exclusively') because of their relevance not to records but to a new rock aesthetic of practice and performance.

What was therefore now operative was a business at least groping after the concept of directly exploiting a new meta-morphic *zeitgeist*. The 1960s left like a stranger; before long the memory of that decade paled in the shadow of hyperinflation, industrial unrest, spiralling civil disorder in Northern Ireland (and, it seemed, most of the Western world beyond British borders); the counter-cultural rock explosion was no longer pre-eminent. Pop, in the form of the Jackson 5 and T. Rex, was launching a renewed popularity offensive. The bands signed in the Progressive fad of 1969–70 began to fall away, either bankrupted, disintegrated in rows over the last baked-bean tin in the squat, in rehab or simply jettisoned as record executives began tightening belts. The survivors, though, carved out a very substantial commercial and artistic niche for themselves in the popular cultural firmament. The appetite for Progressive had not gone away, but had particularized around a core of acts who would go on to concretize what we have so far described as Progressive rock ideology, but would do so in different fashions for divergent (though fundamentally unified) audiences.

The first type of Progressive, led by the evolution of Pink Floyd and Yes towards Western classical models from an experimental beginning, roping in European Romantic devices, proved to be by far the more commercially successful form of Progressive rock. Its sister school, which we shall examine in depth below, toyed with the limits of the 'Progressive' nomenclature, and sought fidelity to the definition in musical thought and social deed. Both forms would sustain a mutually untrusting relationship, but each would occupy a central place in the British rock landscape of the 1970s.

In the final section of this chapter we shall itemize the principal players in the former category, those who most embodied through their early-1970s work a discernible shift away from their roots through the process of distilling the bourgeois, aesthetic aspects of the counter-cultural project to consecrate an entirely new form of rock music characterized by the criteria we have outlined above: ELP, Gentle Giant and Yes.

THE TOUGH GET GOING – PROGRESSIVE'S FIRST RECORDED LEGACY

Sighs John Peel,

> It's a shame about ELP, because actually, Keith Emerson is a nice bloke, a genuinely pleasant human being. I remember when they first played the Festival Hall, I was surrounded by a lot of dickheads in leather trousers who thought it was wonderful. I remember some berk in front of me talking to some smart Hampstead friends, saying, 'Oh man, my mind's completely blown, it's really blown.'[49]

Emerson, Lake and Palmer originated in a few casual jam sessions early in 1970. Since Cream, the record industry had ensured that supersession juggernauts of guitar-battling earnestness had become as common a currency in rock as was merger-mania in the City of London. Band relationships, strained by poverty, overwork and hallucinogenic excess (or any combination of the three) made for a febrile scene. The fluidity of personnel in rock made such summit meetings relatively easy to arrange. Emerson was presiding over a band holed below the waterline by internal friction (the Nice). Bassist Greg Lake decided to make good his escape from a band he saw as doomed (King Crimson) and Emerson and Lake's blandishments lured drummer Carl Palmer from the ranks of Atomic Rooster.

The trio's get-togethers were picked up on by the press and major record labels (although the independent Island were the first to show real interest). No matter that they were merely road-testing Emerson's knockabout 'Rondo' and King Crimson's armour-plated '21st Century Schizoid Man' (an item regrettably dropped by the group) – they were touted as a new phenomenon in any case, and to a degree, went on to become just that,

ELP debuted at Portsmouth Town Hall on 25 August 1970 (not, as biographies have it, at the Isle of Wight Festival four days later). Their debut album was released by Island in October, charting at No. 4. Still hailed by many as the band's best effort, it established the blueprint for a musical style which, for all the bullish puffing of the band's 'progressive' credentials, they would develop hardly at all. The Hammond histrionics and biff-bang riffs opening the album (an unacknowledged rearrangement of Bartók's piano showpiece 'Allegro Barbaro') offer a suitably vulgar but arresting opening. But here, as in the long 'Take a Pebble', the band's penchant for milking ideas dry weighs heavily. 'But,' claimed Lake with some justification a couple of years later, 'if the public want us to be artists then that's what we are.'[50]

Artists? In the piece 'Knife Edge', the Bachian contrapuntal treatment of a theme from Janáček's 'Sinfonietta' is artless compared with the Nice's treatment of 'Rondo'. The heavy chorale chords (interestingly modal, in the vein of Duruflé or Langlais) that introduce Part One of 'The Three Fates', 'Clotho', genuinely invite the listener into a harmonically ambiguous world which promises much but only segues vilely into 'Lachesis', a piece of similar facility but hobbled by the bad taste of the edit between the two. Part Three, 'Atropos', is the album's best track, a charming combination of Keystone Kops piano, cha-cha-cha bassline and Xavier Cugat percussion playing silly buggers over an Emerson/Lake riff. 'Tank' hedges from the promising atonality of organ, piano, bass and drums to humdrum tonality through the horrid agency of an unremarkable drum solo. The pre-Raphaelite imagery of the closer 'Lucky Man' is forgettable, the melody more so, and only the flanging and phasing of Emerson's Moog, flitting from one channel to the other and through a range of frequencies which augured well for future experiments with the instrument, rescues it. Emerson was soon to be publicized and photographed in deep communion with the creator of the instrument, Robert Moog. By the second album, *Tarkus* (a No. 1 smash in early 1971), the band's style had been set in stone; the twenty-minute title-track suite gets into its stride with a speedy, dissonant, syncopated keyboard-led theme over which further riffs, ideas and countermelodies are layered. But the band's tendency to solo in traditional forms – beginning and ending on downbeats, or using blues voicings – rarely lends the music any passion. Lake's enervatingly portentous lyrics and throwaway comedy songs such as the homophobic 'Jeremy Bender' and the rock'n'roll pastiche 'Are You Ready Eddie?', which must once have seemed engagingly perky, have aged embarrassingly.

But the emotional immediacy of pop music, its orgasmic tensions and releases, no matter how scorned by the Progressive cognoscenti, were emotional responses apparent in popular song just as much as in the nineteenth-century Romantic art music that the likes of Emerson wished to emulate. Was ELP really to be such a hidebound opponent of the *jouissance* of music, and substitute technique and form in its place?

ELP's third album, a recording of their stage favourite 'Pictures at an Exhibition', attempted to answer all those questions. In addition to the signature 'Promenade' introduction, the band adapted the first two and final two movements ('The Gnome', 'The Old Castle', 'The Hut of Baba Yaga' and 'The Great Gate of Kiev') of Mussorgsky's masterpiece for solo piano and interpolated material of their own.

The cavil that ELP were, like those orchestral-rock pioneers of the late 1960s, attempting to 'improve' Mussorgsky's work, is neither borne out by contemporary testimony nor by observance of the facts. Mussorgsky's suite had been for years adapted by the great and humble alike in numerous configurations. That Emerson should have tried to join their ranks cannot be criticized *per se*. In fact, the varying dynamics of the reprises of the big 'Promenade' tune – even with ghastly lyrics appended to it in one instance – are intelligent and tasteful. Lake's lyrics were often predictable; much was made of 'Life' and its philosophical ambiguities, with references to Gothic fallbacks like 'tortured dreams' further empurpling the prose.

The rhythmic subtleties of 'The Gnome' are distributed among the band smartly and effectively, and although 'The Hut of Baba Yaga' is speeded up to emphasize its visceral drive, there is neither over-extension nor solo indulgence. 'Baba Yaga' is one of the best examples of Emerson's instinct for adaptation; the *allegro* tempo is taken at a breakneck rapidity, but the volume and sustain afforded by Emerson's organ playing generate tremendous vitality.

'The Great Gate of Kiev' suffers from a superfluous flourish of Hammond improvisation from Emerson; in another context, its *concrète* wailing would have been of interest. Here, it merely resembles a trade-fair exhibition ('Yes, gentlemen, that is the amazing world of the Hammond organ'). But the sublime contrapuntal interlude of 'The Great Gate' – with the 'Promenade' theme reprised over repeated piano lines – inspires ELP to perhaps their greatest triumph, with Emerson's organ filigree beautifully offset by Palmer's ride cymbal. Unfortunately the swelling bombast of Lake's lyrics detracts from the otherwise electrifying trio arrangement of the suite's last bloated pages.

Gentle Giant also began life in Portsmouth on the south coast as pop band Simon Dupree and the Big Sound, whose billowing anthem 'Kites' (1967) had been one of the first pop singles to employ a bank of keyboards simultaneously for melodic and colouristic purposes – organ, Mellotron, piano (with vibraphone for luck). Bizarrely, three of the members of this impeccably provincial English pop combo would later form the core of the even more impeccably English Progressive rock band Gentle Giant. The Shulman brothers, Derek, Phil and Ray, were born in Glasgow's Gorbals, and had followed their saxophonist father to

Portsmouth when the latter was posted there in World War II; keyboardist Kerry Minnear, ex–Bath Boys' School, a graduate in composition from the Royal Academy of Music and author of a piano concerto, perhaps fitted the Progressive bill better. Wanting to 'get out of the blues thing and do something experimental'[51] as did most of their contemporaries in 1969, the Shulmans plucked Minnear from Clapham bedsit penury, and formed Gentle Giant from the ashes of the Big Sound. They convinced Progressive manager Gerry Bron, and Vertigo – as they tended to do in 1970 – stepped in waving a recording contract.

The mundane origins of the band (a fading naval port), their slightly subfusc take on Englishness (Gothic script with everything) and a fondness for exaggeratedly portentous self-promotion made many early listeners sceptical. One sleeve note read: 'It is our goal to expand the frontiers of contemporary popular music at the risk of being very unpopular. We have recorded each composition with one thought, that it should be unique, adventurous and fascinating … from the outset we have abandoned all preconceived thoughts on blatant commercialism'.[52]

Ponderous upstarts, without a good tune between them – that's how history views Gentle Giant. But the packaging hid an originality of conception and execution immediately apparent on both their first, eponymous album (1970) and *Acquiring the Taste* (1971). Not only is the vertical complexity of the music daunting (tenor sax, alto sax, trumpet, clarinet, recorders, claves, tambourine, gong, cello, bass violin, violin, viola, guitar, bass, drums, moog, celeste, Mellotron, electric piano among others), but horizontal developments are of astonishing precocity. The Dutch Progressive musicologist Jan-Paul van Spaendonck praises Gentle Giant's ability seamlessly to extend pop voicings and themes by using classical technique, notably in the four-part fugue with which the theme to 'Black Cat' (1971) is introduced, and then counterpointed, for a string ensemble, with the surging introductory motif.

Spaendonck goes on self-righteously to assert that 'only a trained musician' can appreciate the grace of the band's developmental methods, but also notes that the panache of such technique contrasts well with the 'collaging' of Jethro Tull's attempts at contrapuntal canvases, in which complexity becomes not a compositional tool but a badge of worthiness; whereas complexity becomes an end in itself in Tull, with Gentle Giant it is merely the means to an end.[53]

The band's influences were, by 1973, being enumerated by Duncan Fallowell as 'Elgar, Stravinsky and Bartók', in a review of the band's best album, *Octopus*.[54] The pieces are short (none more than six minutes long) and the music retains intimacy; if not direct in utterance, then the sheer discipline of composition grabs the listener by the lapels. Fallowell also commented appreciatively that with Gentle Giant, despite their liberal usage of canon, fugue and counterpoint, theirs was no half-baked nostalgia for an ersatz medievalism; 'there are parallel fifths, but no revivalism'.[55]

This was questionable; the insistence on archaic typographies for their album sleeves aside, the band's Rabelaisian leanings (exemplified by 1972's 'The Advent of Panurge' and 1971's 'Pantagruel's Nativity', not to mention 'Raconteur Troubadour' (1973), combined with the recherché harmonies, seem to hanker after an affected timelessness. But much Giant music employed sharply irregular and chromatic melodic profiles, unorthodox and relatively harsh for their time. Polyphonic construction, like that of 'Pantagruel's Nativity', extends that chromaticism still further to a 'floating' harmony, inferred but not identifiable. 'Knots' (again from *Octopus*) 'uses highly chromatic harmonic patterns realized through a dense contrapuntal [largely vocal] texture' according to Allan Moore.[56] Ironically, straight rock metres are not uncommon – only the ingenious use of emphases, and the relative novelty of counterpointed harmony create the illusion of great difficulty.

The start of the 1970s saw Yes plugging on, but this time vertiginously downwards, returning to a surfeit of dead-end gigs belying their early next-big-thing status; the *Time and a Word* orchestra scam oozed desperation, a bid to heft Yes's ambitious Progressive pop into the Deep Purple/Nice league. The feeling is of a top-heavy treatment of humdrum tunes. 'Jon [Anderson] could have benefited so much from a bit of musical education,' Bill Bruford admits. 'He wanted to do so much, and it was difficult for him to express it.'[57]

The band ditched guitarist Peter Banks for the jazz and sophistication of ex-Tomorrow face Steve Howe. Rooted originally in jazz, blues and flamenco guitar (notably that of Carlos Montoya), Howe added chordal complexity to the band's tunes, and also added a cutting edge to a sound which, on *Time and a Word*, threatened to evaporate. His solo on 'Starship Trooper' from *The Yes Album* (1971), for example, smothered the repetitive three-chord patterns of the finale in gloriously unorthodox fashion, employing multinational voicings in a non-blues solo pattern. This was no burglarizing of different constituents from different genres but a methodical honing-down of those constituents into quite a separate style of music which defied any pigeon-holing. Sixteen-tracking enabled grafting and rearrangements of riffs and melodies to construct greater wholes. But besides painstaking method in recording, penetrating inspiration such as the clever contrast of 7/4 and 14/8 metres in 'Perpetual Change' and the tender-tough transition from choir to funked-up bass/drums bridging 'Your Move' and 'All Good People' came 'out of nothing', according to band members.

What was evident by the follow-up *Fragile* (1972) was the deployment of the band as vehicle not for standard tunes but for sometimes mere fragments contributed by band members into which the learned lessons of other musics were ploughed, often with a wilful disregard for provenance.

'Jon would sit for hours in front of the TV with his guitar – that he couldn't play. His mind was like blotting paper to the point where plagiarism was almost a factor,' states Bill Bruford.

The classics – Sibelius, in particular – there were loads of classical references in Yes, but other things, too. Jon would bring these bits to the rehearsals and he'd go, 'Play this' and give us the *Bonanza* theme – which later turned up as the first riff into 'Yours is No Disgrace' – and someone would go, 'Hang on, Jon, that sounds a bit like *Bonanza*.' He'd go, 'No, it doesn't! If you can come up with anything better play that!' And an argument would start. And so we said, 'Oh all right, we'll play that then.' People – especially Americans – tend to assume that there is some grand masterplan behind these compositions, which is generally untrue. It was a mess of amateurism, shamateurism, which then met Rick Wakeman, who was so professional. Jon's modest little tune might grind to a halt after four bars and he would say, 'Right, now I want it to go into this twinkly angel section,' and Rick would say, 'I know *exactly* how to do that, and what's more, you won't even see the join.' He could modulate, sew the thing up, and before you knew it you had some genuine form. The thing was a much better piece of music with Rick than without. It was the best thing we ever did, hiring him.'[58]

Tony Kaye, the band's original organist, had been sacked in 1971, and the twenty-one-year-old Wakeman, widely touted as the hottest property in British rock, got the call. A star with folk-rock band the Strawbs, Wakeman was an unstarred alumnus (*not* a graduate) of the Royal College of Music. He'd been overawed by fellow students' dedication and supplemented his grant by sidelining in pub bands and an inordinate number of sessions, from Black Sabbath to Clive Dunn's 'Grandad', as well as the Mellotron lift-off in Bowie's 'Space Oddity', the piano introduction to Cat Stevens's 'Morning Has Broken' and the plinky-plonk of the then *Ask Aspel* theme.

Aside of pinning down keys with a piece of wood and some nails to enable a chord to be held while he soloed with both hands, the use of a paint-roller on the keys and some Emersonesque rocking of the organ, Wakeman was a very musicianly musician. 'He ... had a burning organ sound. He played it correctly. It cut,' says Bruford.[59]

In addition, Wakeman's lifestyle ('early grunge' remembers Jon Anderson,)[60] lubricated with Scotch (he had passed out during his first clarinet lesson at the Royal College) was littered with incidents of ruggedly bohemian mayhem (he once threw Salvador Dalí off stage in Paris when the painter climbed up to interrupt an electric piano solo, something that would later also provoke a drunken Ray Davies to violence when Yes supported the Kinks on an early US tour). It allowed the liberation of tensions within Yes. Dope was used in the band (save by Bruford), while Wakeman stuck to Scotch and pints; Wakeman's combination of bourgeois classical training and petit-bourgeois artistic values added both musical and social stimulus.

In this formation the band would cut the album that broke them internationally, *Fragile* (1972). 'Someone handed me a copy of *Billboard* in the taxi on the way into New York,' remembers Bruford, 'and *Fragile* was No. 4. Suddenly it was Barbra Streisand, Frank Sinatra and Yes. I thought: hang on, there's some money in this. I'm more prosaic than most about success, but that really was an eye-opener.'[61]

What helped was a symbiotic relationship with engineer/ producer Eddie Offord, who enabled them to indulge a collective fondness for refinement of, above all, atmosphere. The colours and depth of the organ and acoustic-guitar dream-sequences which interpolate the band's famous 'Roundabout' (1972) are testament enough to a filmic, representational musical language derived from European classicism in which entire musical moods, as well as styles, are violently contrasted. As Bruford told Tim Morse of Wakeman's influence: 'If the only thing he'd done was the solo in 'Roundabout', that alone was worth its weight in gold ... a wailing solo without a note of jazz in it. There's no phrasing in it, no breathing like a jazz player ...'[62]

Singular also to the Yes image so memorably committed to the rock pantheon on *Fragile* was the cover – an uncommonly striking variation on the other-worldly, mystical imagery predominating in the sphere of record-sleeve design. The polystylistic Roger Dean here called upon shades of Friedrich, Segantini and Gaudí; it established a Yes marque which would help set in train the shaping of a marketable Progressive rock aesthetic, although vocalist Anderson later claimed that the band wanted to 'package' their music as early as 1969.[63]

The sixteen-bar tune lifted directly from the notation of the percussion line in Bruford's 'Five Percent for Nothing' is an infuriating cul-de-sac, half a minute of teeming counterpoint and dissonance to which the band would return all too rarely. The basslines continue to shine, with Wakeman reprising the chorus's bassline on grand piano in a sombre, autumnal introduction of the central section of 'South Side of the Sky', and bass and organ riffs play jump-cut hide-and-seek with great effect on 'Long Distance Runaround'. Only in the closer, 'Heart of the Sunrise', with its Crimsonic metre and interesting relationship of the 'song' section to instrumental workouts, does the band's collective inspiration gel consistently and unflaggingly over an extended span.

That inspiration sustained itself over the entirety of *Close to the Edge*, which even today draws grudging respect from Yes's most trenchant critics. Certainly its ambition is matched by the heartfelt commitment of the playing, even though the organization of the music is almost total. The title track segues from the choreography of riffs, effects and systems-music repetition in 'The Solid Time of Change' (overlaid by a visceral and overwhelmingly busy Howe solo) through two Andersonian pop interludes sporting pyramid harmonies, to a Wakeman solo spot and a cleverly recapped further pop conclusion; 'And You and I' is a *tour de force* of atmosphere, contrasting opaline twelve-string against Wakeman's cavernous Mellotron, light and shade divided across the four sections with pleasing architectural skill; and the closer, 'Siberian Khatru', is a modal monster, chilled by Wakeman's terrifying Mellotron strings, charging on in irregular tempo to a series of climactic barbarian chants interspersed with lightning twelve-string soloing from Howe.

Rolling Stone asserted: 'Every element is utilized to enhance or modify *mood* [my italics], and you never get the impression that a particular passage was included because Wakeman just found a hot new sound on his moog that they *had* to get in there.'[64]

The band had hardly skimped on effort in achieving this end. Recording occupied over three months at Advision Studios, and some notices accused them of over-attention to detail. Remembers Bruford,

> *Close to the Edge* got drawn out longer and longer and in the process we found out that Simon and Garfunkel had taken three months to record *Bridge Over Troubled Water* so we had to

take three months and two days. That's what we copped all the criticism for. But it was the done thing. Everybody did it, not just so-called 'progressive' bands. You wanted bigger sales, a bigger band. Chris nearly broke the band in the early days by ordering more and better equipment, which he would order with abandon with no idea of the band's finances. I knew we couldn't afford it.

It started off so simply – in 1971, for our first American tour, the whole back line went as excess baggage, with the plane waiting on the tarmac. All these businessmen would look out and tut-tut at the Mellotron, two guitar cases, and drum boxes being winched up into the hold of the plane.[65]

Such amateurism notwithstanding, there were unmistakable signs that the Progressive music phenomenon that the Underground and counter-culture had spawned was now being mainstreamed. By 1972 albums like *Sounds Progressive* were appearing in the shops; cover versions by anonymous sessionmen of underground hits like the Gun's 'Race with the Devil' – it was recorded, according to Vernon Joynson, at the wrong speed – and 'introduced by Kid Jensen',[66] who had cut his teeth at the independent Capital Radio of London as a specialist rock DJ. It was an almost calculatedly insulting subversion of the anti-commercial, Romantic ethos of the genre.

Chris Cutler remembers: 'Psychedelia had created an optimism – and a certain awareness of the political nature of resistance ... centred on changing oneself first.'[67] He describes a generation who climbed the ladder of psychedelia, then kicked it away.

Richard Neville, the erstwhile editor of *Oz* magazine and all-round Voice of Hippydom, was offered a then-considerable £3,000 advance from Jonathan Cape for the tiresome book *Play Power* on the evidence of one Paul Johnson-endorsed piece in the *New Statesman* to outline the joys of the counter-culture for Joe Public. Clearly, people were starting to make serious money out of what had been the Underground, and not just those the Underground had tried to undermine, but its own denizens too. Charles Shaar Murray states:

The line from hippy to yuppy is not nearly as convoluted as people like to believe and a lot of the old hippy rhetoric could well be co-opted now by the pseudo-libertarian Right – which has in fact happened – get the government off our backs, let individuals do what they want. That translates very smoothly into *laissez-faire* yuppyism, and that's the legacy of the era.[68]

Perhaps the ultimate summary of the transition to the consecration of Progressive rock ideology as cultural and consumer commodity, however, is attributable to Chris Squire, who as a member of Yes was among the prime movers of the dislocation. Commenting on the changes of 1972, he told Yes biographer Dan Hedges that the period killed the idealism of the band. 'By that time we'd been to America. America has a nasty habit of ... changing things.'[69]

4: PEOPLE'S PROGRESSIVE?
(PROGRESSIVE ROCK, CULTURE AND POLITICS 1973–76)

THE OTHERS ...

If some Progressive rock musicians found America and professionalism, there were plenty of Progressive musicians who didn't. By 1973 the Progressive boom had bust for the scores of acts landed in the rush for signatures of 1969–70. What had happened?

'I think people stopped producing records by most of those bands because a lot of them were piss, basically,' opines John Peel.[1]

The founding of a rock aristocracy (Progressive or otherwise) into which record company money could be ploughed at the expense of others hinted at new 'Establishment' values within the rock industry. Whereas in its salad days of 1967–70 rock still lacked an idiom, by 1973 it had found its voice and the acts to put it across, considerably diminishing the desire to unearth new talent. Finding new market niches (a department of the industry as yet unformed and understaffed) aside, it was thought unprofitable simply to retread formulae already in place. Progressive, too, was turning into an expensive genre (Yes were not the only band spending months in pricey studios to record albums), and this meant less money spread thinner over fewer bands – an economic truth that would eventually cut the ground from under Progressive rock.

Victims of this scorched-earth policy, Next Big Things who never were, included Second Hand, whose 1968 debut *Reality* shows symphonic leanings prior to Yes's debut the following year. Indeed the cover art too presaged later things, being a totalized packaging concept with the clear intention of resembling a 'second-hand' record. Press reaction was good, and continued to be so for the band's three-year career; the group's second effort was a suitably eclectic soundtrack to the surrealist film *Death May Be Your Santa Claus*, in which the handiwork of Lennon and Ono can be detected. But good notices mattered little; extinction came soon. Of all failed early Progressives, the opinion among latterday cognoscenti seems to indicate that Second Hand received the most unjust treatment from the music industry.

Other contenders that might have been, thrown out with the bathwater, included Steamhammer, signed to a major label (Columbia) as early as 1968 – before Yes or Jethro Tull and only a year or so after Pink Floyd's link-up with EMI – and by 1970 reduced to trudging around the Continent to compensate for homeland indifference. The power trio T2 stormed the Isle of Wight Festival in 1970 and their leader, guitarist and keyboard player Keith Cross, was likened to a new Eric Clapton. They signed to Decca, cut the album *It'll All Work Out in Boomland* (boasting a thrilling twenty-one-minute Progressive blues extravaganza entitled 'Morning') and vanished. The acronymically named Gygafo (Get Your Gear And Fuck Off) deserved to succeed for wit alone. Mere musicianly lassitude sabotaged other aborted projects. The promising-sounding Stars, a band formed by Syd Barrett and ex-Pink Fairy Twink in 1972, broke up during their first gig, when Barrett wandered offstage and disappeared.

The communitarian paradigms of original 1960s Progressive ideology had been inherently compromised by creeping commerciality – just as the hippies had thrown their 'Breadhead!' insults at rock's entrepreneurs in 1968, so the insults seemed to be borne out by the facts in 1973. On the one hand, Progressive was lavish, canonical, culturally aspirant, and on the other a vibrant, grassroots music which often shunned – or remained indifferent towards – commercial success.

Dreams of Anglo-Saxon hippyocracy had imploded at the Isle of Wight when Mick Farren and the White Panthers stormed the fences and caused a near-riot, but there remained a hardcore repository of aesthetic and political Progressive ideological strands: first, the cosmology of English eccentricity, mysticism and pastoralism, which defied the grubby reality of the hippy apocalypse in the bloodied wake of the Altamont Festival stabbing to create an other-worldly parallel existence governed by gnostic arcana and spiritual liberty, most publicly in bands such as Gong and Quintessence; second, a spiritual autonomy of the musician-creator always close to Romantic ideology, which indirectly informed the unconventional performances and practices of Henry Cow. Third, there was the notion of bohemian community. All three strands interweave in the story of 'alternative' Progressive, which helped create a superficially disparate but ideologically related dark side to Progressive's elite.

BACK TO BASICS: FESTIVALS AND THE CANTERBURY TRIANGLE

Festivals were grotesquely unpleasant. People had them anywhere, everywhere. The ones in the hills above Buxton were probably the worst. But everyone had a worst festival. Most of the time you simply didn't get paid. Bands would be ripped off. Punters would be ripped off. But bands especially. You'd get people coming up and saying, 'Oh man, they should be playing for free', which pissed me off. What they meant was that bands should in effect give people money to listen to them play miles from where they'd rather be.'[2]

Thus John Peel, with feeling. Peel acknowledges, however, that lower-league festivals at least – those on Tooting Bec Common, Windsor (later Watchfield), Plumpton and that Somme of festivals, the Great Western Festival at Lincoln – did keep alive a heady atmosphere of anarchic disorganization which contrasted ever more strikingly with the Progressive elite's flowering infatuation with professionalism and precision.

> You couldn't always be sure what would happen. Lincoln, 1972 – I was MCing. It poured with rain the whole time. The farmer who rented us the field actually put straw down for us – unusual care for the consumers – but it didn't make any difference. And at one stage in desperation I just put on this folk disc by the Cheviot Ranters, railwaymen from Hexham or somewhere. And the crowd loved it. It was a cue for a straw fight – suddenly, the sky was full of sheaves of straw being flung from one side of the site to the other.[3]

This grassroots and shit-on-boots earthiness, ostensibly the culmination and maturity of rock's organic longings back in 1968–9 when guitars and muddy fields seemed the most natural and decorous of partners, may have largely been superseded, but such instances proved that British rock culture still had a celebrant, slightly bohemian element of chaos to it. It engulfed not only stoned and exhausted festival-goers, but London's multi-racial, working-class district of Notting Hill, which had done so much to foster the counter-culture, Progressive's spiritual parent, was as vibrant with the extreme and outlandish at the end of the 1960s as at the start. But with the smell of cordite and blood from Prague, Paris, Kent State University and Belfast having politicized the counter-culture, the passive resistance of the early 1960s now hardened. The revolution had been deferred, and indeed its dilution by the beautiful people who'd discovered just what tremendous *fun* hippies could be (Andy Williams and Lauren Bacall visiting Apple's London boutique) left a sour taste. As the revolution's hardware seemed to become the property of middle-class consumers, a backlash was waiting to happen.

In 1970 idealism still hung heady and heavy in the air like resinous smoke. Jeff Dexter could call for a musical bank, a collective enterprise for the shared good of all musicians, and be taken seriously. Society was still apparently there for the changing. But with the effeminate delicacy of Progressive and hippy ethics seemingly impotent in the face of Establishment practices (Soft Machine at the Proms etc.) there were those who brought more confrontational stances to bear, mostly associated with the cellular politics of London's Notting Hill. And while the world could still be changed for a happy hippy tomorrow, others still had the power to change it back to yesterday. For example, as late as 1971 Jerry Wiggin MP submitted an Anti-Festival (Night Assemblies) Bill to the House of Commons. Even *The Times* said that the Bill, a precursor of the Criminal Justice Bill of 1994, 'wanted watching'.[4]

Wiggin's last stand for Middle England was thrown out in May 1972, but clearly the counter-culture still attracted opposition. Perhaps it was because the 1960s had reached high places that its edge had been blunted; while the likes of Wiggin may have tried to stop festivals, the very organization of those festivals was now interesting men of no less respectability. Great Western Festivals, organizers of not a few Progressive gatherings in the early 1970s, numbered among its shareholders Lord Harlech, De Vere Hotels and Hambros Bank.

What had happened? Here was rock, the campus youth's cultural neutron bomb, safely stowed in the opposition's arsenal. Among those willing to fight by other means were the Edgar Broughton Band. Alleged anarchists from Warwickshire signed to noted anti-Establishment body Harvest Records (prop. EMI Ltd), this was the band, the reader may recall, last encountered in a layby with their frontman's mum boiling soup in the back of the van. They obtained mythical status with their tireless slogging round the festival network, which they inevitably enlivened with a football-terrace chant of inspiring banality, 'Out Demons Out'; 'It's an attack on the pig mentality,'[5] Edgar Broughton insisted. Most Broughton material was rooted in the urban blues tradition which Progressive sought to supersede, but recordings – and much more so live tapes – indicate that, behind the off-the pig rabble-rousing there was a genuine spirit of deconstruction, with songs beaten into submission by the time they reached the middle eight in an apple-pie-bed of raucous guitar feedback and hollered slogans.

The Pink Fairies, originally an informal and loose-knit drinking club of eighth-rate London faces who got their kicks from trashing gigs (such as King Crimson's second night at the Speakeasy), incorporated sometime Pretty Thing Twink and a post-Bolan Steve Took. They became a 'band' when Twink voted with his feet (the likes of Took and Mick Farren unable to find theirs most of the time), joining Russell Hunter and the Deviants. The remnants of Farren's Technicolor Dream goon-squad, they dropped the 'Social' and in doing so became ever more anti-social, ambling on amid bohemian pranks, burning down a venue in Colchester by letting off fireworks on stage and later commandeering a van, ramming the doors of the Essex University refectory and distributing free ice cream. One set at the Roundhouse won them a contract with Polydor which never amounted to much; but their Pinkwind partnership with Hawkwind helped set in motion a dynamic of free-gigging impromptu musical events which persisted long into the 1970s and established a locus of alternative hippy culture.

Among these was the Phun City Festival at Patching in 1970. A benefit for *IT* (then the dock for running gay contact ads), it comprised a 'rock festival, poetry gathering, Guerrilla Theatre, Sci-Fi Convention, Bikers' Grand Run, Electric Cinema, National Pinball Championships and a Giant Rip Off Market'. Organized in a week, it featured the Blackheath Foot and Death Men, a 'psychedelic Morris troupe', and at one point the entire stage was physically lifted and moved by volunteers from the audience.

The contemporary illusion of glazed hippy inertia in the face of imminent social breakdown and rampant urban motorway-construction doesn't hold water when the hard-nut lyrics of Third World War, another associate of the Semtex-and-spliffs crashpad of early-1970s Notting Hill, are considered. A 'political underground' act, they were able to write excellent, sensitive melodies, but in general their music and lyrics were ugly and real – like life itself. On 'MI5's Alive' they bemoaned 'kissing the monarch's arse ... letting the bad air out'.[6] These august commentators shared bills at free festivals with proto-crustie pioneers Here and Now and East of Eden, but most notably featured at the Police Ball benefit for *Oz* magazine with Arthur Brown, Viv Stanshall, the Pink Fairies, Egg, Roy Harper and Gnidrolog.

Such sentiments inevitably had their political equivalents, and Mick Farren's White Panther Party filled that role admirably. 'There were only two White Panthers and Mick Farren was the leader,' claims John Peel.[7] Farren had reportedly been among those enforcing with axe-handles at Phun City and had led the charge on the fences at the Isle of Wight, with Deviant David Goodman instrumental in holding the organizers to ransom and forcing them to erect a fringe stage for the Pink Fairies and Hawkwind at the risk of losing their power supply.

Among the patchouli-plastered platoon of acts that emerged blinking from the collectives of Notting Hill were Quintessence (whose first single was called 'Notting Hill Gate'), formed from an ad in *Melody Maker* with auditions at the local All Saints' Hall. They specialized in Roland Kirkish flute-and-guitar-based rock, with mantric chanting encouraged in the audience, amplified into the band's own compositional methods, best exemplified by *Moho Mantra* (1968). Amazingly, the band cut five albums in four years, the last being *Indweller* in 1972.

Hawkwind's credentials should have earmarked them as possibly one of Notting Hill's less likely acts – half of the band, according to *Melody Maker*, were supposed to be sleeping rough at any one time. Band saxist/vocalist Nik Turner, nevertheless, uttered the cautions on drugs that were then, hilariously, almost mandatory for all acts interviewed in *Melody Maker* – 'we want people to get stoned on the show, not on acid'.[8] The media monomania about the band's drug connections led to what manager Doug Smith estimated to be sixty-eight busts in three years. Turner stayed above all this – if only because the police never found the heroin he stashed in the bell of his sax. The band acquired notoriety by playing illicitly and for free at the Isle of Wight Festival, Turner painting himself silver for the occasion. They played gigs as though their lives depended on it, including one at Wormwood Scrubs, and claimed they were 'too progressive for most Progressive clubs'.[9]

Doug Smith remained remarkably sanguine towards his charges:

> Hawkwind weren't really space rock, or science fiction. The reality was that it was a good way to drop acid and play a gig. When [bassist] Lemmy joined they were still dropping acid, they were still doing speed like you cannot believe. I remember [guitarist] Dave Brock walking across the stage, kicking Lemmy up the arse and saying, 'Fucking slow down, cunt!' Then there'd be other nights when Lemmy would be speeding out of his head and he'd think, 'Can't take this any more' and the mandies would come out and they'd ... get slower and slower'.[10]

But for all the extraneous floss (their second album came complete with a twenty-four-page 'Hawklog'), Dik Mik's contrived handle and wheezy electronics, the 'Space Ritual' roadshow, Hawkwind's music remained obdurately pedestrian. True, the band's live improvization and electronic experimentation were impressive, but their playing was marred by rhythmic conservatism and a harmonic language which remained strictly street-level. Theirs was music still irredeemably blues-indebted.

Progressive took itself seriously. The pretensions of hippy thought, its embrace of selfhood, being in the world and the relation of subject to subject (all such discourse possibly – or possibly not – under the influence of mind-altering drugs) meant that from the start the Progressive ideology struggled to fulfil missionary aspirations.

Neither Hawkwind nor Henry Cow adopted anything like

the chaotic, save-petrol-burn-cars textual or political stance of the Situationists. The mid-1970s offbeat Progressive band National Health would later be seen throwing trays of cutlery around the 'Old Grey Whistle Test' studios, with gigs featuring bassist John Greaves trying to set fire to drummer Pip Pyle's cymbals while keyboard player Dave Stewart played 'The Marseillaise' standing on his head. But while this and, more specifically, the preference in Henry Cow and associated acts for environmental transformation as a precondition for political liberation may have recalled the chaotic precepts of Situationism, the unavoidable trap of operating as a part of the society of the Spectacle for both society's and the artists' benefit proved that the Situationists' suspicions of hippydom proved to have good grounds. In fact, the Notting Hill community bands even had an in-house graphic designer (albeit on a somewhat ad hoc and strictly unofficial basis), the legendary Barney Bubbles. Bubbles, who took drugs 'with everything' according to one source (even to the extent of crumbling hash over steak and chips) designed the initial Hawkwind sleeves and also others, not least Dr Z's *Three Parts to My Soul*.[11]

To cast early-1970s rock culture, in consumption and production, as being quintessentially humourless would be a mistake; *vide* John Peel's accounts of straw-fighting at Lincoln. But what remained inviolable was an aesthetic monotheism, a belief in a cultural commodity jealously protected by those who saw it threatened by uncomprehending outsiders: policemen, teachers, parents and later, critics.

Subsequently the humour that did reach Progressive was ultimately as obscurantist and exclusive as the movement's other cultural trappings. Theatre of the Absurd cast-off surrealism decanted itself through the English public-school system to give the world Monty Python (signed to Progressive Charisma Records for recording purposes), Grimms and the Bonzo Dog Doo Dah Band. This was humour that rested on shared appreciation of often arcane satirical codes, which in the case of these artists hit on just the emblems of traditional Establishment values Progressive claimed to resist. But humour was kept distinct from, rather than infiltrated into, rock discourse. Rock was too important, too valuable, to be laughed at or even with.

There were acts who attempted to deconstruct rock practices; Principal Edwards' Magic Theatre (named after the Dean of Exeter University) were signed by John Peel to his Dandelion label (although Peel has since disowned them). Incongruously fronted by the Caithness-glass vocals of Vivienne McAulliffe, they were none the less an anarchic force, sporting both a choreographer and a writer (Gillian Hadley) and a dancer (John Hill) to add to a stage act of legendary idiocy, distinguished by long, lunatic compositions of failed funhouse attempts at virtuosity and slapstick silliness such as 'The Death of Don Quixote', 'Third Sonnet to Sundry Notes of Music' and the epic 'Pink: A Mystery-Cycle'.

Tea and Symphony were, if anything, an even more rudimentary rendition of the small-stage, community-theatre-prefiguring Dada embodied by Principal Edwards' Magic Theatre. Says psychedelic discographer Vernon Joynson of the vinyl legacy of this multi-media ensemble, 'This is a pandemonium of wilful, oblique and obscure tunes, all filled with a manic musical magic which will either appal you or take you by storm. Improbable instrumental combinations and unexpected barbed-wire dissonances are treated with excellent musical craftsmanship.'

'What you've got to remember,' John Peel concludes, 'is that the drop-out trip was irritatingly middle-class attitudinalizing. Such suffering that was experienced was, by and large, suffering which could be ended by a phone call to mummy and daddy. There was a lot of crap talked about it.'[12]

One festival that thrived on such bucolic idylls was Andrew Kerr's Glastonbury Fayre, first held in 1970. Kerr was an unconventional local landowner who decided to rent out a field to the kids not only because he wanted to make some money but because he wanted to see some bands for himself. The stage he constructed was pyramidal in shape, in homage to the Great Pyramid, hailed as a centre for global occult energy since the days of Blavatsky's Theosophists. Intentionally a free festival, Coca-

Cola trucks and non-vegetarian food vendors were strenuously refused permission to trade at the site.

Quite apart from the worldwide fame the festival has since accrued, its success at the start was borderline but played a central part in establishing alternative Progressive mores. The rediscovery by the hippies of occultist and alternative beliefs in the 1960s, as well as Indian and Chinese philosophies, had inevitably ended in a sweaty embrace with existing, similarly internationalist currents in British alternative thinking, from the theosophy of Cyril Scott and Vera Stanley-Alder through the cosmography of Notting Hill veteran John Michell and even to ariosophists and sun-worshippers. Here was the unshakable belief that Glastonbury was a sacred site of pre-eminence matched only by Stonehenge and the Great Pyramid. Joseph of Arimathea had allegedly visited on a pilgrimage in the first century AD. Ley-lines were said to bristle around it like iron filings around a magnet. Glastonbury was one of those elevated locations at which man could commune with the essence of the world, etc. This was the 1970s, after all.

In the words of the painter Nicola Lane: 'The world would be changed to a sort of Tolkienesque landscape ... there were conversations about how the force, the positive power of the hippies, would overcome the forces of evil and corruption ... all the bad things kind of vaporized.'[13]

At Glastonbury, that dream was made flesh. The insalubriousness which gave festivals a bad name was here merely celebrated as the embodiment of the ideological purity of 'natural' music making, in conditions as close to nature as possible, sealing an imagined bond between musical creativity and the *Erdgeist*. This would then become a kind of holy amateurishness, a musicianly vagabondage, drawing on traditions of minstrelsy and itinerant exclusion which both underlined nostalgia for a lost, non-industralized Utopia and championed musical creativity. Non-payment of fees at festivals was not a problem for these people, it was a prerequisite.

Although Marc Bolan's doomed Tyrannosaurus Rex (mere months away from their miraculous T. Rex metamorphosis into bubblegum heroes) played at the first Fayre in 1970, their feathered and tasselled mantle as tramp troubadours to the turned-on and tuned-in was inherited by Gong, a pick-up band trawled by Daevid Allen from the ashes of French drop-outs who'd even dropped out of 1968.

They had recorded first the unashamedly occult-heavy *Magick Brother, Mystick Sister* in autumn 1969 and then 'scored' the Jerome Laperrousaz motorbike movie *Continental Circus* with a narcoleptically disjointed series of wafer-thin riffs, blaring sax and guitar interjections and sub-Floyd improvisations. The LP *Camembert Electrique* followed in 1971, and despite the fluidity of the lineup (Robert Wyatt was on the sessions) Gong began to establish a style, harmonically blues-rooted but apt to wander obsessively down avant-garde or folk avenues with interlocking rhythms of ever-increasing complexity and chromatic germ-themes in apparently random interplay between saxist Didier Malherbe and twenty-year-old guitar prodigy Steve Hillage. The blasting and squawking of Malherbe, and Hillage's effects-riven duets with Allen – whose 'glissando' technique consisted, acording to most sources, of holding down various chords on his guitar and feeding back – were startling. There is a fascinating dislocation of preconceptions on the band's first recordings, being in effect the direct inheritance of random sessions which Allen had cut in Paris in the late 1960s; the sheer visceral thrust of the band's sound, added to the frayed and fizzing textures, recall contemporary garage-band racket.

The influence of Soft Machine also resounds throughout Allen's work; dependable pop melodies and run-of-the-mill, wheezy late 1960s beat-blues arrangements are spiked with the deadliest hallucinogens; disorientated and diverted, odd harmonies suddenly shone upon them like flashlights. There are the moments of inspired lunacy, such as 'Goldilocks', a song in which the nascent free jazz of the Softs comes to the fore, and 'Why Do You Come Knocking at My Door', a primitive but effective use of vocal tape-loops to create a sound collage of considerable interest. Vocal trickery was at the core of Gong's sound, with Allen's purposely inebriated rant offset by the ethereal laryngitic gymnastics of one Gilli Smyth, a Welsh white-witch who dropped out and went, like Allen, to Paris. Dubbed somewhat self-consciously the 'space whisper', its erotic undertones brought an extra dimension of diffuse hedonism to the Dionysiac riot of the music. This truly was total performance, sensual anarchy, if not in the language of the music, then in its delivery. Free gigs and festivals dominated the band's career; audience participation too was encouraged.

In 1967 Pink Floyd's producer Joe Boyd noted with earnest appreciation the passivity and attentiveness of the band's UFO-period audiences; Rick Wright of that band scoffed later to *Record Mirror*. 'In America the audience comes to listen. In England they come to pick up scrubbers.'[14] The reverential and contemplative aspect of bourgeois musical consumption was, for better or worse, already a staple of Progressive ideology – Gong, however, were a rare act inasmuch as they challenged this performer–spectator dynamic. The presence of Parisian performance poet Daniel Laloux helped destabilize normal interaction. Their behaviour, modulating between concentration and chaos, was uncannily similar to Frank Zappa's Janus-faced juggling of rock Situationism and conservatorial seriousness. Incidentally, Gong's music's bluesy shades, practically submerged in distinctive and unusual chord voicings, possess a hypnotic swing and bustling rock punch comparable with Zappa's post-Mothers *Hot Rats*-era work. But whereas Zappa's surrealistic humour tapped everyday concerns, Gong's flirted with cosmic gnosticism in an occult attire of pointed hats and strange symbology that speckled the band's public image and arcane vocabulary. (Occasionally this was anchored to conventional occultist belief, such as the obsession with lunar/solar imagery and theosophy, as in the track 'Fohat Digs Holes in Outer Space' (1971), directly – if maybe satirically – referring to theosophists' nomenclature for the all-encompassing and all-creating ethereal fire.)

Soft Machine alumnus Kevin Ayers joined Gong on vocals, and it was this lineup that stormed the Glastonbury Festival in 1971. The band were so inspired they promptly broke up, then reconstituted themselves, Allen flitting between France and Deya, where the old hippies of 1963 were entering dissolute dotage. Despite recording the body of their *Radio Gnome Invisible Trilogy* (*The Flying Teapot*, 1973; *Angel's Egg*, 1974; *You*, 1974) and featuring on the Glastonbury album, and the barbiturate-powered freakshow at Dingwall's dancehall (London) under the Greasy Truckers banner in 1973, this ramshackle outfit spent most of their time in France and as such exile themselves from the central thrust of this book; their outlook was shaped more by French cultural currents than English ones.

'People like Gong weren't nearly as eccentric as history would have them be,' says Virgin Records producer Tom Newman, who attended most of the band's recordings at the Manor Studio.

> Gilli was into the occult; but she believed in all things that have since come into the mainstream, aromatherapy etc. In my own experience that was the first I'd seen of it crossing into the music business. Tim Blake (later to join the band on synthesizers) was a lovely chap, but he felt that he was a bit of a Swinburne, a kind of wasted Romantic poet thing; very camp, wore makeup a lot.[15]

Apart from the roots laid down in France by Allen, that Gong relocated is of no surprise to Robert Wyatt, for whom the Continent was a hotbed of musical radicalism:

> Europe had the audience, basically. It's also partly to do with radio. English radio had oases of openness like John Peel's programme. Basically it's either pop music or it's Mozart. But on the Continent they really did have lots of weird little radio stations. They had their official radio stations, which often were much more boring even than ours but perhaps because of that they had a much more anarchic network of alternative musical dissemination and also I think there was a political dimension, in that there was a stronger radical tradition dating back to the Resistance. That gave radicalism a moral authority. There was this attitude of contempt towards deliberately gearing art towards the market. Independence was a very strong idea. A lot of

concerts were promoted by local authorities, arts councils etc. Not just in Italy, but in France, Germany, Holland and Scandinavia as well ... A great deal of stuff was subsidized just as the posh arts are here. That meant you could be neither classical or pop music – it gave you space, and a lot of groups on the Continent used it.[16]

The attitude of Soft Machine was itself increasingly unconventional. Mike Ratledge began consciously developing a 'fuck-you' attitude to the audience. Drummer Wyatt, however, told *Time Out* magazine in 1970: 'I'm not a revolutionary at all. I'm really a homebody, an average middle-class bourgeois. I enjoy getting on with the grocer and the dentist.' All this not long after Soft Machine refused to do a benefit for one left-wing magazine on the grounds that the band needed the money more than the magazine did, because they were making the world 'a more beautiful place'. Wyatt continued:

For us, each set is like performing a ... ritual ... a prayer, for example, which you might say every day or night ... but which has different meanings each time it's used. We can see where the end is. It's been worked out beforehand, note by note, and it's just a matter of the exact way in which we phrase it in getting there. I can think ten minutes or more ahead to what I shall do when a bit comes up as a result of something I just did ... the discipline of the musical life, when seriously done, is in itself a totally satisfying and absorbing lifestyle.[17]

This sounds craftily disingenuous. The Softs' music was radical enough and while they had substituted jazz verse-chorus techniques for the aleatory psychedelic pop of their formative years, they were exploring chromatic composition and free soloing, with Wyatt working alongside Lester Bowie's uncompromisingly harsh Art Ensemble of Chicago and Mal Dean's hard-impro Amazing Band, free-jazz legends the pair, by which time Wyatt had transcended rock performance norms by playing every inch of his kit; literally everything in sight.

For a long time I didn't have a proper drum kit. When I played with the Amazing Band I didn't have a drum kit at all. We recorded one track where I just hit anything to hand. My first hi-hat was one of my mum's typewriters.

The drums themselves were rather synthesized, artificial, awkward instruments. Max Roach said that it was hard to get anything going just from sticks and metal boxes. It's very hard to breathe life into them sometimes. You can thwack the shit out of the fuckers like John Bonham [of Led Zeppelin] – but early Tony Williams [in Miles Davis's 1960s quintets] was a bit of an eye-opener in terms of where to go, what to do and what not to do, in terms of effectiveness. I just have a very low boredom threshold. Things like 'in tune' and 'in time' were just sort of bourgeois concepts – the Heath Robinson approach came naturally.[18]

Keith Moon's destructive frenzy was all very well, but here was showmanship of a different kind, which upset not only traditional drum practice but also mystified with its non-rock credentials, employing what Chris Cutler would later call 'small sounds' as opposed to theatrical rhetoric, and harking back to the world of John Cage. Anyone could kick over a Premier kit, but not everyone would think of playing the shells with his fingernails in a solo, producing a performance of musical legitimacy (as opposed to the anti-musical, purely Spectacle-geared antics of Moon) but using unconventional methods to do it.[19]

Even vocalizing, Wyatt was unsatisfied; he was

fed up with songs where the main accents would make you emphasize the words in a way you wouldn't if you were just saying them. At the time I thought there was a great deal of whimsy and eccentricity.

My Grandad used to write comic stuff influenced by Hilaire Belloc and I thought of him and Edward Lear as my ideal English antecedents in terms of words. I wrote nonsense lyrics. For me it was part of an English tradition of making up funny words. That's what we do here …[20]

'It was clever. It was clever in so far as that it was obviously clever, not obviously "look at us, we're being clever", which was so prevalent in Progressive rock, and that was what clinched it,' says John Peel.[21]

Historically, Soft Machine's progress was as feckless as its music. Wyatt left after *Fourth* (1971), Elton Dean after *Fifth* (1972), and Hugh Hopper after *Sixth* (1973). The recruitment of guitarist Allan Holdsworth for 1975's *Bundles* was seen by some aficionados as simply straitjacketing the Softs' fundamentally free-form music in hackneyed jazz-rock paradigms. A minority, however, claim it was a vivid and colouristic revolution in the entire feel and timbral materiality of the band's sound. Whatever, his replacement, ex-Wolf guitarist John Etheridge, brought a more fluid, transparent style whose sheeny texture and jazzy Rheinhardtish attack consolidated the band's new-found harmonic vocabulary post-Holdsworth but loosened up the sound, detaching it from the Marshall stacks' power-point where Holdsworth's fuzzy, effects-laden style seemed to be rooting it. That Etheridge proved no Renaissance man was not his fault; the last original Soft, Mike Ratledge, quit just before *Softs* (1976), and was replaced by Rick Wakeman's brother Alan, by which time the writing was on the wall as big and bold as any 'George Davis is Innocent' slogan.

Of other associates of the mid-1960s Canterbury/Wilde Flowers scene that spawned Soft Machine, Richard Coughlan (drums), organist David Sinclair and guitarist Pye Hastings formed Caravan in 1968; they became Underground darlings overnight with a hypnotic, sybaritic psychedelia showcased on an eponymous debut album and on *If I Could Do It Again, I'd Do It All Over You* for Decca, which respectively featured covers displaying the band kaftan-clad in the desert and lolling in a verdant post-Woodstock glade; it included their evergreen crowd-pleaser 'For Richard'. But as the Technicolor leeched out of the Underground, Caravan's hipster whimsy found itself suddenly friendless. The band's third album, *In the Land of Grey and Pink*, featured lyrics concerning 'grumbly gremblies', boy scouts and cautions to the listener not to 'leave your Dad out in the rain'. Beyond the Learish daftness, the band found themselves treading water, merely gesturing with vaguely vogueish adjuncts such as a wobbly and scrawnily-stringed orchestra (*Caravan and the New Symphonia*, 1973) and electric viola.

Matching Mole, a band formed from scratch with American guitarist Phil Miller (from Carol Grimes's Delivery), bassist Bill McCormick, and Caravan organist Dave Sinclair, showed to what extent Wyatt, like the superstars, had refined his art, yet it still overflows with spritzy invention, from the beautifully lachrymose triads of piano and organ on the ballad 'O Caroline' (a love song made for closing an album, which opens this one). The lyrics of the following track, 'this is the first verse ... this is the chorus ... or perhaps it's a bridge ... or just another part of the song that I'm singing,' highlighted a postmodern stance not new to pop – the Bonzos had pioneered it (among others) in the 1960s, and Wyatt himself had dabbled with it as early as the Softs' second album (1969) – but here, sung with Wyatt's ambivalent timbre, it's especially hard to know exactly what Wyatt *feels* about the words he's singing, thereby upending the cosy rock listener–artist relationship. Wyatt's tribute to Schoenberg, 'Pierrot Lunaire', arose 'not because I sit around listening to Schoenberg, but because I admire the didactic, distanced sort of effect he developed with *sprechgesang*' (literally, speech-song).[22]

The 'drone' effect of much Soft Machine has been replaced by a greater emphasis on more haphazard time-signatures, from which evolve what melodies there are. The rhythm section is particularly busy – not unlike contemporary Miles Davis records such as *On the Corner*, which also utilize a 'soundstream' effect or 'drone', but with Wyatt, the tensions of asymmetry of melody and rhythm that unsettle the listener and alert him/her for further developments are much more upfront, more urgent, more explicit.

Wyatt's horrific accident in 1973, when he was paralysed from the waist down after a fall from a window at a party thrown by Kevin Ayers and members of Gong, focused his exceptional writing ability; the album written in Stoke Mandeville Hospital in the immediate aftermath of the accident, Wyatt's solo LP *Rock*

Bottom, embodies the now considerable confusion circulating about the usage of the word 'progressive' in rock circles. This was clearly far more harmonically advanced than Yes or ELP, even if it lacked their panache at broad-canvased thematic development or arrangement; in fact, it bypassed conventional organization altogether.

Surprise elements, restricted to explosive atonality or the additions of incongruous blue-notes to the chord patterns of pop-song melody lines, became in Wyatt's hands base elements of a wholly individual muse, whereby soundscaping (Brian Eno's synthesizers, looped voices, and a further elaboration on the improvised/composed distinctions of the Matching Mole records act as emotional substitutes for tunes. Rock-band dynamics are replaced by specific interplay between small ensembles of musicians, usually in duos or trios, where, as on *Rock Bottom*'s bitterly poignant 'Sea Song', the intuitive working out of the song between bassist Richard Sinclair and Wyatt (keyboards and vocals) makes a mockery of the limited soundstage to create a set of textures that most contemporary bands needed three months behind a twenty-four-track mixing desk to achieve.

Wyatt's lyrics are also unique; at a time when confessional songs delivered by an 'I' subject relating to personal experience were considered the province of the acoustic-based singer-songwriter, Wyatt fitted them to his complex time-signatures, arbitrary *divertissements* and often dissonant choices of arrangement. On 'Sea Song', the arbitrary choice of emphasis for syllables makes Wyatt's charming apostrophe of his beloved (who he loves most late at night, when she is drunk) all the same strangely imitative. Wyatt's emotional effects were achieved not by consultation of a borrowed, pre-ordained musico-emotional template derived from the words and music of a necropolis of half-remembered poets and composers. No, Wyatt does what he does by drawing on his own experience; how else to explain the chilling introduction of Mellotron chords, the stinging filaments of Mike Oldfield's lamenting guitar solo and Wyatt's haunting treble which opens 'Little Red Robin Hood Hit the Road' from 1974's *Ruth is Stranger than Richard* set, a grandiose prelude to a brisk and unceremonious metamorphosis into a discordant vamp over which Ivor Cutler intones gobbledygook verse?

Hugh Hopper, who outlasted Wyatt in Soft Machine by a year, also stretched himself with the exceptional *1984* (1973), which trod a similarly contrary path. This time, however, the harsher, more abstract elements of the original Softs conception were the basis of experiment. *1984* uses tape-loop samples of the kind that had provided backing both for Soft Machine live performances and Daevid Allen poetry readings: 'a lot of ... clicking a comb or crunching a bit of paper. I don't think a lot of it was very successful, but I remember sitting for about three or four hours at Advision trying to record the sound of a mosquito so that I could use that as a bit of a loop.'[23]

Hopper maintained that listeners had to be 'very stoned' to enjoy *1984* – possibly an exaggeration, as the dichotomies between free improvisation and composition/ collage attain an ambiguity almost as tantalizing as that set up by the (allied) likes of Gilgamesh and National Health years later.

Souled out and jazzed up, what could better explain Hopper and the attendant universe? As adept at free jazz as at Progressive, Hopper guested on a multitude of projects, playing with Lol Coxhill, Wyatt, Keith Tippett, Japanese avant-garde percussionist Stomu Yamashta and Isotope. United by the dialectic of composition and improvisation, these projects serviced the dense music of *Hoppertunity Box* (1976), by which time textural and harmonic freedom had led Hopper almost entirely (though not exclusively) into the modern-jazz fold that was also animating his erstwhile colleagues. That inspiration drives these musicians even today.

Richard Sinclair, bassist of Caravan, and accomplice of much early Canterbury Wilde Flowers–Soft Machine experimentation, put it best: 'I think we've got a particular sound, Kent. We've sung it in our schools ... we were all at school in this sort of area. I was part of the C of E choir; up to the age of sixteen I was singing harmonies that were very English.'[24]

Also distantly linked to the Canterbury constellation were Egg. The brainchild of Kenya-born bassist Montgomery Campbell and London-born keyboardist Dave Stewart, they had initially formed Uriel with Stewart's guitar-prodigy schoolfriend Steve Hillage, but were reduced to a trio with Hillage's departure for university in Canterbury. Stewart recalls:

> Steve's mum and dad gave him a Fender Stratocaster and amp at the age of fifteen. He became phenomenally good phenomenally quickly, so good that I decided to give up guitar and switch to organ, which enabled two groups, Uriel and Arzachel, to come about. When he quit for Canterbury he thought he'd get in with the main men there but I think he was a bit disappointed in the end.[25]

The remnant band began reworking Campbell's compositions, 'which, according to Stewart, were incredibly complex. Mont could write it all down, and not only did I have to learn it, I wanted to learn it, how he did this music.'[26]

Of his days in Egg and in his later band National Health, Stewart says:

> We didn't consider ourselves Progressive. We thought of ourselves as English rock musicians doing our own thing. Progressive, we thought, was Genesis and Yes, and all that stuff, which we hated. Their music, we thought then, didn't seem sufficiently original. It seemed then that what Yes were all about was recycling classical chord voicings. Of course that was what we were doing in Egg! But it all seemed to be about their *shows*, about the spotlight on the geezer in the white kaftan up front. We saw – or supported – Genesis, and there was Peter Gabriel with the front of his head shaved booting a bass drum, and the front row were going "Knife" ... "Knife" ... "Knife" [referring to Genesis's perennial show-stopping climactic number 'The Knife'] and it just seemed so moronic. We didn't see ourselves in that vein at all. I remember a journalist asking me, 'What kind of show will you do?' And I said, 'I'll probably put a clean shirt on,' because I hadn't a clue what he was on about. When I tried to do a Keith Emerson and jump over the organ I sprained my ankle.

The priority was to make music that was interesting. To us. We couldn't foresee what hundreds of thousands of people were going to think was interesting so we judged it off our own bat. It came out pretty complicated – 19/8 rhythms, polyrhythms, polytonality. It was hard to learn, hard to play and probably hard to listen to. We saw that as a worthy cause. Others saw it as a bit of a waste of time. But at the time it seemed necessary to exert oneself … intellectually. We encountered an attitude – it wasn't just us! – that the more original your music was the more valid it was. Originality, that was the key word. The more it sounded like you, the better it was. [27]

Egg were fatuously pigeonholed as a classical-rock band by an intellectually idle music press. Classical leanings are readily acknowledged by Stewart, but their choice of sources, not least later Stravinsky (the severely modal, neo-classical Stravinsky of *Dumbarton Oaks* and the *Ebony Concerto*, as opposed to the colouristic, extravagant Stravinsky of *The Firebird* and *Petrushka* that so animated Yes's Jon Anderson) set them apart from the epigonism of most classical wannabes in the rock firmament. 'Boilk' (1970) alludes to Bach's cantata *Durch Adams Fall ist ganz verderbt* in its chromatic chords – and on the band's third and posthumous album, *Civil Surface* (1974), woodwind quintets were featured; while they fail to arouse much enthusiasm among even diehard aficionados of the band, there is a fastidious grace and unmannered naïveté about them which confirms that here was a band seriously dedicated not to reworking emotionally rewarding music in an emotionally immediate medium (i.e. that of rock) but to reinterpret musical rigour of the past in a musical rigour of now.

The band's second LP, *The Polite Force*, takes these measures much further; the genial pop riffs of the nostalgic romp 'A Visit to Newport Hospital' prefigure a mass of breathtakingly complicated themes and developments. Polytonality becomes atonality on 'Boilk', but only through tape manipulation and switched-off Bach via seasick Mellotron. The band's real originality derives from the creation of a distinct harmonic language from interworked themes, fragments, full blown melodies; 'Long Piece No. 3', comprising side two, piles additive rhythm upon additive rhythm to underpin a series of harsh, often jarring melodies which seem to have been conceived simultaneously with the rhythmic figures.

OTHER OTHERS: WOMEN, BLACKS, FOREIGNERS

'Progressive rock,' one of the musicians interviewed for this book told me gravely, 'was very blokey indeed. Too blokey, in fact.'[28]

In 1970 Chris Welch reported to an astonished world that just-married Ian Anderson of Jethro Tull was a damned fortunate chap because his wife was, er, *hip to his scene*. Mrs Jenny Anderson, Welch told his readers, listened to Frank Zappa 'while she did the housework'.[29] Nicola Lane recalls: 'You weren't really encouraged to be a thinker. You were there really for fucks and domesticity. "My lady". So Guinevere-y. It was quite a difficult time for a girl.'[30]

The Underground, cloaked by a paisley-printed wrap of right-on-ness (and indeed with the occasional complicity of vocal feminists), peddled an image of women which not only compounded that promulgated by the capitalist bourgeois order they purported to despise, but concealed it in a tissue of flimsy libertarian sophistry, fuelled by fantasies of womanhood derived from the same nineteenth-century Romantic idealism that informed much Progressive ideology.

Says John Peel:

We all thought we were being fantastically generous to women, letting them in on what we were doing. Even Germaine Greer, who was a very frightening woman even then, appeared with no clothes on in the underground press and everyone thought it was brilliant. I had a Schoolgirl of the Year competition on the radio – although it did have a vaguely surrealist aspect – one year it was won by a typewriter, one year by half a rhinoceros, because people would send in photos of anything.'[31]

Gong's Daevid Allen wrote songs called 'Pretty Miss Titty' and 'I Am Your Pussy'; the thoughtful and level-headed composer David Bedford's orchestral experiment of 1971, *The Garden of Love*, demanded 'six beautiful girls to dance and turn pages' in its score.[32] Richard Branson told Robert Wyatt's wife Alfreda: 'I don't talk to women about these things,' as she tried to negotiate a contract for her incapacitated husband with Virgin.[33]

The Beatnik ideology which prefigured Progressive ideology had rebelled against the home and the family, then identified solely with traditional nurturing aspects of womanhood. Sex, by Beat and Bohemian standards, was, ideally, free, uninhibited, anti-familial, improvised, spontaneous – rather like music. Rock sex too was meant to be 'free' – ignoring the respective roles played by male and female components in the sex contract. The 'natural' ideology of hippyism was found wanting in its gaucherie, when faced with the realities of the sex contract in the late 1960s; while it propagated earth-motherly solidarity with the eternal feminine (Gilli Smyth's Mothergong project was about birthing experiences 'both physical and spiritual')[34] and untamed expression of womanly sexuality, it ignored extant attitudes towards sex in which female receptivity, passivity and dependence on men was taken for granted. Led Zeppelin guitarist and textbook 1970s rock icon Jimmy Page once admitted: 'I'm just looking for an angel with a broken wing, one who couldn't fly away.'[35]

The feminist invocation of 'our bodies, our selves', putatively welcomed as a manifestation of the individualist impulse in the counter-cultural agenda, was eventually rejected by a male-oriented hippy *Weltanschauung*. To hippies, the invocation of *choice* to *reject* promiscuous sex was the reaction of the repressed. Mary Whitehouse's media-amplified moral crusade against 1960s permissiveness was, inevitably and rashly, identified with feminism. Folk-leftist Phil Ochs believed that the women's movement was a CIA plot to emasculate the counter-culture.

Rock ideology, which gave the world the conflicting images of male performers and instrumentalists both as sensitive, quasi-feminized creators and as super-heroic embodiments of

Nietzschean stamina, promulgated women as 'free spirits', sultry G-stringed temptresses like Sonja Kristina of Curved Air who, the embryonic A&R boys emphasized, was a girl of 'today', able to choose her sexual destiny. Most of Curved Air's almost exclusively male audience knew what choices they'd like to see her make. Jenny Fabian's novel, *Groupie* – for which the word 'tawdry' might have been coined – is an nauseatingly insalubrious account not only of the late-1960s rock milieu but of the way so-called 'Progressive' musicians (in this case, Family) believed themselves (and indeed were blithely puffed as) independent of showbiz behavioural traditions, but casually dipped toes (and wicks) into the kind of fleshly temptations familiar to popular artists for centuries past.

Womankind was presented and consumed as commodity. King Crimson's *Cadence and Cascade* (1970) was freely admitted to have been 'about two groupies'.[36] Crimson, and specifically their lyricist Pete Sinfield, muscularly bolstered the canon of masculine fantasy still further with their 'Ladies of the Road' from 1971's *Islands*: 'a flower seller's daughter/as sweet as holy water/said 'I'm the school reporter/please teach me' – well I taught her/high-diving Chinese trender/black hair and black suspender/said, "Please me no surrender/just love to feel your Fender"/stone-headed Frisco spacer/ate all the meat I gave her/said would I like to taste hers/and even craved the flavour.' Disbelieving readers may wish to check the sleeve for proof.

Author Sinfield says, a trifle sheepishly:

'Ladies of the Road'; everybody writes at least one groupie song. We shouldn't. But we do. It is the ultimate sexist lyric *of all time*. I couldn't imagine anyone taking it too seriously, because in those days you were still able to say things like 'my lady' with a capital M and a capital L. The other thing about groupies was that most groupies were actually very funny and very intelligent, especially in America. They certainly freed me from my English shyness. One of these girls might say 'Y'all wanna take a shower with us?' And I'd say, 'What, with *you*?' And then I'd double-take and go, 'With *all* of you?' My public-school upbringing, you see. It liberated me from that.'[37]

Girls were either urban libertines like Fabian or they were relegated to rustic folkie flakiness, Elvira Madigans with guitars, 'natural' conduits for 'natural' sounds. Folk music was earth music, girls were of the earth, so where was the problem?

The problem came later. The role created for women in Progressive ideology was one where artistic creation was minimal – only artistic *interpretations* of things created by men were legitimate, a role as patronizing as maintaining that women's role in art was the conveyance of male artistic ideals. There were no female instrumentalists of any note employed beyond those in bands like Fanny, whose name really says it all; in that rock context, women were packaged as slut-streetwalkers, degraded 'victim' of the urban capitalism their blues-based music seemed to signify. Progressive implicitly conveyed an ulterior femininity, of intense liberation and untamed sensual expression, freed of the capitalist-contractual notions of sexuality which seemed part and parcel of the blues and its descendent music. But the feminine aspects of Progressive ideology and practice also betrayed a male view of female sexuality, marginalizing female participation in the worldview. Only in left-field acts – Henry Cow, Holland's female-dominated Supersister or various 1980s Japanese Progressive rock acts – would the gender fundamentalism of the genre be challenged and blurred. In the meantime, the passive role played by women in the ideology of 1970s rock led to excesses which to a 1990s audience seem merely offensive. As music writer and editor Tony Herrington recalls of the *NME* in the mid-1970s: 'Despite this pervading editorial ultraleft, liberal atmosphere of right-on-ness, the gigs page would be covered in pictures of women with their tits out, for no other reason than that they'd got their tits out.'[38]

Women, as a rule, went into the business as ancillaries of artistic transmission – they became photographers like Penny Reel, Jill Furmanovsky or Lynn Goldsmith, or publicists like Charisma's Gail Colson. Few went into journalism, with *Sounds'* Penny Valentine and later *NME's* Angie Errigo honourable exceptions. Performers were restricted to brave and independent avant-garde adventuresses like wind player Lindsay Cooper and cellist Georgina Born, who played significant performing (and compositional) roles in Henry Cow, a band of scrupulously applied equal opportunity where women were expected to hump gear and drive trucks. The most visible of the (few) rock women of the era, Fleetwood Mac's twin-babe team of Christine McVie and Stevie Nicks and Jefferson Airplane's Grace Slick, were presented as focal points first, creators second. No matter that, having authored the tracks 'White Rabbit' and 'Rejoyce', Slick had provided psychedelia with two of its musical defining moments, and that McVie and Nicks were skilled musicians. Robert Wyatt recalls: 'As Pete Townshend said, there were a lot of rope-ins going on. People roped women in because they looked a certain way and dressed a certain way.'[39]

The same unwitting exclusion applied to ethnic minorities. Beyond the also-ran underground band Locomotive paying the rent in 1967 with an ad hoc but smash-hit rendition of Prince Buster's ska classic 'Rudy's in Love' that dismayed as many blacks as it dismayed skinheads as it dismayed hippies, black music was effectively rendered anonymous, sno-paked out of the entire Progressive project. 'It was never conscious racism so far as I could tell,' admits John Peel. 'It just happened. Like with women. We thought we were *letting them in on what we were doing*. But we weren't.'[40]

Black instrumentalists in Progressive were practically unknown, despite all the fine words about the imagined egalitarianism and shoulder-to-shoulder colour-blindness of the 1960s. Romeo Challenger, who would later go on to drum, sing and be racially abused for fancy-dress Ted revivalists Showaddywaddy, did a stint with Leicester hard-rock band Black Widow; but aside of itinerant jazzers (usually South African exiles) like trumpeter Mongezi Feza or saxophonist Dudu Pukwana, there was scarcely a black face to be seen in Progressive. Even the 1970s ubiquity of Eastern philosophy, then swilling around youth culture like sacred cow-dung, didn't help; in fact, it rendered ethnic minorities – specifically Asian – even more as representatives of 'otherness'. This was possibly what hobbled the career of Quintessence, led by two Indian immigrants (although Raja Ram, their celebrated flautist/violinist was one Ron Rothfield, who hailed from Australia): the pervasive stereotype of Asiatic culture as consumer source for mystical panaceas and nothing else. They were, and remained, novelties.

What didn't help was that black immigrants constituted a relatively small proportion of the youth population and hence numbered proportionately fewer than whites in popular music, even soul; and black tastes were a thorny problem for hippies. Before the arrival of Mickie Most's stable of bubblegum block-busters Suzi Quatro, Mud and Sweet, the most visible musical enemy of Progressive was Tamla Motown, then regarded as the Fordist Antichrist of mass-produced pop pap, conveyer-belting innumerable 'manufactured' artists singing 'manufactured' hits.

'Rock and roll disinherited its terminology and black roots,' declares Robert Wyatt. 'Chuck Berry and Jimmy Smith and Ray Charles were disappeared. Then the more vacuous black pop music came along and people assumed that that was all there was. That turned into disco and black music got called "that commercial stuff". Rubbish, of course, but that's what people thought.'[41]

Letters were written to *Sounds* criticizing John Peel for playing 'too much black pop'; Stevie Wonder, armed with his credentials as singer-songwriter from his earliest 'Fingertips' days, was an exception, as were Hendrix, James Brown and Screamin' Jay Hawkins, black artists who, for better or worse, conformed to the prevailing white notion of rootsy artistic 'integrity' and 'authenticity' – those old standbys again.

It is interesting, if perhaps a little disingenuous, to speculate on what might have happened to Progressive rock music and values – and ideology – had Hendrix lived. Commentators routinely, and rightly, point to Progressive rock's whiteness and imply that Hendrix's rank as instrumental hero was largely a 'token' gesture by white rock fans and cognoscenti. But close inspection of contemporary testimony reveals just how important Hendrix, and more specifically his treatment of the blues, was in white rock culture. In his final year, in the teeth of disapproval from the black militants who had befriended him, Hendrix toyed with a raft of putative collaborations with white players including guitarist John McLaughlin – but most interestingly, he envisaged a collaboration with Keith Emerson and Greg Lake, and the free-jazz and avant-garde leanings of his late recordings suggest an unself-conscious adoption of a style already favoured more by white consumers than black consumers and one whose musical provenance is at best difficult to discern. The last developments in Hendrix's career as a composer and improviser suggest a *volte-face*, embracing other musics as much as the impeccable black blues traditions that had hitherto informed his music. Most of those interviewed for this book recall that Hendrix's popularity was overwhelmingly among a white constituency; had he continued into the 1970s, his attitude towards that constituency might have been at least interesting, at best revolutionary.

Of the rumoured collaboration (which anecdotal evidence suggests was aborted by Emerson and Lake when a 'wigged-out' and bodyguarded Mitch Mitchell came to open negotiations), Pete Sinfield observes:

> Greg was trying to balance out Keith because Keith was extraordinary on stage and Greg used to stand there and, er, play his bass. I don't think Jimi, after Mitch Mitchell, needed another drummer who could hit everything very quickly and very loudly, like Carl [Palmer]. He needed a jazz-type drummer, because rock'n'roll concepts are odd to jazz drummers. They don't really want to play straightforwardly. Like Tony Williams. That wouldn't have been Carl's style.'[42]

But Hendrix's aesthetic also chimed with an unreconstructed view of blackness among white consumers fuelled by the counter-cultural relevancy of blackness as embodied in the *Shaft* and *Superfly* Blaxploitation films. Outgrowths of the male macho urban outsider fantasy of sexual potency, they were the dopplegangers of contemporary *Easy Rider* freedom-fantasies of white youth. Hendrix, hero of guitar erotica, *was* sexual potency and outsiderism. In the counter-culture, blacks were read exclusively as victims of 'the system' – save John Shaft and Hendrix, figures of resistance through outsiderism; the Jackson Five, meanwhile, viewed as servants of the system, seemed to play the music the system wanted to hear: anonymous, homogenized. Hendrix was different because he fitted white Romantic adeals of originality in all things.

Ironically it was perhaps the most English of bands, Genesis, who broke the black taboo by signing American drummer Chester Thompson in 1976 and asking another black American, bassist Alphonso Johnson, to join the band on guitar the following year. By then, of course, the fascination with the multi-racial universe of US jazz-rock fusion had implanted itself in many UK musicians' minds and opened them up considerably.

The alleged internationalism of the hippy project had been undermined by the reaction of foreign police forces to longhair assertion irrespective of nationality post-1968. In the UK, foreign travel was still for the most part restricted to package holidays or hippy hitching. Communication with Europe was still plagued by breakdowns in TV transmission from ice-skating tournaments, football matches and the Eurovision Song Contest. When the UK joined the EEC on 1 January 1973 Europe's presence was suddenly nearer yet paradoxically no nearer, commercially and culturally unshackled, yet forbiddingly alien. Leeds United, Arsenal and other British football teams were suddenly being beaten up or just beaten by Continental sides from Murmansk to Malaga. Strikebound Britain seemed to be lagging; 'Tomorrow's World' was full of this French, that German or the other Dutch scientific initiative.

Rock was no different. The singles success registered by Shocking Blue ('Venus') and Frijid Pink ('House of the Rising Sun') in 1970 may not have convinced many of a Continental shift, but it raised enough eyebrows for agents to consider importing other acts. In came Burnin' Red Ivanhoe from Denmark, Ange from France, Premiata Forneria Marconi (PFM) from Italy ('who could have been another King Crimson' – Pete

Sinfield) and – most sensationally – Focus, a Dutch act based on the staggering improvisational talents of keyboardist/flautist Thijs van Leer and award-winning guitarist Jan Akkerman, who wrought numberless moods from original, folk-derived or classically-purloined themes, often with a spirit of irresistible clownishness and genre-bending dexterity which escaped English Progressive bands.

Europe, with a more distinct dichotomy between the music of the middle classes and that of the young, underlined by the cultural chasm opened up in 1968, often saw the Progressive ideology taken even more seriously than in England, where a degree of youthful cultural autonomy had been apparent since Bill Haley's onslaught in 1954. In Europe, rock had been slower to obtain significance and had therefore taken on a more distinct identity as a music of resistance. Most European nations boasted substantial Progressive scenes and acts; Norway had Prudence, Sweden Zamla Mammaz Manna, Finland Wigwam. Even fascist Spain produced bands, such as the excellent Triana. Italy was a particular hotbed of Progressive, a quintessentially musical culture like that of Germany's encouraging numerous bands, among them Le Orme, Electric Frankenstein, Reale Accademia di Musica and Quella Vecchia Loccanda. The Iron Curtain also proved no obstacle to Progressive, as any hearing of Czechoslovakia's Collegium Musicum or Modry Efekt, Poland's SBB or Hungary's grotesquely glam-attired stadium-fillers Omega will soon make apparent.

'There was an Anglocentric attitude towards Europe,' says Bill Bruford, 'a feeling of "Ah, we've got all that. We've got Keith Emerson, what can *they* show us?" Magma, though, turned heads; they appeared to be an elemental force that was completely unlike anything else.'[43]

Christian Vander's Magma, 'for the life, for the death, for the life after death',[44] were a French band who effortlessly mingled Coleman/Coltrane-derived jazz soloing, Orff-style chorales, Bartókian time-signatures, electronics and free improvisation in a mammoth musical vision to tell the story of apocalypse and after in a megalomaniacal conceptual dekalogy (related in an entire extra-terrestrial language dreamt up by Vander – a fabulist's bastardization of Hungarian, French and Leon Thomas's scat-singing on Pharoah Sanders records), transfixed musicians then and now, although they inspired more acolytes in Continental Europe than the UK, where their following remained strictly cultic. A handful of visits were made; after recording their 1972 *Mekanik Destruktiw Kommandoh* album at Branson's Manor studios, Magma stormed the 1973 Reading Festival, belatedly rode the slipstream of the short-lived jazz-rock-fusion bandwaggon with tours in 1974/5, and won the adulation of snooker megastar Steve Davis, who funded an unlikely return of the band to the UK in 1988.

There were also Can, Tangerine Dream and Faust – the crusaders of Krautrock – purveyors of mantra-like improvisation, Gothic electronica and auto-destructive post-serial noise respectively, issuing from a wholly different cultural mediation of American popular music and one in which the value of rock as resistance – not to mention the questioning of the very harnessing of rock's social conditions of production to capitalism – was important. This cultural parentage places them outside the remit of this narrative, but nevertheless, the immeasurably more febrile musical and social nature of Progressive in Germany warrants careful attention by any student of popular culture. It seems incredible that as yet only one reliable English-language book (Julian Cope's *Krautrocksampler*, published by Head Heritage in 1995) even begins to grapple with its complexities. But as we have seen, a combination of industry sloth, amateurism or parochialism reduced Euro-rock to a mere nomenclature in an industry rapidly filling up with them, another obsessive's 'bin' in HMV shops.

SHAKERS OF THE CITY WALLS: (BOMB)SITES OF PROGRESSIVE RESISTANCE

The Situationist project of disruption, danger and chance which flitted within and without the grasp of the masses in 1968, remained embryonically embedded in Progressive even after its corporatization between 1969 and 1971. There were those, in short, who felt that society, or at least individual consciousness, could be changed through rock'n'roll, both its performance and its ethics. While the Angry Brigade, England's own urban guerrilla outfit, never embraced rock as a potentially potent source of propaganda, their contemporaries in far-left agitprop were never far from rock; the sterner the sermons preached by a band against commercialism, the more likely that revolutionary hangers-on would be drawn to it.

This took the form of two very different strains of Progressive rock. One was rigorously disciplined, possessed of civic notions of focused subjection to the collective will as a means to a revolutionary end, as exemplified by Henry Cow; the other was play-powered dissolution, celebrant, populist and irresponsible – the Notting Hill scene.

Henry Cow were formed by politically motivated musicians and Cambridge University students Fred Frith (guitar) and Tim Hodgkinson (sax) in 1968. Frith was a mental-hospital ancillary at the time and had, in the words of Canadian avant-garde specialist Andrew Jones, applied the teachings of Cage and Cardew to the blues of Alexis Korner and the jazz of Wes Montgomery. Mythology would later term the Cow a 'Dada blues band'.[45] Dada *was* a factor; preconceptions of instrumental technique, already in chaotic flux thanks to Hendrix and Townshend and the found-object interference with instruments by AMM and Pink Floyd, were seized and shaken up; Frith played his guitar with and through anything to hand. Drummer Chris Cutler had already been exploring the possibility of rock to exercise head and heart in the Ottawa Music Company, a twenty-six-piece 'rock composers' orchestra' he had formed with his keyboardist friend Dave Stewart (Egg) perhaps reflecting the considerable influence of Cutler of avant-jazz mystic, keyboard virtuoso and bandleader Sun Ra.

Henry Cow's future looked bright; the band had won John Peel's BBC 'Rockortunity Knocks' competition the previous year, and while the music was of an already formidable tonal and rhythmic abstraction, there were lateral tracings into the work of Soft Machine to interest an audience still with the tinnitus of the experiments of 1967–8 ringing in their ears. The appetites among group members for discovering new forms of reorganizing sound, both in composition and in performance (whether improvised or not), whetted the band's appetite for novelty all the more.

Cutler is forthright:

There was a polarity between people like us and people like Yes and ELP who were trying to play 'classics for the people' – they did some very interesting things, and I don't want to denigrate that. Some of ELP's treatments of the classics were valuable, because they say something about the compositions and their adaptability, and the suitability of using electric instruments to interpret them. But to me that was all backward-looking. Bands like Henry Cow tried rather to bring in non-pop influences that were a bit more contemporary, Schoenberg, Varese, Stockhausen, Bartok, Ornette Coleman, Sun Ra, *musique concrète*.

Much of our music had to be written down because it was compositionally complex. Normally someone comes along with a guitar or a keyboard, plays the chords, sings along, and everybody starts to help arrange it. Composing's different – you organize your musical forces in a highly complex way moving from one musical disposition to another so that the players can't simply be left to work out their own parts. When you're composing harmonies vertically or contrapuntally, it's best to write it out. [Henry Cow] worked in different ways on different songs. Some things, like 'Amygdala' [1973], are completely scored, every single note. But we worked, as all rock groups do, on looser structures, too and in totally un-planned improvisation. We were in a fairly unusual position, I suppose, because there weren't any heroes or leaders; Henry Cow was very much a collective enterprise, so even if a composer brought a fully-scored piece to the group we'd feel free, as a group, to change individual parts, chop sections out, or say, 'We need something else in here and then develop it. It was a very productive way to work, extending the power of scores. Henry Cow didn't rely on scores – though they were a marketing tool – and we didn't bring our scores to the stage. Everything was committed to memory. It's very hard to play convincingly when you're reading, but once you've internalized a piece of music, you can make what comes next appear fresh and necessary – play it, ideally, as though you'd just thought of it.

Improvisation was part of our brief from the very beginning. Henry Cow was a band interested in extremes. For instance, I would say that our compositions were probably more complex than anybody else's, with the exception perhaps of Frank Zappa's, while, improvisationally, we followed the Coltrane/Ra/Coleman school. No pre-arrangements, no tonal or chordal centre, no rules. In a collective improvisation, the pleasure is to wind up somewhere no individual could have palmed. One learns a lot about one's instrument in open improvisation discovering new kinds of techniques, which later became incorporated into composition.[46]

Perhaps this can best be illustrated with reference to the blistering and initially conventional-sounding Frith guitar solo in 'Teenbeat Reprise' on *Legend*. The rhythm section's (and Frith's) irregular downbeats encourage a harmonic elasticity, but that doesn't diminish the roller-coaster exhilaration of the song. The effect of both radical composition and blowing is heightened by the use of distance and perspective in the mix – radicalizing the studio. (Archie Shepp and Albert Ayler's 1960s free impro hadn't cottoned on to that). Cutler's 'small sounds', used not just by percussion but by all instrumentalists, occupy places of importance by dint of their placing in the mix, achieving a *pointilliste* effect, texturing multi-tracked voiced syllables, the organ and piano phrases dissolving slowly into tinier and tinier entities, as on 'Ruins' (1974).

Exquisite textures result, such as the studio superimpositions of guitars and organ at the start of 'Teenbeat'. The stereo soundstage will offer discrete groupings of instruments apparently playing lines both harmonically and melodically independent of each other which are united by the soloist in the centre.

'Linguaphonie' (1974), a forbidding collage, utilizes, with important emotional effect, vari-speed tape manipulation. This enables contrapuntal backing to Hodgkinson's horn solos or Frith's guitar pyrotechnics.

While the word 'symphonic' might not superficially apply to the vertical or horizontal scale of the music, it *does* apply to the Cow's emotional range. At the serene heart of the long 'Ruins', the horn gravely soliloquizes while the viola tells its own sorry tale in a misty chromatic landscape. Percussion tickles and goads the two instruments. Frith's viola/violin work also dismisses notions that Cow music was always truculent and abrasive; there is languor here too.

Cow explored nervelessly; the concise paragraphs of *Legend* mature and expand for 1974's *Unrest*, with longer sections of vamping behind long solos allowing greater swing. The emphasis is on a greater commitment to ideals, particularly on the hyperactive side two. While the rock aspect rocks harder, the music's rough edges get rougher too and the phrases less synchronous (reaching a manic pitch on the white-hot 'Upon Entering the Hotel Adlon', two minutes fifty-six seconds of high-speed ensemble and simultaneously-soloed free-form fury).

Politically, Henry Cow were always committed to the Left, playing benefit gigs around Europe. Cutler asserts: 'We were fairly serious individuals ... We were serious about rock, and its potential. And we were serious about politics. We weren't happy to see the defeats of the late 1960s rest as defeats.'[47]

Dada haunts the band's boisterous manhandling of polymathic compositional techniques. Hodgkinson's 'Nine Funerals for the Citizen King' boasts a line which begins 'and underneath the spectacle ... ' (referring, surely, to Guy Debord's leftist polemic about the bread-and-circuses narcotic of the 'society of the Spectacle') and climaxes 'as long ago as 1919' (pikestaff-plain reference to Dadaism's birth in Zurich). The band also initiated a sequence of concerts in London – for which they appropriated the Dada title Cabaret Voltaire – which saw them seated in armchairs on a set decorated to resemble a Victorian parlour complete with sideboard and tasselled standard-lamps. Robert

Wyatt muses:

> Perhaps it's an ironic consequence of the British Empire that you do get to see a lot of people with funny hats on making funny noises with their mouths. Some are left sitting with the strange images of Empire stuck in their brains. It's the opposite of pomp and circumstance – domestic as opposed to public'.[48]

The band participated in offbeat theatrical projects such as an avant-garde production of Euripides' *The Bacchae* at the Explorers' Club in 1972 with Ivor Cutler, Derek Bailey, Ron Geesin and David Toop, and they would later go on to perform in conjunction with the Manchester Royal Exchange Theatre Company in a 1978 tour sponsored by the Arts Council.

David Ilic has since suggested that Henry Cow's performances unfailingly 'subjected their material to ... continual, rigorous self-examination, with numbers dissected, reassembled and reworked during performances to the ultimate end of irrigating the material to keep it fresh for players and spectators'.[49] The basic rhythmic *matériel* of rock, bass/drums, employ not standard rock pulses but imbue the music with an irresistible vigour. It is easy to imagine that the music could be played by a string quartet, or indeed any tight-knit musical groupuscule in which players act independently and collectively – for instance, the arrangements mean that few Cow musicians perform the unitary functions of most rock players in the sound of the band. But Cutler's drumming in particular is an impulse that arouses insatiable anticipation; what will the next trick be? The return of tonality? Its disappearance?

Later work substitutes study for swing: *In Praise of Learning* (1975) was recorded with sister avant-gardists Slapp Happy. Placing the voice of the latter's singer, the tenebrously expressive Dagmar Krause, at the front of the soundstage diminishes the surface complexity of the music. But a more austere, less spontaneous climate blows in to compensate. The instrumental pieces, 'Beginning: The Long March' and 'Morning Star' are granitic sculptures of multi-layered sound organization. There is a cogency, a tough and uncompromising single-minded vision argued in each meticulously engineered song.

The imposing 'Beautiful as the Moon: Terrible as an Army with Banners' contains a lusty Frith solo whose very difference from the saturnine surroundings emphasizes the discipline of the rest; again, throughout the final pages of 'Living in the Heart of the Beast', largely tonal harmonies rise in strange keys; like Frith's solos, it emphasizes the academic and sternly fastidious nature of the rest of the piece. Its brilliant harmonic finesse shows the unconvinced just what skilful composers are at work here. If people were tempted to advance the theory that their wilder dissonances belied their ability to play or compose 'real' music, these sort of sequences, martial and hectoring though they may be, destroy any such opposition.

Ironically, given the tastes of both groups for economical sound, the arrangements are fuller and deeper, reinforced by electronics and effects. The depth empowers the band elsewhere; those 'small sounds' are afoot again, with little percussive noises sounding right through the textures on 'The Long March' like cathedral bells. But this is as far as rock practice goes; Krause sings monodies rather than melodies, toying listlessly with tonality.

The German Krause had been, like the rest of Slapp Happy, exposed to the avant-garde sonic-Teutonic terrorism of Faust and was steeped in oppositional music; with a few exceptions (mostly in their early music), normal verse-chorus structures are upset in Slapp Happy songs, which are more redolent of twentieth-century classical vocal music. Expressionist mono-drama is evident in staccato, polysyllabic singing with chromatic accidentals rendering the music more difficult than unduly odd rhythms – although the emphases of the long verses on 'Riding a Tiger' (from *Desperate Straights*, 1975) are among the most infuriatingly strange in rock. Brecht–Eisler cabaret songs play their part too – chamber arrangements for piano, bass, guitar and drums playing in an arid soundscape with sardonic samples of other styles wittily appearing here and there – the title track from *Desperate Straights* is an astounding satire, an unending circular waltz-pastiche of Jacques Loussier, Burt Bacharach and Erik

Satie's *Vexations*.

'Art is not a Mirror – It is a Hammer!' John Grierson's aphorism was boldly reproduced on the cover of Henry Cow/Slapp Happy's *In Praise of Learning* album. This was problematic in terms of semantics for a start. Was the music 'art'? More specifically, could it be independent of the capitalistic social *realpolitik* in which it was created (ex-Stowe boy and Cow label boss Branson's business methods are discussed elsewhere in this book).

As we shall see later, Cutler and Co's ethos was to couple radical values to radical art. But measure the worth of same against a rock culture that enabled books like *No One Waved Goodbye* (Robert Somma, Charisma Books, 1973) to be published. The book, a pre-emptive slant on the schema of rock-star-as-victim, maintained that Janis Joplin, Hendrix, Morrison and the rest had been hounded to their deaths by the vices of capitalism, an argument to which, in the light of the contemporaneous miners' strike, the *NME*'s Bob Edmands wrote a stirring rejoinder:

> Would you rather die of an OD or a rockfall ... the least we could have expected ... was the odd benefit for the miners' strike fund – but George Harrison's too busy buying Oriental antiques by all accounts. Sadly, it is no longer hip to come on strong with dialectical diarrhoea. The real thing is much more acceptable.[50]

That rock was unsuited to urban dissent, its blackboard-jungle credibility having been tamely subsumed by corporate America some two decades before, was increasingly self-evident. Could a re-visitation of rusticity, in the van of the atavistic hippy ideology of the retreat to nature, provide a viable alternative for means of resistance? We found out soon enough.

WIDE-OPEN SPACES: CALLING THE COUNTRY TO THE CITY-FOLK AND PROGRESSIVE ROCK

It would be inappropriate to proceed further without examining the influence of folk music on Progressive rock and vice versa. After all, the explicit nature of hippyism's Romantic rejection of urban industrial capitalism for a communion with the 'natural' made the cross-fertilization inevitable.

We have already examined the phenomenon in various forms. But given that folk purists castigated the espousal of electronic amplification of folk music as a betrayal of its authenticity, we must remember that the marriage of folk and rock music was always on rock music's terms. Rock saw folk mostly as a means to an end of bolstering its own concerns. The left-field singles success of Notting Hill vagrant heroes East of Eden, whose out-of-character hoedown single 'Jig a Jig' in 1971 was almost entirely due to the bawdy sawing of Dave Arbus's violin, tuned into still-vibrant rural yearnings in record buyers.

The most obvious example of the biased congress between rock and folk was the misleadingly named folk-rock; it enjoyed periodic vogues, notably at the end of the 1960s when, as we have seen, the bucolic nature of hippyism was still viable cultural currency. The Earth-motherly aspects of the mandolins, guitars and violins, wielded by the likes of the Incredible String Band, Mellow Candle, Trees etc., must have seemed like potential goldmines. But while these acts remained largely folk-oriented, others decided to go the whole hog and jump ship to rock full time, taking only their harmonies with them. It proved to be an unintentionally ironic endorsement of Constant Lambert's celebrated witticism that the only thing one could do when one had finished playing a folk song was to play it again louder.[51]

Such a band were the Strawbs, an acoustic duo whose recruitment of John Ford (bass), Richard Hudson (drums) and a pre-Yes Rick Wakeman (keyboards) gave their uncomplicated chords and melodies both oomph and potential for development, which on 1970's *Just a Collection of Antiques and Curios*, recorded live at the Queen Elizabeth Hall, is self-evident. *From the Witchwood* (1971) clearly tries to accommodate the substantial writing skills of Hudson and Ford as well as Wakeman's endless talent for improvisation into the music, and fails. Titles like 'Sheep', 'Cannondale' etc. may score idyllic points but the earthbound nature of the band's musical language offers little of either evocative or authentic musical enlightenment. This was neither music to delight the aesthete or engage the grassroots sensibilities of folk connoisseurs.

It is tempting to harp on the topic of folk-rock. Its relationship to Progressive is, however, at best incidental. While Progressive espoused pastoral imagery and apparently 'folky' textures, it is important to take these in context. For example, Genesis's twelve-string sound, patented on *Trespass* (1970), often cited by fans as a folk influence, owes more to Crosby Stills and Nash and Joni Mitchell's appropriation of folk guitar than to folk guitar itself. Similarly, the fascination with the rustic often reflects a view of the countryside inherited through the refracting lenses of a century of popular, mass-cultural idealizations of rural life (e.g. from 'The Monarch of the Glen' to the Southern Railway's elysian poster art to, ultimately, Pink Floyd's 'Grantchester Meadows'). The immediacy of expression implicit in real traditional English folk music jarred with the accelerating refinement of the ruralist idylls extolled by hippy utopians – indeed by Progressive ideology generally.

As *fin-de-siècle* Romanticism had sought a mythical medieval utopia, so hippyism looked further back to a time innocent of internal combustion and the cost thereof.

It's maybe churlish to dismiss this nostalgia altogether. Substantial numbers did attempt to live the ideal; where forty years earlier rambling legions of earnest young men and women in cycling shorts had headed, the same process was repeated as hairies by the hundred schlepped into the backwoods. Tepee communes were founded, newly-weds restored derelict oasthouses in Dorset and the first moneyed graduates of the counter-cultural rat race began their own retreat to the countryside.

The atavistic urge also manifested itself in the mainstream. The BBC drama series 'The Six Wives of Henry VIII' had been a TV smash hit in the early 1970s (and was in the process of being reinterpreted by rock icon Rick Wakeman); 'Greensleeves' could be heard everywhere. Baby-faced medieval woodwind scholar

David Munrow was the toast of the chattering classes, colour supplement editors and record producers.

The extent of this cultural phenomenon can be read by rock's wholehearted embrace of it; while Progressive's commercial honeymoon had waned by 1973 and record companies were now no longer signing anything featuring woodwind and a Mellotron, the success of two bands that year attests to a post-hippy medievalism that equated itself with folk. Giles Farnaby's Dream Band, a curious lineup formed from folk band the Druids and Trevor Crozier's Broken Consort and named after the renowned sixteenth-century English composer and lutenist, rehashed medieval folk material with some bass-led virility – on EMI to boot. But bigger and better by far were Gryphon, brainchild of Royal College of Music graduates Richard Harvey and Brian Gulland. Both were woodwind virtuosi, dedicated to early music, Gulland concentrating on reed instruments (specifically crumhorns), with Harvey both a composer and recorder player of formidable facility.

The band became the first act to be played on all four BBC radio stations in one week. Their debut album interspersed traditional medieval material with original themes in raffish pastiche style. Purists sniffed at the integration of acoustic guitar and modern-day percussion but it did give Gryphon a more consumer-friendly sound, an opalescent and vaguely contemporary sheen to the gruff tones of the Gulland–Harvey woodwind consorts; not unallied in arrangement to the more overtly folky material of ex-Fairport associates Shirley and Dolly Collins.

Gryphon were not hidebound revivalists; modernity had plenty to offer them: stereo imaging and delay techniques for 'The Unquiet Grave'; ditto double-tracking voices (both spoken and sung) into, and tacking a manic excerpt from 'The Entertainer' on to the closing 'The Devil and the Farmer's Wife'. There's a whiff of the academic however; the music has little of the spry vitality of a Munrow performance and the arbitrary interpolation of different themes from quite different periods into pieces such as 'Kemp's Jig' (a sixteenth-century English tune to which is added a thirteenth-century Spanish tune) smacks of verisimilitude. Did they *need* to pull such a stunt?

But Culture found them irresistible (did the 1970s stresses and strains placed upon the British self-image demand a lingering rewind of Elizabethan glories?). Gryphon went from cold fish to hot property overnight. Peter Hall commissioned them to score a National Theatre *Tempest* (duplicated as the 'Midnight Mushrumps' suite on their second 1974 album) and film soundtracks for *Pope Joan* and *Brother Sun, Sister Moon* were also forthcoming. Most famously, they provided the theme to the cinematic story of that defining moment of rustic atavism, *Glastonbury Fayre.*

Harvey and Gulland's expertise in medieval music and its demanding counter-subjects enabled them to write idiomatically with more modern harmonies; 'Juniper Suite' (1973) is one of the tightest, loveliest pieces of thematic development and cross-reference in the entire Progressive genre, weighing in at a breathless four minutes and forty-three seconds. The gift for additive rhythm and tangential development – suddenly wrenching the music in a completely new direction – also invited comparisons with neo-classical Stravinsky. *Midnight Mushrumps* saw the band cast their hats towards a rock audience, with conventional electric instruments added. Melodic contours remained distinctly medieval, although authorship was now almost exclusively within the band. Guitar lines are more salient, with solo lines allotted; instrumentation, even without electronics (such as with drummer David Oberle's tuned percussion instruments) is fattened up.

By *Red Queen to Gryphon Three* (also 1974), electric instruments outweigh acoustic ones and Harvey is spending almost as much time behind keyboards as with his recorders. But the band lack cohesion in places; the group chords often sound shrill and trebly, and fail to anchor the contrapuntal developments which, stretched over eight or nine minutes as they are here, begin to flag in terms of inspiration. Refinement of orchestration is also at a rudimentary stage, all the more underlined on the very different *Rain Dance* (1975). By this time the band were touring with Yes, with whom they shared management, and the influence of the latter band blooms forth on a still more electronic effort, into which have now crept blue-note pop harmonies and a vivid sense of colour. The rich lustre of Yes's sound is detectable, with each instrument being used to the maximum of its capabilities in concert with every other instrument (in groups of two, three or more); effects and treatments inclusive, not least on the just-too-clever Harvey composition 'Ein Klein(es) Heldenleben'. This sixteen-minute tribute to Richard Strauss's 1898 tone poem also posits two contrasting Strauss-like themes at the start of a rhapsodic sixteen-minute extravaganza.

That the relentless marketization of the rural idyll by commerce could be better illustrated than it is by the transmogrification of Gryphon from jovial troubadours to symphonic rock auteurs seems strange; but it *was* achieved: by Virgin Records and jobbing guitarist Mike Oldfield.

This collaboration began with the inception of Virgin Records' Manor Studios in 1971. The Manor was, in effect, a material professionalization of Progressive's back-to-the-land idealism (freedom from journalists optional). Branson had found the Oxfordshire mansion for sale in the pages of that revolution-rag, *Country Life*. The previous owner had been declared missing and her executors put the house up for sale (only for her fifteen-month-dead corpse to be found in a personal lift stuck between floors).

The Manor experience was thus the ultimate in rock-rural escapism: literally, if city vibes hindered 'musical creativity' this was the answer. For studios were only part of the lavish leisure complex Branson promised. This included a large number of metal detectors if anyone wanted to go scouring the local prehistoric and Roman sites and, reported *Sounds*, three girls to act as hostesses and 'do the housework'.[52] Tom Newman remembers:

> I just wanted a place to record. My girlfriend was working for *Student* magazine, which was Richard's mag. She told me he was a very entrepreneurial character who might be interested in the pop business because that was where the money was.

The staff were starving because Richard was paying them about a quid a week; I went round the back of the Queensway Wimpy Bar and stole a huge bag of chips for them. But I got on well with Richard and I told him what he should get into. He sold records; now he could make them, too.

When we first set the studio up and started recording bands to get the machines working, it was a very shoestring affair. There were about seven big studios in London and only about five independents. It was a very small industry and the money was made by two or three majors. It was risky thing and it would have failed if we hadn't released Mike Oldfield when we did.[53]

Oldfield, one of the most important and one of the most signally unifying icons of Progressive ideology in the mid-1970s, was a refugee from folk who in 1970 had joined the Whole World, another mutant offspring of the Canterbury scene. This was led by ex-Soft Machine vocalist Kevin Ayers, who had joined the Wilde Flowers in 1963, but split for Ibiza in 1965, returning to help form Soft Machine in 1966. He had deserted them, mentally and physically wrecked, after a second US tour in 1969. His solo debut *Joy of a Toy* subverted the bedsit balladeering of Al Stewart, and 1970's *Shooting at the Moon*, recorded with the Whole World, offered little more, though it was flawlessly played. That said, titles like 'Pisser Dans Un Violon' hinted at more darkly surreal legacies of Canterbury bohemianism. Oldfield would be encouraged to solo unaccompanied on guitar and then do somersaults on stage; keyboardist David Bedford would play his electric piano with bricks. Saxophonist Lol Coxhill's idea of cutting a solo album was recording himself improvising under railway bridges.

Bedford (b. 1937), the brother of conductor Steuart Bedford, was a highly regarded young shockworker of post-serial extremism, and in addition to teaching had been clambering in and out of pianos on stage and composing large-scale works throughout the 1960s (in which choirs would routinely squall words like 'hell' and 'mad'). A Who fan, he was supplementing his income by playing rock when Ayers called. The Whole World helped out on Bedford's 1970 Blake-inspired ensemble/ performance piece *The Garden of Love* (broadcast by Radio 3). It was scored for organ, swanee whistle, bird warblers, two electric guitars, saxophone, drums, flute, clarinet, horn, trumpet, double bass and the aforementioned 'six beautiful girls'. This twenty-minute piece, incorporating a section in which the 'girls' play organ with fists, elbows and forearms (while the band swig beer on stage), later dancing with the audience in the aisles while the group bulldoze into a hair-raising finale of atonal improvisation, won bemused approval from classical and rock critics alike.

Enfant terrible though he was Bedford's formal training wouldn't quite relinquish him. Ayers sighed that Bedford dichotomized the music into 'funny' (Coxhill's solos or jokes) and 'serious' bits (i.e. composition, performance).[54] Oldfield, meanwhile, resented the 'unfocused' nature of the band[55] – in short, an ordered, bourgeois mentality was manifesting itself in the Whole World, at odds with the disruptive ethic which the band represented.

In Bedford's defence, however, it must be stated that he had the humorous resourcefulness once to contemplate scoring Oldfield's forthcoming smash *Tubular Bells* as a percussion piece, *Variations on a Rhythm of Mike Oldfield*, for eighty-four different instruments including milk bottles, vacuum cleaners etc.. He could, plainly, reconcile the extremes of the various musical worlds he chose to frequent.

Ayers was obliging enough; he recognized Oldfield's itch to diverge, lent him a tape machine, and told him to go away and turn his aspirations into recorded sound. Bedford befriended the guitarist and, interested in his ideas, referred him to Frederick Delius's orchestral English rhapsody *Brigg Fair* to try and provide some artistic template for the ideas Oldfield related to him. This, believed Bedford, was the soundworld Oldfield sought.

Only slightly, *Brigg Fair*, essentially a theme and variations in which a traditional Lincolnshire melody is subjected to a series of ambitious symphonic treatment over a quarter-hour, does possess the shimmering limpidity of texture that Oldfield would deploy on *Tubular Bells*, but its structure is expertly controlled.

Oldfield's forty-nine-minute work employs a handful of themes which occupy discrete sections of the whole, with superficial cross-referencing. Recapitulation and development, inversion and vertical variation are surrendered to (very gradual) horizontal variation in timbre and arrangement. Palmer, in a discussion of *Tubular Bells*, provocatively offers Sibelius, Vaughan Williams and, penetratingly, the crossover French musical-theatre composer Michel Legrand as influences.[56]

In 1972, by chance, Richard Branson sidekick Simon Draper offered Oldfield the chance to feature on Branson's new label Virgin and to come down to the Manor Studios and run ideas past the executive. Oldfield took the demo-tape he had recorded with Ayers's and Bedford's advice. Branson loved it; Oldfield watched him type out a ten-album contract at 5 per cent royalty rates. At the Cannes MIDEM festival an industry executive told Branson, hawking *Tubular Bells* to interested parties, to ask Oldfield to apply some 'meaning' with unspecified vocals. But the vocals that did appear were the Piltdown Man's strangled grunts and Vivian Stanshall's outrageously postmodern Master of Ceremonies role, in which each instrument was individually and camply introduced in a sequence of majestic and bolero-like accumulation.

Oldfield's work stands little formal comparison with the complex late-nineteenth-century classical music he most readily refers to; but its idiosyncratic construction *and* its hybrid instrumentation (flageolet, mandolin, Mellotron, percussion, organs and guitars of various specifications, and, naturally, tubular bells) wrongfooted critics of all persuasions. The conductor and musicologist Bernard Benoliel, for instance, lauds it not for its formal surefootedness but specifically for its 'emotional impact'.[57] At the time, Oldfield modestly admitted that Bedford had helped with nearly all aspects.

Critics who saw the first performance in the Queen Elizabeth Hall in June 1973 attempted classical dissection which failed to address the piece's essential heterogeneity, its postmodern dislocation of two counterposing genres of music which as yet had no critical vocabulary to evaluate it. The album sold hugely; although initial curiosity only exploded into cult adulation when William Friedkin used a section of the music for his movie *The*

Exorcist, which was issued as a single in the US and hogged the charts for a lengthy spell.

But the factors which captivated most attention in the public furore about *Tubular Bells* were essentially bourgeois in origin; the extraordinary tenacity and dedication and single-minded genius of the lone artist (Oldfield), the apparent 'novelty' of his adaptation of rock themes to a classical format, and, most of all, the mastery of technology (the studio). It soon leaked out that Oldfield had used hundreds of drops-ins and edits (to correct wrong notes) on the album. But this evidence of technical exactitude and discipline, far from diminishing the album's appeal to rock critics and to the public at large, actually accentuated it.

Robert Wyatt says now of Oldfield: 'He tuned in very well – also gave me and Alfie [Mrs Wyatt] a drive in his new sports car at 100 m.p.h. down this tiny little road. He'd suddenly become incredibly rich and didn't know what to do about it. He didn't know what to do about suddenly being Mike Oldfield.'[58]

On 10 November 1973 Soft Machine and Pink Floyd reunited for their first co-headliner since the Fourteen-Hour Technicolor Dream, at the Rainbow in Finsbury Park, London, as a benefit for the stricken Wyatt. Music cognoscenti looked on and journalists scribbled the evening assiduously into inky posterity; the crowd listened in barely concealed indifference to the Softs; only when the Floyd, resplendent in the post-detonation dazzle of an album called *Dark Side of the Moon*, hit the stage, did the event lift off as a public spectacle.

In the six years since Alexandra Palace, Progressive rock had come a long way; perhaps on this evening in Finsbury Park, just a few miles from the deserted venue of the Technicolor Dream, the acme of its ideology was asserted that chilly evening. One week later, Yes would begin touring England with *Tales from Topographic Oceans*. The consecration of Progressive rock ideology was complete in November 1973. The counter-cultural ideology was gone; in its place was nebulous bourgeois acquisitiveness and Romantic rhetoric which, while not an artistic retreat, represented the primacy of the final, determinant and fatal phase of Progressive development.

5 YOU WANT TO RECORD *WHAT?*
(PROGRESSIVE'S POMP: THE FUTURE IN A GATEFOLD SLEEVE 1973–75)

THE CONCEPT ALBUM AS CONCEPT: PINK FLOYD

Allan F. Moore maintains that 'concept albums' possess only slight thematic unity, being constructed not as continuous pieces of music but as individual songs running consecutively within larger ones.[1]

While Progressive rock musicians may have been stereotyped as classical musicians *manqués*, they seldom attempted to transcend basic limitations of ability or the economics of production. With the rule-proving exception of Oldfield's *Tubular Bells* (and the obscure case of Cosmic Eye, who occupied a full forty minutes of LP vinyl in 1972 with their track 'Dream Sequence', but in a cack-handedly florid and bombastic fashion much less co-ordinated than Oldfield's) few attempted substantial compositional development. Soft Machine, who freely welded songs together, had occupied much of the time with free (solo) improvisation. Compositionally, Progressive musicians never (or very exceptionally) aspired to beyond half an hour of continuous music. Very few classical instrumental pieces, particularly in the Baroque and Romantic canons which many Progressive musicians drew upon as inspiration, attempted to retain thematic unity across single uninterrupted spans of thirty to thirty-five minutes, except in unusual cases of extreme compositional discipline as demonstrated by the likes of the fifty-minute single-movement symphonies of the Swedish composer Allan Pettersson (1911–80). Opera, of course, with multifarious textual and imagistic concerns to be taken into creative consideration, is a different compositional matter entirely.

Concept albums were, of course, not only a 1970s phenome-non. They formed a defining aspect of 1960s rock auteurism key to the founding of Progressive aesthetics. By 1973, however, they began to assume a character identical to that of their creators; they were the texts of a Romantic rock aesthetic but proved forerunners of a new social and economic sensibility in rock.

Chief among them is Pink Floyd's *Dark Side of the Moon*. Still among the highest-selling albums of all time, it spent an astro-nomical 736 consecutive weeks on *Billboard*'s albums chart. It became a cult of its own; Hipgnosis's unfashionably plain cover image of the diffusing prism became one of the greatest visual signifiers in popular culture, comparable with Warhol's soup can. The critic Sheila Whiteley has even read (somewhat arcanely) the depiction of the passing of white light into colours as an allegory on the 'scientific' dimension of the album's painstaking assembly as music.

Perhaps more importantly, *Dark Side of the Moon* was instru-mental in the construction of 1970s lifestyle. As one observer said: 'Millions of people across the globe ... have fucked to *Dark Side of the Moon*.'[2] It was the first rock LP to assume the status of a consumer durable, something that people bought not because of affinities with the music but, like colour TV in the early 1970s,

because it was a badge of cultural participation. The commodi-
tization of rock, and of Progressive aesthetics (a grenade in punk
hands some four years later) became inevitable. Certainly its
success changed attitudes within the industry as to the viability
of Progressive, and engendered sales of such magnitude as to
make a professionalization of the rock industry essential if such
commercial phenomena were to be adequately exploited. Some
critics have also pilloried it as the acme of stone-hearted studio
pedantry and the championing of method over immediacy in
performance.

From the start the album seemed to attract preferential
treatment unheard-of in the then-shabby world of rock promotion. It wasn't released, for instance, but 'premiered' by EMI at the
London Planetarium in March 1973.

Much has been written about the album's themes of
schizophrenia, death and money, supposedly the first evidence
that the space-rockers *par excellence* were now devoted to more
worldly concerns. Some, given the album's profits and the
aforementioned materialistic currents blowing like a chill breeze
throughout the unbendingly sombre musical landscape, believe
Waters's monomania concerning the rock star's cruel lot began
here. The celebrated satire on rock wealth in 'Money', with its
acquisitions of football teams and Lear Jets, locked Waters onto an
ontological collision course with the reality of rock stardom.

So, Waters was telling us, it's all incredibly lonely and empty up
here. Doubtless; but while the irony of the lyrics was being
unisyllabically pointed out to detractors there is a strain of self-
righteousness here which would distend horribly by the decade's
end and *The Wall.*

The collaging and editing techniques, the multitudinous
effects of sound manipulation, were never more in evidence; a
heartbeat, rendered in ambiguous stereo from one channel to
another, opens and closes the album. Cash-registers sounding in
7/4 open 'Money'. Alan Parsons members: 'It was literally a fight
to get the delay effect on "Us and Them".We spent a tremendous
amount of time hooking up Dolby units and realigning machines
at the wrong speed to get that effect.'[3]

The band had considered recording an entirely *musique concrète* album; elastic bands, Sellotape and aerosols were among the rudiments for this planned sequel to 'Alan's Psychedelic Breakfast' (1970), but listening to the musicians one returns inexorably to the issue that the noises would have been used not for their intrinsic qualities as noises, but as literalist representational music: 'We used aerosol sprays and pulling rolls of Sellotape out to different lengths. The further away it gets the note changes,' enthused Gilmour, who also got a 'really good bass sound'[4] by stretching an elastic band between two G-clamps. On *Dark Side* the sounds appear to be there to illustrate concepts rooted chordally and rhythmically in often commonplace time-signatures and harmony. That doesn't say that the found sounds aren't deployed on this album with more guile than on any other Floyd recording; they are often haunting, sometimes painfully so; the engineering itself becomes of specific emotional import.

Perhaps because the music is largely conventional (save for some aching, poignant lines from Gilmour and an interesting range of orchestrations and harmonizing from Wright's keyboard artillery) and the melodies are strong and direct, the noises occasionally occupy disruptive positions. The band are playing straight, emotionally involving pop songs. Wright's blue notes in the chorus of 'Time' derive from Miles Davis's 'So What' and give the piece a satisfying melodic body. And so the noises service the music, are subordinate to it, but also create a disturbing dualism against its essential directness.

But there's that inescapable literalism about them which echoes Schaffner's point when comparing the relationship of the music, and the lyrics, to the inner-space terrors of those created – and experienced – by Syd Barrett. 'The difference [between random Barrett-era effects and later ones] was the difference between a conscious exploration of madness by observers themselves fundamentally sane, and the visionary delirium of an artist who was actually going mad.'[5]

This element of calculation helped the Floyd establish a rock legend of dubious stature. The bourgeois obsession with the work ethic would indeed pay off handsomely by dint of the exactitude of the work involved in the creation of this record, a process in itself often paid homage to in rock historiography. Alan Parsons attributes some of the album's success, as well as being manna for the hi-fi industry, to a further trick of the engineer's art. '*Dark Side of the Moon* was perfect fodder for American album radio at the time. It was very programmable. If a jock wanted to play two or three tracks one after the other, he'd had his work done for him because all the segues were carefully worked out within the grooves.'[6]

THE CONCEPT ALBUM AS CONCEPT: TALES FROM TOPOGRAPHIC OCEANS:

Yes's seventh album began life in January 1973 with the incongruous meeting of King Crimson's new and eccentric percussionist Jamie Muir – a man given to wearing animal skins, eating blood capsules and throwing chains while on stage – and Yes vocalist/writer Jon Anderson in the course of Crimson/Yes drummer Bill Bruford's wedding. 'Jamie turned Jon on to Paramhansa Yogananda's *Autobiography of a Yogi*,' explains Bruford. 'And Jon got a bee in his bonnet about it. The rest is rock history, I'm afraid to say.'[7]

The resultant album, four-sided, four-tracked, musically and lyrically conceived by Anderson in a series of late-night meditative sessions with guitarist Steve Howe, has perhaps come to be the ultimate icon of Progressive – it is certainly offered by journalists as irreproachable proof of the genre's moral and artistic bankruptcy.

Defending the album is a mighty task. For a start, its chief publicity gimmick was a sixty-five-foot balloon advertisement designed by Roger Dean ('$40,000 worth of hot air and fabric', wrote Yes biographer Dan Hedges wryly).[8] The gatefold sleeve contains a long-winded liner note explaining Howe and Anderson's interpretation of the four-part Shastric scriptures outlined in Yogananda's book. Four months were spent rehearsing and recording the album, only for the critics to eviscerate both it and the subsequent concerts, in which the grand conceit of the recording was seen to be compounded by the fact that the gigs were given over to replaying the entire album from start to finish.

The album concretized Yes's artistic *raison d'être* and perhaps the 'maturity' of Anderson's lyrical style: alluding to nothing other than esoteric logic of symbolism, a non-narrative Babel of mountains and rivers, songs and skylines, preachers and teachers.

Anderson's lyrics probably draw more fire than any other single commodity in Progressive, described as they are in almost unanimously negative terms ranging from incomprehension to hostility, but they are none the less of enormous contemporary interest. Music papers once ran small ads from people offering to 'explain' Yes lyrics (for a fee).

In 1995, two American theology graduates published *Yes ... But What Does It All Mean?*, which purported, 'in four interlocking essays about Yes music' (itself a crib from the *Topographic* sleevenotes) to reveal all.

If one can negotiate the cover picture (a transfigured Anderson clutching a harp, while one raised hand receives divine inspiration through forked lightning) the analysis of Yes's music is exhaustively impressive. But the interpretations of the lyrics seem to confer an even more nebulous runic quality to the words and seem completely to downplay the probability that for the most part, their purpose was less representational than purely musical and onamatopoeic.[9]

Producer Eddie Offord is more forthright. 'The rest of the band gave [Jon] such a hard time about his lyrics. They'd all say to him, "Jon, your fucking lyrics don't make any sense at all." '[10]

Anderson, and at a later date Tony Kaye, would claim for the defence that this use of words was less literary than colouristic, much in the vein of Leon Thomas's work with Pharoah Sanders, or to a lesser extent the Kobaian language which Thomas helped inspire in epigrammatic Magma drummer Christian Vander for his compositions. In the post-hippy, post-Hesse lexicon of popular culture, however, Anderson's expostulations provided just the kind of initiate exclusiveness in Yes's lyrics that his fans heard in Yes's music. In fairness to Anderson, the assonances (as opposed to alliterations) of his style, the emphasis on open vowel sounds and the profusion of soft consonants do lend extra texture to the music in places.

The album's creation (like its gestation) was a shambolic affair in marked contrast to its ultra-refined public image. Rehearsals took place at ELP's Manticore Studios (actually a refurbished Odeon cinema in south-west London); Anderson himself had little idea where the music was going: at one stage he urged Offord to build a bathroom in the studio because white tiles, Anderson believed, added a new dimension to his singing. Not at Morgan Studios, Willesden, they didn't, and so the experiment was expensively shelved. Seeing his band split between recording in the country or in town, manager Brian Lane decided to add some 'rustic' atmosphere. As well as pot-plants being installed, Wakeman's keyboards were balanced on bales of straw, a picket fence surrounded White's drums and a cardboard cow took centre stage. 'About halfway through the album the cow was covered in graffiti and all the plants had died. That just kind of sums up that whole album,' recalled Offord.[11]

On tour Wakeman, whose uncertainty over the music's quality soon became open hostility, would nonchalantly crack open twelve-packs of beer and eat curries while playing; the fibreglass stage set designed by the Dean Brothers (thematically related to the album cover) proved so exasperating to the band's squad of roadies that one day they smashed it up. 'It wasn't gear to them ... you couldn't plug it in,' comments Steve Howe.[12]

Topographic is at least twenty minutes too long, not because of the band's eagerness constantly to angle for new ideas but, as with ELP, their tendency to overfish old ones. The construction of large-scale structures from the harmonies and melodies out of Anderson's motifs is simply overdone.

Crucial to the record's success, however, is the immediate languorous attraction of the music. The harmony still builds in traditional blocks, but the sophisticated usage of the constituent intervals in those harmonies (notably in the 'They move fast, they tell me' section on track 1) makes for pleasurable listening, updating Brian Wilson's orgiastic harmonies from *Pet Sounds et al.*, in an agreeably intimate small-group electric setting. This sonic Radox eventually sinks the album, though, particularly in the unimpressive second movement, a somewhat tokenistic

acknowledgement of Wakeman's untiring keyboard resourcefulness. This time recapitulation takes nearly half the side, and
Wakeman's interjections on Moog and Mellotron sound forced
and out-of-sorts, suggesting an allowance made to mollify a
player understandably ill-at-ease.

'The Ancient' also suffers from flatulence; the opening systemic
percussion figures make an interesting comparison with the
opening of King Crimson's contemporary 'Lark's Tongues in
Aspic', but are used tonally to build a complicated metre and
bass-line to an unadorned guitar solo unsure of any rhythmic
anchor, contributing to probably the most interesting music on
the whole album. Unfortunately, strung over nine minutes in
various guises, this solo is overblown, although some motifs from
the first and second movements make neat appearances. An even
more superfluous Spanish guitar solo leads into a dreary pop-
song coda, which ill-prepares the listener for the vigour of the
concluding movement, 'Ritual'.

This piece is kicked into life by the upward swoop of Squire's
bass. Squire's subsequent soloing over the developmental section
steadily establishes tension (the music rises through the registers)
which is released in what could have been a percussion segment
of excruciating tedium but works because of its sheer shock
value. It is not a drum solo; all members of the band are involved
in what is essentially a percussion workout held together by
merely the most rudimentary bassline. The heavy breathing that
can be heard – like that of Pan through a rainforest – is dense,
impressionist stuff prefiguring the band's next effort, *Relayer*
(1974), and it leads into the final variation on the 'Nous Sommes
du Soleil' theme which itself ushers in a postlude of enough
ambiguity in tone, mood and key to provide the album with a
curiously unfulfilled ending; compositionally, the last note lands
as a satisfying cadence just where it should do in relation to the
whole piece. But there is a traumatized shudder about the final
resting place of the music.

Wakeman duly flew the nest, carping at *Topographic* ('it's like
wading through a cesspool to get to a water lily'),[13] but merely
going on to carve out his own niche in the history of *folie de*

grandeur with *Journey to the Centre of the Earth*, a forty-minute work immodestly augmented by the sixty-eight-voice English Chamber Choir and 100 members of the London Symphony Orchestra and the hammily declamatory narration of David Hemmings. Wakeman relates in his autobiography that, incredibly, his record label A&M, basking in the afterglow of fat profits for Wakeman's first solo album and his status as one of the rock world's premier instrumentalists, refused to release the *Journey* album, deeming it unsellable. Only the word of the company's president prevailed, and was vindicated by the album's almost instantaneous number-one status worldwide. A relieved Wakeman celebrated by performing the entire work in the open air in front of 15,000 people at London's Crystal Palace, complete with inflatable dinosaurs rising from the stage-front lake where Pink Floyd's high-volume rendition of their trance-epic jam 'Echoes' four years before had killed all the fish. Wakeman's music had no killer intent; it would have been hard-put to have incurred assault charges. Regrettably, and oddly, Wakeman's genius for improvisation, ornamentation and transforming the mundane for his employers didn't extend to his own music.

Wakeman also had another problem: Progressive rock had been going for long enough for some of its tricks, such as over-attention to the cod-classical, already to sound lame. This latter foible hardly plagues Wakeman's music, but when imitation raises its head, Wakeman's own inspirations tend to sag. Unlike his former employers, Wakeman could not assimilate the classics, he could seemingly use them only as floss.

Wakeman compared badly with Yes – although this did not hinder his sales. There is, inescapably, a homophonic stolidity about Wakeman's melodic syntax and a similar attitude to the arrangement thereof; few harmonic tricks are played, few motivic resources are reprised with anything but clunking obviousness. Wakeman, tellingly, and with commendable honesty, never denied the fundamental commercial intent of his music, nor made any verbal claims for its pre-eminence, but as Soft Machine had shown, pop voicings and experimental forms could coexist and earn money. Behind Wakeman's keyboard virtuosity (undeniably impressive in the right context) there was professionalism, ingenuity, emotional literacy, but little compositional depth.

THE CONCEPT ALBUM AS CONCEPT: JETHRO TULL

Aqualung (1971) started the trouble. A collection of songs it may have been, and little advance on *Benefit* (although as with all Tull albums, there is appreciable differentiation). Side 1 treats the Aqualung character, a tramp so named for his respiratory complaint, in a restrained and quasi-cyclical form, in a handful of virile, sophisticated pop songs straining at rock's strophic forms. Arrangements are deeper and wider (the recorders on 'Mother Goose', and liberal splashes of Mellotron, the counterpointed flute soloing and the treated 'choir' effects of side 2's 'My God', the opening segment of another cycle, this time ramblingly assaulting established religion). The procedures of melody and bassline accompaniments were increasingly straining away from each other, and if the lyrics were now tending towards the provocatively obscure, they were none the less possessed of some style, not least in their occasional Blakean allusions. Critical notices were mixed; some sniffed pretension, others juicy experiment.

Of Tull's 1972 album, however, many agreed that Ian Anderson had overreached himself. A forty-five-minute piece which doesn't quite achieve unity due to the edit required for the break between LP sides, *Thick as a Brick* was not roundly booed but was at best tepidly greeted.

As with Yes, a singer named Anderson and his personal view of the lyric-writer's role in rock proved too much for most writers. With Jethro Tull's Ian Anderson, concern was centred less on the obscurantism of his namesake Jon Anderson in Yes – this criticism zeroed in on the wilful (and illusory) conceit of much of his versifying. In a demolition-derby review of the 1973 album *A Passion Play*, Stephen Holden of *Rolling Stone* nutshelled much of the sentiment and prefaced many more anti-Progressive critiques as yet unborn. Some of his tirade was unjustified criticism of Anderson, yet it was written with an assassin's panache and considerable literacy. 'A jumble of anarchic, childishly precocious gestures that are intellectually faithless to any idea other than their own esoteric non-logic,' charged Holden of Anderson's lyrics.[14]

This is unfair – those words, while overly derivative of Eliot, particularly in their stark oppositions of fable and flophouse, street and dream, are very effective, his delivery even more so. The band does lack fire, although this is possibly due to a nervy over-attention to detail.

The musicologist Nors Josephson's declaration that *Thick as a Brick* is 'the most impressive variation cycle' in Progressive rock (he uses Beethoven's 'Diabelli' Variations as a rather exalted model) is offset by the comparative (though not terminally damaging) lack of dramatic coherence to the piece (an accusation hardly applicable to Beethoven's work), although, as he maintains, the inversions and reprise of the initial material culminating towards the end of the album-long composition is masterly.[15] The 'concept', a somewhat self-conscious and mannered lionization of individual genius (in this case, an eight-year-old poet named Gerald 'Little Milton' Bostock) against caricatured bourgeois Philistinism, scarcely sees the light of day through the thickets of Anderson's imagery, but this doesn't detract from what, in hindsight, is quite a respectable, if periodically water-treading, stab at advanced extensional technique.

The band are still recognizably a rock band doing rock-band things; similarly, the album lacks the later Tull characteristic of smart lacing of the melody from chord to chord via ensemble and solo; they largely chug away pleasantly, the guitar solos dutifully occupying frames between sung verses and wearing bluesy threads. But signs of a fresher future are evident: the splendid wrong-footing shift of emphasis in the 'you curl your toes ... ' section. Side 2, in fact, has an almost palpable sense of adventure, from the echoing arabesques of Anderson's flute ('see there! a man'), and the foregrounding of the folkishly strummed acoustic guitar, to a more irregular verse structure and the ensemble ostinati of the final 'let me tell you' variation, which is reassuringly off-beam.

Anderson's ambition flared too indiscriminately in *A Passion*

Play (1973), where the writing is militantly episodic, from the echopexed fuzz guitar, trilling and scalic sax flourishes at the primeval chaos at the opening of the first side. Some moments, like the double-tracking of acoustic guitars backed by soft organ chords some ten minutes into *A Passion Play* behind the 'all along the icy wastes' section, are sublimely beautiful, but the listener is often left bemused, knocked hither and thither by yet another new theme or arrangement.

On side 2 there is 'The Story of the Hare Who Lost His Spectacles', a shaggy-dog story self-consciously introduced by a theme of caricature infantilism played on a nursery-school rhythm section of xylophone, piano and clarinet. But again the twenty minutes pass by laboriously. Tull have now given their music a third textural dimension, and in that respect have met Yes halfway; guitars no longer perform only allotted guitar roles, drums no longer occupy drum spaces (compare the drum solo on *Thick as a Brick* to that on 'Ritual' from *Topographic* for evidence) but, as with Yes, the temptation to overemphasize novelty and an incoherence in developing what stable music there is, defeats them. Jan-Paul van Spaendonck observes that Tull's music is 'great ... but not from a classical point of view ... they're mere collages, whereas Gentle Giant's pieces [by comparison] ... are really consistent compositions'.[16] Others echo him; Dan Hedges bemoans Yes's linearity on *Topographic* as confusing constant variety with high art.[17]

Stephen Holden dismissed Tull as the 'ultimate exaggeration of self-indulgent whimsy, an intellectual tease inflated with portent but devoid of wonder'.[18] What Anderson hoped to achieve with *Brick* and *Passion Play* and their musico-textual puzzles, however, is unknown, due to the piqued petulance with which he shut himself away from all communication with the press in the wake of the vitriolic notices both albums received.

THE CONCEPT ALBUM AS CONCEPT: EMERSON, LAKE AND PALMER

Gigantism was seriously big in 1973. ELP, now fully-fledged rock technocrats, experimented with effects machinery, and a fully portable stage (all in the range of music press hacks and lensmen – with hubristic intent brought on by record-company investment came slicker co-ordination of publicity). Their 1973 album, *Brain Salad Surgery* (nine months in the making, the publicity breathlessly informed us), was dominated by the outsize suite 'Karn Evil 9', whose twenty-eight-and-a-half-minute span comprised three 'impressions' and straddled one and a quarter album sides. It augured well; the elaborate sleeve, the work of the Swiss designer H. R. Giger (whose dreamlike, monochromatic elisions of the organic and the mechanical foresaw the cinema of David Lynch), was an ideal representation of ELP's continuing schizoid relationship between stainless-steel futurism and flesh-and-blood Romantic-creator mythos. The album opened with two brutal exemplars of this dualism: a clodhoppingly mannered rendition of Parry's setting of 'Jerusalem' followed by a demonic adaptation of the fourth movement ('Toccata') of the Piano Concerto No. 1 by the Argentinian composer Alberto Ginastera (b. 1916).

Lake had been up until now 'helped' to write song-words by Dik Fraser, (who has recently graduated to putting on the Pope in Central Park, but was then a roadie, first for King Crimson and later for ELP and Genesis).

Sinfield says emphatically:

> I was out of King Crimson. For my own safety. Once they dropped a Mellotron and it missed me by that much. Down in this club in Plymouth. And those things were fucking heavy. And I thought – whoops, that's it, bye-bye. Because I wasn't really a member of the band. Greg called me. 'I need help with the lyrics.' And, boy, did he need help. I was seduced away by the world's worst publishing contract, ever. I got a third of Greg's royalties. It sounds OK, doesn't it, until you realize that Greg only got 25 per cent of the band's royalties. Oh well.[19]

Ginastera had declared himself pleased with Emerson's supremely demented piece of electronic audacity and almost angrily asserted virtuosity. The original's wobbly tonality – not to mention the careful composition of its hectic, complex rhythmic abandon – is treated to a sensational series of different orchestrations, concentrating on phased fuzz bass, organ, electric piano and Moog. 'Toccata' is as cacophonous a piece of rock music as existed at the time, and one we will return to later. Electronic drums were used on 'Toccata', whereby a second mike was placed inside each of Palmer's drums to trigger a small cigar-box-sized synthesizer during the middle section, but the technology was so primitive that touring with it was out of the question.

Ginastera gushed that ELP had 'captured the essence of my music'.[20] A shame that 'Karn Evil 9' does not warrant such laurels; a tale of individual heroism (but of course) in the face of futuristic supreme-being technology gone apocalyptically wrong, it was heralded superbly in subdued but ominous fashion by a suitably sonorous and menacing Hammond organ introduction of smoky minor-key truculence, one of the most understated but effective uses of Emerson's dexterity on record. The trouble is, the band then resort to ping-ponging frustratingly between the inspired and the intolerable; Emerson's synthesizers (including early polyphonic machines) *do* galvanize the band's sound, and the broader symphonic brush is suited to the more craftsmanlike embroidery of the melodies and verses from chord to chord with Yes-ish refinement. But the utterly absurd bipartite structure of the piece's 'First Impression', the all-too-familiar over-indulgence of Emerson's solo spot and the phenomenally trite sci-fi libretto ('Let the mask of war be drawn,' Lake orders his cybertronic analogue) of the third part (spoiling one of the band's most exciting and committed workouts, full of vigorous and fertile riff-development and fierce, diamond-hard textures) pull the plug on the enterprise.

'Karn Evil 9' was, in Emerson's opinion, 'a logical extension of *Tarkus* (1971). But whereas *Tarkus* was my dabbling in fourths and fifths, "Karn Evil 9" dealt with counterpoint ... the beginning ... is counterpoint ... but then I gave up! The moment I got together with Greg and Carl they'd say: "That's very clever – now let's get on with the song." '[21]

Emerson's respect for Leonard Bernstein seemed to translate

itself helplessly into his band's music – its oscillation between serious and stupid, between eye-watering banality and facetious brilliance. Bernstein's own smart-arse sallies, graphically splurged from *On the Town* (1945) to *Mass* and *Songfest* in the 1970s, at least showed a composer who knew when to stop, when to terminate the trickery. Emerson, Lake and Palmer appeared to have no such sense of innate self-control (and would later fall foul of Bernstein himself).

The band participated in a *ciné-vérité* project for BBC2 on Boxing Day 1973, one of the very earliest TV–album tie-ins, which showed the band looning affectedly if sometimes amusingly, but served mostly to foreground the extent of their hardware, with much prominence given to the three articulated trucks in which each member's equipment was transported (their names emblazoned on the roof of each trailer, presumably in case the roadies couldn't tell keyboards from drums).

ELP's stage shows did little to confound those who believed the band had become slaves to conceit. In 1970 Carl Palmer had told Chris Welch that the public got bored with six-minute drum solos, 'so I'm cutting mine down to three minutes'.[22] How short musicians' memories are; by 1974 he was stretching out way beyond that, climaxing by activating a giant bell, pulling its cord with his teeth.

A young man of admirable self-confidence who had once hustled lessons with Buddy Rich by gatecrashing the drummer's hotel room and impressing him with sheer chutzpah, shamelessly out-gimmicked his master; while Rich might set his drumsticks alight by generating friction during a solo, Palmer's grandstanding was so exaggeratedly vulgar that it jarred; Rich's sideshows were just that, merely a novelty adumbration of performance. Palmer's transgression of this simple prescription, and his adoption of megalomaniacal grandiloquence above and beyond the call of duty is perhaps Progressive rock's least forgivable trait.

'You always knew when Carl's drum solo was coming up,' Tony Tyler wrote in 1977, 'because he'd take his shirt off first.'[23] Tyler had been editor of the Progressive-infatuated musical instrument magazine *Beat International* but left in 1970 to handle ELP's publicity. He didn't last long. Sinfield remembers, 'There got to be kind of paranoia in the band about playing fast. You got to the point whereby you'd plead with them, please play it slower.'[24]

Equipment was also showing signs of hypertrophy. There was a discrete quadraphonic PA, and a flying piano rig which levitated an entire grand piano and spun it through 360 degrees – with Emerson still pounding gleefully on it. Palmer was approached by British Steel, who offered to make him cylinders for his exponentially expanding drumkit. Originally to be an eighth of an inch thick, they turned out to be half an inch thick, which meant that two people were required to carry Palmer's bass drum alone; the whole outfit weighed a ton and a half. It was, in Pete Sinfield's words, 'a beautiful object that didn't sound very good'. Palmer was also fanatically picky – not least, according to Sinfield, about Hilton hotel pillows. He would demand: 'I want one hard-hair and one soft-hair' – Spinal Tap before its time. Lake, taking his cue from the Incredible String Band, would perform on stage only if a certain carpet were *in situ* for him to stand on. Pete Sinfield went with the bassist to buy said carpeting: 'I've seen people do it since. It does absorb the sound, but it didn't do Greg much good. It cost thousands, a beautiful thing. Perhaps the roadies used to have to hoover it for him, perhaps they didn't, I can't remember. In a way I thought, if it helps the stagefright, OK.'[25]

Lake has since claimed that the gimmick originated from an incident with a 'live' microphone; understandably nervous about electrocution, he bought himself a rubber mat to perform on, and then decided to disguise it with a carpet – albeit one that cost £6,000.

Sinfield again:

Greg was determined. He came from a poor background. Greg told me once that the people next door had tinned peaches for tea. Ergo, he'd wanted tinned peaches. He was one of those classic keep-up-with-the-Joneses cases. He was a Roman throwback, the freed slave who kind of went out and bought everything. He was so determined that nobody would better them, nobody would rip them off, that maybe he went too far.

I heard a story that Keith told a journalist that he would be happy ending up being a pub piano player. Fine. Keith *would* be a pub piano player but he'd still have a medallion round his neck with gold and diamonds which reads 'Keith'. Sorry, Keith. But it *is* true.'[26]

Ironically, Lake was later to claim that it was only long *after Brain Salad Surgery* that 'everything became "ego driven".'[27]

PROGRESSIVE POP: GENESIS, OR BRIAN WILSON LOOSE IN THE SIXTH FORM COMMON ROOM

Genesis had metamorphosed from two Charterhouse School bands, the Anon and the Garden Wall; we left them in the clutches of Jonathan King's UK Publishing. Behind the boxy contemporary pop soundscapes of *From Genesis to Revelation* (deliberately Bee Gee-ized to tap King's current obsession), lurked a definitive bourgeois Anglo-Saxonry, based less on the band members' Home Counties upbringing than on their exposure to English sacred music (the Choral Society was a sacrosanct component of Carthusian tradition – Anthony Phillips talks nostalgically about 'hymnal piano interludes' that were left off the band's debut album)[28].

Keyboard main-man Tony Banks also harboured long-standing pianistic leanings towards Rachmaninov, as unashamedly romantic as the Percy Faith and Liberace harmonies which soused the musical palates of middle-class Britain in the late 1950s – the Britain that bore a generation of Progressive musicians.

The result was an immediately attractive musical language whose dominant features, in Allan Moore's terms, were chord progressions dominated by thirds of the type found in much Baroque sacred music and which filtered through to the English choral tradition through the impeccably upright likes of Wesley and John Stainer.[29] Indeed one of the best-known composers of British sacred music of this century, Basil Harwood (1859–1949), was a Carthusian. Baroque techniques were brazenly apparent, summarised beautifully by Josephson in his analysis of Genesis's 1972 epic 'Supper's Ready', which widely uses both Baroque arpeggios and diminished seventh chords.[30]

A common enthusiasm for an acoustic twelve-string sound of particular brilliance and harmonic sensibility patented by guitarist Anthony Phillips and bassist Mike Rutherford eked out a new soundworld after King lost interest (this was, after all, the Progressive folk era of Mellow Candle, Trees *et al.*, while Crosby Stills and Nash were reviving the European folk-musical inspirations of ethnic American music). Given the blue-note inflections introduced by soul-freak vocalist Peter Gabriel, the resultant melange was often soaked in a sentimentality that went down not at all well on the road. But perceptive minds at Charisma Records saw the consonance of the band's image with contemporary post-Woodstock pastoral mores and recruited them and, with Tony Banks giving enhanced orchestral scope to the Mellotron, the band began to accrue a mystique of Olde Englishe romanticism that would serve them well for years to come.

Producer John Anthony told one band chronicler: 'When I first saw them I was really into William Blake ... and that's what filled my head ... close your eyes and the sun shines in big rays through the clouds.'[31] Overexposure to King Crimson's *In the Court of the Crimson King* had clearly taken its toll on Genesis, as it had on so many other young artists of the time, but already the diatonic riffs and melodies, and the Palm Court-orchestral melodramatics to which they subjected emotionally telling sections ('The Knife' from 1970s *Trespass*) offset the confessional, slightly Donovanesque nature of some of the melodies and lyrics with the perennial undertow of twelve-string arpeggio (e.g. 1970s 'Stagnation', 'Dusk') and the developments were wholly pop. This was in effect a further refinement of the Procol Harum/Yes work of the late 1960s.

Songs rarely contained more than two contrasting sections, with chorus-verse structures followed faithfully enough, although some pieces, from 'Looking For Someone' (1970) through 'Musical Box' and 'Return of the Giant Hogweed' (1971) to 'Watcher of the Skies' (1972), added often grandiose codas to the overall structure. If any doubt the role played by pop in the band's development, the barefaced presence of a riff from Lennon/McCartney's 'I Am The Walrus' cropping up incongruously in the middle of the *Trespass* opener 'Looking For Someone' must silence them.

Pop dynamics and structures, classical voicings and rock arrangement, ever more masterfully integrated, would push the band towards an entirely personal pop language in which boundaries between pop and rock would blur, but which would, nevertheless, later be subsumed in the general critical feeding-frenzy on Progressive at the end of the 1970s.

This approach matured on 1971's *Nursery Cryme*. By now musical touchstone Phillips had left, driven out by the exigencies of relationships mutated by touring. New recruits were Londoners Steve Hackett and Phil Collins (the latter already aware of exploitative tendencies towards Progressive after experiences with Flaming Youth, a promising psychedelic outfit steered popwards by bespoke songwriting duo Howard and Blaikley).

As with Wakeman's advent in Yes, Collins brought both hard-nosed professionalism and humour to the stiff-upper-lipped powder keg of raging amateur impotence that was Genesis. He and Hackett were more rock-orientated and brought backbone to the skeletal textures of *Trespass*; on 'Return of the Giant Hogweed', 'The Musical Box' and 'Fountain of Salmacis' (all 1971) Collins's pulse and Hackett's reticent yet dourly aggressive electric growl broadened the group's soundstage and made them rhythmically more fluid and flexible, enabling Banks's Hammond organ and Mellotron to stretch out. The soundstage is very wide – the acoustic straining to attain a resonance to give a greater panorama to the band's textures.

In the van of the camp-rock theatrics of David Bowie, Arthur Brown and Alice Cooper, with their debts to the Theatres of Cruelty and of the Absurd, Gabriel's increasingly picaresque wardrobe of costumes illustrated the fruity fancies he was constructing in his song lyrics, particularly in the archetypally English eccentricity evident in 'Harold the Barrel' and the

'Willow Farm' section of the 1972 'Supper's Ready'. To Duncan Fallowell he was 'the restless kid Hamlet ... a frail Saxon poet to Ray Davies's bargee pierrot'.[32] Gabriel eulogized on, among other things, Victorian senile eroticism ('Musical Box', 1971) and village-green sadism ('Harold the Barrel', 1971). A fox's head, a woman's full-length red dress, Rameses II makeup, coupled with surreal tales (including one account of a young woman who stripped naked on a tube train, unzipped herself and fell apart in halves) told to cover for the tuning of guitars, made Gabriel a cult frontman. *Foxtrot* (1972) confirmed the band's ascendancy. By now not only were the themes more secure harmonically and developmentally (cf. the metamorphosis of the verse and chorus of 'Watcher of the Skies' from the apocalyptic Mellotron intro which rings up the curtain on the album), but Collins could do ever greater mischief with them (his laidback shuffle tempo which totally transforms the otherwise undistinguished theme of 'Get 'Em Out By Friday') without for one minute compromising the essential hummability of the tunes.

Side 2 of *Foxtrot* was almost entirely given over to the twenty-three-minute, ten-part 'Supper's Ready'. At the time, Gabriel claimed, possibly tongue-in-cheek, that the song told of 'the ultimate cosmic battle for Armageddon between good and evil in which man is destroyed, but the deaths of countless thousands atone for mankind, reborn no longer as *Homo Sapiens*'.[33] Multitudinous fragments, each of greater or lesser but never negligible musical interest given their Beatles-ish heritage, are drawn from Genesis desk-drawers and poured into this masterpiece, which despite the profligate diversity of tempi and atmospheres on show retains a remarkable uniformity of mood. The finale, although rather a pompous apotheosis of sound, dissolves in studio fade-out rather than conclusive *sforzando*. A sense of tension-and-release worthy of emotionally manipulative, rhetorical composers from Samuel Wesley to Puccini is everywhere; Josephson draws parallels between the development of the recitative in section 1 to the 'operatic' takes on same in sections 2 'The Guaranteed Eternal Sanctuary Man' and 7 'As Sure as Eggs is Eggs (Aching Men's Feet)'.[34] Calculated, yes, but it is an achievement of engaging pop songwriting whose application to a twenty-three-minute concrete structure does no harm whatever to its constituent parts.

What was apparent from early on was the increasing rapidity of the band's professionalization, which faithfully reflects well the general pace of same in the industry and indeed in the consolidation of Progressive ideology. *Nursery Cryme* was publicized with an endorsement written by Keith Emerson after a viewing of the band at the Lyceum in London:

> These days it's hard for a new band to step over the line and gain recognition ... in the light of such hardship it is important that the original conception should be carried through, worked on, and improved on; and to hope that sooner or later, someone's going to 'dig' you. If nobody does, so what! You are a musician and that's what matters. There are a lot of people 'digging' Genesis at the moment, but not enough; sooner or later they are going to make it, and you'll have wished you had been in on it at the start.[35]

Quite apart from Gabriel's fox head (later replaced by a plastic 'old man' mask), he turned himself into a flower to perform the 'Willow Farm' section of 'Supper's Ready' on stage, and shaved the front of his scalp. Collins meanwhile invited the audience to boo, it was said (though never so simply), to get them off their complacent backsides. 'Our role as musicians,' said Gabriel, 'is somewhere between the orchestra in the pit and the old fashioned, but out-front, rock and roll group ... Instead of the band being the focus of attention, therefore, it will be the mime or dance or whatever we are orchestrating. I appreciate,' he finished drily, 'that this may well be providing more bourgeois escapism.'[36] Having made inroads into America, the band continued to court middle England, racking up even larger audiences and even healthier sales with *Selling England by the Pound* (1973).

On this album Gabriel's unassuageable hankering to tackle more earthly concerns in the gang warfare of 'The Battle of

Epping Forest' suffers from the prolixity of the vernacularly uninitiated. Banks's classical echoes resound like thunderclaps throughout the riotously melodramatic 'Firth of Fifth', whose cheesy Schumannesque piano intro is transformed into a stunningly executed piece of recapitulation as the middle-eight keyboard solo, itself reworked as a sumptuously wallowing quasi-melodic guitar solo which installs Hackett definitively in the band's soundworld. There is a uniquely other-worldly and curiously symphonic quality about his sound, rather like Hackett's childhood hero Hank Marvin heard across the centuries by H. G. Wells's time-traveller. Quite apart from the near hit-single 'I Know What I Like (in Your Wardrobe)', which implied imminent success, this was the work of a band shaping up finally to convert the easiest of goals.

That conversion in the end was unusual and somewhat laboured. Genesis ditched a Mike Rutherford suggestion as to a concept album based around Antoine de Saint Exupéry's fable *The Little Prince*, which Gabriel thought 'too twee'. The leader later commented: 'It was 1974 ... pre-Punk, but I still thought we ought to base the story around a contemporary figure rather than a fantasy creation. We were starting to get into the era of the big, fat supergroups... and I thought, "I don't want to go down with this *Titanic*".'[37]

Having forced his yarn (a kind of pilgrim's progress as undertaken by an alienated New York Puerto Rican) on his sceptical band, Gabriel led them to Headley in Surrey, where he attempted to cobble the epic together. The result met mixed reviews on its release in November 1974, but has since proved to be Genesis's most consistent back-catalogue seller. *The Lamb Lies Down on Broadway* was a concept album, but echoing Moore's sentiment it did not hang together musically; only with a prior textual knowledge of the tale (a text of a necessarily gnostic kind, as ambiguously intimated on the sleeve) could any listener trace much thematic connection between one song and another, all dealing, via first-person lyrics, with the picaresque career of Gabriel's character Rael.

The album, later taken to the stage in its entirety on a 1974–5 world tour, not only necessitated a new panoply of stage props for the ever-chameleonic Gabriel but stalled the group tendency towards longer songs and workouts exemplified by the likes of 'Firth of Fifth'. There were startling, and tellingly dramatic, uprushes of instrumental, studio-created space and power (the cataclysmic entries of drums and Mellotron on 'Hairless Heart' and 'Fly on a Windshield' for example) but by and large the album consisted of ramshackle and discrete songs constructed unpretentiously but originally around hastily arranged melodic fragments bound together over four sides of vinyl to tell, or (to put it more succinctly and accurately) *intimate* a story.

BONFIRES OF THE VANITIES: KING CRIMSON AND AESTHETIC SACRILEGE

In the midst of all this arch refinement came King Crimson.

There can be no doubt that Robert Fripp reconstituted his band with a number of musicians who would transform his compositions into some of the most burningly confrontational rock yet heard, but his music was put together in the same cultural conditions as that of his peers, and shares many of its artistic concerns:

> A frequent criticism at the time was of 'self-indulgence'. In practice, when you let rip this is always a risk. In principle, to consider acting in accordance with one's musical sense-of-rightness as indulgent is a terrifying commentary upon the extent to which our culture has become aberrent in its values ...Young musicians of the time who were self-indulgent were not, as far as my perception went, playing what was true for them but what they believed to be in fashion.[38]

Fripp was a believer in music, a cheerful zealot besotted with its essentialist qualities. All Fripp did was simply to transcend borrowed nineteenth-century Romanticism and lend his own vernacular, mediated perfectly through a multiplicity of twentieth-century influences already profuse and continually in flux – Fripp was a voracious listener to new music and had a mind enquiring enough to benefit from the experience.

The new band was assembled with Fripp's customary care and included Bill Bruford from Yes (Fripp told him, 'I think you're ready to play with King Crimson now'),[39] John Wetton from Roxy Music, unknown violinist David Cross and percussionist Jamie Muir, who would vanish into a monastery after *Larks' Tongues in Aspic* and diminish the band's sonic impact considerably.

Both *Larks' Tongues* (1973) and *Starless and Bible Black* (1974), not to mention the later *Red* (also 1974) have been admirably and elegantly analysed by Allan Moore, but Fripp's aesthetic choices must be obvious to even the most musically obtuse listener.

Solos appear to erupt uncued by the metre of the piece, not simply as a means of getting from one constituent part of a song to another. Texturally, Crimson rewrite the script from the very first note of the album, introducing what sounds like a poly-rhythmical thumb piano. The warm Mellotron strings of yore are gone, as are the resolutions on to filmically melodramatic chords and cadences (compare 'In the Court of the Crimson King'). Few conventional emotional triggers are evident; hierarchies between instruments in the mix seem to vary throughout the album. As with early Pink Floyd and Yes, every instrument is used from the bottom of its range to the very top.

Fripp was no anarchist; the formal intricacies of his compositions attest to that. His genius was to evoke a new system of emotional responses for Progressive rock which would turn on not only listeners but the musicians who were playing it. Genesis guitarist Steve Hackett once commented that King Crimson 'were like musical karate, and I found that fascinating'. Military precision, he continued, was counterpointed with 'the balls of rock, the fluidity of jazz, the form of the classics and the technology of combining a small group of people in an orchestral sound'.[40]

But this was necessarily an orchestral sound in which discipline was not a master but a brother of spontaneity. Fripp remembers, concerning his orchestra: 'Mellotrons, for instance, we controlled by foot pedal. If a foot slipped, the whole orchestra lurched.'[41] He also acknowledged that 'excited drummers sometimes hit microphones with their sticks', but found it a cause for celebration rather than affront. To illustrate the point, 'KC repertoire is not a sacrosanct and final body of work but ... organic, malleable', Fripp wrote later.[42]

On stage, contrary takes on album material, and incorporation of micro-samples of same into lengthy collective improvisations proved sensationally that while Fripp located himself in a Western artistic context just as much as the next Progressive musician, his aesthetic was striving to *transcend* the bourgeois, formalized attitudes now shaping the music of Yes *et al.* The title track of the band's next album, *Starless and Bible Black* (1974), seems to resemble an attempt to take this tension between the discipline of tightly constructed basslines and the individual musicians' urges to stretch out within them.[43]

Interestingly, there's a more conventional structure about the first number of *Starless*, 'The Great Deceiver'; there are thrilling variations of tempo and orchestration in each repetition of verse and chorus. For instance, the first verse is sung by Wetton, then the band play a complicated figure underneath it, making ambiguous the emphasis of the words. 'Lament' (the sourest and most sardonic barb yet aimed by Fripp at an increasingly oppressive record industry) also reprises material in a fashion less like *Larks' Tongues* than *Close to the Edge*. The abrasive timbre of the music is unaffected, even if the Hell's kitchen of (Muir's) percussion is disappointingly absent. 'The Night Watch', probably the closest thing to a conventional song that the band ever attempted, showed how fecund was their inspiration even with everyday structures of verse-refrain; adding cembalom to the introductory pages of the song adds a bleak layer of atmosphere to this appropriately dark-hued apostrophe of Rembrandt's painting.

Fripp was now tending towards earthy, uncontrasted primary colours. His use of the Mellotron is no longer for the simple emulation of *other* musical sounds, but achieving the unique body of the machine's sound as a perverse orchestral backcloth to simmer beneath riffs and broken phrases as at the start of 'The Mincer'. Finally, as Moore says, the closing 'Fracture' dumps normative rock triadic-chord construction altogether, yet still totes the album's catchiest riff.

Crimson's sound ciphers were not those of nature, of mountains and rivers or of whispering winds; they were either of the city — alarms, buzzers, impact, steel on steel — or of inner landscapes, abrasive contact, primal screams, coital sighs. It's wrong, however, to paint Fripp as a kind of Punk prophet without honour, a loose screw within the Progressive superstructure. Fripp didn't buck the received notion of rock *auteur* as dandified aesthete; in his 1974 diaries he reports that he is reading Watkins's *The Old Straight Track* and hints at the malevolent influence of a ouija-board on the band's fortunes in the USA. Then, after he dissolved the band, he went to 'improve himself' at J. G. Bennett's International Academy for Continuous Education in Sherborne, Dorset.

Bill Bruford says: 'I remember in 1974 when Robert told me he was splitting up King Crimson. "I don't want to be like all these dinosaur bands," he told me. I remember thinking, "Well, this is a drag because we're just about to really make it big, but I guess he's right. And he was."' [44]

6 DECADENCE AND DESTRUCTION
(PROGRESSIVE AND PUNK 1975–78)

TAX FEVER

Modern rock ideology has it that the big bands of the 1970s simply became too big for their platform boots; that laziness and decadence were innate in their music. This inexcusably ignores the part played by external factors in Progressive's defensive decline in the mid-1970s.

Bands like Pink Floyd, Yes and ELP had been well on the way to being rock's first megastars, along with scruffier deities like the Rolling Stones, Led Zeppelin, Deep Purple and the Who, the pioneer sterling-millionaires of the rock era. It was perhaps the furthest imaginable departure from the kick-out-the-jams communitarianism of the late 1960s. Many of the artists popularly conjured and perceived as – and indeed in many cases living the mythology of – long-haired, Labour-voting yobs were now long-haired, Tory-voting *nouveaux-riches*. But the significance of that status led them also to contend with an element of social history in the Britain of the 1970s often overlooked post-Thatcher: tax.

Tax fever had begun with Ted Heath's ill-fated Conservative administration's introduction of Value Added Tax in 1973, and gained steam with the punitive tax measures announced by the incoming Labour administration of 1974, designed to fund their reflation of the economy. What it amounted to was that from 5 April 1974 onwards, individuals in the top tax bracket were taxed at 83 per cent on monies earned within the sterling zone, taxable as long as the artist officially resided in Britain. Residency was governed by a given number of 'tax-free' days.

And why not? In 1974, according to Simon Frith, 'At least a hundred British rock stars were earning £100,000 or more a year.'[1] Given the zeros attached to the modern contracts of Jacksons or Madonnas, such a figure is hard for a contemporary audience to compute in terms of buying power. The fact that ELP earned £5 million in 1974 is perhaps less difficult to assimilate. Unsurprisingly, really, as ELP were led only by the Rolling Stones, the Who and Led Zeppelin as world concert draws in 1973–4.

A hue and cry arose about the drainage of talent from this country such tax measures would occasion. As it turned out, this usually referred to irreplaceable UK national assets such as Roger Moore, but by 1976 events were drawing near the brink as even middling rock stars like Genesis and Gentle Giant were recording abroad – stymied by the demands of the UK-residence rules governing taxation – and the big league quit the country, full stop. And so, one by one, the dinosaurs swam for it as the taxman's net closed around them and, perhaps fatally, also fell out of the UK public gaze and seriously alienated their most favourable and loyal grassroots markets in so doing.

WHAT THEY DID ON THEIR HOLIDAYS: PROGRESSIVE SUPERSTARDOM AND AESTHETICS

Pink Floyd, at least, were active in the UK in 1975, recording *Wish You Were Here*, which it is probably no exaggeration to say was (at the time) the most eagerly anticipated rock album ever released. Even the announcement of its issue date was headline news. These hosannas were grounded on no more than the fact that it was simply the Floyd's follow-up to *Dark Side of the Moon*, which represented, for many, the acme of the genre to date.

Given the mythological status that its predecessor had earned in two years, disappointment with *Wish* was perhaps inevitable. *Dark Side of the Moon* was still hogging the charts and gorging on pockets when its successor hit the racks. But verdicts were, none the less, conciliatory; the *NME*'s Pete Erskine, although never a Floyd fan, generously reported that the Floyd were 'intelligent enough to make the crossover from greatcoatland to coffee table'.[2]

Its inevitable failure to live up to the omniscient mystique of its predecessor, however, proved the Floyd were fallible. It was an unsettling stumble which perhaps confirmed that Progressive was indeed showing its age. The album's plodding, flat-footed metres are now patented almost to death; only the much-imitated and oft-rendered legato pedal note which introduces the Barrett tribute 'Shine on You Crazy Diamond Part 1' (the now-crazed Barrett was to turn up in the studio for the sessions and inform a bemused band that he was ready to 'do his bit')[3] is remotely memorable. Synthesized sonorities dominate the album – Rick Wright obviously had a lot of new toys and wanted the world to listen to him playing with them. But the musical evolution is less rhythmically based than before, on pieces such as 'Echoes' (1971) or 'Set the Controls for the Heart of the Sun' (1969). The sounds now appear out of Wright's perfumed paradise of sound. French jazz legend Stéphane Grappelli had been asked to perform a violin cadenza at the end of the title track, but was apparently drowned out by the effects whirlwind generated by those pesky electronics – a fair indication of how withered the Floyd's taste antennae had become.

Yes proved themselves particularly elusive at a time when critical reappraisal of rock mores – a shift away from aestheticism and instrumental sophistication – made a definitive artistic statement of their own beliefs, whether in concert or on record, essential. After the mauling of *Topographic* they triumphed with the stunningly audacious *Relayer* (1974) and toured the USA, but unwisely did so with an unremitting regularity that strained an already tense outfit to breaking point.

Yes skipped the UK, save for one brief tour in spring 1975 and an appearance at that summer's Reading Festival. Tax-plagued, they turned to their adoring US market with three vast tours between 1974 and 1976.

Wakeman's deputy was Patrick Moraz, a Swiss-born player who'd made a reputation in jazz and early synthesized sound-tracking, before almost losing it again in Refugee. This had been a catastrophic Charisma Records attempt to reconstitute the Nice with Brian Davison, Lee Jackson and a spare keyboard showman (there were plenty lying around, after all, in 1974). But Moraz, while possessing more chops than is decently healthy for any one musician, was no mere speed merchant, no muscle-flexing, technique-toting he-man, but a genuinely exploratory artist, captive to but willing to fiddle around with the body politic of mainstream popular rock and jazz. This had left him with a more innate sympathy with the rhythmic subtleties of metre and melodic construction emptying out of contemporary US jazz-rock fusion, and also with the poetic harmonic possibilities therein. In short, Moraz was no second-class Keith Emerson. He was a first-class Patrick Moraz.

In 1974 Yes were not, as accepted wisdom has it, reviled by the media – hacks may have slated *Topographic* on record and in the flesh, but they still hove into band-führer Jon Anderson's view when *Relayer* was announced. To their credit, Yes replied by at least acknowledging a debt to the real world that seemed to have escaped them on their previous flawed epic, despite – or in concert with – the overcast desert landscapes of Roger Dean's cover.

The oil crisis of 1973, with its louring potential for world war, may have run like a subterranean river through the musical conception of the album, originally intended as an adaptation of Tolstoy's epic *War and Peace*. Certainly the music is sterner than anything else in the Yes canon, while tonality is only prodded rather than overturned, and cadences tend to fall where rock cadences do, the emotional scope of the music takes on a matchless breadth.

Hedges's claim that Moraz tackles seventeen changes of keyboard in the first twenty-two bars of 'The Gates of Delirium', the side-long opener, is not only questionable but, like the apocrypha of Moraz playing an Awful Lot of Keyboards (accounts range between fourteen and twenty-four) is irrelevant. Moraz's importance lies in his enriching of the band's expressive vocabulary. The contrapuntal synthesizer solo closing the final track 'To Be Over' (whose graceful, Straussian waltz and dainty chordal progress is pure poetry) is surprising. But the way the music often confounds its own linearity, crumpling up and reforming itself at odd moments (the introduction to 'Gates' and the surpassing strange processed a capella cha-cha-chas muscling unannounced into the jazz rock of 'Sound Chaser') adopts a seat-of-the-pants approach hitherto unknown in Yes's studio work. This is pure Moraz, filtering through contemporary jazz mores without the harmonics, or with the harmonics subtly disguised, with the blues filleted in favour of symphonism. The notorious free-form charge-and-battle extemporization of 'Gates', with its rilling, atonal squirts of guitar and synthesizer and battery of treated special effects ends in a scorching sequence that sounds nothing so much as an out-of-control flail-tank. But perhaps the band is at its most telling at its quietest, cathartically resolving the row in 'Soon', an ordinary-enough tune harmonized with exquisite beauty and textural expertise. The coda's comfy-chair relaxation of C major is clouded by the distant modal threats of E flat and B flat.[4]

But that sense of distance, of the unattainable, the allusive and elusive, maybe defused the contemporary pretensions of the music and would also invest subsequent projects, especially Anderson's towering *Olias of Sunhillow* (1976) with a lofty languor quite alien to rock syntax. There was, and still is even among Yes fanatics, a notion that *Relayer* is the beginning of the end of the band as innovators, that it is an extreme example of studio infatuation, with the creation of music not through instruments but through the mixing desk. Certainly live, the amazing textural variety of 'The

Gates of Delirium' is lost; the Yes marque, Yes's distinct individual soundworld (paramount in the evaluative criteria used among fans in those days) seemed to be as much a creation of the production console as the choice of notes that each instrumentalist made. The concerts simply mislaid it.

We shall return to the accusation of contrivance later; but while not unfair, it does hide other issues of musical authenticity and also of circumstantial necessity. Far from being the cold, calculated manipulation often suggested, the processes undergone in the studio to obtain such delicacy were often far from the monkish craftsmanship sessions commonly imagined. The fourth section of Yes's *Close to the Edge*, for example, with its remarkable change in tempo and texture, exists as recorded artefact simply because Eddie Offord threw away the original mix and kept a reject. Additionally, in Bruford's words to Tim Morse,

> There was a cleaning lady ... she was very vicious and would throw away everything ... but it was a disaster because the record was halfway made, so there was tape all over the room ... I woke up one day at four or five o'clock in the morning and everybody was searching in this trash can for the missing section.[5]

Yes appeased hard-core fans in 1975 with a clutch of solo albums; the press were turning restless, although the reviews of the individual albums were passable. Moraz's *The Story of i*, located in a specifically European jazz-rock context, is really beyond the scope of this book, but suffice it to say that it contains much outlandish music – every Yes fan should hear *The Story of i*, as it points a direction in which the band could have gone that might have prolonged the intense music of *Relayer* and conceivably taken mainstream rock music down a wholly new track. But even this pales in comparison with Anderson's *Olias*.

It is Anderson writ large, as fey, space-age space-case to some, visionary musical pioneer to others, but it is probably the most complete manifesto to Progressive ideology (infinitely more so than *Topographic*). A voracious reader of the theosophist Vera

Stanley-Alder and fascinated with the quasi-Art Nouveau sci-fi imagery that Atlantic Records, with the help of Roger Dean and Donald Lehmkuhl, had put together for Yes, Anderson had obviously set out to best them all.

The record is intimidatingly packaged; a triple gatefold, in relief paper, it is stunningly illustrated not by Dean but by an obscure newcomer, Dave Roe, who would go on to design sleeves aplenty for the sci-fi novel market but, ironically, would never design another Progressive album cover. The style is particularly interesting, a refinement of Dean's singular impressionism, this time unashamedly mixing influences, both Hokusai limpidity and Frank Frazetta *Sturm-und-Drang*. This is all rendered irrelevant, however, by the music within. Even if we believe the musicological edicts that Yes music, and much of Progressive, was directly Beatles-descended in terms of texture and harmony, this album strays about as far from accepted textural practices of mainstream rock (while remaining eminently listenable to a mainstream rock audience), as it is possible to get.

The dissension from the rock lexicon audible on the last two sides of *Topographic* and *Relayer* here comes gloriously to fruition; metres and tonality are approachable, but the melodic profiles and particularly the instrumentation are utterly original. Both qualities are best exemplified by the staggering pedal note which underpins the opening 'Ocean Song' and the Ligeti-esque choral passage which follows, derived from long hours grafting and regrafting in Anderson's own studio.

The musical language is largely tonal, but is delivered in a fashion unexplored by even the most dedicated rock studio auteur up until that point. The likes of Stockhausen, Cage and Boulez had, of course, gone light-years beyond Anderson in developing electronic timbres, but Anderson was the first to display such cerebral refinement in timbral technique on a mainstream *rock* album, especially one in which the musical language was comparatively straightforward.

The orchestration is equally ambitious: Anderson played more than thirty instruments on the album. His technical ability is modest, but this hardly matters. The music is conceived in terms of a series of atmospheric tableaux, either shimmering in polychrome or disrupted by volcanic uprushes of exotic percussion. Anderson's lyrics are the usual assonant gobbledygook, but at least take the narrative bull by the horns, and intermittently extend his coloristic lexical remit to its logical conclusion – he invents his own sci-fi dialect.

Would that such good taste had been in evidence with Rick Wakeman's stabs at musical fantasy. He had spent his first few months out of Yes's orbit putting together another solo album to capitalize on the success of the *Journey to the Centre of the Earth*. He had taken *Journey* around the world, its dinosaurs in particular proving a great hit; 'We just thought this was incredibly funny,' says Paul Schütze – an experimental musician and writer now living in London and then an adolescent observer of the Australian leg of the tour, 'and it seemed, so did Wakeman. It looked like he was pissing himself laughing at this.'[6] Wakeman's next wheeze was to deck out himself and his long-suffering band (derived from a Buckinghamshire pub outfit) in armour, chainmail, stout mead-cups, school-panto wizard hats and cardboard broadswords for 1975's *King Arthur and the Knights of the Round Table*, an opus originally earmarked for open-air performance in a medieval pageant at Tintagel Castle in Cornwall. Kyboshed by the local authorities, Wakeman merely transferred proceedings to Wembley Arena. On being informed that the only possible dates available for performances coincided with the arena being frozen over for an ice show, Wakeman briskly informed his promoters that *King Arthur* would be performed on ice. And it was. The forces were identical to those used for *Journey*, with an extra choir bunged in for good (if inaudible) measure.

By this time the press that had so deified him only two years previously were out for his blood. The consensus was, if Wakeman's credentials as composer and keyboardist were so good, why did he have to keep hiding behind Babylonian set-pieces?

Wakeman's extravagance didn't end with the music, however. He owned a collection of vintage Rolls-Royces which comprised his Fragile Carriage Company; at the end of 1975

Ken Russell recruited him to help score the execrable movie *Lisztomania*, in which a suitably embarrassed Wakeman appears as Thor, the God of Thunder. No ifs, no buts; Wakeman was a major star. The mere association of him with Liszt, the creator of keyboard virtuoso mythos (even in such shockingly silly fashion as Russell created), helped cement the image of Wakeman as keyboard genius. He became a reluctant commodity in 1970s middle-class culture, as colour supplements winnowed out the most 'tasteful' of the counter-cultural leftovers.

Nobody could say Wakeman didn't deserve his success; his commitment to music, as to alcohol, was prodigious. After the première of *Journey* in 1974 he battled back from a coronary, and then in 1976, having been informed out of the blue that he was £700,000 in debt, he fought off financial ruin. It's interesting, therefore, to speculate on exactly where Wakeman would have gone after this album had Patrick Moraz not quit Yes, as it is fascinating to conjure the band's likely future.

The latter had, however, become exhaustedly alienated by Yes's gruelling roadwork. Before anyone outside the band knew what was happening, Wakeman was back. By spring 1977, a new album, recorded at Montreux, was in the can.

In 1976 prevailing rock ideology was as yet wholly unhindered by revolution. That year the music journalist Tony Palmer made for London Weekend Television an epic seventeen-part history of popular music entitled *All You Need is Love*. Although acclaimed upon broadcast, this then-monumental project has enjoyed little re-exposure. Palmer's story, though told with erudition, terminated in a stolid endorsement of an artistically teleological, progressive (though not strictly Progressive) rock ethic (rock as new art form) which, even as Palmer outlined musical history, was being eclipsed by a wholly new musical and social movement.

CHEAP HOLIDAYS WITH OTHER PEOPLE'S MONEY: PUNK, THE BEYOND, AND THE HERE AND NOW

In hindsight perhaps the most surprising aspect of the public reaction – and indeed the initial reaction of the rock business –

to Punk's ramshackle rise between 1976 and 1977 was the fact that both the alleged – and factual – antics of 'punk rockers' were treated with such vivid dismay as social aberrations. Quite apart from the visual impact of torn tartan, safety-pinned extremities and dayglo hair in a Britain in which nearly half the population could recall austerity and national service, Punk roused a moral panic not seen since the 1950s.

But why the outrage? As we have seen, the writing was on the wall for the 1970s ethos long before John Lydon first snarled from the cover of the *NME*, pub-rock was burning across the land from the Thames Estuary like an oil-refinery flare, and in the USA the future of rock'n'roll was an unshaven dude-with-attitude from the car lots and goods yards of Asbury Park, New Jersey, brandishing a woolly hat and a Telecaster guitar: Bruce Springsteen.

The last of the free festivals, Watchfield, had ended in skull-cracking, hippy-smacking truncheon carnage the previous summer. Britain was becoming a violent and unpredictable place; in 1976 Notting Hill's annual carnival exploded into two days of street violence, unemployment topped 1,500,000, inflation touched 25 per cent and the International Monetary Fund were called in to bail the Callaghan Labour administration out of bankruptcy. Paul Theroux's novel *The Family Arsenal* mirrored Punk's apocalyptic vision with its random savagery, meted out by a drifting gang of psychopaths in 1970s London; the subculture of viciousness and collapse tapped in *A Clockwork Orange* and the evergreen 1970s pulp-fiction bestseller *Skinhead* had barged from margin to mainstream. In the wake of a worrying increase in fascist aggression from the National Front, street confrontations with anti-racists spilled over into rioting. But when punks arrived on the street corners of a nation to which the media were fond of administering the last rites, they were seen as 'the cult of hate' (the *Sun*), not so much signs of the times than aberrant interlopers into them.

Punk's musico-cultural role has, like so much of rock history, been misrepresented. The idea that it was an 'assault' on some 'rock Establishment', a howl of rage against a pampered nobility, is only a half-truth. The Sex Pistols' celebrated 'never trust a hippy' dictum has underwritten an entire chapter in rock history. Julie Burchill and Tony Parsons reported that Rotten became the Sex Pistols' vocalist only because Malcolm MacLaren was so won over by his 'sadistically mutilated Pink Floyd T-shirt with the words "I HATE" scribbled in a biro trembling with furious loathing above the Dodos' moniker'.[7] But was this the whole story? In July 1977, invited to bring a batch of his favourite records along to a Capital Radio interview with DJ Tommy Vance, Rotten turned up with a Peter Hammill (of Van der Graaf Generator) album in his bag. Joe Strummer and Mick Jones of the Clash emphasized the urban, dispossessed roots of their music, but in language no different from that used by the likes of 'hippy' Mick Farren, who in the Notting Hill of 1970 had indeed been among the chief proselytizers of the music that rock historians claim punk sought to 'destroy'. Study of contemporary sources reveals that punk's mantras claimed a share of rock's ill-gotten booty; punks glorified consumption, but more for unruly, bohemian purposes than those genteel bourgeois pursuits now accumulating around rock's nobility. Drink and drug debauchery, the most visible acts of superstar indulgence, didn't count; Sid Vicious attests to punk's gleeful embrace of all that rock could do to the metabolism. The target for scorn, rarely if ever voiced, though detectable in many interviews, was what Yes engineer Michael Tait said of his employers: 'Where the band was 99 per cent of their lives, it's now only 80 per cent ... they've got wives, children, and schools to worry about.'[8] Pardon? Was this rock'n'roll or the Women's Institute?

Back in the 1970s, when the genre was still a mere two decades old, long before it developed the ability to sustain an affluent middle-class audience, it was still for many people a proletarian phenomenon. Its practitioners were portrayed – fictionally – as predominantly drop-outs, slummy, uncouth, ill-concealed analogues of Dylan the beatnik rabbit from kiddie TV favourite *The Magic Roundabout*. Even in the work of young artists such as novelist Martin Amis, pop musicians were still fair game for potshots at degraded dissolution, as can be seen from the fiendish portrayal of the sociopathic musician Andy Adorno in *Dead Babies* (1975).

The reality, however, was becoming somewhat different; Yes and ELP lived and recorded abroad for much of the time; Wakeman was a director of eleven companies. As early as 1970 Keith Emerson had praised Greg Lake for having a 'really good business head'.[9] Lake later went on to tell *Melody Maker*: 'If the cats doing it today put enough into it they'll be heavy themselves one day ... Input equals output.'[10] At least Lake's well-meaning proto-Thatcherism sounded more emollient than the Moody Blues' brand of capitalism. Their Threshold Record stores were, the band told an indifferent world, 'a service to the community'.

The Moodies' woodwind player, Ray Thomas, saw it like this: 'If the shops are prospering the community is prospering – businessmen making money makes businesses make money.'[11] Why the Moodies' first commercial venture with their new store beyond the stockbroker-belt comforts and affluence of their native Cobham was to the nondescript town of Andover in Hampshire has never been established.

Roger Waters of Pink Floyd was 'coptered into concerts on the band's 1977 'In the Flesh' tour; the other members had to make do with limousines. Waters was a man, according to one observer, who lived 'the life of a gentleman landowner who's very happy to pay people to do the work'.[12]

Nice work if you can get it, particularly if you can get away with appearing to despise it all and still earn money from it. Waters's dissatisfaction with this state of affairs was pandered to by journalists like the obsequious Karl Dallas (see below). But in any case, the money was there to burn; after the oil crisis, the rock industry had recovered its composure and could go on treating its stars like royalty, even as punk surged up on the rails. But were such material benefits beginning to sap musicianly creativity?

By the mid-1970s the superstar status attained by many Progressive musicians courted super-hubris. Yes's Steve Howe commented of 1976, 'It was an era of technology that baffled me. I saw everyone getting more and more equipment, and I began to wonder maybe if the whole thing wasn't beginning to get out of hand.'[13] Live presentation of the music had also assumed mind-boggling dimensions. Other media helped determine that evolution; from the mid-1970s onwards, advances in television technology (particularly important for the American market, where more concerts were filmed for televisual distribution) *à propos* image resolution enabled rock stage shows to develop a wider range of colouristic effects to enable cameras to reproduce the effects accurately; hitherto these cameras had been unable to switch from light to dark scenarios and vice versa.

While puny by later rock-show standards (which were indisputably set by visually obsessed Progressive acts) Genesis's world-tour rig in 1977, featuring forty-eight Boeing 747 landing lights, proved an undoubted draw. Whereas the precursors of rock theatre, Arthur Brown, David Bowie, Alice Cooper and Iggy Pop, had depended largely on the human element, deriving their stuntwork from theatrical traditions, Progressive bands relied (and sold themselves with relish) to a greater and greater extent on electronically generated spectacle. Even Hawkwind's cramped budget allowed them to supplement lights and lasers with a fire-eater, the odd village-pageant Martian costume, and a dancer, the statuesque Stacia.

In the middle of a Pink Floyd gig in Detroit, a smoke bomb timed to explode in the middle of the early track 'Careful with That Axe, Eugene', detonated the speaker housing it. Roger Waters recalls:

Inside this bin, holding it down, is a ... fourteen-pound stage weight. There was nothing left of this bin; it disappeared. The top of the bass cabinet it was standing on, which was made of three-quarter-inch marine plywood just ... it just wasn't there any more. How nobody was killed, we will never know. A guy sitting thirty rows back in the audience copped a piece of this marine ply ... in the stomach. Every single speaker in the gear blew immediately. Of course, the audience thought it was fantastic. They were on their feet for ... seemed like hours.[14]

When Pete Erskine asked Dave Gilmour if an audience applaud a solo rather than a bucket of dry ice, Gilmour maintained that the dry ice was 'all part of the dramatic effect'.[15]

One *Melody Maker* journalist asserted in print that the equipment was solely to 'heighten the effect of their music'.[16] None the less, the aspect of production that most defined Progressive in the 1970s was not visual hardware, but the technology of sound. Instruments, like instrumental prowess, became fetishisized as much for size and superficial efficacy as for their intrinsic qualities.

Equipment – and its boys-with-toys foregrounding of expertise and stamina – was central to Progressive. As usual, rock historiography has judiciously filleted the truth. While obsessional devotion to hardware was commonplace – as any browsing of the likes of *Beat International* in the 1970s will attest – the reason for the stunning profligacy of outlay on equipment was simple: analogue equipment, particularly monophonic synthesizers, needed to be deployed in bulk for the intended musical effects to be achieved.

Gimmickry, however, was never far behind. While Progressive might have haughtily disdained bubblegum pop with its star-shaped guitar bodies and stripey drumsticks (remember Dave Lea of Slade?), it had its own brash vulgarities. Even violins and drums were affected, Curved Air's Darryl Way and Eddie Jobson renowned for their use of transparent fibreglass electric violins. Percussionists were less convinced; 'Gretsch and Ludwig ... were traditional craftsmanship drums, but then they all seemed to take a terrible turn for the worse ... they brought out the perspex shell kits, everything suddenly went apeshit. The early seventies. Everybody seemed to suffer,' one Progressive drummer commented later.[17]

But Progressive did give a mighty shove to reproduction technology, most notably in the production console and, specifically, with regard to keyboards. Guitars changed their basic makeup hardly at all – Fenders, Gibsons *et al.*, though now with a cascade of imitators clamouring noisily and profitably in their wakes, and with a new auxiliary branch of the technology in pedal boards and effects. But keyboards changed radically.

At first the popularity of the Hammond organ on many Progressive albums was due less to the suitability of the instrument to the genre than to the ubiquity of the instrument in popular music, as with the aforementioned guitars and bass guitars. It was simply a popular cultural icon, an affordable electronic musical instrument for amateur and professional alike, which enabled the mechanics of its practice and performance to be disseminated over as wide a constituency as possible in its domestic and amateur heyday of the 1950s and 1960s. This lent the madcap antics of Keith Emerson all the more piquancy; the breathtaking range of sounds he wrought from it gave the instrument a whole new cachet. Pete Townshend and Jimi Hendrix's abuse of their guitars had opened up one sonic universe; Emerson opened up another.

There were, however, instruments whose very *raison d'être* would serve Progressive rock without any mediation from their players.

The Mellotron was a precursor of modern electronic sampling technology inasmuch as it had been developed from an American device, the Chamberlain Musicmaster, consisting of a keyboard-activated frame of tapes sampled from other instruments, whereby each key set tapes in motion to reproduce the sound recorded thereon. Birmingham electrical engineers Les, Frank and Norman Bradley were contacted in 1962 by the Chamberlain's patentee, Bill Fransen, with a view to mass-producing the machine, and Mellotronics Ltd, with support from bandleader Eric Robinson and magician David Nixon, was set up in Streetly, in the Midlands.

The result was a back-breakingly heavy twin-console keyboard instrument that resembled a fine piece of mahogany furniture but also produced one of the most distinctive sounds in all music. Quite apart from the 1,260 possible sound combinations which appealed to special-effects departments throughout the motion picture industry, the string-orchestra, solo flute and choral effects not only replicated violins and cellos and chorus effects to disconcertingly accurate effect, but the primitive tape-frames also lent a unique surface to the sound which purists swear is unobtainable digitally. True, the instruments were notoriously unreliable; anything but scientifically controlled temperatures would distort a Mellotron's tape-frame and render it hopelessly out of tune. Mark I Mellotrons used Meccano chains to drive the tapes;

mark II machines used chains from Reynolds bicycles.

The curiously reedy, dry flute setting was used particularly effectively by the Beatles on 'Strawberry Fields' ('Living is easy'); but perhaps the most notable early users were the Moody Blues, whose Mike Pinder had bought his first Mellotron mark II from the Dunlop social club near the Streetly factory. The convenience of the instrument (it rendered an orchestra superfluous) quickly immortalized it as the single most identifiable piece of Progressive-rock hardware, the instrument which both revolutionized the imagination of musicians and was itself revolutionized by the use to which those musicians put it.

Numerous revamps and rebuilds of the Mellotron appeared between 1966 and 1986; reliability problems were never quite ironed out; similarly the instrument's inherent obesity ever really cured. The Novotron was put on the market in 1978, along with the Birotron, a copycat project supported by Yes's Rick Wakeman which, thanks to its use of tape-loops as opposed to set lengths of tape, enabled players to hold down legato notes indefinitely. Wakeman, however, was so disillusioned by the Birotron's chronic incapacity that he kicked his offstage and left it there.

Artificial sound generation had been a preoccupation of the musical avant-garde for many years, from Thaddeus Cahill's two-hundred-ton telharmonium of 1906 through the groundbreaking experiments of the Italian Futurist Luigi Russolo to illustrate the sounds of speed and heavy industry which Futurism so lionized; Leon Theremin gave sci-fi B movies their very own instrument, and the invention of a genre of electronic music around Pierre Schaefer's Paris experiments in Paris in the 1940s and Karlheinz Stockhausen's Darmstadt and Cologne experiments of the 1950s made electronics a definitive influence on the cutting-edge post-serial avant-garde of the 1960s. The links between counter-cultural rock musicians and the avant-garde in the 1960s were cemented by the former's use of artificial sound generation and amplification, to the extent that Pierre Boulez, in the process of lobbying the French government for the inception of a special laboratory for research into electronic sound in modern composition, lectured at the

Roundhouse during his tenure as chief conductor of the BBC Symphony Orchestra between 1969 and 1975. Ron Geesin and David Bedford were only two of the many classical young turks of the 1960s who flirted with the possibilities of technologies hitherto reserved for rock music but as yet practically unexplored.

A breakthrough came in 1969 when EMS (owned by electronic pioneer Peter Zinovieff) patented the VCS3, the first fully portable synthesizer – perhaps the most durable example of co-operation between the avant-garde classical and rock milieux. Originally priced cheaply (£300) it was relatively affordable. While the VCS3 was notoriously poor as a melodic or improvisational instrument, its prowess as a sound generator was unrivalled.

But in terms of pop and rock utility, Robert A. Moog beat EMS to the punch; his Mini Moog, a variant on the classic modular synthesizer system patented by its inventor in the mid-1960s, summarized the latter's inexhaustible if unwieldy galaxy of sound reproduction in a machine capable of being set up quickly and conveniently on stage.

Moog was also the first (in 1976) to patent a mass-production polyphonic synthesizer, the Polymoog, whose keyboard was actually touch-sensitive. Into the breach that Oberheim and Moog had opened came hordes of imitators, good, bad and exceptional, not least the fine instruments of Alan Richard Pearlman, whose ARP firm produced the classic, warm, enveloping incense of sound which characterized the 2500, 2600 and Odyssey models. Pearlman had worked as an engineer on the US Gemini and Apollo space programmes and his 2500 was used as the synthesizer which 'starred' in the final sequence of Spielberg's *Close Encounters of the Third Kind*.

The portentous announcements of the first polyphonic synthesizers in the late 1970s, which rendered many keyboards obsolete, coincided with Progressive's demise; the cost of making the music in the studio had become crippling, live performance became more so. Some tried to buck the system, to cut costs and keep creativity alive. Tom Newman of the Manor remembers:

When I first started the Manor I tried to encourage Richard [Branson] to start an electronic research and development arm. We had a guy called Ivor Taylor who started SEC later on, designing compact, high-quality mixers. I was desperate to see a shift in technology from the big recording studios where you had to pay £100 an hour for twenty-four-track facilities. I felt that that was choking creativity because it meant that the only other alternative was a Revox, recording straight on to stereo and at the time there were all sorts of synthesizers and they were starting to pin down the idea of compact keyboards. It seemed obvious that some kind of multi-track recording should be made available to kids. Captain Beefheart showed me this little device which was basically a Walkman but which you could plug your guitar into and play along with. A Rockman, it was called. I thought that that was the future. I pushed Richard to try and invest in what I called a studio in a suitcase. I wanted it a bit bigger than a briefcase – an eight-track tape recorder and a mixing console and a sound generator. So that you could go anywhere, plug in your guitar and record. A bit like a laptop word processor. It still hasn't actually happened. But the shift from big studios should have happened five years earlier.[18]

By this time (the 1980s) Progressive, hobbled by its own seven-league boots, had also the slur of unfashionability to cope with. No matter that the music's exorbitant costs could be scythed. And there was still lingering conceit to be taken into account. The music journalist Mike Barnes, acquainted with the 1980s Progressive act Twelfth Night, recalls: 'One night at a gig Rick [Battersby, the band's keyboardist] told me, "You see that Mellotron? It doesn't work. I've got samples for the sound. But people who are so desperate to see it onstage aren't going to be any the wiser that it doesn't make a sound."'[19] This prefaces another keyboardist's plaintive and perplexed reasoning: 'Using a Casio in Prog is not the done thing. You have to show you've got all these keyboards.'[20]

Apart from bands turning their stage shows into musical-instrument trade fairs, the other most obvious manifestations of this creative bloatedness was the wholesale professionalization of the genre, an insidious process which many interviewees for this book initially bemoan but ultimately salute: 'If it hadn't happened, I wouldn't be sitting here now,' said one. In short, more money had been made available thanks to rock's staggering fiduciary returns in the 1970s – and new attitudes came with the lucre. The average promotional budget given to an album in America in 1971 had been $50,000; in 1975, CBS spent five times that promoting Springsteen's *Born to Run* – top-line Progressive budgets were probably comparable. The rise of FM radio in America (its cheapness of operation and reduced reliance on commercial breaks and consequent spans of uninterrupted music made it a natural outlet, if not for Progressive then for rock), which had coincided with the birth of the rock market and helped define it in Frith's terms as a community of consumers, had helped consecrate the market, and the existence of a market meant playing to it. From the debut of Frank Barsalona's Premier Talent Agency in the USA in the late 1960s, the first agency set up specifically to break rock acts, the emphasis had been on selling, and the professional etiquitte of selling, the need for a manager.

Virgin's diversification from mail-order to high-street retail to recording to distribution was another example. But the faceless bureaucrats of 'the industry' weren't the only moguls; the individualistic ethos which gave birth to Progressive and had spawned experiments like Apple and Threshold Records still bore fruit, instead of renting their equipment from others, the Who bought theirs and began renting it out themselves. By the late 1970s, they owned a substantial share in Shepperton Studios for holograph research, laser development, video and dubbing facilities – designed to expand the scope of rock 'production' even further. The assumption of sound-engineering duties by bands in the early 1970s had become an expansionism with covetous eyes on the rock industry's ancillary functions. Individualism had grown from guitar soloing to business speculation.

'The first US tour that was organized from beginning to end

in terms of fan merchandise that I know of was Yes's *Topographic* tour of America in 1973/4,' says Roger Dean.

> There was no company we could go to for tour merchandise. I organized the printing and the shipping from England and we shipped two tons of paper every other day. This was a company called Brocken who went round in a little van. We took Brocken to the States and they were dead against it. We said, 'It'll be a doddle, we're handing all this to you on a plate.' Well it wasn't a doddle, but we were handing it to them on a plate. Brocken are hauling down hundreds of millions a year now. That was the first tour that tourwide merchandise and marketing the imagery was organized on a coast-to-coast basis.'[21]

By this time the absence of multi-media marketing, of explicitly linking image to music as described by Dean had begun to be replaced by the ever more elaborate expenditure on themed visuals – such as specially designed tour programmes.

In the mid-1970s Dean capitalized on Progressive ideology when he began planning a portfolio of what were in effect its most representative visual artefacts: the *Album Cover Album*. Hipgnosis's Storm Thorgerson had a similar idea and agreed to merge the project with Dean's. The explosion of interest in LP sleeves had also opened up a flourishing graphic-art market steeped in fantasy; Abdul Mati Klarwein, H. R. Giger, Patrick Woodroffe and Rodney Matthews covered almost as much adolescent wallspace as Crown paints.

Most other merchandise still reeked of well-intentioned amateurism, Manfred Mann's Progressive outfit, the Earth Band, sold their 1973 album *The Good Earth* with a deed entitling each buyer to one square foot of Brecknockshire in Wales. Gentle Giant's *Giant for a Day* (1978) exhorted consumers to cut from the cover a mask of the band's genial mascot to 'be a giant for a day' (having already had jigsaws manufactured of the cover for their 1977 *The Missing Piece* album). Beyond button badges and posters, however, little emerged beyond uninspired variations on the themes represented on record sleeves.

Perhaps the most outrageous attempt made by rock creators to keep pace with rock production resulted, in 1977, in one of the most outlandish examples ever of hubris in rock, a dazzlingly white elephant which went under the title *Consequences*. Publicized at the time as a musical breakthrough, it has since become a forgotten monument to megalomania or bravado, according to one's musical tastes.

Consequences was a triple-album boxed set of music by multi-instrumentalist Lol Creme and drummer Kevin Godley, who left the band 10cc in late 1976 to perfect the Gizmo, a (then) revolutionary synthesizer developed in association with electronics staff at UMIST in Manchester. The rapidity with which normal synthesizer technology overtook the Gizmo's (admittedly broad, if problem-plagued) capacity for manipulating sound has led to an unfair eclipse of the instrument in rock history. Certainly Creme and Godley's unashamed deployment of it over six sides of a triple album speaks volumes of their confidence in the machine.

The album was released in October 1977 and retailed at an eyebrow-raising eleven pounds. It came with a twenty-page booklet authored by rock writer and broadcaster Paul Gambaccini, logging the evolution of the project over the previous twelve months. The Gizmo, handled by its creators, then took centre stage, along with a handful of other conventional instruments and the unlikely allied talents of the jazz diva Sarah Vaughan and the comedian Peter Cook. The tale this oddball quartet spun was effectively three concept albums in one, an account of natural elements ganging up on mankind, only to be tamed not by the power of technology but by the simple means of acoustic music. This took the form of a piano concerto 'written' by the story's musician hero, Blint, whose battles with the Establishment are satirically detailed by Cook.

Quite apart from the virtuoso–hero myth popularized by Progressive, this self-negating attitude to the technology of the musical-industrial complex then dominating rock was illuminating if a little perverse. Creme and Godley had spent the first two sides of this mammoth effort displaying the awesome power of what then seemed like that complex's ultimate product, the Gizmo, in an often-imposing orchestral impression of the uprising of nature.

The album closes, though, with Blint's concerto for acoustic piano. It testified to the continuing existence (if not exactly rude health) of the calculating, ironic instincts which had made 10cc one of the most original British pop acts of the previous four years — instincts which Creme and Godley would later carry on into pioneering work on rock videos. The packaging, a totalized and ultra-stylish concept which tended to sidestep normal Progressive aesthetic paradigms of ornament and archaism, was a cleaner, altogether more modernistic approach and was a taster of the smart satires on rock as product as consumer durable practised by the ZTT organization in the 1980s. But tragically, the pair's evangelical devotion to engineering and craftsmanship, which had been the flipside of 10cc's mastery of pop, was the most evident hangover from Creme and Godley's past, and it strangled the life out of the project. *Consequences* became, and remains, a flawed colossus.

Neither the album nor the Gizmo ever caught on; they were obliterated by punk and the hairshirt critical attitudes that followed in its wake.

Dave Laing writes,

> The generality of musicians in 1976 identified good records with expensive ones. And since the only source of adequate finance for the studio costs of a good recording was the major or large independent label, the only path to artistic success musicians could imagine lay through convincing those labels that one's own work would prove commercially viable.[22]

As Laing rightly asserts, Progressive's obsession with technology, with expertise and innovation, so wedded it to the studio and the great expense of making time-consuming recordings, that it became ever more deeply in hock to record-company capital, an arrangement that alienated audiences and made bands' own survival even more dependent on industry whim. The expansion of the record-buying market had led to a push for higher and higher sales, and commensurate investments to ensure profits and prestige. This 'platinum strategy', predicated on a push for million-selling LPs every time, reflects the truism that record companies speculate to accumulate; and as Frith points out, a million-selling example of an expensive LP will be more profitable than 50,000 sales of a cheaply made one.[23]

CBS had upped the ante in the early 1970s by increasing the advances offered to bands, increasing the numbers of sales necessary for break-even and, inevitably, the amount one had to spend on promotion. These economics affected Progressive only incidentally − some of the most striking Progressive music and imagism can be found on small independent labels far from the big-budget boys and untethered to corporate music-making; similarly, some of the most lavish industry budgets went to non-Progressive artists.

These 'rockonomics' demonstrate how a supply/demand flux forced grandiloquence on some of the practitioners of the genre while the vast majority continued to play their music in the same crummy halls and studios as everyone else. The fact that big budgets were spent by Progressive bands on Progressive vanities − the Dean Bros. stage sets for Yes, for example − cannot, however, be used as a stick to beat the genre. Fleetwood Mac, Rod Stewart, Elton John used their (bigger) budgets with just as much giganticist aplomb, but history has forgiven them.

But let us now return to Tony Palmer as surveyor of prevailing rock ideology; examination of his work is as important for a revelation of rock aesthetics as investigation of money and equipment in rock is to understanding the 1970s musico-economic context.

Palmer's cogent polemic reads curiously, post-1976−7. His repugnance at the venality of the star-making machinery reflects counter-cultural concerns, but contemporary rock-star mythology undermines his arguments. His profile of Mike Oldfield embodies all the worst aspects of this; Palmer harped on the player's continuing insistence on privacy (the result of very real and deep-seated emotional trauma) and thereby helped consecrate a Chattertonian/Romantic mythology around the sensitive, isolated young composer. Palmer's romanticized portrait was contrasted, inevitably, with the public and vulgar excesses of most rock stars' lifestyle.

In the wake of Roger Waters's well-publicized and million-selling sneers at the record industry on both *Dark Side of the Moon* and *Wish You Were Here*, the initial anti-capitalist impulse of rock had become a paranoid stasis, trapped in a gilded Weberian cage. Monied Progressive rockers still despised the industry, even as it fell over itself to advance them ever larger sums. The familiar refrains of anti-materialism – that wealth meant nothing, and was solely useful as a motor of the genius's privacy and autonomy – best exemplify the mystique generated by record companies now cognisant of the idealized, Palmerian image of the rock auteur – a generation of images which itself consumed millions of dollars. When Palmer claims that, '[Jimmy Page and] Oldfield, stand against the triviality of glitter rock ... the banality of the Osmonds,'[24] he is simply reiterating the (industry-nurtured) myth that somehow the music of Progressive musicians' albums reached their fans' turntables by a morally purer route than the music on the cheap teenybopper trannies. This revision of the Romantic-creator mythos of early Progressive rock and its strident posturing against the capital it so obviously now embodied didn't end there; there was also cultural legitimation to be had from the likes of the *Sunday Times*'s venerable rock and jazz critic (at that time a position akin to being the organizer of discos for the MCC) Derek Jewell, whose hyperbole grew with the dimensions of the Progressive fancies he droolingly lauded. 'Richly they [Pink Floyd] deserve their place among the symphonic overlords of today's popular hierarchy ... they reeled off, apparently effortlessly, a performance with musical textures so ravishing and visual accompaniment so surprising that, for once, the thunderous standing ovation was completely justified.'[25] This on a 1974 concert which guitarist Dave Gilmour recalled as 'probably the worst we've done on the whole tour'.[26]

The pre-Progressive bourgeois youth adoption of jazz and art-school aesthetics, the consciously slumming aspirations to lower-class values and styles, had now become a new middle-class aspiration governed by material privilege. The play ethic of the late 1960s had been replaced by a studio-bound work ethic. While this would produce unique and excellent music, it also produced a sessionman-virtuoso culture. Two of the most regrettable manifestations of these phenomena were 'project' albums and a renewed interest in supergroups.

MONEY TO BURN? SUPERGROUP STRATEGY, ELP, GENESIS AND YES

Between 1975 and 1979 a host of 'superstar project' concepts appeared: a rock *Peter and the Wolf*, Andrew Lloyd-Webber signing up Jon Hiseman's reborn Colosseum II for his *Variations* album (1978), a jazz-rocked-up rerun of the famous Paganini Caprice. Mandalaband, a colossal white elephant of a group, having cut a reasonable debut album in 1975, went supernova in 1978, assuming the mantle of supergroup manqué, bringing in all of Barclay James Harvest, 10cc (hadn't they learned from Ramases?) and seemingly half the musicians in the north of England to cut *The Eye of Wendor: Prophecies*, the first (disastrous) part of a mercifully aborted Tolkien-inspired trilogy. This is (unfortunately) not to forget Jeff Wayne's *War of the Worlds* double-set. An album remarkably consistent in its tedium, it was a homogenized musical package which was to adults in 1978 what *Saturday Night Fever* and *Grease* were to their children.

The accredited, post-Cream supergroups weren't far behind. Every week the press resonated with some rumoured collaboration between unattached Progressive players, perhaps the most famous being a triumvirate of John Wetton, Bill Bruford (both ex-KC) and Rick Wakeman, splashed prematurely in an October 1976 *Melody Maker*, a PR glitch that effectively killed it. 'Although for the first time I was actually writing entire songs,' confides Bruford twenty years on. 'And to be fair, Rick did incredibly interesting things with that material. We couldn't get Rick out of his house, though, he was trying to avoid someone.'[27] Wetton and Bruford would later play in the UK, 'an alliance between two jazz guys, me and Allan [Holdsworth, guitarist], and two pop guys, Eddie [Jobson, violinist/keyboardist with Roxy Music and Curved Air among others] and John'.[28] The resultant eponymous album (1978) was, perhaps predictably, an uneven affair.

But what had enjoyed novelty value in the late 1960s – the exponential growth of new technologies, new ways of thinking and new techniques in music against a perceived background of beneficent social change – became old hat in the 1970s. But the often overlooked irony about 1977, a time which according to rock *epos* slew the chimera of Progressive, was that Progressive bands sold more albums than ever that year. Yes and ELP, who had been out of the public eye for nigh on two years, strolled back into the casino and hit the jackpot. Yes's *Going for the One* was their first ever British No. 1 album; ELP cashed in by releasing two albums, the Top Ten *Works Vol. 1* in March, and its follow-up, *Works Vol. 2*, in December.

But the real jackpot-sweepers during the superstars' R'n'R were Genesis, for so long the Cinderella of Progressive, who established themselves as stars, if not in terms of musical originality then in terms of sheer bravura. Genesis weren't regarded as dinosaurs. They sang surreally of contemporary concerns, their music emotionally charged but never overripe. But Gabriel's abrupt departure in 1975 had even the friendly critics composing obituaries for the band. At first, noises about their continuing were muted; it wasn't until the release of Steve Hackett's first solo album, *Voyage of the Acolyte*, in the autumn of 1975 that the band re-emerged with the announcement that drummer Phil Collins – who had already handled a few vocal duties for the band, particularly during Gabriel's more outrageous on-stage calisthenics during *The Lamb* show – was now Gabriel's permanent replacement.

Hackett's album helped reinvent Genesis. Tony Stratton-Smith remembers: 'It was a very useful indicator to everyone that interest in Genesis was still at a very high level.'[29] Despite initial critical uncertainty – many of the opinion that Hackett was overly anonymous – the resulting album assumed its place as a Progressive classic. In some places melodic inspiration – and mix – pall.

But musical conservatism doesn't devalue the gentle delicacy and economy of means prevalent in tracks like 'Hands of the Priestess', a gorgeous theme picked out by twelve-string, flute and Mellotron, an instrument which dominates the album; its string mode was rarely less melodramatically but more effectively utilized. The sonorities obtained are uniquely nostalgic and autumnal, and when used in tandem with woodwind, particularly on the exquisite 'Star of Sirius', the effect is simply breathtaking (in a style that the Moody Blues spent an entire career trying – and failing – to master). Hackett's own playing is typically idiosyncratic, utilizing a few arpeggios here, a busy cascade of notes there; mostly his prodigious gifts manifest themselves, as usual, through well-timed use of effects and pedals.

The undemonstratively lyrical compositions of *Voyage* helped prepare a sceptical public for the new Genesis lineup which appeared on the album *A Trick of the Tail* in February 1976, to unanimous surprise and delight. A crafty and well-crafted album, *Trick* finally expels the boxy sound the band had endured hitherto; in Genesis biographer Armando Gallo's words, 'Finally you can hear the drums!'[30] Collins's vocals, more fragile and vulnerable than Gabriel's, clean up the sound still further. *Abbey Road*-style harmonies mingle with Chopinesque piano chords; the emphasis, as on the follow-up, *Wind and Wuthering*, is on consonant, scholarly extended pop which continues to mine the emotional seams of its predecessor.

Josephson, in a dazzling analysis of the track 'One for the Vine', points out that the Baroque/sacred progressions of the band's earlier music are now bolstered by techniques drawn from early Romanticism – he highlights the developmental process applied to the piece's initial themes and compares them (again somewhat grandiloquently) with Beethoven's Fifth Symphony, in method if not mastery. The opulence of the sound is polished by David Hentschel's engineering to enhance the orchestral illusion.

Bill Bruford depped for Collins on stage: 'I didn't care for the music because I'd had no input into it. It was the first time I was ever a hired gun, with no say in the music. But playing it on tour was fine.'[31]

Gabriel's influence was purged. The band also enjoyed first-class management strategy: their new music courted old and new fans alike, a tie-in tour was timed to perfection, and then to consolidate their popularity, *Wind and Wuthering* was cut and released to support a vast world tour. And despite an early critical mauling of Bruford's replacement on drums, the American jazzer Chester Thompson, the band's January tour of England (including the cleverly publicized reopening of London's Rainbow Theatre – another managerial masterstroke – on New Year's Day), was hysterically received, progress mirrored throughout the world until the end of the tour in June.

The show was visually dazzling, but also well-drilled, neither a minute too long nor a minute too short. There were no ELP-style histrionics, just a superbly staged impression of mothership-scale power. 'Genesis simply power forward, carrying all before them,' gushed a young Ian Cranna of the *NME*.[32]

Emulating the vogue for live double-albums in the wake of Peter Frampton's multi-platinum 1976 chart-buster *Frampton Comes Alive*, Genesis's own live double, *Seconds Out*, released in October 1977, was inevitable. Even as the Ramones, the Clash and the Pistols grabbed the headlines around them, Genesis still got the plaudits. '*Seconds Out* might just be the greatest live album ever,' the *NME*'s Phil McNeill reported solemnly.[33]

Bloodier-minded Genesis fans regard *Seconds Out* as the studio tracks with clapping. And it is fair to admit that there is a certain perfunctoriness in several numbers, not least the tooling rendition of 'Supper's Ready'. There is a sense that Genesis had really gone as far as they could go with *Seconds Out*, unable to top their pre-existing visual or sonic achievements. There is also the lingering sense that a little too much of *Seconds Out* is contrived, played and put on to vinyl only as part of the Master Plan which had taken them so successfully from Gabriel onwards and would continue to propel them upwards into the megastar bracket.

And Steve Hackett left. The guitarist reflected: 'I just didn't think there were enough risks being taken with the form or the content of the songs.'[34] But what of it? As their next album, *And Then There were Three* (1978), would prove (particularly, and tellingly, in the anodyne US market), Genesis knew they could live without Hackett, and that they might even go on and take over the planet.

Another beneficiary of the big-name furloughs was Jethro Tull. The critics who had so piqued Anderson in 1973 did not, *pace* common opinion, diminish Anderson's horizons; the band turned their attention to a projected film, *War Child*, which never got beyond the talking stage but appeared as an album in 1974. The tendency towards shorter, self-contained songs reconciled Anderson and his tormentors, and the band returned to the stage. But the metric and harmonic experiments of the *Benefit* and *Aqualung* periods, grossly inflated in 1972–3, returned with a vengeance and with an artful refinement that possibly constituted some of Tull's, and Progressive's, most intriguing music.

The band's signature discontinuities of verse-refrain structures found more concise utterance on *Minstrel in the Gallery* (1975), a searching and accomplished effort. Diffuseness was now distilled into a sprightly, idiosyncratic collection of powerful numbers. Verses are of varying lengths, eschewing regular patterns, and the irregularity of the rhythm section's accompaniment becomes more and more extreme. Allan Moore suggests that the technique of additive rhythms, pioneered on *Benefit* ('so-called because they do not derive from taking a temporal unit – a bar – and dividing it into equal portions, but from taking a smallest possible unit and adding together an unspecified number of these to produce generally uneven-length beats')[35] proceeds to a level unmatched elsewhere in rock. By way of illustration, he cites the swingeing, cavalier 'Cold Wind to Valhalla', which 'switches between 4 and 6 beats per bar, while the instrumental interpolation consists of 4½ – effectively extending each bar'.[36]

In addition, I would suggest that Tull's ability to transpose themes texturally and melodically is the key to explaining the greater emotional intensity of the music – notably the decorative riffs of the title track and the bluesy four-square refrain derived from the complex introduction, and compounded riffs adding melodic and rhythmic interest to 'Black Satin Dancer'. New textures are quickly established, the most salient being the folksy acoustic guitar piloting a course through the album, with lower-string lines and chordal rhythmic upper-string accompaniment.

These tones were underplayed in 1976, the year of the ill-favoured and ill-starred *Too Old to Rock and Roll, Too Young to Die*, an aborted theatrical conceit; but 1977 treated the band well. *Songs from the Wood*, a refocusing of the folk influence, shifted shiploads; cued by *Minstrel*, the barbed, rickety grandeur that Tull had left behind with *Benefit* had been rebottled in punchy numbers with enough melodic contours to satisfy latterday FM-radio demands. Once again, the band's riffs are unremarkable, but counterpointed – such as with synthesizers playing off mandolin on the title track – and the impact is mesmerizing. The melodies are little more than fragments, but these hold together fleeting riffs and chords (soloing is very restricted, but the apparent independence of the bass/drums unit, constantly reinventing lines underneath straightforward structures, is among the most radical phenomena in mainstream rock). The soundstage is deeper by far than anything the band had created before; the introduction to the title track is, as Moore points out, miraculously refined, with glockenspiel and flute ornamenting parallel a capella voices in multiple metre.[37] The folk element, emphasized in the lyrics, re-establishes itself. Hooks are plentiful, but insubstantial, and the riffs are shared around the ensemble with frightening skill.

Tull were then handed the honour of playing the first gig ever transmitted by satellite from the USA to the UK in September 1978. Within a year, however, they would be just another beached whale abandoned by a changing musical tide with the unaccommodating *Stormwatch* album, and the band would split up, leaving only Anderson and Martin Barre to pick up the pieces and start again.

Anderson's pre-eminence within the ranks of the band was winning him few friends beyond it. Jethro Tull were among the 'blackest' of the *bêtes noires* singled out for punk retribution in 1977. It is difficult to deny that Anderson's lordly helmsmanship of the group had something to do with this. While never characterized in the same hippy-with-the-iron-hand terms as his namesake Jon Anderson, he became identified with the *auteur*-as-autocrat ethos. Punk's iconoclasm marked out Anderson's high-profile benevolent despotism as a prime target. The actual personification of Jethro Tull in the eyes of many neutral onlookers, to many in the rock community he had started actually to embody this personalized role. His touchiness at dissent, so well catalogued with the débâcle over *Thick as a Brick*, among others, didn't help. Despite eloquent and well-argued testimony for the defence, he was consigned to the rock aristocracy. Steve Clarke, in an uncompromising *NME* review of Tull's *Heavy Horses* (1978), mocked Anderson's opinions on the fate of the shire horse: 'One wonders how many fields he's had to plough in his time.'[38]

And how would Yes adapt? Would they bother? Their *Going for the One* (1977) was launched right into the crucible of the 'summer of Punk' and yet sold in millions and even featured a hit single. All this from a band who had deserted the studio for nearly three years; it must once again be repeated that in 1976–7, in a punitive era of short-term contracts and record company dominance, this was indicative of truly Imperial indulgence.

But contrary to received mythology, the music press came not to bury but to praise. 'A triumphant return,' fawned *Melody Maker*'s Chris Welch.[39] Phil McNeill in the *NME* was more measured:

> It's probably too late now for Yes to start making music which sounds like anything except ... the outpourings of some failed Royal College of Music entrant – which is a shame, because *Going for the One* shows Yes are potentially still a great band, even if they do misuse their abilities most of the time ... at no time does this album become overly pretentious or verbose or tedious.[40]

The cute Anderson ballad 'Turn of the Century', with its glorious Spanish guitar and piano dialogues, is a masterstroke of textural finesse. From Anderson's chromatic monody, harmonies arc developed with extraordinary sensitivity, although the decentred nature of the piece seems to result from the musicians having to strain to fit phrases to Anderson's phrasing of the lines, a problem which had first become apparent on *Topographic*. Indeed, melodies are few and far between; Andersonian chants, elaborately harmonized, or riff-scraps, such as the four-note chorale which underpins 'Parallels', dominate, with extra emphasis on a thick orchestration of state-of-the-art electronics, notably the foregrounding of the orchestrating brilliance of the prodigal Wakeman.

'Parallels' is a bullying piece of music-making which careers along with intimidating speed and violence, culminating contrapuntally in one of Yes's most adrenalized climaxes yet. The finale, the sixteen-minute 'Awaken', was spliced into three parts, featuring alternating downward or upward riffs and suitably falling or climbing decorations – including a bizarrely Baroque-postmodern middle section featuring Wakeman's pipe organ (actually recorded over the phone from a church in Vevey, four miles from the studio in Montreux, Switzerland). With White's handbells and Anderson's harp, the piece was truly orchestral in its sweep.

Unfortunately it also lends the music an air of contrivance; there's a hyper-arranged feel about it. On *Olias*, that was fair enough – the whole album had been conceived as a one-man-and-his-studio experiment and possessed enough organic unity to work as such – but 'Awaken' was curiously misshapen, and the interesting questions raised by *Relayer* about whether or not rock should be an entity that lived and died in immediate perform-ance – whether rock's art lay in calculation or spontaneity – was swamped by overextended vocal phrasings (words and music at war again?) and empty Baroque flourishes which only led the listener to question what better material such decoration might have obscured.

Enthusiasm for the band, however, showed little sign of abating. By 1978 they were in the shops again, this time with *Tormato*, but this time they came to grief. Sales were mediocre, and although gigs at London's Wembley Arena that October duly sold out, they couldn't dispel a feeling of foreboding. Steve Clarke wrote peevishly (and, as it turned out, with alarming prescience) that 'one couldn't help but get the feeling that in fifteen years' time Yes will be here again, this time celebrating twenty-five years in the business'.[41] The 'Yes in the Round' concept, placing the band on a revolving stage in the centre of the auditorium, was plagued by hitches, the stage once turning through only 180 degrees before the mass of understage wiring became hopelessly fouled. One evening, the stage's motors burned out and twenty people were commandeered from the first two rows to push the thing around.

The band had, damagingly, split with Eddie Offord, who had, in Steve Howe's judgement,

> become unreliable ... on tours, Eddie could do that crowd over, but he could also let us down and give us a shit sound. We did manage to keep a good rapport, even though he was leaping around like a maniac half the time, but it got to the point where we didn't think it was very funny any more.[42]

But Offord had a knack of bringing out the best in musicians; with his departure Yes lost the vital source of restraint that had prevented their five egos warring unmanageably. Offord sighed to the press that producing Yes was like 'trying to produce five producers'.[43] The cloying whiff of excess and decadence on *Going for the One* becomes, on *Tormato*, a shiver of wan indecision and lassitude; both are diminished by the disappearance of Roger Dean's designs from the album covers. Yes, devoid of one of their most immediately recognizable trademarks, suddenly became just another band.

ELP too returned from obscurity into the Punk maelstrom with a loudly-trumpeted album and a loudly-trumpeted surprise hit single, but they also returned to loudly-trumpeted raspberries.

What prompted ELP to do what they did to their listeners, their critics and ultimately themselves in 1977 can only be guessed at. What is certain is that it consigned them to eternal rock notoriety. Even discounting Punk, had not the musical climate changed enough to convince them that epics were out of fashion, both on record and in concert? Apparently not; practically their entire comeback was conducted in clodhoppingly stereotypical tradition.

First up was a double-album entitled *Works*; if this wasn't pretentious enough, the subtitle *Vol. 1* promised more excesses to come. Containing a paltry one side of group work, the rest was taken up with the fancies of band members; Keith Emerson even performed his own Piano Concerto. After originally planning (and then axing) gigs in England as part of a series of concerts to celebrate the Queen's Silver Jubilee, they didn't play a single UK concert during 1977, although they appeared happily enough in the characteristically futuristic and architecturally overblown Olympic Stadium in Montreal with their spacious version of Copland's 'Fanfare for the Common Man'.

Whimper followed bang in December when *Works Vol. 2* (mercifully, only a single album) appeared. Greg Lake himself had forecast all this turgidity in March 1977: 'We've been working ... in Montreux. The trouble is it's a hard environment to create in. It's so grey. There's nothing there. You get sod-all inspiration.'[44]

Perhaps such venal utterances – mirroring the music- were merely ELP's ironic goads to the punks who goaded them, but humour was never ELP's strong suit. The band threatened to wax litigious when *Gay Times* ran an ad based very loosely on an outline illustration of Emerson and Palmer from the inside sleeve of *Trilogy*, their 1972 album. Stories of excess continued to abound, most unproven but few denied. Lake, it was said, kept live lobsters in his bath to feed a seafood habit, installed urinals to obviate the strain of lifting toilet seats and, on being asked by a connoisseur friend about his wine of choice to accompany a meal, replied, 'the most expensive.' Declares Pete Sinfield,

> Gregory is a classically vulgar person. ELP ... weren't brave enough to be funny. They had to have all this bombast which covered up this fear of not winning. Often at cost. For *Tarkus* onstage, they had giant robot armadillos, spewing out polystyrene snow, which filled up the innards of the grand piano one night at Brighton. Keith had the guts to say: 'We

seem to have a small problem here.' And the roadies took the entire piano apart and put it back together, to *vast* cheers. After *twenty* minutes! But having said that, they could take themselves so *terribly* seriously. They really thought that they were the aristocracy of rock. They would expect people to come over to their table. But they didn't mix well with the rest of the business and it had to do with the whole ethos of ELP.[45]

The next wheeze was to tour North America with a full-scale orchestra, a financial calamity which some saw as little more than comeuppance for the band's brimming arrogance. Sinfield says:

They should never have taken [the orchestra] on the road. Keith wanted to play his concerto on the road and Stewart Young [the manager] allowed himself to be bullied. They lost thousands. Godfrey Salmon, who put the orchestra together, was amazingly brave. There were moments of sheer joy when it worked, though – like during a power failure at Madison Square Garden.[46]

Works Vol. 1 is not without merit, though, and Emerson's stab at a concerto competent enough. Having intelligently ingested and understood the rhythmic and melodic angularity of Bartók and Prokofiev, Emerson's virtuosity is never less than impressive, and once in this setting it sits easier upon the musical stage than it does in ELP's rockier workouts. Carl Palmer's contribution is flashy but negligible, and Greg Lake seems content merely to spin out a few more dowdy songs.

Originally, Emerson had wanted Leonard Bernstein to conduct the orchestra for his concerto. Bernstein duly materialized at the band's rehearsal studio in Paris, sweeping into the studio with camel-hair coat and entourage. After a while, however, he raised his hand and said, 'Stop! How can you be so primitive?' Sinfield remembers:

Sometimes what Keith wanted to do with the classics did work, sometimes the Lenny-babys of this world said we were primitive. Oh, and *Works*, the title ... was my idea. I suppose if you're gonna be pretentious, you might as well do it big. They had all these bits floating around. But 'Bits' didn't really sound right. Let's face it, I could have done worse. I could have called it 'Opuses', or 'Opi'.[47]

Even Progressive militants have trouble defending *Vol. 2*, although 'When the Apple Blossoms Bloom in the Windmills of Your Mind' does have a perverse charm. 'Tiger in a Spotlight', however, a cheesy plod, shows just how low the band's collective inspiration had sunk. If further evidence were needed, 1978's *Love Beach* marked the final detonation of ELP's heat-death. Recorded in Nassau, the album sports a cover showing the trio, medallion-emblazoned chests bared, posing on a palm-fringed beach, looking, as Ian Penman of the *NME* put it, 'as though they were being chased by a giant Barry Gibb'.[48]

Pete Sinfield suggests:

We all became far too technical for our abilities. We had a certain vision of pushing the envelope – what an awful expression – lost the plot, and were spoilt by the decadence. We were hugely popular in the US – and in Japan especially. Because they saw us as being brave, and, in a very simplified classical form, different. We were seen to be trying. The problem was we failed so often. But trying at least, I suppose, is important.'[49]

NEW DIRECTIONS FOR OLD?

Progressive rock – known pejoratively by the mid-1970s as 'techno' or 'flash' rock to differentiate it from its sibling heavy rock, which had shared the 'Progressive' umbrella in the late 1960s – had been sold to a generation on its subversion of established cultural norms – commercialism, suburban gentility ... now, irrespective of the actuality of such revolutionary attributes, it stood to have them, and its entire *raison d'être*, appropriated by another. How would it come to terms? How would it – how could it – go on Progressing?

Phil Collins claims:

> I thought punk was a great idea – like someone shaking an apple tree until all the bad ones fell off and you'd just got the good ones left ... I never thought of [Genesis] as being like Yes, ELP, Tull or Floyd, so when they came along and said, 'All that lot are crap,' I was agreeing with them and then found that they thought we were like that too, which was a drag ... we were more open and direct'.[50]

Anyone listening to the material that Genesis took on tour with them in 1977 might justifiably demur; while the Blakean stormlight and Tchaikovskian intervals of 'Firth of Fifth' and 'Supper's Ready' come across delivered with chilling power and disarming grace, it is hardly music that might readily have been chanted on Chelsea or Leeds football terraces.

Collins was among those who sought a new direction for Progressive with his espousal of jazz in the fusion band Brand X. An in-demand sessioneer by 1975, he encountered bassist Percy Jones, an alumnus of the Liverpool Scene, guitarist John Goodsall and keyboard player Robin Lumley (a distant relative of Joanna's) and the four set themselves up as Brand X.

A rock subculture which prided itself on technical ability such as British Progressive rock had been won over by US developments in jazz-rock fusion. This took the blueprint of Miles Davis's exotic and atmospheric melange of jazz harmonies and rock voicings and rhythms in the late 1960s and used the flexibility of harmonic and rhythmic language to foreground star soloists within a distinctive and controlled idiom. Simon Hopkins has since written perceptively that its chief exponents, keyboardist Chick Corea and guitarist John McLaughlin (an émigré alumnus of the Brit R&B scene that had produced many Progressive musicians), were in a way too compositionally gifted, and reduced the fluidity of Davis's polycultural sonic explorations to overly academic and Western-looking symphonic-scale frames for individual flair.[51]

McLaughlin and a swarm of US Davis-wannabes picked up considerable airplay and record sales in the UK, and provided most musicians of the epoch with a benchmark of technical proficiency not witnessed since Cream. Musicians everywhere knew that the goalposts had been shifted — now, if a guy could play like McLaughlin, a guy had a chance. Seeing the possibility of cashing in on the jazz-rock boom, Charisma offered Brand X's peculiarly English take on the style, with their curiously sedate melodies standing out oddly against the furious barrage of light-speed solos — after a few impromptu jams. The ninths, elevenths, unison lines and limpid arrangements redolent of US jazz-rock were offset by strangely mannered poppy chords and verse-chorus structures on their first album, *Unorthodox Behaviour* (1976). But onstage the band were transformed, jettisoning structure for lengthy and atmospheric extemporizations on riffs and semi-riffs, supported by the swaying fretless basslines of Jones, the intricacies of percussion maestro Morris Pert and prettified by fireworks from Goodsall — possibly the most underrated rock guitarist of all time — and Lumley's keyboards — heavily influenced by the Mahavishnu Orchestra's Jan Hammer — ensured that the band's stage priorities were atmosphere, contrast of mood and melodic elasticity.

Their second album, *Moroccan Roll*, was issued in the glare of publicity that surrounded Collins and Genesis in the first half of 1977 and suffered not a bit for it. Musically, however, it didn't distinguish itself much from its predecessor, although much of Goodsall's work was again electrifying. One somewhat irksome characteristic of the album was its inauguration of a vein of self-indulgent humour. Presumably this was introduced to 'humanize' the band in the light of Punk's assault on the lofty citadels associated with 'musicianship'. Brand X were photographed puffing rollups, lounging or lolling around, or laddishly clowning in everyday clobber.

Not that this affected the band's live album, brought out simultaneously with Genesis's *Seconds Out* that autumn. *Livestock* brilliantly spotlighted the band's improvising talents. Particularly notable was Collins's 'Isis Mourning' and John Goodsall's beautifully languid 'Euthanasia Waltz'. 'Ish', by Percy Jones, was a superbly directionless piece of abstract spacefunk.

The combination of jazz inflections and improvisatory zeal reimported into rock from the States should have cleared the decks for the revolutionary notions of the Canterbury and alternative crew; after all, hadn't Daevid Allen and Hugh Hopper, the men who'd kicked off the whole Canterbury crowd in the 1960s, been noted jazzers?

The Canterbury cosmology, however, from the severe, ascetic geometries of Henry Cow to the blissed-out solos of guitarist Steve Hillage, used improvisation less as a solo endeavour than as an interactive catalyst, which was in direct opposition to the increasing contemporary obsession with individualism. It had, indeed, nurtured its own brand of fusion since Soft Machine's Proms pomp and had spawned allied bands of minimal melodic excitement but maximal technical difficulty (both in composition and performance), such as Isotope and Gilgamesh.

This was in reaction to such disappointments and embodiments of epigonism as Soft Machine's *Bundles* (1975), which were signs of a general retreat into the musicianly arcana of speed and 'difficulty' at the cost of compositional ingenuity. Allan Holdsworth's opening guitar solo may clock in at an avalanching seven minutes, but this does not excuse a reduction of the band's music to a simple mainstream-jazz chorus–solo–chorus regimen dolled up in flashy new electric trappings, and a regimentation of their pop-soul themes to rules already being careworn by their American fusion creators.

Yet another band determined to explore the comparisons and contrasts between jazz and rock were Isotope, whose attention to virtuosity and precision matched the Softs' but presented the listener with an altogether more forbidding prospect. Their three albums featured phenomenally concentrated and harmonically extreme jazz-rock, in which the chief interests were Hugh Hopper's bass playing and the ever more complicated relation of melody to metre. Hopper also turned up on two albums by another twice-removed Canterbury band, Gilgamesh, whose keyboard player Alan Gowen pledged himself to the notion that the improvised and composed elements of his music should be indistinguishable to the listener. But by now the early fondness for improvisation as a determinant of the relations between soloist and ensemble was being abandoned – nothing new in jazz, but in jazz-rock the parameters were still being set, the moral high ground there for the taking. This retreat to more conventionally organized writing was not a bad thing *per se* (particularly in the face of the irresistible US jazz-rock assault), provided the soloists were of a suitably original stamp; this was the aim of one of the more raucous and (temporarily) more popular post-Softs lineups, National Health.

'National Health,' says Bill Bruford, 'were a very European-directed rock group. The first time I came across written charts. Not jazz or purporting to be, but a genuine white European rock.'[52] A creature of the amiable ongoing chaos of Canterbury players both original and *parvenu*, they were directly descended from campus favourites Hatfield and the North.

Formed in 1972, the Hatfields further refined the decentred mentality of the many 'Canterbury' and more left-field Progressive acts already cited. The informal aspect of many of these acts and the consistent interchange of personnel made for a fertile musical environment in which ideas were more or less constantly in circulation around many different players. The core Hatfields were Richard Sinclair (bass, vocals, ex-Caravan), Phil Miller (guitar, ex-Matching Mole), Dave Stewart (keyboards) and Pip Pyle (drums, erstwhile Gong sideman) and they formed a loosely co-operative pool, generating a productive flux of concepts: Dadaist humour (in the band's name, taken from 'the first signpost on the M1'),[53] to song titles like 'Fitter Stokes Has a Bath', 'Gigantic Land Crabs in Earth Takeover Bid', 'Walking Up to People and Tinkling' etc.), chromatic harmony, free and simultaneous improvisation, jazz chord progressions.

Stewart, who had kept improvisation at arm's length in Egg, took on a much freer role – perhaps understandably given the flexible nature of live performances, which coupled extemporizing fluidity and compositional discipline with a delightful invention to allow the integration of other musicians. The accommodation of the four Hatfields (not to omit their female backing singers, the Northettes, one of whom, Barbara Gaskin, would later become Stewart's artistic and domestic partner) seemed to extend the developmental abilities of each musician. The Hatfields' non-album track 'Clocks and Clouds' nods, at the very least titularly, to György Ligeti, and demonstrates the band's modernist pedigree.

National Health's eponymous debut album, released in summer 1977, received good notices and retains an askew charm, dominated by a wheezy, rough-and-reedy sound at odds with the amniotic sybaritism of most Progressive production jobs at the time. The inventive material has been criticized for its excessive compositional rigour, particularly 'Borogoves' and 'Tenemos Roads' which, despite nimble ensemble work and languorous, lush instrumental interludes of an agreeably modal stamp, develop from initial statements of tonality through complex thematic developments in major and minor keys – often based on tempo changes – which enable soloists Phil Miller (guitar), Alan Gowen (keyboards) and Stewart to create delicious effects combining double-take rhythms and adventurous soloing. This naturally discourages the traditional soloists' trick of using downbeats to emphasize climactic releases, and the chromatic musical language allows the soloists greater leeway while retaining at least some loyalty to the compositions' harmonic sequences. In Allan Moore's opinion, the language of this and other similar bands can best be exemplified by using short contrary-motion periodic development in melody and bassline, separated by ninths or sevenths with jazzy harmonies filling in the remaining spaces.[54]

'I never really believed in English jazz-rock,' declares Stewart in the 1990s. 'I think that the only thing we had going for us was that compositionally we could hold our own.'[55] The degree of communication between the rock and jazz milieux at the time can best be illustrated by reference to guitarist Allan Holdsworth, who in the space of a year (1976–7) recorded jazz-rock with Soft Machine and with New York sessionmen under his own name, as well as cutting a meltingly delicate album of guitar–piano duets with archetypal jazzer Gordon Beck, before ploughing blithely on into the Progressive supergroup UK.

But by the mid-1970s rock structures were becoming more salient even in the music of Henry Cow, notably on 'War', which opens *In Praise of Learning*; the tendency can also be heard on Cow's live *Concerts* album, culled from a pan-European tour embarked upon after a split with Virgin Records. Was this a reversal of the trends in mainstream Progressive, a lurch rockwards when mainstream rock musicians were lurching towards jazz?

Hardly, when one considers the vitriolic split with the increasingly commercially-minded Branson and his expansionist Virgin.

The band's political outlook changed not at all. 'It was hard, it was hell,' Chris Cutler said of that time. 'But it was wonderful ... we did things, and were satisfied with the results ... we were living absolutely 160 per cent and examining most things most of the time.'[56] Cellist Georgie Born remembers the collectivized dynamic of the band (only unanimous decisions allowed, often through countless hours of debate) as a phenomenon encompassing 'very serious issues concerned with abuses of power'.[57] Cutler himself admits that 'the women probably got oppressed by the men'.[58]

Born herself had replaced bassist John Greaves, who'd quit, exhausted by the demands of the Cow lifestyle, in 1976. But the Cow and their associates ambled on through a Europe riven with ideological dissent; terrorism in Italy and an onstage attack on Lou Reed in 1975 prevented foreign acts playing there for a while, but Henry Cow got in, paid for by leftist local municipalities, playing to huge 'and totally diffuse' publics at cultural festivals.[59]

The Eurocommunist heyday of decentralized socialism was afoot, a semi-organized distillation of the spirit of 1968 which pitched the small and beautiful against the centralized and ugly, and Cutler, Krause and friends were part of the period's soundtrack. Robert Wyatt, now wheelchair-bound, was along for the ride, and the band included a number of his compositions

('Gloria Gloom' and 'Little Red Robin Hood Hit the Road') in their increasingly intense live repertoire. 'Beautiful as the Moon', which makes up side 1 of Henry Cow's *Concerts* as part of a medley with 'Terrible as an Army with Banners', continued to be developed, according to one observer, with some live performances stretching it some forty minutes.[60]

The Punk phenomenon was of little interest to these musicians; aside of the steepling financial difficulties besetting Henry Cow at the time, the populism of Punk left a sour taste; Wyatt recalls that for the Cow, 'radical politics had to have a radical language'.[61] Cutler later told Patrick Wright: 'If you want to talk about being progressive, you can't treat people as though they only respond to banalities ... progressive content in a reactionary form marks a real collapse in contemporary art culture.'[62]

Henry Cow themselves split in 1978, with the words 'We will not settle into the role of being Henry Cow and reproducing our past to earn our pensions.'[63] Cutler's permanent revolution was alive and well, though. With Frith and Krause he formed the Art Bears, a band whose harshness of musical language might not have seemed out of place in 1978, but whose exploitation of extant studio techniques, not least in the webs of electronics and analogue multi-tracking that skein their debut *Hopes and Fears*, betrays a fully up-to-the-minute fascination with studio technology that locates them at the cutting edge of contemporary rock musicianship.

There were attempts at reconciliation between Punk and Progressive. Negotiations were tentatively broached at a skatepark under Notting Hill's Westway flyover. John Peel remembers the semi-legendary Punk propagandist and devotee of disruption Mark Perry lining up his Alternative TV crew (proto-Dadaists all) alongside a shambolic Notting Hill pick-up outfit (both in terms of personnel and musical influences) called Here and Now at a benefit for said skatepark in 1978;[64] later that year the same pairing would headline the Stonehenge Free Festival with Inner City Unit, formed by ex-Hawkwind saxist and singer Nik Turner.

Turner's *Sphinx Xitintoday* (1977) crystallized this bizarre alliance of riffing brotherhood, buoying his bully-boy sax and declaimed choruses upon a synthesized orgy of swooning sound from Gong alumni Steve Hillage (guitar) and Tim Blake (keyboards).

History has still not adequately catalogued the reasons for the *rapprochement* between Perry ('This is a chord. This is another. This is another. Now go out and form a band')[65] and the transcendence of the hippyism Punk allegedly never trusted. But read logically, the gurgling density, motivic simplicity and essentially disorganized sound created by the Hawkwind/Hillage axis should have appealed to thinking punks.

Hillage's work will be discussed later in the examination of another counter-culture, but his stubborn liking for rumbustious, saturated sounds even amidst the perfumed delicacy of his melodies and the astronomics of occultism he brought to both his lyrical and musical procedures (mantric utterance was big with Steve) contrasted with axe-hero riffing to garner grassroots kudos. Hippy culture had left a residue, a rump of diehards for whom enlightenment could only mean rock of a specifically 1960s derivation. They may have bought the stylizations of Yes and Genesis, but salvation was through the guitar and the effects box. Given that much of this music could trace at least some of its parentage to counter-cultural leftovers in west London (the unfinished dope uprisings of Hawkwind, the Pink Fairies and the Deviants) was it so surprising, in the decade of little-man defensiveness, Liberal Party councillor Chrissie Mayer's community politics (these bands were community bands, after all), E. F. Schumacher's 'Small is Beautiful' philosophy and others, that the scruffiest legacy of Progressive – its disadvantaged, dandruffed sibling – should have listed towards the similarly disaffected shout of Punk's more culturally active footsoldiers? Perry and his followers wanted chaos; Hillage and Here and Now the New Jerusalem. It must have seemed to both camps like a fairly profitable dialectic.

NEW DIRECTIONS FOR OLD: TEXTUAL REORIENTATIONS POST-1976

The first major Progressive album to appear after the first public exposure of Punk in autumn 1976 was Pink Floyd's *Animals* (February 1977). The band had nurtured a relationship of singular ambiguity with the press ever since the mammoth success of *Dark Side of the Moon*. *Wish You Were Here*'s even more jaundiced worldview seemed like Roger Waters's prickly riposte to accusations of ivory-towerism, and *Animals*, despite its well-publicized budget and gimmicks (the giant inflatable pig Hipgnosis set up for the cover art breaking from its moorings above Battersea Power Station and floating across London) seemed to go some way to consolidating this confrontation with life in the 1970s as it was lived by mere mortals.

A more credible and ultimately more durable stab at productively marrying musical relevance with lyrical creativity was undertaken by Peter Gabriel. Since his backdoor escape from Genesis in 1975, Gabriel had retreated to his home at Bath, 'making babies and growing cabbages'.[66] A projected rock opera called *Mozo* tardily took shape but disintegrated; by this time, though, a first solo album was already in the can. Charisma hooked its release up to the Genesis publicity juggernaut rolling in the wake of the *Wind and Wuthering* album and tour in spring 1977. With a favourable response from a somewhat confounded critical community, Gabriel felt the time was right to reappear to his public, and took the album on the road.

The path chosen was logical enough; the retreat from hippy-trippy pastoralism embodied by his pre-*The Lamb* work was extended into a yet leaner, sparer musical landscape which, despite exquisite lyrical interludes like 'Here Comes the Flood', intimated more King Crimson density than Genesis delicacy – and a return of catchy pop to boot.

Where Genesis mollified, Gabriel wanted to disturb. His recruitment of Robert Fripp and his audio-vérité approach to the production console for his second solo album atoned for his Genesis aestheticism, as did his much-publicized performances at Punk festivals in 1978 (he had already played in New York supported by Television and would later use Sham 69 as support act in Belgium). 'I refuse to see it as anything other than a pop album,' said Gabriel of his second LP. 'The playing on the album is ... very hard edges ... there's actually more synth on the second album but it's used in a different way. It's used less like a string section.'[67]

Fripp's relationship with Gabriel was mutually nourishing. Gabriel at first sighed, 'There's a certain amount of experimentation which I like to do which he [Fripp] wasn't inclined to,' but later praised the ex-Crimson man: 'I think Robert had seen my situation with Bob Ezrin on the first album and was trying to do the very opposite. I think the dryness of it was something he was very keen on as I was.'[68] The morbid misanthropy of the music and lyrics in 'Mother of Violence', with its surly, sullen obsessiveness, its reek of junk food and TV, led the *NME*'s Nick Kent to allude to de Niro's psychopathic Travis Bickle character in Scorsese's film *Taxi Driver* to contextualize the song's suppressed rage.[69] The steel guitar on 'Home Sweet Home' and the unsettling acoustic undercarriage of the raucously contemporary 'DIY' served to isolate Gabriel all the more from the saccharine and grandiloquent confections displayed by his former employers on their 1978 album, *And Then There were Three*. But perhaps the most obvious sign of this naughty-boy approach was the projected *Lamb* movie which was beginning to occupy more of Gabriel's time than ever.

Gabriel's choice for director was the maverick Chilean Alejandro Jeodorowsky, the man behind the bloodthirsty and thoroughly bizarre *El Topo*; a cinematic genius, Jeodorowsky has nevertheless frequently been characterized as a warped film-maker, his work a lyrical cross between the psychological abysses of David Cronenberg and the *grand guignol* of Dario Argento. It's perhaps the bluntest symbol possible of the frankly unsettling artistic outlook taking hold of Gabriel.

The singer continued courting newer and rawer musical styles, getting himself a No. 2 crop into the bargain. The fans loved it; most of the Genesis faithful, while somewhat bemused by their erstwhile hero's innovations, dutifully went out and boosted the Gabriel bank balance.

The *Lamb* movie never saw the light of day. But such setbacks hindered Gabriel's ascent not at all. By 1980 he was rivalling his ex-employers in the big-league stakes, and certainly in critical terms had long since cantered over the horizon ahead of them.

What did Progressive's *bêtes noires* think of their would-be executioners? The attempts at peaceful coexistence tottered between the absurd and inspired; virile supergroup UK, supported by japester US New Wavers the Fabulous Poodles; Pink Floyd drummer Nick Mason producing the Damned's second album, *Music for Pleasure* and, perhaps most joltingly of all, jazz-rock axe hero Allan Holdsworth jamming onstage with Chiswick's Benny Hill of Punk, Johnny Moped.

John Peel remembers scores of letters from Progressive fans who were 'not so much angry as hurt – as though I had betrayed them, as though I were a favourite uncle who'd decided to vote Conservative. It was *How could you?*'[70]

Bill Bruford observes that at the time he

> wasn't very aware of Punk – most musicians just concentrate on a daily basis on the job of playing an instrument – nobody saw it as a landmark revolution in music. It was a lot of noisy kids and musicians love noisy kids. When Punk came along I didn't feel like I was anything to do with Prog rock. It was 'Not guilty, m'lud'. I'd got off the gravy train.[71]

Bruford's sometime paymaster, Robert Fripp, later declared that he'd waited six years for Punk to come along.[72] Jon Anderson typified much of the discourse: 'A lot of good came out of the New Wave. But a lot of people were shown up for what they are – businessmen who want to hustle kids.' Of the Pistols themselves:

> If you're going to go out there and abuse everybody people are going to throw it straight back ... they hadn't even started thinking about where they were in relation to music. I thought they were doing it on a commercial level only. The thing is, you have to have more [musically] to back that sort of thing up'.[73]

Anderson was not being unfriendly. But his comments perhaps, sadly, indicate just how far mainstream rock musical thinking was now straying from the grassroots.

Greg Lake fulminated: 'If you're talking about aggression – real aggression – that's ELP. It makes Johnny Rotten look like a fucking walk in the park.'[74] Could Lake be referring to 'When the Apple Blossoms Bloom in the Windmills of Your Mind', maybe? Or 'Still ... You Turn Me On'? The more sanguine Emerson clubbably owns up to being fond enough of Punk, but suggests that punk 'behaviour' was a bit old hat after ELP themselves 'threw up in airports and that stuff ... we were far worse than the Sex Pistols'.[75] Tom Newman describes himself as very pro-Punk.

> It gave us a lot of good things. It started indies off in a big way. It made the industry much less corrupt. It was a kind of cleansing by fire if you like. At first I had trouble with it because around that time I was getting into Debussy and the finer points of 'culture' [laughs] and then along comes this raging inferno. But after a year or two, when it started merging into this Gothic Romanticism with Siouxsie and what-have-you, I saw the true value of it.[76]

Nick Mason, who further blurred the Punk–Progressive boundary by (disastrously) producing the Damned's appalling 1978 LP *Music for Pleasure*, assents:

> The worst thing about it was the record companies were becoming bigger ... and going public ... They wouldn't take risks, and the bands were more and more expensive to promote and maintain. They'd rather outbid each other for a million-dollars-plus to buy the Rolling Stones than invest in new bands.
>
> The business had changed – in the 1960s, the record companies seemed to sign anything with long hair; if it was a sheepdog, so what. But there was this problem whereby the thing had become ... dinosaurs rumbling across the earth. There was fuck-all else for anything else. What punk did was say we can make records for twenty quid again. It was about energy and *wanting* [my italics] to perform, not about who's

the greatest musician in the world. It was absolutely necessary.[77]

True or not, the accusation of elitist, technophiliac remoteness came as a shock to some Progressive acts, the modestly innovative Gentle Giant, for example. 'We were ... a cottage industry,' admitted guitarist Gary Green later.[78] The band made their own instruments, creating a kind of electric ukulele with the E, A and D strings of a violin, a plank, guitar tuning pegs and pick-ups. Pixiephones were bought from Woolworths for elaborate chiming fugal sections in one of the band's most elaborate pieces, the polyphonic 'So Sincere' (1974), merely for pentatonic scale and overtones which were otherwise beyond the reach of contemporary technology or the band's wallet.

'There was a gloss on Progressive rock,' counters Dave Stewart, 'it was "Ah, it's all about geezers poncing around playing classical riffs on their guitars." But people forgot that there'd been great bands like Comus, Magma, Henry Cow, that had played some really good stuff. It was like Year Zero. Nobody could get arrested with anything.'[79]

Despite the apparent industry agenda of a musical war footing between crumblies and kids, the 'war' remained a cold one. Dinosaurism wasn't confined to Progressive rock. But Progressive's peculiarities – both in terms of its expense and its style – were to prove its undoing. Most Progressive musicians were workaday musicians trying to get gigs doing something they could do, something frequently misunderstood in the deterministic universe of rock journalism.

Progressive rock's demise was assured the moment when everything that was Progressive crystallized – the other world, art for art's sake, music for music's sake, art and music for utopia's sake. Whether it was represented by *Topographic Oceans* or by Henry Cow, utopia was out. Whereas the likes of Fleetwood Mac and Rod Stewart could continue to market a commercially successful, artistically undemonstrative stance, Progressives, more connected, in their espousal in their morals and politics, with that other world, never stood a chance. Record buyers never cared much for Punk's strictures – they kept buying records by superstars – but superstars who didn't seem hopelessly out of place. Musically or politically, the 1960s were exposed and alone in a suddenly much colder climate.

7 MISADVENTURE
(PROGRESSIVE'S CULTURAL OBSOLESCENCE 1979–82)

ENGLAND'S NIGHTMARE

On 4 May 1979 Margaret Thatcher ascended the steps of 10 Downing Street. A nation looked on in admiration – it is hard to recall now that they had borne her there on a tide of hope. After the subsequent events – industrial apocalypse, social fragmentation, riots – it is hard to perceive Margaret Thatcher as a saviour. But while her 1983 and 1987 election triumphs were the work of a defensive electorate cowed by threats of miners and Marx, in 1979 such spectres weren't needed (certainly she never polled so heavily again).

She mesmerized rock, too. As Simon Frith wrote in *Melody Maker* that April: 'Chris Welch's recent star-chats have been riveting. The old pros are Tory to a man. Their obsession is the defence of traditional values; the Protestant ethic, the Family, Effort and Reward and Responsibility.'[1] Checking up on that statement reveals precious little to that end, although Frith has clearly identified prevalent trends. And when, that summer, Jimmy Page of Led Zeppelin was telling *Melody Maker* that he had had no qualms about voting for Thatcher, Frith's point appeared superficially tenable.[2]

Pete Sinfield looks back: 'I don't think that Peter Gabriel voted for Thatcher. Robert [Fripp] didn't, I don't think. I know I didn't.'[3] Meanwhile, though, rock names like Mike Oldfield (and, more tentatively, Peter Gabriel) became immersed in psycho-guru Werner Erhard's crypto-Thatcherite cult EST, whose status as just another beautiful people's mystical cop-out rocketed to *zeitgeist*-hogging importance with its obsessional stress on the subject's individual responsibility for his/her present, past and future. From the collective prescription of theosophy to the individual prognoses of EST, the whole outlook of a generation had altered in the space of a decade.

Ironically, the cultural erasure of Progressive rock coincided with Margaret Thatcher's accession. The genre which was then and still is characterized as the most English (and bourgeois) of all popular music withered and died during the Thatcher years, themselves the consecration of a super-English popular politics.

The notion of a rock resistance to right-wing politics was, however, still strong enough to be taken for granted among the vast majority of rock consumers. But by 1979 the business of publicizing the resistance was no longer that of Progressive. Many names were irremediably contaminated by the excesses of the 1970s ('I watch my krugerrands going up and down on the international market,' said Carl Palmer)[4] and also by inexcusable outbursts (Eric Clapton's intoxicated and ultimately inexplicable endorsement of Enoch Powell being a case in point). That farce so enraged two members of the audience that they determined to organize resistance to what many saw as an inexorable colonization of rock by far-right notions. Rock Against Racism was born. The prevalent suspicion of the time, that rock stars were turning reactionary through simple over-exposure to the evils of capitalist acquisition, may look a trifle simplistic today, but the concerns of RAR had cause enough – in David Bowie's sympathy for fascism, for instance, which was much more disturbing and troublingly obvious than Clapton's saloon-bar aside. Bowie lived the dream, with its trappings of Berlin, amorality and the 1930s, all the predictable jetsam of glamorized brutality and totalitarianism. This was the man who also arrived to a flashbulb welcome at Victoria station giving Nazi salutes. To the rock concords of the 1970s had now been attached the values of Conservatism (Paul Weller also joined the jamboree in 1977 when he vowed to the *NME* to vote for Thatcher when he got the chance).[5]

It seemed the right time for the alternative agenda of the Henry Cow universe to take centre stage, now that the crude determinism of punk had been replaced by the more experimental musical and textual language of bands like the Slits, the Gang of Four etc.

In the late 1970s, Henry Cow's impending retirement had been paralleled by a concretizing of the links between culturally oppositional bands – Italy's Stormy Six, Sweden's Zamla Mammaz Manna, France's Etron Fou Leloublan. In 1978 these bands met at Sunrise Studios in Kirchberg, Switzerland, and hammered out a blueprint for a network of gig bookings and record distribution, as well as a provisional political manifesto. At the same time Chris Cutler set up his own soapbox for musical subversion, Recommended Records in Wandsworth, south London. The manifesto was unwritten, but as commentator Alan Jones writes, ' ... groups and composers [had to] share an engagement with (i) instrumental possibilities [new techniques and treatments]; (ii) compositional possibilities and (iii) the expressive possibilities [engaged content] of the above'.[6]

Cutler's 'recommended' records were entirely that: records by those artists whose musical and artistic vision he sympathized with. Among the acts was Cutler's own Art Bears, whose *Hopes and Fears* album radically deconstructs pop's linguistics, in a manner similar to that employed by advanced classical/post-jazz acts like Cassiber, News from Babel and South Africa's Kalahari Surfers. This was music Cutler saw as eating away at, if not yet destroying, the barriers separating class from class. But it wasn't all drivetime music for Frankfurt School devotees; the knowing meta-kitsch of France's ZNR disproves that. Here was the very artificiality of the modern world being given expression in music comparable to the textual pranks being played by the likes of the Pop Group, music which would reorganize the way ears schooled in pop listening techniques would receive and react to certain sonic messages.

In 1979 Progressive and its offshoots proposed a comparable artillery of musical confrontation. Lindsay Cooper, having packed her bags in the disintegration of the Henry Cow caravan in 1978, began work on a project called *Rags*, a hyper-esoteric collection of songs about London needlewomen in the nineteenth century – songs of struggle and liberation. The album would not appear until 1983 (on, inevitably, Recommended), but Cooper had already set up and was hard at work with the Feminist Improvising Group, along with (ex-Henry Cow) bassist/cellist Georgie Born, avant-garde Dutch trombonist Anne-Marie Roelofs, experimental American harpist Zeena Parkins and singer Dagmar Krause:'We could veer off into theatre, tap-dancing, or whatever.'[7] Cooper suggests that the feminized element of the act generated a creativity which might have been diminished in the presence of men. However arguable that point may be, the discourse of opposition was still being recited and developed loudly and at length in 1979.

Progressive acts – less radical than the likes of Cutler and Cooper – were also finding themselves starkly at odds with the mainstream, even though their music used accessible, tonal traditions happily enough. This curious phenomenon yet to be adequately analysed by any rock historian or journalist, is my next centre of investigation.

DIEHARDS

The retraction of the record industry in the face of further oil aftershocks in 1979 mortally wounded Progressive. The final eviction orders were up in the February, when the *NME* readers poll catapulted new-wave acts into top slots across the board. Genesis finished fourth in the best-band category behind the Clash, and Yes slunk home in ninth place. Tony Banks scored highly in the best keyboardist stakes, although Wakeman and Emerson lagged badly.

That said, the year did witness the release of a couple of albums which belied the parlous state of Progressive's body politic. First among these equals was The Enid's immense *Touch Me*.

Formed in 1974, The Enid ploughed a lonely and often frankly unorthodox furrow through Progressive's Waterloo years, their erratic career progress graph somewhat ironically and unfortunately matching that of diametrically different bands such as the Slits, bumping along from dodgy deal to dodgy deal, wowing London critics at the Hammersmith Odeon one night and getting the bird at West Runton Pavilion the next.

Not that stardom would have found them easily, even in Progressive's heyday. Their leader, the portly and avuncular keyboardist Robert Godfrey, hardly courted sellability. He had passed up a promising career as a concert pianist to become the musical director of the fledgling Barclay James Harvest; having played a Brahms concerto at the age of fifteen, he studied at both the Royal College and Royal Academy of Music, graduating from neither. He was

> sucked into a kind of middle-aged famous composers' gay circle with Tippett, Henze and Britten ... I got very upset and frightened and it interrupted my work. I left there, went back to Finchden, tried the Academy with Vivian Langrishe. I got on very well with him but by this time I had got involved with hippy culture. I met Barclay James Harvest and talked them into doing gigs with an orchestra.[8]

In the mid-1970s Godfrey was offered a break by Charisma Records and cut a concept album, *The Fall of Hyperion*; described now by him as 'stupid',[9] it was indeed deplorable, a directionless melange of symphonic bluster and empty pianistic virtuosity. It sank without trace and a chastened Godfrey regrouped, chucking in his lot with guitarist Stephen Stewart.

Godfrey and Stewart set up their own band under the cryptic name The Enid, referring to a fictitious girlfriend of Godfrey's.

Personnel came and went (Steve Hackett keyboard sideman Nick Magnus joined for a time), including a lead singer named Peter Roberts who committed suicide on New Year's Day 1975, shortly before rehearsals for the band's first recordings ('We were instrumental ever after,' said Godfrey, 'he was impossible to replace.')[10] Armed with a Tarot concept named *Voyage of the Acolyte*, Godfrey tried to drum up support from Tony Stratton-Smith. The troubled Charisma were unable to offer the band an option, however, and Stratton-Smith passed Godfrey's concept to the more bankable Steve Hackett who, it seems, was suffering from concept block. Undaunted, the band took the already recorded album to EMI, and in 1976 the record appeared under the considerably improved title of *In the Region of the Summer Stars*.

Right from the off this was strange stuff. Although solidly tonal and frothily classically influenced, it wasn't mere Nice/ELP-style reworking and pastiche, but rather a much more workmanlike and wide-ranging deployment of classical chord voicings, intervals and developments in compositions impelled by rock metres; 'the romance and dynamics of classical music',[11] in Godfrey's terminology. Synthesizers were used extensively, perhaps as much as by any other British band at the time. Fleet-fingered soloing was also downplayed, although ensemble virtuosity was powerful. Side 2 was particularly memorable, occupied mostly by the continuous 'The Last Judgement/In the Region of Summer Stars', a joyous orgy of irresistibly passionate sound and fury. Lifting a figure from Mahler's 'Resurrection' Symphony (No. 2) did the music no harm at all, either, and fingerprints from Stravinsky, Elgar and (most obviously) Rachmaninov were everywhere.

Godfrey recalls: 'The Mahler quote was absolutely in keeping with the programme. Being obsessed with Carl Jung and his ideas of archetypes, I saw the Resurrection motif as a very important part of that story. "The Lovers" is pastiche Rachmaninov, a bit like the *Warsaw Concerto* – that sumptuous analogue of orgasm.'[12]

Godfrey took the lion's share of compositional honours but he was ably supported by guitarists Stephen Stewart and Francis Lickerish while drummer Robbie Dobson kicked up a storm, despite Godfrey's assertion that the problem we've had with drummers is that there's never been very much for them to do. Very often the music would work just as well without drums, but if you've got a drummer you have to give them something to do. 'Albion Fair' [1979], for example, that's not got much for a drummer to do – but by God drummers do everything they can to make up for it.[13]

Despite the fact that the band's early years were spent in the shadow of punk, EMI kept faith; The Enid's quirky appearance and stage act (Miles affectionately termed them 'nutters'; they could and did cover anything and everything from 'Pretty Vacant' to 'The Dambusters March')[14] built them a sizeable campus following.

The second Enid opus, the satirically-titled *Aerie Faerie Nonsense* emerged in 1977. The showpiece track, the side-long 'Fand' was another vast piece of structure and arrangement which suffered only because it remains somewhat dwarfed by its elder-sister composition (and artistic mirror-image), Bax's symphonic tone-poem *The Garden of Fand* (1916). The rest of the album, however, was a so-so exercise in retreading the melodic and harmonic pastures of *In the Region of the Summer Stars*.

But when the brilliant young Scots keyboardist and composer William Gilmour joined the band in 1978, The Enid was transformed, as 1979's *Touch Me* amply illustrates. This time the album consisted of just two segmented pieces. The orchestrations were superbly embroidered and the use of Tony Freer's oboe and cor anglais lends the music a gloriously unaffected pastoral feel, the decentred nature of the narrative even more unsettling and the music even more postmodern, with Godfrey's thunderous piano octaves swinging wildly in allegiance from Gershwin to Rachmaninov within the space of a couple of bars. Synths are yet more in evidence, though the album's masterstroke – apart from a cornucopia of splendid melodies that the band never matched before or afterward – is that contrivance is absent. The lengthy sixteen-minute 'Albion Fair' is missing eight minutes of music, including a double-fugue that was written but never recorded. Loud and soft passages alike serve the whole instead of appearing merely as cornball effects; Godfrey and crew never got closer to reworking the spirit of classical expression than here.

'The music isn't demanding,' maintains Godfrey. 'It isn't that difficult to play.'[15] The death-defying precision ensemble passages and breathtakingly glittering arrangements of *Six Pieces* (also 1979), which constituted that album, might lead some to dispute Godfrey's diagnosis. Either in stop-start syncopations or in broad-gesturing *nobilmente* passages, a William Walton influence is perhaps most apparent here.

Godfrey continues:

Willie [Gilmour] and Martin Russell, a bassist and keyboard player we got in, they were both university graduates in music. They weren't that Romantic in outlook – they were much more interested in writing absolute music. Tony Freer only stuck around for one album – that was a shame, but there was a situation with a woman, and she decided she wanted to take over everything...[16]

Not that these criteria stood much chance in the anti-Progressive deluge that was getting under way in 1979. Even apart from the critical broadsides aimed at the music, The Enid's entire *raison d'être* received more than its share of flak. Despite accusations that, even if the band were busting a gut on stage the music would still sound stilted, it's worth noting that (as Godfrey has since declared), Enid guitarists come exclusively from the Hendrix/Page end of rock music as opposed to the more circumspect Howe/Hackett axis. 'The Enid is very heavy', Godfrey said. 'Enid fans have tended to ... have been more into the leather jacket.'[17] (He is right: said fans once bottled off a local punk band supporting their heroes in Tunbridge Wells.) There have been too many one-night stands in terminally anonymous English towns like Halifax or Banbury scattered throughout the memories of various Enideers for these accusations of effetery to stick. Music journalist Mike Barnes remembers,

The Enid were a weird bunch. They attracted the most bizarre following. You went to their gigs, and you'd see punks. You went to punk gigs and you'd see Enid fans. The Enid for me were symptomatic of just how catholic audiences were by the end of the 1970s. A mate of mine dragged me along to see them at Bristol Colston Hall. I liked them, and I went backstage. Godfrey told me they were playing the Rainbow in London and was I going to be there? I answered that I could afford the train fare or the ticket, not both. And he convened the band, they had a whip-round, and offered me the train fare. Amazing. How many Prog bands did – or were supposed to be hip enough to do – something like that?[18]

The year 1979 was also good to Bill Bruford, who since the break-up of King Crimson had been stand-in Progressive drummer-by-appointment, playing with Gong and Genesis, among others. Having released his debut solo *Feels Good to Me* and played on the ill-fated supergroup's first UK album in 1978, pundits complacently predicted more of the intensely concentrated English variant on the jazz-rock crossover that he had developed on the aforementioned when the debut release of his eponymously named band appeared in February. While they weren't wrong, they hadn't bargained for the sheer assurance of the music that Bruford produced. It may not have offended the neighbours, but it was melodically aerobatic and soulfully tight to an extent unheard of in both English and other fusions of jazz improvisation and rock at the time.

Bruford's trump card was his choice of musicians – they were prodigiously gifted, but so expensive the cost of hiring them would later drive him to break the band up ('They're driving me to the poorhouse,' he once allegedly told Steve Hackett).[19] Allan Holdsworth (guitar), Jeff Berlin (bass) and Dave Stewart (keyboards) weren't in the world's top rank of sessionmen but they were formidable players and arrangers, soloists who always subjugated show to substance. Sporadic touring engendered muso worship, and it was a shame that Holdsworth left in the spring of 1979 to return to session work. His replacement, 'The Unknown' John Clark, had an impossible act to follow, although he acquits himself well on the live *Bruford Tapes* which Polydor rushed out in early 1980, with the band roaring through a series of consistently excellent numbers.

Dave Stewart remembers:

'He [Clark] was an acolyte – and sometime pupil – of Allan Holdsworth's. Allan recommended him, and he sat in with me and Bill in Bill's garage: an electric piano, a Mini-Moog, a drumkit, a guitarist and room for bugger-all else ... I'd sent him a tape of a piece, 'Sample and Hold'. We started playing and it was awful – clashes everywhere. John's cassette player had gone wrong, and he'd learnt it in the wrong key. He was in B flat, I was in B. I said, 'Can't you learn it in B flat?' and he said, 'Sod that, I've learnt it in B flat, can't *you* learn it in B flat?' He was confident, and I was impressed. We had a gig in a week in Amsterdam. John had a week to learn material me and Bill had taken a year to write. He played it note-perfect, and he even went down the front of the stage and started throwing the old guitar poses. Brilliant![20]

The melodic and rhythmic rigour – if not the dissonance and textural freedom – of King Crimson was only shadily apparent in this music. The unceasing invention makes the occasional bursts of sweet-toned lyricism – 'Travels with Myself (And Someone Else)' and part two of 'The Sahara of Snow' – all the more enjoyable and replace Crimson's scatter-gun polytonality with modal gestures conjured from nowhere as emotional trump cards. Stewart's unerring harmonic resourcefulness in his solos breathlessly develops his National Health work into a chunkier rock context, and the Bootsy Collins-on-speed bass solo with which Jeff Berlin introduces the album's closing track, '5g', has to be heard to be believed. Progressive or not, the unmistakable acrid lyricism, quirky time-signatures and offbeat humour are undiminished. But by the end of the year it was all over. While they hadn't actually beggared Bruford, financial pressures finally poleaxed the project.

Bruford continued to prosper musically, however. He rejoined the reconstituted King Crimson in 1981 and cut three albums with them. In addition to this unlikely re-formation, Bruford undertook a very different project with another Yes alumnus, Patrick Moraz. In the years since leaving Yes, Moraz had taken up where he had left off, composing well-upholstered and thoroughly civilized European instrumental rock music. He cut a couple of albums of this lavishly crafted material but unfortunately lent it as much character as a grain elevator. Among these efforts was an album of live electronic and piano improvisation, *Future Memories Live on TV* (1979). Released on the French Carrere label, it was a concert given live on Swiss TV, and while much of it is the kind of aimless synthesizer atmospherics which usually soundtrack TV documentaries about corn-circles, the pianism is awe-inspiringly percussive and inventive. Moraz clearly was a talent to be reckoned with, though his next gig restricted his steel-fingered stuntwork; this was supporting the sagging structure of the superannuated Moody Blues. Bruford rescued him from this lucrative but musically sclerotic position with an offer to cut an album in 1984 entitled, unpromisingly, *Music for Piano and Drums.*

The ideological exclusion of Progressive rock expression was laying down its deepest roots in the media at this time. The spectre of New Age was on the horizon and instrumental music that did not occupy the territories of bellowing iconoclasm beloved of Einsturzende Neubaten and Test Department was proscribed entirely. Yet Moraz and Bruford won through, and followed this up with *Flags* in 1985, which attracted similarly good verdicts. Bruford recalls:

> I loved the idea of piano and drums and I knew Patrick had a jazz heart in him. He was bored to death with the Moody Blues and I gave him the opportunity to stretch out and see exactly what he could do on one piano. Four years, two albums, some gigs. It was fairly adventurous and did me no end of good. It was very cheap too. Musicians play music for lots of reasons, and usually for the last reasons non-musicians can imagine. I played with Patrick because it was easy. I didn't need

a road crew, I didn't need a lighting rig. We had no equipment.
I could say to the promoter, 'Provide a Steinway, and I'll rent a
drum set.'[21]

No such critical indulgence was ever granted to Steve
Hackett. From his departure from Genesis onwards, his reception
was an indication of just how much Progressive had slipped in
influence. He may have been a Progressive king but he ranked no
more than a baronet in the post-Progressive rock aristocracy.

Please Don't Touch (1978), Hackett's first release after his split
from Genesis, could perhaps be dubbed as quintessential: a
curate's egg of splendour and silliness which summarized his
unenviable position as lord of the shrinking empire which he
surveyed; the fretful inconsistency of the product unconsciously
mirrored a genre in crisis.

Touch is overburdened with guests; Richie Havens's dyspeptic
drawl provided telling contrast to the pastoral sonorities chiming
around him. Soul chanteuse Randy Crawford's regal presence on
'Hoping Love Will Last' was less melodramatic than mystifying,
her gospelly intonation as out of place amongst the Mellotrons
and woodwind as a tumbleweed in a daffodil bed. The album
could also be better-paced; there's always the sense that Hackett
wants to get on to the next idea double-quick, which strangles
some good ideas at birth, like the quicksilver twelve-string work
of 'Narnia' and 'Land of a Thousand Autumns'.

In August 1978, a band was hastily put together to get Hackett
out on the road, and it proved highly successful; that winter the
lineup recorded *Spectral Mornings*, Hackett's best set. The musical
cohesion of *Voyage* combined with the manic catholicity of *Touch*
to create a memorable album. 'Clocks', in particular, was a
metronomic masterpiece of chilling power; the turbo-charged
spookiness of the Hackett guitar sound redoubling its fury. Light
relief was provided by 'The Ballad of the Decomposing Man', a
Residents-style piece of vocoder-led Formby pastiche, in
addition to two harmonically remote acoustic nocturnes, both
tonally and timbrally offering gorgeous interplay between guitar
and flute ('Lost Time in Cordoba' and 'The Virgin and The

Gypsy'). Topping the lot was the title track, an achingly lyrical band blowout which cocked a snook at Genesis and proved Steve could write Tony Banks songs every bit as well as Tony Banks.

Hackett's stock was high but his second band album, *Defector* (1980), is somewhat of a disappointment when compared with its predecessor. It contains some fine music, however, notably the suitably spacious opener 'The Steppes' with its Antarctic Mellotron. The stand-out track is the bizarre short instrumental 'Hammer in the Sand', little more than a goldfish bowl for Nick Magnus's keyboard talents but betraying Hackett's harmonic literacy and prowess as an arranger.

It may have sold strongly on the back of the juggernaut which Genesis's contemporary Duke album set rolling through the spring of 1980, but financial problems forced Hackett reluctantly to disband the group; scandalously, neither the superb vocalist John Hicks nor bassist/backing vocalist Dik Cadbury, ever worked again at the top level.

THE END – ALMOST

No other outcome was possible now; Progressive was doomed. The year's remaining Progressive output was eloquent enough testimony to this. Rick Wakeman released a poppy, chirpy double-album (the inaptly titled *Rhapsodies*) that actually managed to sound even more insipid than its predecessors. Gentle Giant fled to the West Coast of the US, cut the laborious *Civilian* in search of FM salvation, and were torn apart by boredom and familial worries. National Health broke up after the January issue of their overlooked album *Of Queues and Cures*. ELP had concluded their final disastrous tour of the USA and disintegrated, releasing the posthumous *Live*. It did little but detract from a legend already irreversibly tarnished by the fiascos of *Works* and *Love Beach*.

Others lost in the sandbox were Mike Oldfield, Anthony Phillips and Dave Greenslade. Oldfield continued his fruitless yearly quest to try and fit the musical world into an LP sleeve with the prolix *Incantations*; Phillips's *Sides* was indifferent, and the year also saw the debut of the guitarist's perennial *Private Parts and Pieces* series.

Greenslade's effort, *The Pentateuch of the Cosmogony* was about as far from Phillips's DIY filigree of drawing-room sound as it was possible to get; a double-album presented in unprecedentedly luxuriant fashion, it was one of the most ghastly and expensive failures in Progressive history. It was musically quite sound in places, but went on for about thirty minutes too long and used about thirty keyboard instruments too many in the process. It came in a limited edition of 50,000 with a book of illustrations by sci-fantasy artist Patrick Woodroffe, gifting the music an opulent milieu it often didn't warrant. Now a collector's piece *par excellence*, it must rank as one of the most incongruously inopportune releases ever of any album. While the music press hosannaed the stripped-down angularity of the Gang of Four's *Entertainment* album and raved about deconstructed disco supremos Chic, along came *The Pentateuch*. Selling this must have been like trying to sell a Billy Graham album in North Korea.

This conceptual floundering wasn't restricted to Greenslade; one of the year's sadder episodes saw the classical guitarist John Williams dent his hitherto unimpeachable pedigree by forming Sky. This was a nominally Progressive band centred on Williams's picking and ex-Curved Air keyboard player Francis Monkman erecting milestones of musical mundanity around both dirge-like originals of aspirant classicism or bovine and *passé* reworkings of actual classical pieces which made even the Nice sound like geniuses. Sky combined the compositional gimmicks of early Progressive with the airbrushed aridity of contemporary jazz-rock techniques. Their second album, the double-LP *Sky 2* in 1980, was an improvement on their first, although it rarely transcended the banal. Incredibly, five more albums followed, the last coming as late as 1987. An attempted gentrification of rock, its bad taste holed it below the waterline, much as happened to other colour-supplement favourites of the time; look no further than the LSO's 1978 recording of *Classic Rock Songs*. The London Planetarium, however, devoted one evening a month to 'Laserock', whereby then-new laser effects would be choreographed in laboured fashion to undemanding atmospheric tracks from the likes of Pink Floyd and recent Genesis. One

Andre Dudek recorded a 'rock cello' single, 'The Cello Caprice'; Violinski, the solo project of ELO violinist Mik Kaminski (neat, huh?) charted but plumbed even greater depths. Darryl Way's *Concerto for Electric Violin* at least had a semblance of formal know-how to it.

Another luminary caught napping in the merciless on-coming glare of a new decade was Steve Hillage. The ex-Gong guitarist's accelerating obsession with all things occult reached its apotheosis in 'Rainbow Dome Musick' (1979). Played by Hillage on glissando/electric guitars and keyboards with girlfriend Miquette Giraudy on synthesizers, it was quite revolutionary for the time, although notices were dismissive; New Age music was still seven years away and Hillage's effort was dismissed as an insult to the intelligence, even by those still sympathetic to Progressive ideals. A 1990s listener, however, would probably nominate it as the most durable of Hillage's albums; its bubbling, fizzing, celestial qualities make it the natural progenitor of Hillage's later flirtation with ambient dance music.

Then, however, he was fast approaching Aleister Crowley status in the mumbo-jumbo stakes, as a chunk from his programme notes for that year's Glastonbury shindig demonstrates:

> We're gathered together on the shores of the crystal isle, to exchange our gifts, recharge our batteries and to stimulate this special place as a generator of hope for years to come ... the timeless vessel of fusion is the Grail ... as a vital symbol of receptivity, it reappears in the modern radio telescope, capturing subtle energies from distant galaxies ...[22]

Summing up 1979's Progressive humiliation was Pink Floyd's lugubrious *The Wall* double-album and the quiet but acrimonious sundering of Yes. *The Wall*, too, was to bring unacceptable pressures to bear within Pink Floyd.

An era had passed for rock music in general. The ballyhoo that accompanied the release of *The Wall* was one of the last acts of reverence for rock auteurism before its reinvention as 'mature rock' in the post-Live Aid 1980s. Radio 1 broadcast a special show around the album; interviews with the band were everywhere. The Floyd were among the few bands left to be accorded such treatment. Even the now militantly anti-Progressive John Peel hailed its arrival. Hard-headed critical assessment, though, returned verdicts of misadventure; the *NME* from the outset turned heavy guns on the album, assigning it to the avowedly anti-Progressive, pop millenarian Ian Penman, who described it as 'ideologically beached, and, for the Floyd, archetypal'.[23] The painfully polite response of the *Melody Maker*'s Chris Brazier was almost as depressingly mannered, predictable and devoid of actual musical or textual insight. Brazier merely fretted that he was 'unsure whether *The Wall* was brilliant or terrible' but opined that it was still 'utterly compelling', while failing to tell us why.[24]

Rock historiography perhaps devotes more space to *The Wall* than to any other Progressive album; to the outlandish Christmas No. 1 success of the single 'Another Brick in the Wall (Part 2)', the empty Bob Geldof film-of-the-album in 1982, the band tensions the music so destructively exposed. Its pretensions to chronicling totalitarian excess sit ill with the esoteric lushness of much of its music; by then such sentiments did not seem apt coming from Progressive musicians. Seeing a Progressive band of culturally extravagant status and towering wealth singing about oppression and inciting classroom insurrection seemed just excruciatingly embarrassing. This was fatuous thinking, of course, but by this time, it was inevitable that culturally, the Floyd had missed the bus. *The Wall* is an immense – and immensely flawed – album, and for Progressive to have drawn any strength from it, it should have at least matched 1977's *Animals* in terms of cultural relevance and melodic invention. Despite some studiedly impressive moments, *The Wall* never really comes to life.

The music did have its moments: the ecstatic marching riffs of 'Run Like Hell' are impressive, and the Floyd indicate that their penchant for acidic poignancy has lost little of its flair with 'Hey You' and 'Goodbye Blue Sky'. The apostolic Karl Dallas would later insist that it was 'arguably the most important project in the history of the genre', and that Waters's disingenuous shrilling against the rock industry laid bare 'the weary treadmill of all that superstardom'. Dallas flayed Waters's critics: 'When you have spent a year's toil and thousands of pounds on doing your best, it must be galling to have it rubbished in five lines by some idiot.' In the same breath, however, Dallas falls victim to the kind of circular logic that stymied Waters's own social critique. 'One of nineteenth-century literature's more unhelpful bequests to the twentieth century is the Byronic image of artist as hero-victim,' lectures Dallas, as a prelude to his doing just that with Roger Waters.[25] Waters and Dallas are inextricably part of the star-making machinery, and are equally culpable for its evils. Dallas, normally a thoughtful, humane critic, even tries to argue that the Floyd were an essentially working-class band with an essentially working-class following, and that quadraphonic music and 'great visuals' actually offered a palliative to the realities of life in Thatcher's Britain, surely a calamitous misreading of the *zeitgeist*.[26] Waters, diarist of rock madness and fearless critic of excess, had presumably been party to the monstrous mega-dollar follies the Floyd planned to promote *The Wall*'s scream against corporatism, such as 'the Slug', a portable, inflatable, fully integrated concert complex, 354 feet long by 82 feet high. A real site of resistance.

Waters's dog-in-the-mangerism later fell under the critical eye of Richard Cook who, in his assessment of 1983's Floyd album *The Final Cut*, wrote:

> Waters's walls have sealed him up permanently. Every diatribe he releases as a Pink Floyd album will be filed beside the others ... what will bother [consumers] isn't how effective a catharsis each one summons; it won't be how much they can assimilate and learn from a personal, provocative vision. What will bother them is why there aren't any good tunes as good as 'Money'.[27]

If Waters believed that the stadium show had become a sham, why play in stadiums at all? Why, having gone to all the trouble of constructing a wall between the band and the audience and having lookalikes perform the music, did Waters insist on giving them the same old gunk? Why was the music, by 1979, so mushily static, so uninspired? For a transfiguring experience from the Floyd, Dallas might have suggested the expedient of giving punters their money's worth. But isn't that merely sealing oneself inside walls again, voluntarily, as Cook describes? Ironic perhaps, but the Floyd's sense of irony had apparently deserted them with Syd Barrett.

The point about rock stardom, of course, is the power of *choice* it lends its stars, especially ones so obviously in control of their destinies – indeed, those who have made fortunes out of appearing to be sublimely, superhumanly in control – as the likes of Floyd and ELP. If *The Wall* was an anti-show, it was just as big a spectacle as all post-1969 Floyd had been. It broke no cycles, and did not attempt to do so. It negated itself.

The impression was that the Floyd had just left it too long. Their day had passed, and *The Wall* seemed, if not outdated, then somehow menopausal.

In 1979–80 Michael Jackson took the USA by storm with his brilliant *Off The Wall* album (a title of substantial if unintentional irony), the definitive statement of Disco, and the UK reverberated to the strains of the Police and the Jam, the first superstar spawn of Punk. The new wave of British Heavy Metal which would have such a huge impact on both sides of the Atlantic was in full cry. The arrivistes had arrived, and *The Wall* couldn't exclude them.

The Wall's valedictory watershed status became evident the following spring when an almost-as-long-awaited album, Genesis's *Duke*, appeared. Not for this the reverence that had greeted the Floyd's latest outpourings. Genesis's notices weren't measured in acres and for the most part the sentiments in them weren't measured either. Suddenly, after the enormous failure of *The Wall*, reviewing Progressive albums was no big deal. The defences breached, the critics poured through.

Chris Bohn of the *Melody Maker* took unerring aim; he accused Genesis of 'not playing to their strengths', with their theme neither 'interesting in themselves or in a solo framework'. He went on, 'Warhol's influence on pop has largely been among those who had something to say before a means of saying it, while conventional art rock has relied less on what's said than its mode of expression.'[28]

The spring of 1980, however, turned Genesis from rock stars definitively into megastars, kickstarting the phenomenal success that would lead them to lay claim to the status of the world's biggest band by the end of the decade. The new album further emphasized the melodic conciseness of 1978's *And Then There were Three*. But both to appease hard-core fans (impatient at the band's inactivity and unresponsive to the new material) and to attract new followers, Genesis undertook a massive hearts'n'minds tour of small British halls, ransacking their back catalogue in the process. The strategy worked; tour and album sold prodigiously. But it also inaugurated a relentless defensiveness; hurt by the criticism of the post-Punk generation, they sought endlessly to justify their new music, and convince people of the validity and relevance of their contemporary concerns.

This might have been more palatable had the new music not been so feebly anonymous. As Bohn says, the pop songs, 'Turn It on Again', 'Please Don't Ask' and the risible 'Misunderstanding' were simply dull, heavy with the shadows of uneasy reskilling. But another problem was that the old-style rhetoric was pretty weak too. Banks's 'Heathaze' was so slow it almost ground to a halt. Similarly his 'Guide Vocal' theme wallowed in the sentimentality with which he had come close to saturating the previous album (although when fleshed out into the crowd-pleasing Progressive closer 'Duke's Travels', it worked wonders).

To highlight the Genesis comeback further, Peter Gabriel also resurfaced as a hot commercial property that spring. In fact, he was first to the tape with a Top Ten hit, the enamel-bright and percussive 'Games without Frontiers'. With its typical Gabriel wordplay most famously singing of kissed balloons and pissed on baboons, it was a pipe-opener for that April's superb *Peter Gabriel III* album. While Genesis merely toyed with modernization, Gabriel met the 1980s head on. But where so many others got it wrong, Gabriel succeeded in continuing to win friends by not actually *trying* to look 'up-to-date', merely by following his creative instincts. 'Biko' showed that his political conscience was in good working order and this really became the signature tune for Gabriel's 1980s resurgence. An acidic melody supported by the harsh clangour of exotic percussion, it marked the beginning of his immersion in Oriental and African musical cultures which would take a massive stride forward with the fourth album some two years later, and turn him into one of *the* rock faces of the late 1980s. His band are tighter than ever: Tony Levin produced some body-punches from the Chapman bass stick, Jerry Marotta provided meaty, implacable drum support and Larry Fast contributed austere synthesizers.

Gabriel's album was used to pillory Genesis: if Peter Gabriel could still sound contemporary, why couldn't his peers? Gabriel had called in Jam guitarist Paul Weller for 'And Through the Wire' on his new LP. Could one see Genesis calling in one of the Members or UB40? One could not.

Underpinning critical hostility towards Progressive is the age-old rock presupposition that the music is meant to be dysfunctional, to hurt, to offend mum and dad. *Real* music has them pounding on your bedroom door. This is, of course, a questionable notion, but it infuses the contemporary beliefs that the terse sounds of Gabriel and the new Crimson were somehow more 'valid' than the calorific harmonies of most Progressive acts, which were dismissed as 'empty melodrama' or 'bombastic irrelevancies'.

Any lingering hopes of a Progressive renaissance were finally extirpated by the departure from Yes of both Jon Anderson and Rick Wakeman. But that news, disturbing as it was to the faithful, paled beside that concerning the identity of their replacements, Trevor Horn and Geoff Downes, who were celebrated at the time as the vogueish electro-bubblegum duo Buggles.

Perhaps only Bud Flanagan and Chesney Allen would have constituted a less appropriate choice for Yes. Horn and Downes were session journeymen who had, according to Dan Hedges, pooled their resources in 1979 to make 'the perfect pop album. Ultra-clean. Everything very thought out.'[29] It was conceptually rooted in the contemporary cyberfad – their image of high-tech sterility and alienation boosted by Horn's pop-eyed-boffin appearance behind his saucery spectacles. This startlingly unoriginal thematic flavouring shamelessly raided cybernetic Brave New World themes (which Gary Numan had recently plundered) with track titles such as 'Kid Dynamo', 'Astroboy and the Proles on Parade'; the album's trump was the adherent 'Video Killed the Radio Star', a meteoric 1979 hit. Progressive fans grimaced; the Buggles not only embodied but actually relished the 'plasticity' of the pop they so loathed. Even new-wavers, the Joe Strummers and Paul Wellers of this world, were deemed preferable. They at least had 'integrity', 'guts'; they were rockers. Maybe; but they lacked the acumen and good fortune which Horn used to land himself and his friend prestigious positions.

Thanks to managerial links between Yes and the Buggles, Horn managed to hustle his way into the Yes circle. Horn had a song which he (somewhat hubristically) imagined might get on to the next Yes album. Having sung the song to an impressed Chris Squire, Horn first found himself a candidate for Anderson's position and then his official replacement.

The revamped Yes emerged to a disbelieving world in late May 1980 and issued their first – and only – album with the Horn/Downes lineup in August. Unsurprisingly entitled *Drama*, it made a good start in building bridges with alienated fans by sporting a Roger Dean cover. But despite the change being talked up with panicky enthusiasm (Chris Squire on Downes: Geoff ... is the best keyboard player Yes have ever had. He *listens*'),[30] the music collapses like a soggy soufflé. The opening 'Machine Messiah' pings along at a fair rate of knots with some engaging melodic turns, but is ultimately symptomatic of the ill-considered marriage between the vastly divergent styles of Yes and the Buggles. The pick of the crop, 'Into the Lens', succeeds only thanks to a powerhouse steel-guitar solo from Howe and the 'baroque, Byzantine' little filler 'White Car'[31] proves a pleasing indication that Yes could also be believable miniaturists. The US tour that followed the album's release attracted mixed responses, and much the same lukewarm reaction greeted the band in England.

As with any matter concerning this notoriously bickersome band, accounts of the Anderson–Wakeman split are sketchy. It seems that Anderson's insistence on more and more delicacy in the band's music (the 'Wimp Factor' as Downes lumpenly glossed it)[32] distanced him from a band already falling out of love with itself. Underlying tensions erupted, and Anderson left. Wakeman, meanwhile, seemed to spend most of his time out of the country and restricted himself merely to phoning in the odd Polymoog adumbration every now and then before following the leader right out of the group.

Dan Hedges wrote at the time: 'It's Yes after an oil change and a 30,000-mile tune-up, moving out of the cosmic 1970s and into the 1980s. No skinny ties or short-back-and-sides yet, but ... more current. A test run for the new lineup that improves with each listening.'[33] What he overlooked was the fact that the writing had been on the wall for Yes long before Anderson left. As *The Wall* had confirmed, Progressive, in its original incarnation, had sounded its last tired trump. Only musical product which paid lip-service to contemporary trends or which was of unimpeachable and hitherto-unheard musical brilliance could hope to buck the trend. Certainly no respray of Yes, a band already critically untouchable, was going to change matters. Any attempts to reconcile itself with its present when its immediate past was so strewn with what was then assumed to be laziness and complacency were wholly doomed to failure. Horn and Downes were not so much a kick in the pants for Yes as their final convulsive shudder of life. For the time being, anyway.

VERDICT: DEATH BY MISADVENTURE

Three years into Thatcherism and the dinosaurs were almost extinct. True, she began dismantling the tax apparatus that had unsettled and exiled them, but this applied only to the genuine superstars, and despite the incoming Conservative government's tax leniency – which should have had the codgers flocking back and reasserting their grip on the charts after the aberration of Punk – precisely the opposite happened. Even Thatcher couldn't legislate away a sea-change in musical tastes.

To assimilate and attempt to explain the death of Progressive, we need once again to contextualize. Rock values were different in the late1970s. It may seem odd in an era where a four-year gap between albums is regarded as normal, but in the late 1970s such behaviour would have been testament to the fact that an act had disappeared from the face of the earth or fallen victim to terminal sloth. Latterday promotional mechanisms and gimmicks for keeping a band and its produce in the public eye were still in their infancy – video tapes were at a premium; PR budgets were smaller, techniques less sophisticated – in other words, the ephemera with which rock's ancients still flourish in our own time (remasters, repackagings, reinventions) were not as readily available to bridge the gaps between original productions as they are today. A band's workrate had to be more intensive in order to ensure its survival. While today we may imagine that Yes's 1970s recording schedule (eight albums) was hectic by modern standards, then it was seen as an outrageous piece of decadent self-indulgence. It is, of course, nonsense to condemn the acts this way.

Much criticism of rock in the 1970s is unreliable; either it was clouded by fundamental revolutionary fervour during Punk's rabble-rousing house party, or it later became a bad imitation of those same brickbats, second-hand shibboleths ignorant of specific rock production values and aesthetics. It is often over-looked, in our throwaway castigation of rock-star hedonism in the 1970s, that truculent managers and record companies expected major acts to tour and record in almost constant cyclical succession in the 1970s. Yes, in particular, were inveterate workers: doubters can check the band's itineraries during this period.

The rewards, of course, were staggering, and often extravagantly flaunted. But by present-day standards, Progressive bands worked hard; but thanks to the predations of the taxman and the dollar's lure, the crucial British market which had nurtured and maintained them was abandoned by the genre's flagship acts. And in their place, Punk and New Wave moved in.

On a more practical basis, when such values prevailed, there were many other newcomers ready to fill gaps in the market left by big bands on creative furlough – but by 1979 none of these young pretenders was Progressive. They were skinny-tied power-poppers like the Vapors or fodder for the expanding FM market like Sad Café; at the grassroots they were scratchy, politically-correct postpunkers. As early as 1976 the Progressive talent pool was drying up and the investment coffers of record labels were emptying over (less costly) pub-rockers and punks. By 1979 the music-business bubble had burst; Frith claims that world sales, which had grown from $4.75 billion to $7 billion between 1973 and 1978, fell by 20 per cent in Britain in 1979 and by 11 per cent in the USA.[34] Recordings had to find a wider market than hitherto and less money was now likely to be invested in a potentially expensive genre such as Progressive.

Tom Newman summarizes: 'Bands were getting six-figure advances and years to make records. Companies were sucking up to bands and then they realized that they weren't recouping their outlay on the studio time. The accountants moved in. They make things work, but at the same time they spell the death knell for up-and-coming creative and Progressive stuff.'[35]

The change that Punk wrought was not on Progressive stars but on the grassroots that fed the larger stages. Already in 1975 pub-rock had seriously undercut Progressive acts in the marketplace. As public interest in Progressive artists waned, those Smoke-on-the-Water, small-talent-big-dream strummers in guitar shops began seeing profits in greater simplicity of musical means.

Having barred the way for successors and heirs, Progressive welcomed in its assassins. This was embodied perfectly in the phenomenon of the New Wave of British Heavy Metal.

Heavy metal was thought to have been heading the same way as its dinosaur sister, Progressive, at the end of 1978 when a countrywide resurgence in very young Heavy Metal bands appeared. A Heavy Metal disco was opened at Kingsbury in north-west London. 'Thursday night it could get a bit Proggish,' remembers one observer. 'Acid rock night. That night, you didn't just get competitions to see who played air guitar best. You had competitions to see who could play air Hammond organ best – all these guys pretending to be Jon Lord and Keith Emerson, rocking big bits of thin air back and forth.'[36]

By winter 1979, the country swarmed with HM bands. Chief lieutenants of this movement were Radio 1 DJ Tommy Vance and the rock journalist Geoff Barton of *Sounds*. Along with ska, punk and reggae, HM regained a genuine grassroots following both in terms of consumers and performers.

It was the inevitable backlash to Punk's exhortations to 'never trust a hippy'. But instead of a new generation of progsters reasserting the right to wear long hair, chug cider and roll joints, came junior HMers. They hijacked the rockist principles on which Progressive built its citadel: values of musical authenticity and virtuosity. Additionally, they also retained enough working-class machismo to allow Heavy Metal practitioners to hold their heads up in rock's abrasive, urbanized post-Punk aesthetic, depriving Progressive of its middle-class and lower-middle-class fans, for whom rock still 'meant something'. The soulmates of the air-guitar squads with real abilities on real instruments meant that the success that HM could offer starved Progressive of another vital source of lifeblood: new musicians. The vagaries of the rock marketplace were strangling Progressive at its roots.

There were other Progressive bloodlines in new HM; Canadian trio Rush specialized in clunking riffs and bludgeoning bass, but their repertoire also included elaborately constructed suite-like compositions such as the twenty-five-minute 'Cygnus X-1', whose variation of mood, timbre and metre are among the nearest to true English Progressive custom that North America ever got. That the body of their army of adoring fans in the UK usually sewed their name on to their leather jackets alongside the logos of such Jurassic-era axe-thrashers as Vardis and Samson seems odd; but Rush's penchant for stompalong melodic hooks and tendency to live volume and solo overkill sold well amid the HM fraternity. And their lyrics, often inspired by the far-Right Canadian philosopher Ayn Rand, featured social prescriptions of varying toxicity, such as exhortations to 'philosophers and ploughmen' to know their respective places. This was perhaps the logical outcome of an era of accelerating individualism of the haves but the increased defensiveness and parochialism of Western society's blue-collar have-nots in the face of economic recession. Rush were Thatcherite/Reaganite politics made music: all the technique, all the surface of Progressive without its conciliatory nature.

Dave Stewart recalls:

> The New Wave of British Heavy Metal wasn't new. It was there all along. In places like Salcombe and Tidworth there'd be Led Zep wannabes getting out of their heads on Dry Blackthorn cider – but the press picked up on it. At least it made being able to play the guitar acceptable again – and out of that there arose some Progressive revivalists.'[37]

Not in 1981, though; albums from Anthony Phillips and Caravan were ignored; Hackett went into creative recess; Greg Lake attempted a disastrous comeback with an eponymous solo album. Ploddingly rock-based, the characterless result featured an unequivocally atrocious single, 'Nuclear Attack'.

The only consolation was the re-formation of King Crimson and a continuation of the seemingly unstoppable onward march of Genesis, aided no end by the success of Phil Collins's debut album *Face Value* and the single, 'In the Air Tonight'. A collection of morose, timbrally austere pop songs that managed to sound downbeat even at fast tempi, Collins appeared to be a sounding board for the new Genesis which the band continued to plug in interviews to placate foes and – not admitted publicly – to woo new clientele. The spare atmosphere of 'In the Air' was the prototype. By the next group album, September's *Abacab*, Collins's style had been adopted by his adoptive band. The whole of side two, particularly, could have come from *Face Value*.

ELP and Yes went supernova and collapsed into the black hole that was Asia, a hybrid supergroup launched in spring 1982 to derision and delight in equal measure among Progressive fans. The band comprised John Wetton (bass), Geoff Downes (keyboards), Steve Howe (guitar) and Carl Palmer (drums, later to wangle his pal Greg Lake into the lineup as a guest replacement for Wetton). Nothing could have better given anti-Progressive forces a bigger target than this FM-rock band which managed not only to retain the vices of empty virtuosity but combined with them a commitment to musical turgidity and unashamedly money-oriented product.

Asia were luridly launched in April 1982, and the fact that the US AOR market took them to its heart speaks volumes. Asia sold millions, but their links with Progressive rock were as tenuous as George Formby's links with Mozart. Rick Wakeman said: 'I'll probably get shot for saying this – but I think Steve [Howe]'s guitar playing was too good for Asia.'[38]

Wakeman himself was billed for one of any number of idiotic supergroup schemes whose unsellability must have been obvious even to their progenitors (Asia the rule-proving exception). His intended Brian Lane-orchestrated link-up with Carl Palmer and John Wetton had, according to the keyboardist, a no-strings deal with the newly-formed Geffen Record Company, but Wakeman smelt a rat and refused to sign. Within a year, he was sleeping rough on park benches in London – his marriage and career having disintegrated as Charisma Records, his new label, hit the rocks themselves.

Wakeman's decline was alleviated by a short-lived Channel 4 show, *Gastank*, which was in itself, in ironic and unintentional keeping with the times, practically a mortuary for 1970s rock's living dead (Wakeman co-hosted it with Tony Ashton and jammed with everyone and anyone). Stranded in the fission of the 'new' Yes (Horn quitting, unable to take any more), Chris Squire and Alan White were alleged to be taking up with Jimmy Page in a project called XYZ; true to form, it was quietly put to death.

Dave Stewart recalls 1981 as a time of stringency and compromise; he ended up in the pit of a West End sex show, *Let My People Come*, deputizing on keyboards for friend and erstwhile National Health keyboardist Alan Gowen.[39] Gowen's own tragic death from leukaemia in the summer of 1981 was the cruellest and most casual blow fate administered to the ailing Progressive scene. The premier *littérateur* of Progressive, Pete Sinfield, teamed up with the *grands fromages* of Eurovision, Bucks Fizz. Some, like Anthony Phillips, who had had the ill-fortune to launch a musical career based on exquisitely delicate English guitar impressionism in the

Punk winter of 1976–7 and found himself a pariah, survived on library music. The Enid surfaced as Kim Wilde's backing band. Pye, their record company, had folded on the eve of releasing a double compilation album, *Rhapsody in Rock*, and there were bills to be paid, big ones.

Godfrey takes up the story:

Francis [Lickerish] by this time was married with a child. His brother moved into the vicinity with his wife and then decided to conduct an affair with Willie Gilmour's wife. We also had this woman turn up, called Caroline Ashton, saying she wanted to help the band. She got herself ensconced and caused all sorts of trouble. She made Francis believe he was a god and could do anything; there was a failed coup against me, but Francis was the one that ended up being shoehorned out. To keep afloat we had to record completely ridiculous, anonymous singles and we got asked to play these all the time. It was meant to be a kind of subtle two-fingers to the industry but it didn't quite work out like that.

Thank God we at least went on getting gigs after Punk. We had different music, but The Enid had an attitude also, which was 'fuck you', basically, as far as the Establishment was concerned. We had quite a big following after Punk. We'd go up to Middlesbrough or wherever, and play 'Fand'. And you'd get these twenty yobbos at the back screaming 'Fucking get off!' which would turn the other 200-odd people our way, because they felt that we were courageous to do something we so believed in.[40]

Disheartened, the band turned to Wilde and backed her on all her albums up to *Cambodia* (1985). Godfrey remembers: 'Kim was sweet – always was – but … we got paid a pittance. It was recorded in our studio, so we didn't get the kind of rates for recording normal, big-time commercial albums.'[41]

Tom Newman says of this time:

Everyone was confused about what they had to do. Mike

Oldfield was told to start making pop records. He thought, 'What do I do? Do I become the singer? Do I hire a singer?' He wasn't sure if he was supposed to be this leading light of instrumental music or a pop star. People had got used to rules laid down in the 1960s and couldn't adapt.[42]

BLAME THE MESSENGER: PROGRESSIVE AND THE PRESS

This examination of Progressive's last years cannot close without a close look at what most enthusiasts perceive as the real villains of the genre: the rock press. They were accused of rank opportunism in jumping on the Punk bandwaggon and lending it disproportionate support at Progressive's cost. This is, superficially, fair comment, but it conveniently forgets to address the press's role in Progressive's ascendancy. After all, whose bandwaggon had the press pushed, back in 1969? The Archies'?

It was, after all, not the press that cooked up the change in attitudes to Progressive, but circumstances entirely beyond the control of the rock industry and its hangers-on. Progressive, it must be remembered, suckled on the residue of 1960s idealism; by 1972 this was still more than a memory in the minds of most young people. But this was soon to change, and with it the music that the *zeitgeist* produced changed too.

By 1978 the 1960s generation had watched appalled as the Munich killings, Yom Kippur, Amin, the oil crisis, the end of the post-war boom and urban guerrilla warfare worldwide unfolded on TV. The Lewisham anti-Nazi riot of 1977 had a very different import to that of Grosvenor Square in 1968. Detente withered like its architects, Brezhnev senile in Moscow, Nixon cashiered in Washington. Skylab, after Apollo the most potent symbol of post-war technocratic striving, fell uselessly, uncared-for and unnoticed in the Australian outback. The moon stretched out of grasp again.

As forecast in Alvin Toffler's *The Third Wave*, the technology of the immediate future wouldn't be a public technology for the global village, but a personal one; in lieu of space stations would come calculators, PCs and the Sony Walkman. After all, technology could be trusted only in the hands of individual users. In the hands of governments, it became Big Brother. Hadn't Nixon called science to his aid in his Watergate conspiracies by taping Oval Office conversations? Suddenly science was no longer the friend of the common man, but his enemy, a notion entrenched in late-1970s popular culture by novels (Michael Crichton's *Coma*) and movies (*Capricorn One* and *Rollerball*). *Logan's Run* (a *Brave New World* rip-off particularly poignant in its highlighting of tensions between technology, utilitarianism, individualism and utopianism, all proto-hippy lodestones) was a classic of its type.

If the 1960s was flower power, the 1970s was toxic shock. Somehow, by 1978, the 'Yes in the Round' show really did seem disengaged from the *zeitgeist* upon which popular culture feeds. And has anyone who really loves Progressive ever stopped to wonder whether people might not actually have got fed up with it? Or even, to hazard a heresy, grown out of it? Progressive's generation had, by and large, now reached their mid-twenties and had presumably disposed of the bohemian and individualist mannerisms of adolescence; their successors had other musics on their turntables.

The press alone can't be blamed for this. But what about the reportage of Punk and its aftermath? This was discussed in terms of what later writers would term 'rockism' – that rock was still the language of change, that the music was really still dangerous. What underlay this was the conventional modernist notion that music expressed the soul of the performer.

The Romantic/modernist notion of the vocalist, for example, was that the voice was an instrument sung not *with* but *through*, a means of expressing some other quality or entity. For example, the Sex Pistols' music was said to 'express' teenage revolt and inner-city deprivation much in the same way that ELP had been said to 'express' musical genius, an intangible ideal. Music was not prized for its inherent qualities, but always in terms of its power in expressing something else. In this respect, the commentators who praised Punk were dutifully following accepted critical practice.

But these prevalent attitudes began to be questioned by a disparate group of young musicians, among whom numbered such acts as the Gang of Four and the Pop Group. Accompanied by such writers as the *NME*'s Ian Penman and Paul Morley, a critical discourse began to emerge from the theories of postmodern and poststructuralist French thinkers Jacques Derrida, Michel Foucault and Jean Baudrillard and the English sociologist Dick Hebdige.

Clearly, for Progressive rock, with its obsession with transcendence, performance and authorship, this caused chaos. Celebrated instead were disco and pop, musics in which the main component was the beat as Simon Frith wrote, which, utterly simplistic, could not be discussed in subjective terms in the same way as a melody could be described as, for example, 'sinuous' or 'thrilling'. The punk vanguard bands, wrote Frith, emphasized the beat also, for the same reason.[43] The Gang of Four's early material exemplifies this: undermining the idea of rock musicians as elite messengers of a distinct, higher reality. It was not simplicity that was celebrated, but the whole idea that popular music meant, represented, stood for and conveyed nothing apart from itself. The foregrounding of rhythm, music's most objective quality, made music an open text. True to postmodern dicta, all that mattered was surface; there was no substance beneath; the world was now composed of surfaces. A new way of listening to, a new way of writing about, rock and pop was necessary. Those who retained some rhythmic simplicity with a degree of musical literacy – although not one which demonstrated anything redolent of subjectivity, like individual soloing – were then upheld as role models for politically-correct rock – or pop.

This was partly behind preposterous and often appallingly written early-1980s announcements to the effect that the likes of Linx and Haircut 100 were 'subversive'. By 1982 the words of Wham! – get pretty and love the recession – could be actually praised because the text referred to nothing but itself; there could be no 'message' behind the music. And with a surface as apparently literate (surely a subjective value in itself? No? Oh, sorry) as George Michael's rapping on 'Young Guns', well ... was this not the future? For the most part though these 'surfaces' of pure pop sensibility were ineffably dull; Orange Juice, Altered

Images, Depeche Mode, even judged by pop standards, produced music to turn off, unsophisticated to the point of banality, but with the crucial surface glitter of pop simplicity of line and timbre that elated the *NME*. Much piffle was also written about the mind/body dimension of the music (body objective − mind subjective); the fact was, however, that much of the new music was ordinary in terms of danceability, even when compared against the most humdrum of US Disco.

Aside from the laughable subjectivity of this new journalism, the disdain for such textual masturbation among musicians themselves was telling − it was cannily explained away by invoking Barthes's denial of authorial intention.

But the new journalism came to grief by rendering the act of journalism as an object of cult worship by exaggerated technicalities as vacuous as those of the most ostentatious Progressive rocker. In Chris Cutler's phrase: 'They'd all just come out of school where they'd read lots of French philosophers − and wanted everyone to know about it.'[44] *Arriviste* they might have been; but these writers undeniably reflected − if not led − trends in the record industry and in the popular consumption thereof, indeed the entire public reflex towards mass media, by now embracing forms such as video and satellite television whereby the sanctity of the work of art and the mores which formed it − genius, exclusivity, specialism, etc. − were even further eroded.

That the 1980s and 1990s would revive Progressive rock by dint of the very postmodernism that had damned it among the cognoscenti could not have been foreseen. But in the hands of convert minimalists and unashamed imitators, that revival − rendering Progressive rock not real but existing in a kind of hyperreality of simulation and imitation − did indeed take place.

8 INNOVATORS AND SIMULATORS
(PROGRESSIVE AND POSTMODERNITY 1983–88)

THE SHOCK OF THE NEW

Quite apart from the scourging of Progressive in the late 1970s, the early 1980s snuffed out any hope of a rearguard-action revival. New Right politics systematically discredited the utopian and prescriptive postures of the 1960s. Musically, Punk and New Wave reduced record-company overheads, and the media demonization of the genre drove home the nails in its coffin. Most importantly, the changing syntax of rock undermined Progressive: emphasis on the non-American musical currents which had underpinned the Progressive project from 1967 onwards was decisively reversed with the R&B fertilizing of pub-rock, the Iggy Pop–Johnny Thunders–Lou Reed heritage in Punk. Further to this, putatively 'progressive' elements within

Punk asserted themselves; as was suggested in Chapter 7, The Pop
Group, the Gang of Four, Prag VEC sought to radicalize not any
essentialist visions of music – that music was fundamentally
expressive of subjective intentions, honesty, authenticity, sincerity
etc. – but asserted that music's relationship with its consumers
could be changed. To recap, these musicians laid an emphasis less
on orthodox constituents of music-making, such as melody or
harmony, than on rhythm (which is, as Simon Frith has pointed
out, the musical element least open to subjective interpretation
or description), thus emasculating the conventions of musical
representation in Western discourse – no longer could music
accrue recognizable meaning as an emotional cipher except
through meanings generated by the individual listener.

  This rhythm-centred approach, nevertheless, resonated distantly
in the music of two early-1980s mainstream musicians, Peter
Gabriel and Kate Bush, which provided a type of epitaph for
Progressive ideology. Both these musicians drew on non-Western
input to create music, in the words of Allan Moore, 'around rhythm
tracks rather than harmonic patterns'.[1] It was an undertaking that
had occupied Gabriel for some time. Cumulatively revamping his
own textures, he undermined the differentiated approach to
individual instruments (effectively a technique of traditional
arrangement) and blurred the boundaries between timbres. He also
evinced interest in contemporary electronics, and it was surely no
coincidence that he befriended Robert Fripp, who had explored
similar avenues since *No Pussyfooting* (1973). This album, recorded
in collaboration with Brian Eno, itself deconstructed conventional
electric arrangement, with thick, unresponsive, overtone-heavy
sounds obfuscating normal textural relations.

  Additionally, Gabriel's involvement in bankrolling (and
eventually bailing out) the inaugural World of Music, Arts and
Dance (WOMAD) festival in Bath in 1982, reflected a growing
interest in West African polyrhythms; Moore points out that in
the album's centrepiece track, 'Rhythm of the Heat', Gabriel
further develops African affinities with an acceleration of the
tempo in a 3:2 ratio.[2]

  'I'm certain the Third World can have an increasing influence on our culture and in music a very vigorous hybrid will be produced which is based on this non-European influence and the new technology which is going to get very cheap and this facility will open up a new age of electronic skiffle.'[3] These were Gabriel's words to Melvyn Bragg's LWT *South Bank Show* that year. They may have been naïve, but they proved massively prophetic.

The postmodern, plunderphonic nature of Gabriel's purloining of Third World textures to enrich First World music was hardly new, but took a step forward in the use of the Fairlight keyboard computer. This enabled musicians to sample any sound and reproduce it in conventional musical octaves, taking the technology of the Mellotron to its logical conclusion and opening up new sonic and textural possibilities. Gabriel and Bush (almost contemporaneously) used the instrument to generate both arrangements and rhythms, further deconstructing the Progressive notions of authenticity and individual musical/technical endeavour. Gabriel had patented its use on 'I Don't Remember' (1980), sampling smashed milk bottles and banged bricks for the melody.

Rock historiography excludes Bush from Progressive narratives; her early material rested on antique harmonies, utilized occasional metric adventure but ultimately hedged too much on traditional verse-refrain structures to trouble many Progressive anthologists. By *The Dreaming* (1982) Bush was, however, dealing with an Australian Aboriginal Ur-mysticism. Additionally, her employment of other 'roots' sources (traditional Bulgarian vocalists, dijeridus) does indicate that the Progressive/progressive split (i.e. the gap between Progressive ideology and innovatory music-making) had disappeared again. Simply, the end of Progressive ideology had been replaced by a clamour for the moral high ground of rock composition. What could now be deemed Progressive? In a postmodern environment devoid of certainties in any cultural sphere, it was impossible to say – it was impossible for anyone to claim primacy.

But several acts did – or at least their devotees claimed it. One was the reincarnated King Crimson, an updating of Fripp's revolutionary 1970s outfit, who shared musical antecedents with Bush and Gabriel – and Marillion, who claimed Crimson, Bush and Gabriel themselves as influences.

REWRITING THE SCRIPT PART ONE: KING CRIMSON

Since his return to the rock business in 1977, Robert Fripp's residency in New York had further broadened his outlook on musical discourse. From the eyrie of his Bowery loft near Greenwich Village he could survey a vibrant avant-garde artistic scene. Influenced by the pop-art minimalism of the 1960s, its new luminaries – composers Steve Reich, Glenn Branca, Meredith Monk and performance artist Laurie Anderson – pursued the scrap'n'build approach pioneered by LaMonte Young, John Cage and the Velvet Underground in dispensing with Western notions of harmony and rhythm, while dallying with listener-friendliness through sensibilities honed by exposure to Warhol's populism.

The immediate effects on Fripp's own output will be discussed in the next chapter, but his experiences in New York led him to apply his new-found expertise to rock, a medium he still believed to have a flexibility and potential to a degree unmatched by any other contemporary musical form.

Fripp originally approached Bill Bruford and his bassist Jeff Berlin, but he found Berlin's style too 'busy' and instead turned to New Yorker Tony Levin.[4] Fripp admired Levin's work on bass and on the Chapman stick (particularly the latter instrument, whose ten strings and fingering techniques enabled pianistic legato chords to be played with a guitarist's facility for note-bending, vibrato and attack). Fripp also chose a second guitarist, American Adrian Belew, whose band had supported Fripp's other late-1970s project, a 'dance band' of vaguely New Wave bent called the League of Gentlemen (recalling the Dorset soul combo with whom Fripp had started his career). Fripp rehearsed the band from late 1980 and called it, originally and presciently, Discipline; King Crimson, Fripp imagined, was a name that might lead to cash-in accusations from the hated music media.

But by mid-1981, he and the other members agreed – while

on tour in France – that they should rechristen themselves King Crimson. The resultant album, however, retained the title *Discipline*.

Even devotees of the harsher and heavier explorations of the Mark III Crimson were perplexed by what they heard: dizzying, stripped-down polymetric rock'n'roll. If the first King Crimson had been a Rolls-Royce, this was the chassis rebuilt with rocket engines and missing its silencer.

Bill Bruford remembers, 'Music in the States was going well – Peter Gabriel, Laurie Anderson, Talking Heads, the loft scene; it was an exciting time.'[5] For Bruford, the band was 'one of the few gigs for a rock drummer where you could play in 17/16 and still stay in a decent hotel',[6] but it also presented a challenge of a wholly new order.

> The big difference about this band was the acknowledgement of another cultural way of doing things. In the West there's this idea of the soloist, the star who steps forward, does their thing and retires. Robert suggested instead that we work like a gamelan. Everybody said: 'How do they operate?' And he told us. They don't care about soloists, they just co-operate in setting up a huge clanging and banging. You don't have to be a virtuoso to play. In fact in Bali they don't even have a word for musician, it's just something everybody does. Nobody would call themselves a musician any more than you'd call yourself an eater because you eat. We suppressed showing-off; discipline, hence the name. Robert actually erased drum fills of mine as being flourishes of individualism.[7]

Certainly the music on *Discipline* (1981), *Beat* (1982) and *Three of a Perfect Pair* (1984) is of unusual possession and concentration, committed to what Eric Tamm (glossing Fripp) calls a 'single artistic vision' compared to the hybridizing intentions of previous incarnations of the band.[8] The abrasive nature of the music brings most readily to mind *Larks' Tongues in Aspic* from Crimson's oeuvre, but the actualities of the sound are quite different, although just as intrinsic to Fripp's overall orientation of his players, extending the concepts of his solo work into a rock quartet format – both those of composition- and performance-related intellectual sobriety. Urban funk, the non-synchronous phrasing and counterparting of legato and staccato techniques (notably with Belew and Fripp's guitar roles), and the intricacy of interlocking techniques not just between bass and drums and guitar and guitar but simultaneously between all four players, constituted a fundamental reworking of the Progressive ideology. The substitution of intimacy for grandiloquence (the fore-grounding of a compact and undemonstrative unit of players pursuing absolute music as opposed to the projection of singularized individual genius) was daring enough. At a stroke, King Crimson Mark IV reclaimed the word 'progressive' for Progressive rock music.

Tamm comments, 'Because of the reliance on 3rds and 7ths [chords], there may seem to be harmonic activity, but this is an illusion; there are changes or shifts, but no sense of gravitational motion through tonal space ... the music relies more on rhythm and texture than on tonality.'[9] The texture was enriched not by reliance on the virtuosity or sensitivity of individual group members, but through Fripp's increasingly sensitive use of the studio. Whereas Pink Floyd's use of found sound had become increasingly meretricious, with extra-musical material used as illustration, contrasted with the notes, Fripp revisited the original *musique concrète* notions of making noise texturally indissoluble from music, as evidenced on the aural furniture moved from the world around him into compositions such as 'Indiscipline' (*Discipline*), 'Dig Me' (*Three*) and 'Neurotica' (*Beat*).

Fripp's vision may have fractured at times; there is soloing aplenty in King Crimson IV, most notably by Fripp himself, albeit rarely as the centre of musical attention around which the other music revolves and the lurching and soaring of the riffs which both introduce and conclude the stupefyingly hyperactive 'Neurotica' contain some of the most brilliant and virtuosic ensemble playing of any rock band on record.

It is true that the stainless-steel lustre of Fripp's studio sound and the guitar and keyboard sounds he patented would find their way into a multiplicity of New York-derived pop from later David Byrne to Sting, but that is not Fripp's responsibility. But if the guitarist thought his radical rethink of Progressive as progressive would result in a sudden critical acknowledgement of the merits of his music, he was mistaken. Good notices were little more than polite, and even the kinder ones insisted on highlighting the role played by (perceived) technocracy suppressing expression. This was a view perhaps most eloquently put by Ethlie Ann Vare: 'The trouble with having four certified musical geniuses on the same stage at the same time is that if you aren't enjoying the show, you assume it's your fault ... this is a concert, not an IQ test.'[10]

But significant numbers of people liked what they heard. Bruford comments regretfully, 'We were getting written about in the *New York Times*, and serious guys were coming to see us. The term 'world music' was just beginning to circulate and the early days of ambient music were upon us – it was brought rudely to a halt by Robert for no good reason in 1984.'[11]

Bush, Fripp and particularly Gabriel were pilloried by a British rock press who, while maybe not responsible for Progressive's end, were falling over themselves in polysyllabic zeal to ensure the corpse remained firmly interred. Music, of course, didn't count; particularly telling were the two verdicts on Gabriel's 1982 album. Authors Dave McCullough (*Sounds*) and Gavin Martin (*NME*) were, it should be remembered, apologists for the ostentatiously acquisitive jamboree junket of New Pop. 'Genesis, Roxy Music, Gabriel – all comfortably well-off, middle-aged and classed ... characterized by a smugness, a fascismo organization around them ... and a music as predictably fascismo-bland to match ... '[12] Martin ripped into Gabriel's 'white liberal guilt' (a quality wholly absent from contemporary music journalism, naturally) and 'the incredibly selfish notion that we must look to tribal civilizations to understand ourselves (as if they'd been created specifically for the purpose'.[13] Not a note of the music was mentioned.

The triumvirate of Bush, Fripp (who also took their turns in the stocks) and Gabriel undeniably extended rock music in the early 1980s, and the failure of music cognoscenti to recognize the fact is a far greater stain on rock reportage than anything that occurred during Punk. Gabriel's obsession with the conscious and unconscious self may have courted barbs with its whiff of late 1970s Californian New Ageism, particularly his aborted rock opera, *Mozo*, which dealt with the self-transforming 'mercurial stranger' of the Aurora Consurgens, the medieval alchemical treatise believed by Carl Jung to be the work of St Thomas Aquinas. But his song 'Milgram's 37' (later 'We Do What We're Told') concerned itself with psychological experiment; and his entire creative *raison d'être* concerned itself with novel ways of human communication; Gabriel had discussed cinema–theatre crossover projects with the Czech director Josef Svoboda of the Lanterna Magica company in Prague, and also with animator Raduz Cincera, advocate of audience-driven plotting.

But as Progressive mores couldn't satisfy the press even by continuing to progress, then it seemed the only viable alternative was to give up, put two fingers up to the world and give the fans what they wanted – go backwards rather than forwards.

REWRITING THE SCRIPT PART TWO: MARILLION AND NEOPROGRESSIVE

One of the chief phenomena of the postmodern condition, the impossibility of uniqueness in an age of hyperreality and inexhaustible sensory overload and information, the recognition that all output can only be simulacra of previous output, came to fruition in Progressive.

In 1979 a Progressive band called Silmarillion came into being in Aylesbury, Buckinghamshire. Losers in a losers' game? While their peers scratched diligently away at post-Punk chords, not only did the Tolkien-derived name hint at limited originality, it was like a kick-my-butt T-shirt to an industry cleansing itself of the Progressive ethos. Compromising the Tolkien debt by changing their name to Marillion made not an iota of difference until the arrival of Derek Dick, a six-feet-five Scot who counted teaboy, forester and garden-sprinkler quality inspector among his previous occupations. He sang under the gnostic pseudonym of

Fish, and he would develop into the most natural British rock showman since Freddie Mercury.

In piquant contrast to the accusations of pomposity and rock monumentalism levelled at the band, Marillion's progress on the road in the early 1980s was of a depressing insalubrity. At one concert guitarist Steve Rothery's strings slipped and a member of the audience had to go home and get him a replacement set. At another the imposing Fish fell through a hole in the rotted stage. In one of rock's most incongruous billings ever, the band even played second on the bill to sardonic Punk poet John Cooper Clarke.

But by January 1982 a punishing gig schedule (during which further members had been jettisoned) had created enough of a grassroots following to win the band a session slot on Tommy Vance's Radio 1 'Friday Rock Show'. This occasioned massive interest, not least because of the blatant plagiarism of early Genesis with which both the session and burgeoning coverage in the rock press seemed to associate the band. Fish's extravagant stage wardrobe also made an obvious enough target for plagiarism-spotters. To *Melody Maker*, Fish resembled 'a blue whale dressed in army surplus reeling from the shock of a head-on collision with a Max Factor lorry'.[14] The frankly derivative manner in which the band built their songs, with prelude, verse and chorus patterns alarmingly redolent of the older band, also drew critical fire.

But still they attracted unquestioning devotion; it became plain that a sizeable slab of Marillion's fan base was drawn from Heavy Metal. Vance's radio show had leant further and further towards the leather-clad constituency over the years and its championing of Marillion infiltrated the band's grandiose conceptions into the minds of impressionable air-guitarists already steeped in the fable-and-fantasy world conjured up in the lyrics and hoary chord sequences employed by the cornier new HMers. The artistic common ground between Progressive and Heavy Metal, always nebulous, was dissolving. Sensing a further sea-change in street-level taste, EMI swooped to sign Marillion for a six-figure sum. When the debut album appeared in March 1983 it confirmed everyone's prejudice, favourable or otherwise, about the band.

That album, *Script for a Jester's Tear*, was, and still is with
hindsight, an act of towering audacity almost unmatched in rock.
Its success illustrated better than almost any other single album
the fragmentation of musical taste in the 1980s. Just when the last
rites had been administered to Progressive, here was a band who
not only played Progressive rock, but – cripes! shock! horror! –
flaunted Progressive ideology, from elaborate sleeve art (retina-
roastingly garish designs from Mark Wilkinson) to concept lyrics
in an era supposedly liberated from such horrors for ever.

The ambiguities of style (ironically appropriated by Progressive's
sworn enemies in the postmodern pop camp and dog-in-the-
mangerishly denied any application elsewhere)were further strained
by Marillion's choice of subject matter: Ulster in 'Forgotten Sons'
(AK47-toting Fish as squaddie) and domestic violence in 'Punch
and Judy'. 'We'd drag out an idea for about five minutes when it was
really only worth about thirty seconds,' commented drummer Mick
Pointer later, referring to the stern editing the band's material
underwent as fame beckoned.[15] By 1984 *Sounds* readers had voted
Marillion best band and *Script* second best album of the year.

Marillion were the first openly postmodern Progressive band,
functionally if not intentionally. Irrespective of critical opinion, all
Progressive rock had, with its uneasy relationship of high cultural
aspiration and low cultural trappings, by its riot of different musical
styles in the eye of a McLuhanite storm of aural sense-data, occupied
an important place in postmodernity. Marillion's combination of
imagistic practices was as unfashionable as it was possible to get in
1983, short of recording an album of SS marching songs with an Oi!
skinhead band in Johannesburg; an apparently wanton borrowing of
a musical style already replete with debts of its own (i.e. the early
Progressive folk-blues-classical of Genesis) both confounded the
listener with its own borrowed musical surfaces and also asked
important questions about the ownership of rock's language – in a
way, Marillion were one of the first tribute bands.

They stoutly defended themselves against charges of imitation,
but their cheek in not only deploying a backward-looking
musical style but one unashamedly purloined from another band
courted brickbats to an almost provocative degree. The accusa-

tions of plagiarism came from what sold itself as a postmodern rock critical fraternity – thereby undermining its own postmodern credentials, for postmodernity sees to it that plagiarism is not only necessary but unavoidable.

In August 1983 a hard-gigging Scottish band, Pallas, who had been toiling through innumerable gigs against insurmountable odds of audience indifference and cultural obsolescence since the mid-1970s, stormed the Reading Festival and EMI moved once again. Before the year's end, Pallas were in America, recording with Eddie Offord (whose specific – and talismanic – involvement indicates just how seriously EMI were taking the possibility of a Progressive revival). Artist Patrick Woodroffe, last seen fleeing the fiasco of Dave Greenslade's *Pentateuch*, designed the cover of *The Sentinel*, which emerged in February 1984, a month before the release of massively popular Marillion's multiple-platinum second album, *Fugazi*.

Original keyboard player Mike Stobbie remembers that playing Progressive in the late 1970s was pleasant enough.

We started off as Rainbow. Aberdeen's only Progressive band. Then along came Richie Blackmore and ripped off our name. 'One criterion was that new singers had to be able to sing Yes's 'Yours is No Disgrace'. We were impossibly naïve. Brian Wood, our vocalist, copied Peter Gabriel – voice, mannerisms, the lot – to the point that he shaved the little triangle out of his hair on his forehead. I got a Rick Wakeman cape. Then there was a helmet which was made out of sheet-metal. Our drummer was a sheet-metal worker, so, well, why not? Then we pasted on mirrors from a mirror-ball. Incredible.'[16]

The band also brought half of Dundee to a standstill with orange smoke when a smoke bomb used in an outdoor performance turned out to be Army surplus.

As for Punk:

We got through it. We changed our name to Pallas Athene. Not too hip, maybe ... but we dressed up in combat fatigues and brought out an EP, *Reds under the Beds*; if you can't beat 'em, join 'em, we reckoned. Yeah, there were still some funny time-signatures but no Mellotrons. And I suppose because we had that harder edge – we left behind that kind of airy-fairy Prog with twelve-string guitars – we hung around for a bit.[17]

Pallas might have ambled happily along exercising these post-adolescent fantasies for years. But when bassist Graeme Murray contacted Marillion's Fish through a small advertisement in the *Melody Maker* and established their mutual Scottishness, a link was established which led to a nationwide tour of small venues which enabled the rough-and-ready Pallas to break themselves in England, where they were wholly unknown, and give the comparably ballsy Marillion a chance to explore a similarly alien Scots market.

Capitalizing threefold on prevailing adolescent trends towards HM, reflected glory from their Marillion connection and the brief revival of interest in the Progressive genre the latter activated – not to mention hyperactive gigging which by 1983 enabled them to top of the bill at Reading – the band were signed to EMI for some £500,000 that autumn.

Stobbie had by that time left, but he maintained contact with his former colleagues.

Pallas were supposed to be the flagship for the relaunch of Harvest – the EMI Prog subsidiary. As for the gigs ... they got the *Dr Who* special effects team to design a stage version of the Pallas helmet and plumage from the cover of *The Sentinel* [a stylized rendition of the mythological warrior queen Pallas Athene]. They gave it a fibreoptic plumage which changed colour. A long way from bucket helmets. They made the front cover of *Sounds*.

Then they came back to London and found that all their friends in EMI were either leaving or getting fired. They ended up without anyone to help them. The next album, *The Wedge*, was out, and cleaning up in Europe and EMI just withdrew all promotion. Killed it. Whether that was because they thought it was too much competition for Marillion and that the market wouldn't sustain the two bands I can't say – but such things are not unheard of.[18]

Pallas and IQ, the other main foci of attention in the (half-hearted at best, cynical at worst) press bandwaggon of a 'neo-Progressive' revival, can in truth feel relatively hard done by. Marillion, the market leaders, were, quite aside from the considerable talents of their frontman, as musically derivative of Genesis as they were imagistically derivative – at times to the point of surrealism.

The very first bars of the opening (title) track of *Script for a Jester's Tear* have Fish plaintively intoning a Gabrielesque melody line – of inevitably hymnal profile, tortuously led by the over-wrought lyrics across the stepping stones of sombre piano chords. From then on it's like a quiz night at a Genesis fans' convention, so many are the references to the older band for the listener to identify. There's a nod to the Tony Banks keyboard solo in 'Firth of Fifth' ('He Knows You Know' and elsewhere) and innumerable twelve-string guitar arpeggios and tinkling preludes. There is, however, a practically note-perfect lift of the opening ostinato to Mike Rutherford's *Smallcreep's Day* re-used as the bassline for 'Chelsea Monday'.

This may resemble nothing so much as musical trainspotting, but when influences are worn so blatantly on the sleeve that they actually hinder a band's compositional talents then they must be identified and isolated.

Indeed they hobble Marillion dreadfully – negating some very fine musicianship. What Genesis used as natural, organic outgrowths from a very personal vision of the language and syntax of pop utterance, Marillion simply over-used as decoration for otherwise conventional rock music – in which ideas are stated at the outset of a piece and then spread thinly around a lengthy musical structure. Dynamic and melodic variety there may be, but Marillion rarely stray far from the home base of their germ material – not necessarily a bad thing, but one which seriously damages their Progressive credentials. The band were also constrained by an unsympathetic production, which rendered them all but anonymous in textural terms. Hardly their fault, and a pity too, as it robs their music of the sense of transparency, of light and shade, that so much of Genesis's music depends on – there is, as a result, little sense of wonder in Marillion's music – all is submerged in a state-of-the-art session-musician storm of sound. The band's attempts at drama often fail to convince too – the chordal language is rich enough, but unadventurous in terms of how it colours and directs a song. Genesis themselves never ventured much beyond the safe haven of rock's cycle of fifths, but at least their chord *progressions* were not telegraphed. Small details – an extra interval in a chord here or a flourish of orchestral volume there – usually courtesy of Tony Banks' Mellotron – was what gave Genesis, for better or worse, their sense of real theatre and visceral edge, no matter how kitsch it might have seemed.

Not that Marillion were as bad as all that. *Script* is a not unpleasant listen. The playing lacks fire, but that is maybe once again the fault of the glutinous treacle of the production. The band's *commitment* is real enough, with a dedication to, and a palpable, almost schoolboyish, joy in their achievement. Fish's lyrics, while tending towards the gratuitous pictorialism of the cover (their prolixity often drags musical ideas out for longer than is strictly healthy) are often memorable. There are nice images nicely put – girls kissing princes into frogs, soldiers in Ireland dreaming of the dole queue as they evade snipers and ending up in a coffin being sent 'down the Emerald aisle'. But as with much amateur poetry, the unintentional juxtaposition of the naff image ('neon wonderland') with the naif ('saffron sunsets') undermines it. On *Fugazi* (1984) and in subsequent work, Fish has cultivated a rare talent – mostly because he has learned to recognize the poetry one can derive from the very ordinariness of pop lyrics. Peter Hammill's vividness of language, for example, often strikes home because of its location in otherwise unremarkable lines.

Fugazi, like 1985s blockbuster *Misplaced Childhood*, merely paid lip-service to Progressive with the retention of a few keyboard and guitar curlicues, and sold all the more for it. It would be unjust, however, to ignore the middle section of *Fugazi's* title track, exemplifying what Marillion could have been, the music given tremendous vitality by the wrongfooting placing of beats, the more original construction of chords and a strikingly improved means of roping the music between them. This music sings, as all good Progressive should.

IQ, while perhaps lacking the melodic muscle of Marillion (who never wanted for good hooks), did at least offer a more individual palette which, while just as derivative in its way, gave the impression that the choice of arrangements was indivisible from the choice of notes played – that the similarities with older bands arose *accidentally* from their own personal approach to music. This was perhaps inevitable given the greater ambition shown by the band when compared with Marillion – two tracks on IQ's debut album *Tales From The Lush Attic* (1983) break the ten-minute barrier. 'The Enemy Smacks' clocks in at nearly fourteen minutes while 'The Last Human Gateway' almost cracks twenty. This of course can give more scope by note-spinning as well as invention. But the band are tight enough, and are redeemed by a sense of mission, self-belief and even fun; 'My Baby Treats Me Right 'Cos I'm a Hard Lovin' Man All Night Long' may not be subtle satire of Heavy Metal, but satire of any sort in Progressive is a commodity as rare as hen's teeth and to be treasured.

Pallas, meanwhile, probably the most unsophisticated of the three bands, rarely strove to escape the chordal confines of rock, but within these parameters stayed true to a personal conception of Progressive, refusing to be seduced by borrowed ideas of improvization or construction. The result is a music which says not terribly much but says it very well with an undemonstrative lyricism and meaty energy which is more than pleasant. Like It Bites some years later, Pallas had at least some conception of how to rework pop music in their own image, as opposed to merely constructing wonky hybrids.

The re-formation of The Enid, who bought the rights to their back catalogue and began re-releasing them on their own Enid label, was perhaps more interesting for the very reason that no majors came in for the band at all, which enabled a curious little backwater of Progressive ideology to flourish in the mid-1980s.

Whether or not the Marillion phenomenon and its belligerent neo-Progressive stance helped clear a pitch for The Enid's own, more refined Progressive style, is debatable. Certainly The Enid's leader, the irrepressible Robert Godfrey, didn't care much either way. 'Marillion,' he had reputedly scoffed in 1983, 'won't last eighteen months.'[19]

Godfrey and guitarist Stephen Stewart had been tinkering with their own style, tailoring its extravagances to a harsher marketplace, but doing so with ingenuity and wit. They retained the heart-stopping power of Godfrey's classically influenced harmonies but disentangled them from quasi-orchestral canvases and multi-layered syncopations and resettled them in a more regular, congenial, four-square, chunky electro-pop format, often propelled by metres which both required musicianly discipline and offered music to dance to. In Godfrey's words, 'I was influenced by synthesizer music, electronics, by dance music ... but also possibly not having a permanent drummer living with the band, that may have swayed me in favour of sequenced rhythms.'[20]

Godfrey and Stewart, by now the permanent core of the band, set up a society named 'The Stand' to both act as a fan club and to promote Enid music. The response was prodigious and once again the band began to tour. The Stand's bizarre proselytization of unilateral nuclear disarmament (loudly trumpeted in the band's 1983 comeback album, *Something Wicked This Way Comes*), libertarianism, ecology and hippy idealism chimed with sundry themes adrift within an increasingly disparate mid-1980s *zeitgeist*.

Godfrey recalls:

Nuclear war ... was a burning issue at the time and as opposed to the Billy Braggs of this world, The Enid were a bit more subtle about it. More ambiguous, because ambiguity is something that makes people think about things. We weren't saying that nuclear weapons were good or bad – we said, 'Is the holocaust the burning fires of hell coming to punish mankind for his wickedness or the purifying fires of the Last Judgement wiping everything clean and heralding the New Jerusalem?

And just asked that question, which made it better than anything else of its kind.

I also used it to put an enormous amount of pressure on EMI to get our copyright back. I stopped their bands from going to Glastonbury, which was a CND gig in those days, because I found out that Thorn, who owned EMI, made the guidance system for Trident missiles. I rang Michael Eavis [the organizer of the Glastonbury Festival] in 1984 and he accused me of wrecking the festival when I asked him to pull EMI's bands. So I rang Bruce Kent and *he* got Michael to pull them.[21]

What this amounted to was that punks could once again be seen at Enid gigs. As indeed they could be seen at concerts by the enigmatic Twelfth Night who, like Pallas, had been diligently paying dues since the mid-1970s and, although they were led by putative Anglican vicar Geoff Mann, now wooed campus audiences with Mellotrons *and* issues.

It didn't last. The engagement of rock – as opposed to pop – and politics was still in recession. Liberal causes were now seen as the preserve of the popster and the punk, the fiasco of Oi! music and its hijacking of power-chords to neo-fascism notwithstanding. Of previous generations of pop musicians only Robert Wyatt could sing of political or social transformation henceforth and be taken seriously, perhaps because he eschewed the harmonic and melodic language of rock – whether Progressive or otherwise – in favour of a more polyglot style of music drawing on African and European folk music as well as of contemporary pop. To a rock cognoscenti spoon-fed on Punk and post-Punk realpolitik, whereby a transformative agenda had been stolen from the 1970s and remade in the 1980s, the essentially revisionist nature of critical discourse in the 1980s identified rock with the past, although even in the revivifying Phyllosan slipstream of Live Aid's resurrection of the rock damned most still identified rock with complacency and conservatism; even, in some cases, with comedy. Rob Reiner's 1983 movie, *This is Spinal Tap*, was a fictionalized docudrama of a sagging 1970s English rock act slogging through a disaster-prone US tour. Its merciless parody of rock auteurism, cracker-barrel philosophy, volume, virtuosity and above all vulgar stagecraft was aimed specifically at HM. The oafish literalism and pretensions of Spinal Tap's act immortalized Progressive rock practice and performance as something hopelessly obsolescent.

OF FAILURES AND FORGETTING

Why did the revival remain stillborn? Several trends can be identified. The Progressive audience had changed − not much, but appreciably, with the influx of HM acolytes through the agency of Marillion − and their expectations had changed, too. Consumers could find their escapism elsewhere than in Progressive ideology. Progressive's once-vaunted literacy was now devalued by contemporary cultural distrust of the 1960s (save as nostalgia-farm) and the artistic disrepute of its legacy; fantasy no longer meant utopianism and progress but dysfunction and individualization, mythologizing the self in the post-industrial landscape as opposed to the fulfilment of the self in the interior landscape of the mind or the exterior landscape of the rustic or fantastic − step forward Simple Minds (*Live in the City of Light*), U2 ('Where the Streets Have No Name') and Big Country ('Steeltown'). Virtuosity was now the preserve of fretboard-hammering big-hairs, Eddie van Halen, Steve Vai, Joe Satriani, Yngwie Malmsteen. Those wanting their listening pleasure stained with the muck of the countryside now no longer had to make do with finger cymbals and baroque guitars; with the global village getting smaller all the time, ethnicity now meant Salif Keita, WOMAD, ponchos, Afghan hats and gourds.

The rock business had transformed itself. Recovered from the slump of 1979 with epoch-making sales figures like those for Michael Jackson's *Thriller* (1983) and with the limitless profits of the new all-video cable medium of MTV, rock's forgotten amateurishness, in which vast profits were generated almost in spite of its top-heavy corporate structure, was transfigured by money into a super-capitalist machine which geared itself solely to making more money still. Innumerable techniques arose to identify and cater to markets. And then came the rock business's biggest shot in the arm since the Beatles (and perhaps the most significant latterday contribution to rock culture), Live Aid.

Bob Geldof's well-intentioned fundraising ultra-festival in 1985 ended up earning many more millions not just for the rock industry but for the leisure industry after its day-long festivities than for African famine relief, and was duly co-ordinated and funded by record-industry majors as a laboratory incubating new strains of product-propagation to the maximum audience via video, satellite television and marketing. Additionally, its employment of a cast of venerable rockers, thought of as potentially alienating to the hip young audience originally targeted, stole the show and conjured a global market for ageing musicians whom, until Live Aid, the rock industry had written off as unsellable. The performances of Queen, Tina Turner and David Bowie shattered the comfortable teleological economic planning of rock as a source of wealth that had to continually reproduce itself anew to ensure profitability. Henceforward, its products could be recycled, in true postmodern style, targeted with ever greater precision to ever more specialized markets. By 'products', we refer of course not just to past recordings, but to past artists recording again.

Result: a traumatic but sensationally profitable rebirth of rockism. Heavy Metal had made musical ability fashionable again. Live Aid made musical ability and middle age fashionable again, because, with adequate marketing, someone somewhere would buy the product, no matter how grey the hair or how long the solo.

Something, however, didn't add up. While Live Aid's gigantic success diced the already plutocratic rock market into still smaller and more profitable subdivisions of taste (age now had to be taken into consideration too) and the increasing sophistication and availability of reproduction technology opened up a cosmos of consumer choices in musical produce, Progressive, though still remained marginalized. Despite King Crimson's *In the Court of the Crimson King* having been one of the very first rock CDs when the new format hit the shelves in 1983, Marillion's storming of the UK and Genesis (admittedly long since shorn of any Progressive credentials) becoming one of the biggest concert draws in the world by 1987 (by royal appointment too), young Progressive musicians were still encountering implacable diffidence on the part of record companies. Progressive, thanks to the rewriting of the rock constitution by Live Aid, had become a commodity of rock's *past*, not of its future, except as a recyclable commodity. It became one of only a score of genres for the postmodern children of the information revolution to interface with in order to make sense of their lives. In mainstream culture, after all, by 1985 little could be made sense of without reference to something that had already happened.

But even in this ferment of the market, Heavy Metal and country musics enjoyed critical reappraisals in the late 1980s, while Progressive remained a pariah. The commensurate boom in compact-disc technology, with its drastic reduction in the costs of record production and manufacture, should have prepared the ground for an economically viable Progressive revival and for Progressive enthusiasts and musicians to begin adding once again to the genre's recorded corpus. But inexplicably, the kaleidoscopically fragmented post-Live Aid, CD-led marketplace found no place for them. Technology had granted almost every genre of music some niche in the market, but only those with sufficient popular appeal or publicity muscle could be expected to flourish. The irony was immense; the downsized nature of Progressive production (if not of Progressive ambition) meant that Progressive musicians found themselves inhabiting the same DIY terrain that the grandiloquence of their forebears had forced upon punk musicians.

It is illuminating to compare these developments with an account of the brief and tumultuous rebirth of Yes, in 1983/4. Crawling from the wreckage of the Horn and XYZ débâcles, Squire and White had recruited South African multi-instrumentalist/composer/producer Trevor Rabin for a no-horse, no-hope supergroup project called Cinema, to which organist Tony Kaye, Trevor Horn (now safely and gratefully harnessed to his production console) and, eventually, Jon Anderson gravitated. By this time the record industry which had been so ramshackle during Yes's heyday had grown up and got savvy; the nomenclature Yes was therefore given to maximize sales of what might have been a turkey under any other name.

But stylistic changes were also required in the current climate. While Britain might have been reawakening to guitar arpeggios and keyboard solos with Marillion, the USA was undergoing its own punk growing pains and the only sellable rock music in common currency remained straightforward FM/AOR product. What the new Yes did in the circumstances remains a feeble excuse for Progressive in the musical context of this book, yet highly resourceful in terms of contemporary cultural significance. As the returning Tony Kaye said of the resulting album, *90125*: 'We kept it very dimensionally sparse. We wanted it to be modern-sounding, it couldn't just be old Yes and the same old dirge, yet at the same time we knew it mustn't sound like [US FM bands] Styx or Journey'.[22] Atlantic boss Ahmet Ertegun, who had helped smooth the way for projects like *Tales from Topographic Oceans*, got tough; even he, a benevolent jazz-schooled mogul, had caught the prevailing economic wind. He told Squire: 'We have to have a hit single this time.'[23]

That hit, 'Owner of a Lonely Heart', was written by Rabin – on the toilet. Rabin's major chords and the identikit glister of LA studio gold is everywhere, but so is the cut-up editing technique (James Brown horns etc.) and sledgehammer snare-drum sound adapted from US dance music by Horn, which would later play a part in the Art of Noise.

The melodies and riffs are quite smartly integrated into the basic rock tread of the metres, particularly on the hit single, but the head-turning drop-ins and cut-and-paste finessing of musical expectations employed by Horn boosts the album, the first example of a Progressive rock band actively coming to terms with state-of-the-art recording technology in one of the most exciting periods of its development.

What Yes failed ultimately to engage completely with in 1983 was a revolution in the entire aesthetics of popular music, indeed of popular culture, a postmodern detonation of notions of authenticity and originality, a nullifying of stylistic boundaries attainable through technology. As Progressive musicians in the 1970s, Yes had helped the entertainment industry generate ever more investment in electronic reproduction; similarly, and more personally, they had pioneered cross-genre experiments before the popular-cultural critical faculty to appreciate them had developed. By the time such critiques were being formulated, Yes were artistic history, doomed by their Romantic/modernist notions of legitimacy and authenticity.

We shall deal with the issue of postmodernity and its relation to Progressive rock in more detail in the conclusion, but it behoves us to remember that Yes's ultimate refusal to embrace the revolution of sound in the 1980s – albeit swayed by industry diktat – prevented their very real collective and individual musical gifts using contemporary breakthroughs for making music which combined traditional harmonic and melodic inspiration with wholly new means of composition – by way of the sampler. The Art of Noise, Hector Zazou and Anne Dudley would be just three among hundreds who stole the thunder. In the 1970s Yes had enjoyed a mutually evolutionary kinship with studio technology to enhance their own compositional methodology. Now they merely seemed to be using the studio as an adjunct to help apply a surface gloss to ordinary pop music. They had the chance to rewrite again the traditions they had once appropriated – even their own – by means of recycling it into their music by wholly new means, using the sampler-led techniques of disruption and humour evidenced by the work of Malcolm MacLaren. Given Yes's gigantic musical pedigree, couldn't they have come up with something of suitable sophistication? Alas, no. They preferred to go on tour and disinter old favourites, taking a careworn act to stage after stage, to the extent where Warner Brothers actually issued an album, *9012 Live*, which featured, incredibly, only the solos from 1984 live shows.

Not only had technology been revolutionized first by polyphonic synthesizers, then digital recording, and then by the slow dazzle of samplers beginning with the Fairlight in 1980; the world was an ever more diverse source of musical information. With the breaking down of barriers in recording and reproducing technology and indeed of the means of broadcasting it to more and more people, accepted musical maps could surely be redrawn. Even if postmodernism left nothing new under the sun, surely the old could be infinitely rejigged?

'Frankie Goes to Hollywood, the whole idea of the ZTT label was a supreme irony,' laughs Paul Schütze. 'Paul Morley, the arch-postmodern journalist, making music on ZTT Records – now *that* was incredibly Progressive. Take Propaganda, for instance. More than a bit Prog.'[24]

Why not take them? The hyper-stylization of the four-piece recalled the surface obsessions of early-1980s New Romanticism; the extraordinarily knowing and totalized packaging of the likes of Frankie Goes to Hollywood, particularly in the use of ironically enigmatic epigram and motif, displayed an impressive Progressive ideological lineage.

Schütze contends,

It's easy to say that it underplayed virtuosity and promoted surface as opposed to content, but listen to 'Dr Mabuse' by Propaganda. The grandiloquence. These mammoth orchestral samples. That's where the virtuosity comes in. It's not the guitar or the keyboard any more. The fetishization of equipment's still around. This was a concept *label* with virtuoso producers and programmers. There are so many new sounds programmed into Propaganda it isn't true. And if you want to go further, the programming on Grace Jones's *Slave to the Rhythm* means that the difference between that and a Prog album, is, if you think about it, negligible.

I would argue that 808 State were a Progressive band – their music, if you want to examine it closely enough, had immense complexity and skill, but also a veneer of relatively simple beats if you didn't want to examine it.[25]

This is in spite of the relatively blues-based and pop-structured profiles of most of the individual numbers, but Schütze illustrates perfectly the divergence between traditional Progressive musical idioms and accelerating musical technology, which confuses the notion of 'Progressive' yet more to the point of incomprehensibility.

The *femme fatale* surface sheen of Propaganda's Claudia Brucken and Suzanne Freytag may seem light-years from Progressive's more elaborate horizontal developments, but the extraordinary degree of emotional response called into play by the use of imposing orchestral samples is indeed problematic in classifying the music as at least a cousin of Progressive rock. 'The thing is,' continues Schütze, 'the producer's art hasn't yet been admitted to being one of virtuosity. Propaganda's arrangements became so overblown they were almost architectural – overblown in the sense that Soviet sculpture is overblown. So overblown it moves into its own reference of scale where Frankie Goes to Hollywood seems like The Captain and Tenille.'[26] And, of course, very ironic.

A more conventional Progressive language was conjoined with at least a degree of studio manipulation, however, by It Bites. Their achievement came, perhaps not coincidentally, at the public and critical zenith of the career of (the artist then known as) Prince, in 1986–7. The extraordinary achievement of Prince as both studio wizard and musical miscegenator marks him down as – ironically for his blackness, pop sensibility and unashamed showbusiness obsession – Progressive's 1980s dark side. As a devotee of both mechanical sonic contrivance and human visceral response, Prince's aesthetics transpose Progressive mores to a postmodern plane, just to prove that 'Progressive'-type skills were not the sole province of white bourgeois initiates. What resulted could be a music for the heart and head to match the best Yes and Soft Machine – and for the feet, too. Prince was doing no more than using the technology available to him in the 1980s, as were Progressive musicians in the 1970s, to create 'total' cultural commodities of stimulation for those human receptor areas which could be exploited – Prince had the advantage that his techno toys could reach the parts those of his forebears couldn't. It Bites' music provided a Lite English equivalent of less variety but notable cultural curiosity.

An unknown four-piece from Cumbria signed by Virgin Records on the strength of a demo-tape, they proudly trumpeted themselves, from their first appearance on prime-time TV chatshow *Wogan* (while still resident in a Peckham squat), to promote their first hit single, 'Calling All the Heroes', as English rockers unafraid to name Yes and Led Zeppelin as influences. It Bites were among the first mainstream English rock (as opposed to pop) bands to breach postmodernism as a musical device, their stunning debut album *The Big Lad in the Windmill* (1986) mixing satirically clichéd cock-rock posturings (guitarist/vocalist Frank Dunnery's speed of playing and 'fuck that' exclamations redolent of Steve Marriott) with punkish timbral abrasiveness and a harmonic arsenal which recalled the great days of 1960s epic pop more graphically and wrenchingly than any of the 'subversive' new-poppers ever did. Keyboardist John Beck was credited on the band's first album with 'keyboards, backing vocals and ever-present fifth harmonies' to illustrate the band's cinematic major-key melodrama.

They could move the feet too, but did so perversely, as in 'Wanna Shout' where a Prince-ish riff is continually reactivated by dramatic knee-jerks in the tempo of the piece within a basic four-to-the-bar structure. Most of the album's songs are, formally, pop-derived, but invested not only with sampling technology but a harmonic language straining away from the bluesy norms reintroduced by punk, disco and New Romanticism but, crucially, through bluesy methods of *articulation* (the band were never short on histrionics). This, in effect, was a combination of mainstream musical styles (pop, Progressive, Heavy Metal and contemporary black music) not seen since the late 1960s. The musics in question may have been (mostly) anathema to Progressive fans, but hadn't the parental musics that subconsciously found their way into the music of Progressive players fifteen years older (showtunes, classical) also similarly been reviled, and then reprocessed as something quite new?

It Bites, of all the 1980s Progressive revivalists, truly under-stood – if perhaps only instinctively – the contemporaneous impossibility of 'progressing' in the mainstream of rock, and the possibilities that opened up. While their music was far from the cutting-edge of harmony and texture, their coupling-up of accepted popular forms remained faithful to preceding Progressive experiments. While the likes of IQ and Pendragon attempted to achieve novelty with rock voicings coined ten years previously, It Bites subtly (and unsubtly) stole and reused 1980s devices for some of the best-balanced combinations of virtuosity and gut excitement British rock has heard. Mike Stobbie claims that It Bites did 'little that was really new'.[27] But who, by this time, could claim to be doing that? It Bites' sheer èlan, coupled with their ability to grab a wider range of used ideas than their contemporaries, hoisted them aloft and singular as a landmark act.

The band's follow-up album, *Once Around the World* (1988) would, in another epoch, have been seen as the album that broke them as superstars. In 1988, it disappeared without a trace, lacking a suitable single to bolster it *à la* 'Calling All the Heroes'. But again, it's the appeal to heart, head *and* body which is interesting. Comparable pop-rock bands of the era including Big Country, Simple Minds and Then Jericho were schooled in, cognisant of, and faithful to, the ways of Punk and restricted themselves to a broadly orchestrated sweep of a narrow harmonic range, but It Bites restricted themselves to a compact-sounding (if internally complex) arrangement of harmonically wide-ranging yet melodically catchy material. Thus is the heart appealed to, in a fleeting, orgasmic pop sense as opposed to the developmental, 'classical' building of tension and release pretended to by many previous Progressive rock bands. The head is catered to by the interpolation of rhythmic subtleties into otherwise highly danceable phrases (such as section two of the title track).

Meanwhile, more literal, practical crossovers that had been in force since the 1970s – the mutual migrations of jazz and rock players between genres centred around bands of the so-called 'Canterbury' school – tirelessly, if marginally, rolled on regardless. From summer 1983 a loose pick-up band (were such projects ever anything but?) called In Cahoots evolved from sundry Canterbury offshoots, utilizing the bass of Richard Sinclair, the guitar of Phil Miller and the saxophone of Elton Dean. Shoestring-budget albums and extensive French/Belgian/Dutch patronage of their improvisationally extended creations enabled the likes of Hugh Hopper to keep intact their esoteric conception in music in continual flux between regimented composition and Dionysian spontaneity. Ditto the series of recordings made by Phil Miller, each of which poses questions as to the melodic role of soloists, and the soloists' role in melody; but as with Chris Cutler's latterday post-Henry Cow work (not helped by continuing financial crises at Recommended Records), the relation of the music to rock was questionable. The Canterbury constellation of the 1970s had consciously adopted rock voicings as a site for experimentation both vertically and horizontally; by the late 1980s, however, the dissipation of a rock ethic of experimentation and its replacement by radical currents from other musics had led the textural and melodic utterances of these congenitally exploratory one-time rockers away from (moribund) rock.

Or had it? By the late 1980s, as we have seen in the work of various cited artists of both Progressive and non-Progressive persuasions, the stylistic boundaries between genres were all but obsolete. Even the high art/popular art dichotomy was embattled. How and why? Whatever, the Canterbury pilgrims would be there or thereabouts.

The 1980s were the decade when Progressive became an umbrella generic for a musically reviled body of works, a marketing tool, a nostalgic rubric. Progressive ideology was discredited; but come to the end of the decade, it, and Progressive rock, would be on the drawing board again for a radical rethink.

9 REFUGEES
(SPLENDID ISOLATIONISTS: FOUR INDIVIDUALS)

Progressive ideology focuses on the autonomous, creative individual, locked in protean struggle against the forces of philistinism and materialism; was it any wonder William Blake was such a 1970s icon?

This chapter temporarily suspends the chronology of Progressive's history to focus on four musicians who have, in various ways, accrued a singularity for themselves in the narrative of the music. These four are Peter Hammill (ex-Van der Graaf Generator), Robert Fripp (King Crimson), Anthony Phillips (ex-Genesis), and Mike Oldfield.

PETER HAMMILL

It takes, some say, the energy equivalent of a ten-megaton nuclear warhead to make a man from nothing. If so, Peter Hammill must, in his long career, have expended near enough energy to clone himself.

Hammill is Progressive's dark magus, a figure whose inimitable dialect (through his stewardship of the band Van der Graaf Generator and a quarter-century career of fiendish profligacy) unmasks a kind of evil twin of Progressive ideology. He is a man for whom music and text are Promethean sources of individual catharsis and reformation and who has attracted a suitably fanatical and exclusive body of acolytes. He is also, in effect, the first Progressive frontman to become an entity separate from his group, the first actual *auteur* in an *auteurist* genre.

Hammill's particular blend of angst and morbid fantasy is all too easy to dismiss as mere student posturing – he was still at Manchester University when the first Generator album was recorded in 1969 – were it not for his tireless conviction concerning his own inspiration, which substantiates even his weakest creations.

Van der Graaf Generator had actually broken up when the first album was recorded. In 1969, their equipment was stolen and Hammill cut a solo album, backed by his old friends. *Aerosol Grey Machine* (recorded, legend attests, in just twelve hours), however, was credited to Van der Graaf Generator, who re-formed and signed to Charisma Records in 1970. Their early music said little unsaid elsewhere at the time; it was poetically skewed pop, arcanely arranged and cautiously extended. But *The Least We Can Do is Wave to Each Other* did intimate things to come. The Gothic inquisition drama of 'The White Hammer' signposts Hammill's later obsessions, and while the music resolves harmonically and structures itself conventionally enough (Genesis-type grandiose organ chords, chromatic cornet intonation, bluesy basslines on 'White Hammer'), there are suggestions of something nasty in the woodshed: snaggling, niggling Coltrane-ish saxophone from David Jackson, already astounding audiences with his Roland Kirk-style simultaneous two-sax attack, his electric pedal board and grotesque black stage garb.

'After the Flood' has a textural sophistication to rival Yes, but its arbitrary tempo changes, while dramatically gripping, point the way to *H to He, Who am the Only One* (1970). Hammill's declamation fills out hugely to become a coruscating bark, not unlike Bowie impersonating Olivier's Crookback. A lanky, saturnine young man with a long, soulful face, he proudly announced his intention to become the 'Hendrix of the voice',[1] and his aim was true enough.

The deep soundstage and paradoxically close miking, the gruffly roaring timbres of Hugh Banton's organ and sudden acoustic blips – such as Jackson's astonishing shift into a choked, suffocating acoustic on 'Pioneers Over C' – shaped a nightmare. Odd chords and odd ostinati ('House with No Door') helped – indeed the whole project was by now infested with grotesquerie. The very name of the band hinted not at perfumed Progressive utopia but at malformed machinery; their record sleeves were somehow dissonant in themselves, ablaze with imagistic clashes. The band had no bass player (Banton's organ took curdling care of that). Minor keys predominated. Textures were harsh and rich and thick as creosote.

And there were Hammill's lyrics, not only of chilling import but also of increasing slickness and intelligence – so much so that the music began to be led by them, not the other way round. Charisma had promoted the band in 1970 as nothing less than a blend of 'poetry, jazz and rock'.[2] Irregular stanzas made a mockery of verse and chorus lengths; their music resembled less song than operatic narrative. The whole periodicity of rock was torched: cadences landed in unexpected places, legato lines went out of the window, and the soundstage became suddenly much busier, in a manner redolent of middle-period King Crimson. Instruments became concerned not with the linear development of the song towards a fixed point, but centred around what they were doing in a particular bar.

Even when the voice was still, the music seemed intent on turning itself inside out. Witness the tumbling riffs at the end of 'Lost' or the barbarous, jackhammer chords of screeching atonality at its climax. Hammill sang of extremes: torture and despair ('The Emperor in His War Room'), the physical and mental limits of the individual. Influences are too numerous to mention – save for Thomas Pynchon, Poe and Baudelaire. Towards the end of 'Lemmings' from *Pawn Hearts* (1971),

Hammill demands wearily, 'What choice is there but to live?'

His wordsmithery was much in demand; he even wrote the libretto for a preposterous concept album from the Italian ELP, Le Orme. *Felona e Serona* (1973) was a run-of-the-mill B-movie melodrama about warring planets, and didn't deserve Hammill's (dashed-off) input.

The period culminated in the exhausting 'A Plague of Lighthouse Keepers' (1971), a twenty-minute monodrama of serial morbidity after Poe's short story. Ultra-episodic, almost inchoate, the non-synchronous playing outlined above reaches extremes here. When tone-clusters are not used, the harmonic language of the piece is perverse, especially in the tart and unsettling chordal sequence of the finale's hollow grandiosity, which sounds as if it is being played by a ghostly silver band. Such two-fisted vehemence was unique in rock at the time, let alone in Progressive – it was the stuff cults were made of. In a later sleeve note, Hammill described his band as 'serious fun', and that a 'real, chaotic/controlled, tempest/calm thing ... was our *raison d'être*'.[3]

This very loud, very scary outfit broke up, disillusioned and drained, after an Italian tour in 1972. Hammill then recorded *Fool's Mate*, a revamped corpus of pre-Van der Graaf Generator and pre-university songs of plumptious psychedelic pop hedging its bets between Syd Barrett and Al Stewart. Major keys still abound – 'Summer Song in Autumn' is a particularly catchy number; 'Sunshine' seems like a deliberate Small Faces slur, chirpy, tie-dyed with English nostalgia. Others, such as the mini-epic 'Viking' in form and content seem like warm-up exercises for stronger and longer works; the spine-tingling dissonant three-part organ chord which ends the entire album prefigures Van der Graaf Generator's more lunatic moments as well as his own.

Chameleon in the Shadow of the Night (1973), *The Silent Corner and the Empty Stage* (1974) and *In Camera* (1975) personalize Van der Graaf Generator's idiolect (despite the fact that Hammill was already writing 99 per cent of the band's material in any case). Hammill's own guitar and piano playing forms the heart of the songs, albeit a fibrillating one, with the guitar used seemingly as a lead-in to a jungly ensemble sound (compare the multi-tracked primal screams and delay-system-climax of 1973's 'German Overalls'). Neither guitar or piano lines seem to fit anywhere, let alone together. Hammill is no broken flower, no whimperer; his angst is impotent rage, yet rage which has sighted a light. *The Silent Corner*, in particular, flourishes a new richness and the multi-dimensional sound (the sugar-plum Mellotron sonorities on the title track, particularly before the crablike advance of hoarse, chromatic sax riffs is winning, as is the light of flutes in 'Forsaken Gardens'). The *intimacy* is what surprises; Hammill sings not of universals, as might a Yes or ELP, but of individual choices and dilemmas; human drama burns. There are few, if any archaisms. Rock consonance is evident; the procedure texturally and melodically starts promisingly, but is fouled by minor key changes and harsh changes of atmosphere. The multi-tracking of Hammill's voice, particularly on the long 'A Louse is Not a Home' (1974) further confuses; all the lines are sung non-synchronously.

Van der Graaf Generator's re-formation in 1975 didn't stop *In Camera* or Hammill's utter dominance of the group's fine *Godbluff*, where his imagery is as sinewy as ever; while Hammill wasn't above cringing banality, such as rhyming 'limbo' badly with 'akimbo', he could dispense effortlessly concrete imagery ('stub towers in the distance', and sing of the horizon calling 'with its parallel lines') seemingly at will.

Jazz-rock playing practices and an initial move towards friendlier major key chordal language (1975's 'The Sleepwalkers', for example), chunkier rock riffs and a more opaque textural discourse (the introduction of violin and cello) could also accommodate a lack of tonal centre (*Still Life* – 1976) and solos were still just as shrilly disruptive. Some moves were made to contact the normal musical world; 'Sleepwalkers' has dancehall sax and Wurlitzer going off down Mexico Way; 'Meurglys III (The Songwriters' Guild)' –1976 – hesitantly has a fling with reggae.

Hammill's own work, especially on the crusty, uncompromising *In Camera* and *Over* (1977) took no prisoners. Even the quiet bits, infested with effects (notably on 'Gog/Magog (In Bromine Chambers)') sounded revolutionary – the interjection in

'Tapeworm' of a toneless madrigal presents Hammill's genius for the grand gesture. His proto-punk *Nadir's Big Chance* (1976) balanced its unusual conceptual centring with an outrageously fuzzed fury of bellowed rock songs. Hammill's voice, while timbrally expressive (a multi-registered whisper-to-scream miracle) was tonally suspect; it not only ate frequencies, it upset the whole tonal centre of what he was singing. Enslaving music to words, his voice would drag the music around behind it, decentring the harmonic procedure of the piece still more. Hammill made both a mess and a masterpiece of everything he ever wrote and sang.

The final split of Van der Graaf (as they became known) occurred in 1978; Hammill just brazened it out and carried on. That year's *The Future Now* was straighter, narrower, leveller. But side two showcased some of Hammill's most outlandish inspirations, such as the austere, minimal backgrounds of 'Medieval' and the multi-tracked drums which masquerade a melodic line and complicate the rhythmic pulse of the anti-apartheid 'Motorbike in Afrika'.

Hammill has gone on to cut over twenty-five further solo albums in a little over fifteen years. His melodic gift has mellowed, although occasionally the profile of his tunes becomes as bizarre as anything written by Gentle Giant, and as they are never sung the same way twice, they assume an even greater discontinuity. This quality is Hammill's trump; his textural subversion is admirable enough, but his complete disregard for the norms of time in rock, and his consistent confounding of our expectations, should rank him among rock's premier creators.

Ph7 (1979) and 1980's *A Black Box* condense and further extend ('Flight' – 1980 – lasts twenty minutes) VdGG preoccupations. The *pointilliste* effect of much VdGG is enhanced by distortion and by cumulative atonality (1979's 'Careering') and the emotional import of the words and music is less telegraphed; big dramatic moments don't have to have big dramatic chords. Studio craft is back, the incubated, sterile sound of 'The Old School Tie' (1979) being a case in point. The 'Mr X (Gets Tense)'/'Faculty X' medley (1979) mines Progressive rhetoric with face-saving odd chord progressions and even introduces, baldly and shamelessly, the introductory piano vamp from Billy Joel's 'My Life' as a chassis to build a song on. The lyrics hit home as ever; the take on alienation of 'Careering' should be read against the discourse of Genesis and their ilk on the same topic as a set text as how to write intelligent and pertinent rock-song lyrics. On 1979's 'The Old School Tie', Hammill excels himself on political opportunism, a kind of prophesy of spin-doctoring.

Throughout the 1980s Hammill continued to confound; he appeared on stage with the Stranglers, supported Marillion, teamed up with New Wave bands Random Hold and Ludus, and finished his long-term project, a rock opera, *The Fall of the House of Usher*. Unfortunately, what might be seen as possibly the most appropriate vessel for a Hammill *chef d'œuvre* is merely seventy-five minutes of excruciating mannerism; only the breathtaking multi-tracking and fuguing of Hammill's voice as he musically represents the architectural configuration of the House is worth-while. The rest is meandering, formless, electronic non-opera at its warbling worst.

Like Roger Waters's ventures into film music, Hammill's instrumental music – principally for ballets and other dramatic projects – was infinitely more rewarding, and only showed the inconsequentiality of his grander visions. His *Loops and Reels* (1982 – originally a mail-order cassette, later released on CD) and *Spur of the Moment* (1987) – recorded with Guy Evans of VdGG, one of many collaborations Hammill has made with what is now effectively his own repertory company of ex-VdGG talent) are indispensable.

Such music is still often melancholy and minor-key-led; it is angular, non-goal-oriented, means without ends; the melodies of Hammill songs are still as steeply contoured, the words still as elliptical, although the Walt Whitmanesque fondness for polysyllabic, sprawling, free-form lines has been domesticated by a greater adherence to rock-song formats; you can generally tell where Hammill songs are going these days. They are more strophic. That is, except in his slow numbers; picking selections is not easy, but the wrenchingly gorgeous 'Incomplete Surrender' and 'Gaia' from 1992's *Fireships* album are cases in point. The path between the chords, once so brambled, is now smoother, but occasionally the arrangement, which seems to wander haphazardly between those chords, tiptoes on to one which releases a sound, apparently floating free in the music but cunningly tied into the harmonic scheme of the whole, of almost unbelievable beauty. As for Hammill's voice, it retains its old hectoring power, but maturity has deepened and sensitized it. Look no further than the cantorial intonation of the glassy, sepia-stained 'No Moon in the Water' (1990).

Hammill, with the calm courtesy of a lost species of worldly aesthete, refused to be interviewed for this book. When speaking to Mike Barnes for *The Wire* in 1995, however, he distanced himself from his past.[4] Perhaps this is due to the opprobrium associated with the music of that era; perhaps it is personal choice. People grow out of, and into, music. But Hammill's entire career, for this author, has a remarkably unitary narrative flow to it. His handling of pop – for even in his nastiest, dirtiest work with VdGG, R&B and bubblegum basslines or phrases weirdly and surreally appear like party poppers at a wake – is unique and has always been indicative of a mind with serious belief in the form in which he is working – belief enough to exploit its malleability. That is not just the genius of Hammill – that is the genius of Progressive. As such, his status within the canon of the genre, whether desired or not, is assured. His place in the canon of rock is the next logical step. How long will it be before that step is taken?

ROBERT FRIPP

One of Hammill's friends and professional accomplices was Robert Fripp. Another convert to meddling with rock's syntax in terms of how it occupies our time, the predictability of its development, the obviousness – or otherwise – of its cadences, the timeframe implied by its structures), Fripp had been thinking deeply about how instruments take the ear from one place to another in music for long enough in the 1973/4 and 1980s incarnations of King Crimson. Fripp's thing was periodicity.

Fripp's reputation is unfairly schoolmasterly. Given that he's dapper, his intense gaze magnified by granny specs, it's excusable but off-beam. A man for whom rock custom meant superfluous posturing (he played some of the most fantastically intense guitar solos in rock history while sitting on a stool almost from the beginning of King Crimson) and who thought that festivals were the enemy of music and who, even in the 1990s can and does accompany each release with extensive self-explanatory sleevenotes dealing with the spiritual and musical genesis of his work, comes across as humane, challenging, funny, and polite.

The reason behind Fripp's butterfly transformation in the early 1990s is unclear. Certainly contact with the media was obsessively minimized. 'I think,' one colleague of Fripp's told me, 'that at fifty, Robert just felt that he'd had enough of constantly explaining himself.' Infuriated by the intransigence and cavalier attitudes of his record company, EG, Fripp opened a case against them, ongoing during the writing of this book.

Fripp swiftly set up his own label, Discipline Global Mobile, from his home in Dorset and issued what he saw fit, mostly his own work and that of close associates. The result was some of the most polyglot rock-based music heard in twenty years, effectively reviving Progressive ideology single-handed (though no doubt Fripp would blanch at the term).

The difference between Fripp's own music and that of King Crimson is superficially simple. Reasoned analysis, however, betrays their similarity. What harmonic language there is chimes neatly, likewise the obsession with timbre and its expert manipulation. Thirdly, vertical and horizontal standards get a good going over, both in Crimson and Fripp's work. Fripp seems to stray as far as he can from rock whilst maintaining a lifeline of contact with it. His music's tensions and textures could not exist without rock, although the polytonal *massifs* Fripp wrests from one guitar, a MIDI converter and a pedal board take one aback. To '*1999*' (1994) and the 1995 'Soundscaping' series there is a committed intensity which recalls not only the heaven-opening, entropic harmonic ecstasy of Olivier Messaien's organ works, but also the same utter love of the instrument in hand. This is rock guitar we're talking about here, driven to its limit with the intensity of a Hendrix, a Sonny Sharrock or a Keiji Haino. Try offering this Progressive refugee the routine journalistic accusation of lacking 'feel'. *A Blessing of Tears* (1995), a tribute to Fripp's recently deceased mother, drips with melancholy, touching head and heart. The disposal of phrases evident in King Crimson here resolves itself into non-linear development of the first order; normal apprehension of time in a rock context is gone, yet this is obviously rock-derived music, using the tonal language of rock for a unique and personal end. Soundscaping, Fripp concludes, is still 'the best way I know of making a lot of noise with one guitar'.[1]

In 1993 Fripp reactivated the sleeping giant of King Crimson; whether he saw worlds to be saved in so doing is open to debate. The baton of 1980s King Crimson was taken up powerfully and fearlessly by what was dubbed a 'double trio' – two bassist (Levin and fellow stick expert Trey Gunn), two guitarists (Fripp, Belew) and two drummers (Bruford, Pat Mastelotto) The repertoire of the former group was redoubled. The Great Deceivers became Greater Deceivers yet. Fripp valued 'delay, repetition and hazard'[2] in his solo guitar work; here narratives are similarly screwed.

First point: solos are back. Nothing fancy, nothing hard. But the hairshirt asceticism of the 1980s group is gone. The rhythmic cross-purposes are stressed by the existence of two bands (otherwise hard to distinguish) in tracks such as 'Thrak' (1993). It seems as if both trios are tug-of-warring in different directions. Pulse is still paramount; everything aids rhythm, not simply the tooling regularity of a normal rhythm section. This is not post-punk rhythmic fixation, however. Fripp seems to attempt the impossible in making the most objective musical factor – rhythm – subjective, by wedding it closely to the formation and development of musical colours and textures. The abrasive and the velvety are both accommodated within a sound that is wide but not deep – reverb is damped down, but Fripp's longstanding exploration of the guitar has provided the band with an orchestral electronic backcloth which is both unprecedented in their case and unique in anyone's case. Often the only textural sunlight that shines through the swirling fug of heavy, sultry sound-clouds comes from acoustic percussion. But the increasing *pointillisme* of the soundstage – nodding in gratitude to both past Crimsons and Peter Hammill – makes the harmonic thread harder to pick up in complicated passages (loud, fast); the lead instrument (or voice) is hard to singularize, the composition and logic of the chords they lead on to even more so. But the pop input's there: 'VROOOM' (1993) swaggers along on a 'Peter Gunn' riff, and 'Frame by Frame'(1994) is of blues descent.

Eric Tamm's attribution of monotheistic vision to 1980s Crimson – it's here too. The musicians play not as pilots for a comfortable pop itinerary, with not only verses and choruses but chord sequences in the right place, but for a convincing musical vision that (apparently) presents the next bar (at most) as its goal and nothing else. The free-falling, seat-of-the-pants improvisations of *Thrakattack* (1996) suggest that the redundancy of normal pop linearity is now taken for granted.

But what of Fripp's solo output? The 1970s critical opinion, that King Crimson was largely an extension of Fripp's personality, and the progress of Fripp's unique odyssey through music has found too many parallels in the subsequent incarnations of that outfit to enable the accusation to be ignored.

Fripp's sojourn in New York from 1977 confronted him with musics he found amenable; he recorded with and produced acts as diverse as Blondie and the feminist torch song trio the Roches, while working on his own first post-Crimson project, the formidably eloquent *Exposure*. Breathlessly diverse, from the punkoid testosterone of 'You Burn Me Up I'm a Cigarette' (on which Peter Hammill lent rowdy support) to the scholarly found sound of 'NY3' (there is also New York restaurant conversation and an interview with Fripp's mother about the young Robert's toilet training interspersed in the music), the album may be stylistically catholic, but it burns with a visionary coherence that points towards the 'unified' approach of King Crimson IV in the 1980s, in which diverse input became homogeneous output.

The album also marked Fripp's first extended solo exhibition of the Frippertronic projects he had developed with the aid of

Brian Eno on the pair's experimental albums *No Pussyfooting* (1974) and *Evening Star* (1975). In brief, Frippertronics operates on the principle of producing music using two tape recorders set up so that when a single sound was played, it was heard several seconds later at a lower volume level, then again several seconds later at a still lower level, and so on. The system permitted adjustments of various kinds, having to do with volume levels and length of delay; further, the live signal could be disconnected from the loop, so that the already recorded sounds would repeat indefinitely while a live 'solo' line could be played over the top. Tamm rightly invokes the (already related) influence of both raga and minimalism on the style. Fripp liked minimalism well enough but bemoaned its evasion of 'hazard' – an element provided, presumably, in his own music by improvised guitar.[3]

Tamm continues:

> The technological set-up whereby two reel-to-reel tape recorders were connected together and to Fripp's electric guitar; the musical style, that is, the potential for creatively shaping ever-fluctuating masses of sound in real time, ordinarily upon a tonal, pan-diatonic, modal or multi-modal base; and the various uses of Frippertronics – as music performed solo, or as one timbral/structural element within a more conventional song, or as a 'thematic sound' used to unify a large musical collage as in *Exposure*.[4]

Fripp hit the road with his new album, but true to his disavowal of the conventions of rock practice and performance with the epiphanic catharsis of Punk and his own Sherborne and New York experiences, it was far from a conventional guitar-hero tour. Fripp instead played solo, employing Frippertronics extensively, tearing up the formbook as to relationships between guitar players and rock – and for all the harshness and didactic austerity of Fripp's new music, its Babel of harmonies and timbres was still tenuously *of rock lineage*. At first in the USA, then in Europe, Fripp's 'small, mobile, intelligent unit' (as opposed to the 'dinosaurs' he had so gleefully castigated post-King Crimson

III)[5] took the guitar hero into clubs, shopping malls, even pizza parlours (in 1980 Fripp played both the Virgin Megastore in Oxford Street and a Pizza Express restaurant in Notting Hill – a common enough experience for jazz players, but at the time unheard of in rock). For Fripp, the element of spontaneous interplay (even to the extent of a loud fart's effect on performance and performer–spectator interaction) was essential to the creative process – the audience, he believed, had a creative responsibility commensurate with that of the performer.

The same year, 1980, also saw the curious *God Save The Queen/Under Heavy Manners* two-in-one album, a record segregated into one side of Frippertronics and one side of 'Discotronics', explained with Fripp's customary prolixity as 'the interstice between Frippertronics and disco'. *Under Heavy Manners*, released later the same year, revealed an even starker, desensitized inspiration, bold but harrowing, skating between the extremities of music and sound itself. The album includes the notorious 'Zero of the Signified'. It recalls both Roland Barthes's epigram 'to repeat excessively is to enter into loss ... this we term the zero of the signified' and Eno's axiom, 'repetition is change', by consisting simply of ten or so minutes of repeated guitar loops.

This album, with its featureless spaces and foregrounding of rhythm and timbre as chief operatives in the musical scheme, Jamaican-derived title and dub-heavy dancefloor appeal, could be read as Fripp's exploration of the postmodern limits of head and body musics already investigated by the Gang of Four and the Pop Group. Whether Fripp was aware and/or appreciative of their music is still unclear, though his contribution to the cutting-edge audio magazine the *Bristol Recorder* in 1981 suggests he was in touch with contemporary adventures in rock.

That same year saw *Let the Power Fall*, six titles of improvised Frippertronics, and his affected resurrection of the band name the League of Gentlemen from his salad days in 1960s Bournemouth. A joint project with keyboardist Barry Andrews (formerly of Swindon NewWavers XTC) and bassist (latterly of the Gang of Four) Sara Lee, this more explicitly than ever directed Fripp towards 1980s pop. Eric Tamm, however, astutely detects Fripp's restless imagination, unearthing in the music 'a technique of rapidly flat-picking arpeggiated chord-melodies with a staccato attack'[6] and compares it to the *style brisé* of classical music, with melodies subservient to broken chords and the composite rhythms arising therefrom. This recalled techniques employed by Baroque lutenists and harpsichordists as well as in J. S. Bach's suites for solo cello, with 'linear melody so ... suffused with harmonic implications as to make analytic separation of the two impossible'.[7]

Fripp, by now gripped by apparent hypermania, was in the throes of re-forming King Crimson and was also working with Police guitarist Andy Summers, who had preceded Fripp in a band called the Hebrew Fraternity at Bournemouth's Majestic Hotel. *I Advanced Masked* emerged in 1982, to be followed by *Bewitched* (1984). Intense, sometimes meandering, at other times penetrating, these albums of rootless, harmonically diffuse and sometimes navel-gazing musical travelogues through and between the minds of two thoughtful guitarists are of minor interest, simply because they sound like nothing else on release at the time. The porcelain tinkling and gamelan gleam of the chiming Hardy Country (1984) and the halting, poetic poignancy of much of *Masked* teases the listener with its promises of resolution and cadence, and the quest for peace in the music is rarely better heard in Fripp than here. It evokes Hebbel's aphorism, 'in a work of art the intellect asks questions; it does not answer them'.

But despite the seeming surface severity and metropolitan accents of his new music, higher matters still guided Fripp. His 1978–81 projects were dubbed 'The Drive to 1981', to coincide and culminate with what Fripp believed to be an (unspecified) apocalyptic event coinciding with a particular planetary alignment in the solar system on 11 September 1981.

Fripp's thinking had been transfigured by his experiences at Sherborne and his continued involvement with J. G. Bennett's philosophical works there led to his engagement at the American Society for Continuous Education's community and school in West Virginia to give music lessons.

These lectures became Fripp's overriding 1980s preoccupation
– Guitar Craft. Described by his unofficial biographer Eric Tamm
as a 'way of life, centered on the discipline and practice of music',[8]
it is a school of guitar technique which has since mushroomed,
incorporating courses worldwide, with student numbers far into
the four figures. Fripp, naturally left-handed but a right-handed
guitar player, sought to establish a pedagogy for guitar practice
and performance comparable not only to that for left-handed
position and fretting technique but with accepted teaching texts
of other instruments, e.g. the violin's Suzuki method. Much
emphasis was laid on the physical execution of playing guitar
before any judgement was made on the sounds produced. Rote
learning of the chordal and harmonic repertoire of Guitar Craft
was expected. Fripp airily informed his students that 'there is
nothing compulsory. One is not asked to violate cherished beliefs
or accept any of the ideas presented. Rather, a healthy scepticism
is encouraged.'[9]

Tamm's account of a week spent on the expensive and ascetic
Guitar Craft course might cast doubt on that. While no Wackford
Squeers, Fripp appears as a cross between the Maharishi and a
particularly bloody-minded suburban piano teacher. He treated his
charges oddly; 'Wretched, but not hopeless,' he would routinely
smile while listening to a pupil's efforts.[10] Whether Fripp's elliptical,
epigrammatic teaching style wrongfooted his pupils is a moot
point. Similarly, it may have been that his pupils were simply
intimidated by his fame, an attitude inculcated in them by just the
kind of guitaring mythology Fripp wished to destroy.

But, true to the sage gnosis of Bennett's teaching, Zen-like
enigmatism has always surrounded Fripp. For all the lofty
aspirations towards a purer and finer musical experience for both
player and listener, Guitar Craft has spun off its own lucrative
materialist cash-cows – newsletters, literatures, accessories, decals,
cassettes, bumper stickers for God's sake, T-shirts, logos, posters –
the kind of merchandising taxonomy one might associate with
acts like Kiss, but not with Fripp.

Fripp's relationship with technology has also been ambivalent;
he rejected acoustic guitars in the 1970s, only passionately to

extol the essential part they played in Guitar Craft. He has also flirted with MIDI and has swung back behind a console of pedals and an electric guitar for his 1990s soundscaping. The man who mistrusts written media and recorded sound has, as Tamm points out, also been a phenomenally active producer of records for himself and others, and has written with almost breathless zeal about music.[11] He wrote a typically mischievous column for *Musician, Player and Listener* between 1980 and 1982. One item finished 'Perhaps I should shut up.'[12]

Fripp's apparent self-referentiality and self-righteousness have angered critics who have seen in his music a redemptive antidote to the more heated rhetoric of Progressive while maintaining a sense of integrity and adventure. Conceits such as terming his home 'Fripp World Headquarters' and for publishing his own aphorisms as part of Guitar Craft literature don't help, especially as the aphorisms are often, frankly, cracker-barrel homilies and urban folk wisdom. 'Greed is a poor composer'; 'intentional poverty is fine; unintentional poverty is wretched' are two of the better ones.[13]

If Fripp's seemingly intentional perversity can be provisionally explained, perhaps the belief in music as pre-eminent communicator, as divine property – perhaps the philosophical grounding of all Progressive ideology – might just do it. Fripp once told an interviewer that 'music is a quality organized in sound ... music is just a means for creating a magical state'.[14] For Fripp, music is a universal harmony that musicians must find, not create ... 'imagine, just as a possibility, an idea of a repertoire of music which will guarantee, by its performance, to unify the people playing it ... I've seen it happen here [in Guitar Craft]' – Tamm, comparing it with Plato's ideas of musical modes having certain definite, inevitable effects on the human soul, also compares it to Gurdjieff's ideal of objective art'.[15] On *Exposure*, 'The First Inaugural Address to the IACE, Sherborne House' is an outlandish sonic experiment which some critics believe to be a fantastic condensation of the entirety of a J. G. Bennett speech at his Sherborne establishment. Perhaps it is an attempt to tap the 'objective' unalterable harmony of the universal music of the spheres Fripp desires. Scriabin's 'mystic chord', the configuration of notes which infused so much of that master's later music and which he believed to be the earthly sounding of higher, immutable cosmic powers, springs to mind.

But then again, maybe it's nothing like that.

Fripp's recent career, plagued by legal tussles with his former employers EG but brightened by an unexpected marriage to post-Punk chanteuse Toyah Willcox, has followed a similarly frustrating path for observers and analysts. It is as if Fripp simply wants a good laugh at the expense of those who try to cage him in words after years of mutual mistrust.

Gurdjieff believed that only 'an interchangeable, solid "I" could survive'[16] into an unspecified afterlife. Maybe, for Fripp, music is his motive and his means for such striving, rendering his music always a mystery to all but himself. If music is a universal harmony, then all of us have personal musical universes which defy all description and all verbal and written explanation.

ANTHONY PHILLIPS

Lambs and lions lie down together. In 1978, Robert Fripp's promotional tour of the USA was supported by a guitarist who was only a name to many Progressive fans – the name who'd erased himself from Genesis's CV just when it was starting to fill up.

Anthony Phillips is a genial gentleman in his forties with a face in its teens. He has never lost the cherubic bloom of Charterhouse, where he was a member of the pool of callowly polished, musically inspired students who formed Genesis. His departure from the band in 1970, mentally and physically drained from the demands of touring and the economic realities necessitated by professionalism, has led some to dub him 'the Pete Best of Progressive', or a musical Captain Oates voluntarily walking into self-sacrificing oblivion.

Of his big split, 'I was mentally and physically debilitated,' Phillips told Armando Gallo in 1977:

> We were just a bunch of perfectionists. After every gig there were always long, long post-mortems ... there was always so

much wrong. Towards the end, for me, it all sounded so wrong that I always used to come offstage feeling terrible. Music, which was something that I had loved, was becoming something that dissatisfied me profoundly ... There were personality clashes, yes. I would be foolish to deny it. But you see, being so very English, we didn't talk to each other.[1]

Two decades have not changed Phillips's opinion:

It was a personal thing. We were these middle-class kids and despite the fact we'd led this prison-camp existence at Charterhouse, life had never been *that* uncomfortable. But the road changed relationships. There was this great ideal of all living together and getting it together but we got on top of each other and it soured it.[2]

Phillips, the son of a merchant banker, went to boarding school from the age of eight. By eleven he was a Carthusian and he had heard the Shadows.

I picked up a guitar and wanted to play like Hank [Marvin]. Then came the Beatles! Mum bought me Beatles' sheet music at 2s/6d a go. I had a teacher training me on the guitar, and he wanted me to play all these classical chord shapes, but I just wanted the chords to play Beatles songs. Classical music was never an influence. Dad once had a go at learning the violin but he was hopeless.[3]

Phillips had a peculiar relationship with pop. 'There was never any trouble as regards pop music, never any battle between me and my parents, because I either wasn't interested or wasn't there. I do remember they had music to Broadway musicals, *West Side Story* and so on. But a lot of it just passed me by.' Latterly, to the formative regimen of blues and R&B so familiar to 1960s musicians and outlined above, came a love for Family, the Beach Boys and Procol Harum, 'who had that classical influence, and then King Crimson'.[4]

Phillips struck out with single-minded purpose of his own upon his departure from Charterhouse, attending the Guildhall School of Music and winning a diploma in music education. Guaranteed a subsidiary income, and still partnering Genesis bassist Mike Rutherford in impromptu domestic acoustic jams recalling happier adolescent days, Phillips was sufficiently emboldened by 1976 to return to recording with a home-made album called *The Geese and the Ghost*. Charisma were unable to offer him an option, and furthermore Punk was ringing its alarm bells.

Disaster! There was this party line that Punk was the only thing that was cool and the press turned against the guys they'd extolled the day before. I was lucky – I got a deal. A lot of people didn't and disappeared. An American label [Arista] picked up *The Geese and the Ghost* but it sat around for ages here until Hit And Run, my publishers, agreed to bring it out ... only record they ever released.

I can't really imagine why people didn't stand up for any other kinds of music. Punk was great if you wanted a good time, but why should *everyone* have to jump wholesale into a time machine and go back fifteen years? I can remember meeting [percussionist/composer] Morris Pert[5] and he was saying that you had to keep quiet about classical affiliations. America was better – there was Punk, which was fine, but there was mutual respect between the different musics, there wasn't this 1984-style party dictum. And then at the end of the day to have the Pistols turn round and say, 'Oh, we were having you on,' ... well, there should be a lot of red faces in very high places.

Tony Smith went round everywhere to try and sell *The Geese and the Ghost*. It wasn't a-phenomenal-album-that-didn't-make-it-because-of-Punk, but Punk – or rather attitudes to it – didn't help. I met a guy years later at Nottingham University who told me that he'd sold his original copy of *The Geese* because it wasn't cool. He didn't want to be seen with it.[6]

Geese, indeed, commits almost every Progressive transgression proscribed by Punk – with the exception of grandiosity. Conceived and executed as a series of quasi-classical compositions for small acoustic *groupuscules*, centred on varying Phillips–Rutherford guitar configurations, it set the tone for almost all Phillips's later work. There are three acoustic pop songs on the album, also scored for the same forces, which set classical woodwind against acoustic guitar, string quartet or rudimentary keyboard (Farfisa organ or Mellotron). Recorded in Send, Surrey and on Tom Newman's barge in Little Venice, it is sturdily homophonic, hymnal, and resolutely tuneful within a context of gentle melodic profiles redolent of Elgar and/or Samuel Wesley. It was orchestrated with innocent and idiosyncratic delicacy; the flavourful sonorities of woodwind against chiming spider-webbed guitars crossed an allusive, stylized folk texture with the churchy chord sequences that had always dominated Genesis's music. The depth of the soundstage was considerable; small percussion instruments were sprinkled on the textures like diamonds.

But its Englishness – there is hardly a note of the blues on the entire album, its titles (the suite 'Henry – Portraits from Tudor Times', 'Sleepfall; the Geese Fly West') and of course Peter Cross's fabulously rococo cover – combine to create one of the most distinctive packages of individual artistic intent in Progressive ideological history. 'Peter had this gift of English Romanticism with this kind of – equally English – passion for eccentric gadgets – you know, Heath Robinson etc.'[7] Alerted by a friend, Phillips found Cross working alone in a converted greenhouse in his parents' garden; a draughtsman of peerless ability, his unique melanges of the pastoral and the deranged have decorated many Phillips albums ever since.

The Geese and the Ghost remains Phillips's biggest seller, 'just under 100,000, I'm told; 17,000 in New York ... and 749 in Venezuela'.[8] The very simplicity of the music and the facility of Phillips's sound organization stand out. Phillips recalls that the home-brew aspect was the result as much of necessity as choice: 'Remember then most people had no home studio recording equipment, so to record you had to get an advance and had to do

what the label told you. After *Geese* I was pushed in the pop
direction, particularly on *Sides'*.[9] Although developing strong
ideas as arranger and composer later, the album is disappointing,
lacking the sweep and confidence of contemporary pop urges
manifesting themselves in the contemporary Genesis of *And Then
There were Three.*

Private Parts and Pieces (1979), a generically-titled ongoing
work-in-progress series,

> arose partly out of poverty. I was just getting by, library music
> was just getting going. I had to issue a collection of twelve-
> string or solo-piano stuff to boost my income. I had all these
> rough-sounding acoustic recordings. Eno's label turned it
> down, but Arista finally agreed to release it as a free LP with
> the *Sides* album; 'Keep the boy happy', you know. But it always
> picks up the best reviews. People go on about the great sonic
> quality and yet most of it was done at home on a Revox, some
> of it in fake stereo.[10]

There are eight volumes of this series extant at the time of
writing (1996). They largely consist of Phillips's solo compositions or improvisations on acoustic guitar or piano, occasionally
in consort with other instruments. All remain marinated in the
diatonic balm of his debut.

But this does not disqualify Phillips from inclusion in any
book dealing with Progressive; he undertook these works during
the 1980s, in the teeth of uniform commercial indifference, and
in doing so, maintained an indefatigable and uncompromising
stance 'for the ideals of lyricism, beauty and grandeur in the face
of cynical intellectualism'.[11]

Phillips is no crank Unabomber in the cause of musical
conservatism. Indeed, his ability to produce as much fine music
in the (relatively) small rhythmic, melodic and harmonic field of
his choice is remarkable. Is his music conservative? Samey?
Surely, in today's postmodern terms, it is not; his angelic
refinement has now assumed relevance as a truly 'different' idiom.
He is master in a class of one; far from leading to insularity, it has

enabled him to focus his music to a remarkable extent, after a fashion as sharply and effectively as Peter Hammill, and extrapolate from his chosen musical language a syntax which he delivers with economy and accomplishment. The fifth *Private* album from 1985 contains a dozen pieces of twelve-string improvisation, often of fantastic textural and melodic invention yet never straying from Phillips's prescriptions for his music.

A venture into electronics, *1984* (1981) was an attempt at a grand gesture – although Phillips had written the body of a symphony, the work remained unperformed, at least in its original form.

> There was an obsession with rhythm then [in 1981], and drum-boxes. I was fascinated with the idea of combining two elements, classical-sounding synth chords and incessant machine-like rock rhythms. RCA liked it and issued it. It got torn to shreds, of course, but the single off it, 'Prelude 84', was single of the week in some places. Incredible. The notices had nothing to do with the music, just that it wasn't like the book, and they proceeded to tell you what the book was about and how this was nothing like it. Thank God we've moved on a bit since then.[12]

1984 works well; the hook-line of the 'Prelude' gives the album a immense sense of brio and confidence from the off, and while the rhapsodic development of themes and textures over thirty-five minutes of continuous, rhythmically driven music stutters a little at times, Phillips is clearly in charge, developing some ravishing tunes.

Phillips's relative prosperity in the 1980s enabled him to tilt further at symphonic-scale windmills. *Tarka* effectively recycled his orchestral juvenilia as a suite for orchestra and two guitars which had originated in the early 1970s. Showbiz D-listers Simon McCorkindale and Susan George planned a film of Henry Williamson's book, and got wind of the music that Phillips had coincidentally recorded with the author's rock-guitarist grandson Harry.

That meant that a team was marshalled around us. All sorts of oddballs suddenly appeared, particularly in marketing. And the cover! A bod from the record company told us, 'The cover's been done, don't knock it, don't say anything.' For the first time in my life I was lost for words. We weren't credited anywhere. Sometimes anonymity can work for an album, but this time it didn't. Once I walked into a record store and saw it filed under 'female vocalist'. Well, it's called *Tarka* − not 'Tarka the otter', and there's this picture of a woman on the front − for no very good reason.

I'd done studenty orchestral stuff in the 1970s, let's-see-how-this-works pieces, culminating in *Tarka*. Everyone's an influence − especially Holst and Vaughan Williams.[13]

Vaughan Williams's teacher − Ravel − and Bax also peek through the sensuous orchestration of the four-part suite, on which electric instruments are used discreetly, synthesizers deepening the range of the strings and reinforcing the single-release 'Anthem', bearing witness to just how talented Phillips had become as arranger of his often affecting melodic lines. *Tarka* is schmaltzy, but like all Phillips's music it remains charmingly innocent, imbued with single-minded sincerity and an enviable ear for emotional effects that could opt for empty bombast but instead chooses feminine fragility. The process was repeated for 1990's *Slowdance*, more extensively synthesized in the 1984 vanguard but also deploying classical strings and woodwinds.

'I needed money, so I decided to kill two birds with one stone and do something filmic, to try and lure a few people. It was much more Progressive − there was development, light and shade, a sense of focus, whereby the *Private* albums drifted more.'[14]

Phillips denies that his creed leads inevitably to a stale illustrative, representative *raison d'être* for his compositions. 'I've no fixed idea about absolute music or programme music. You think sometimes, oh, I must be describing something, but I don't have any preconceptions. You sit down and you feel up or down and it comes through that way, as opposed to reflecting anything outside yourself.'[15] But the evocative nature of Phillips's music, utilizing so many friendly, cosy classical chords (and often saved from mediocrity by the sheer singularity a twelve-string guitar offers an adventurous harmonist), led him out of the dead-end of post-Punk stasis.

> Loads of us hit trouble after 1977. I knew musicians whose bands had dried up or the market had squeezed them dry who then moved into soundtracks. Some of them were seeing their bands forced to do more singles. I played on a Camel album called *The Single Factor* which was meant to represent that. There was a nice piece we did with big Genesis-sounding, slightly choral keyboard phrases with super soaring guitar over it and they took it off because it didn't have the 'Single Factor'.
> Andy Latimer [Camel's guitarist] was struggling, becoming marginalized. I was lucky. I came across library music almost by accident. A lot have taken that route because it's one way of playing music that doesn't rely on the press and on airplay. Andy found it difficult because you have to adapt your style and sound like other people. My classical training helped me adapt but Andy found it difficult and got really down. Things are coming around for him again at last, thank God.[16]

Comfortably ensconced in a tiny home studio in a Balham back street, Phillips can relax. The genie of Punk has been rebottled, and the teleological urge to constant rock revolution in postmodern, post-Live Aid Britain has enabled him to secure a niche for his music which evades the exacting standards of critical and industry favour but which, thanks to the CD revolution, can be disseminated to those who want to hear it; in effect, the natural outlet for such intimate visions as his. Phillips would never have looked good (or, crucially, sounded good) at Wembley Arena. For Phillips, Valéry's declaration that 'it takes no more energy to write *fortissimo* than *piano*, or *universe* than *garden*' seems almost too appropriate.

'Library and soundtrack is the future for me. The more channels, the more commissions, but it's *very* competitive. But I'm lucky – I got in with Atmosphere Music early, at the right time, and they're still one of the top two companies. Yes, of course, I'd like to do my own albums as well ... '[17]

Private Parts and Pieces 9 – we can be sure – will be due out soon.

MIKE OLDFIELD

When Mike Oldfield found – to his horror – the musical world falling at his feet after the meteoric success of *Tubular Bells*, he was struck down by a recurrence of his manic-depressive symptoms. As Tony Palmer hagiographically pointed out, Oldfield genuinely hated the industry's star-making mill. Interviews he likened to rape.[1] But it is idle to imagine that the industry would let Oldfield off that easily, and indeed Branson and other Virgin grandees and friends coaxed another long-player out of him.

So how to follow *Tubular Bells*? Simple. Merely repeat its developmental techniques through new (but less inspired) sequences of tunes. Nevertheless, *Hergest Ridge* (1974) would hit the top three post haste. *Ommadawn* (1975), a collection of shorter songs, short-circuited any 'new Beethoven' panegyrics (already beginning to appear alongside the Smirnoff ads in the Sunday supplements).

His associate David Bedford released *Star's End* on Virgin in November 1974, a rhapsodic fantasy for orchestra and guitar, bass and drums; Oldfield's soloing over the Delian apotheosis is a particular delight, but alienated many serial-music stalwarts. Commissioned by the Royal Philharmonic Orchestra and conducted faithfully at both recording and subsequent Royal Festival Hall world première by redoubtable English music expert Vernon Handley, the extreme swooning chromaticism of many of the parts recalls Bax, Moeran and of course Delius. The follow-up, the 1975 adaptation of Coleridge's 'Rime of the Ancient Mariner', again warranted (incredibly, to 1990s critical sensibilities) good notices from both sides of the musical fence, despite its drearily clichéd employment of wild agitati for the storm sections.

Unhappily, Oldfield's music, offspring of the alternative Progressive current, quickly came to symbolize 1970s hip affluence. The appeal of its flawless engineering seduced hi-fi 'connoisseurs', but the subtle distillations of artistic pretension, hip-rock stylism and a sanitized vantage point over rootsy ethnicities which Oldfield (probably unthinkingly) brought to bear in his creations struck a chord with a substantial portion of cultural consumers.

Ascendent from and aspirant beyond the petit-bourgeois milieu that had spawned them, a new post-redbrick bourgeois weaned socially and professionally on the liberal arts arose, and Oldfield's soi-disant postmodern crossovers were just the lodestone they needed to align their pasts, presents and futures. Epically satirized by the *Guardian*'s Posy Simmonds and her 'Silent Three' cartoon strip, these liberal lentil-eaters consumed this lite counter-culture just as easily as they summered in rented Celtic-fringe holiday villas. Oldfield had, of course, taken to living near Hergest Ridge itself, in the wilds of Herefordshire, a super-rustic no-man's-land of dale and dereliction where Alfred Watkins had first formulated his ley-line sophistry in the early 1900s. Richard Boston and others were in the early 1970s formulating their embryonic environmentalist agitprop magazine, *Vole*. Oldfield's music deployed cutely olde-worlde and Keltic throwbacks such as the bodhran and uilleann pipes (Yeats was big in Hampstead, remember – we're only five years on from the *fin-de-siècle* crazes of the late 1960s). Other concessions to contemporary obsessions were early-musical instruments such as the kortholt; Oldfield had met Les Penning, a woodwind virtuoso and early-music enthusiast at Penrhos, near his home and invited him to play on his albums.

Such phenomena would be crucial to the establishment of the streamed record-buying publics in the middle and late 1980s which would affect the development and evolution of Progressive rock in the fragmented postmodern record industry, establishing a consumer aesthetic central to that exploited by the marketing men of 1980s New Age.

This is perhaps a little simplistic and a tad unfair on Oldfield's music; after the disappointment of *Hergest Ridge* and its upholstered revisiting of *Tubular Bells*, the technically and emotionally polymathic *Ommadawn* (1975) operates on several levels at once, not least because Oldfield states two themes rather than one near the beginning and doesn't try to develop them sequentially over fifty minutes but allows each its space to breathe and display itself, both singularly and with the other. Greek and Irish pastiche catered to the locations of the then-chattering-classes' leisure time, and for once episodic construction found its niche. The harmonics were harmless, beguiling, just occasionally radiant; there was a greater sense of architecture in the use of harmony than in, say, Genesis's music, or that of Phillips and his ilk, whereby the resolution of harmonic conflict could be relied upon quickly, in a verse or chorus – with Oldfield, it took longer. But the interminable working-out of themes on *Tubular* and, in particular, *Hergest*, is now replaced by a fastidious economy of expression. Oldfield has learned how to cut the crap and now recaps with real panache. The illusion of orchestral texture, with the timpani and chimes at the end of side one, is nicely done, but instruments maintain their own identities (e.g. the Northumbrian pipes are plainly used as Northumbrian pipes for a Northumbrian pipe effect) and betray a meretriciousness that would bedevil Oldfield's albums later.

Certainly the Establishment took Oldfield seriously; conductor and musicologist Bernard Benoliel compares Oldfield not with the nineteenth/early-twentieth-century composers so many progressive musicians had tried to emulate but, interestingly, with the contemporary composers of the 1970s. Benoliel dismisses claims for Oldfield's greatness, but instead concentrates, intelligently, on the inherent qualities of Oldfield's music on its own terms. He points out the emotional intensity which Oldfield brought to Bedford's *Star's End* with his electric guitar playing, for example. As Oldfield's biographer Sean Moraghan writes, Benoliel found 'the originality of [Oldfield's] music lay in his blending of varied styles, and its subtlety was less in its actual material than in the way it was presented, as a result of overdubbing, as a *texture* [my italics].'[2]

Oldfield's continued wowing of the tastemakers included an Arts Council-sponsored film, *Reflections* ('which attempted to reveal,' according to Moraghan, 'often through time-lapse photography and computer images, the symmetrical patterns and structures that existed both in nature and in the prehistoric and more modern architectural monuments made by man').[3] In other words, contrasting tumuli at the bottom of weekend cottage gardens with sculptures in Islington. This association with brown-rice affluence wasn't Oldfield's fault, but the music he would subsequently create seemed to do little but pander to this market, because it became one with it, helped define and create it, providing musical ethnicity handily bottled and tinned for dispensation from Habitat shelves, as in the pastiche old-English treatments of 'Portsmouth', 'Argiers', and the Vatican animation of 'In Dulci Jubilo', all subject to postmodern play with texture and melody. This was music for lecturers to plug into the cartridge machine in the Renault 4 on the way to the Polytechnic.

Oldfield's bewildered, fawn-like demeanour and his marginalization from this bourgeoisification of his music ended in 1978 when he underwent EST (Erhard Seminar Training), a doctrine of personal responsibility that out-Thatchered Thatcherism and helped capsize the libertarianism of the 1960s into the amoral individualism of the 1980s. Oldfield was a model convert; his 1978 album, the top-heavy double *Incantations*, saw him in haircut and ensemble identical to EST staff and on an archetype of the 'beautiful beach' upon which inductees were encouraged to imagine themselves. 'If anybody's in any particular situation, it's their own bloody fault,' he crowed in one interview 'State education is more responsible for people being fucked up than people ... being born [in the first place].'[4]

Oldfield went into orbit. High on post-therapeutic euphoria, the erstwhile introspective who loathed exposure to the world or the machinery of rock, took a massive instrumental and choral ensemble on a Europe-wide tour to promote *Incantations*. He embraced the media, almost too literally; Al Clark told the *NME*'s Bob Edmands: 'I was almost convinced he wasn't going to let you off without sticking his tongue down your throat.'[5] He was said to have marched into London's Capital Radio and invited the entire staff to a party — to which nobody came.

The girls' choir was selected on a looks-only policy; Oldfield, who was dating a model from *Penthouse*, refused to break the news to the parents of those whose voices didn't match their beauty. Among those chosen from Queen's College was a young Emma Freud, who, as Allan Jones reported in an April 1979 *Melody Maker*, impressed journalists as much for her naïveté as her looks. Her incomprehension of a joke told by roadies based around the rhyming slang 'hampton' ('What, you mean as in Court?') is one of Progressive's better road stories.[6] The next joke was on leader Oldfield; the tour cost him half a million pounds.

Incantations opens with a five-minute minimalist exposition of a hectically chromatic phrase voiced in multi-track bizarrerie on flute and synthesizer, easily Oldfield's (and one of Progressive's) most impressive inspirations. Oldfield, coached in an era obsessed with Terry Riley, appreciated the music of Philip Glass and eventually collaborated with Glass's engineer Kurt Munckacsi (a later Peter Gabriel colleague). But the procedure of Oldfield's development is less subtle, less rhythm-rooted; it's too fond of running on the spot, scanning the smooth, synthesized scenery with an appreciative eye; the adaptations of Ben Jonson's 'Diana, luna' lines and Longfellow's ultimate middlebrow mumble 'Hiawatha' is simply dull, with one critic observing that just as the listener thought it could not last another second, it continued 'for another quarter of an hour'.[7]

Oldfield's discovery of synthesizers, paradoxically limited him. It diminished the uncertainties in his music – the uncomfortable refereeing of stylistic clashes. If rock's chief attribute is texture, especially in extended form, Oldfield undermined his own constituency by making his textures more uniform.

Few musicians of his time mixed and matched every aspect of musical construction, multi-culti cutting and pasting with greater zeal than Oldfield. But by 1979's *Platinum*, this was overshadowed by a pre-eminent coupling with mainstream rock, or even pop, as the trademark Oldfield sound was swamped by studio gloss. A sudden post-EST mania for pop respectability was the sole unifying factor, with the pastiche 'Charleston' just that; like ELP's music-hall romps a mere component of a product, much as the folk input had become just an accessory. Oldfield could now merely employ the excellent Battlefield Band as his live support act to maintain his buyers' illusions that his music still possessed the same heady countryside odour as the mud on the tyres of their Range Rovers.

To return to 'Charleston', this trait was all too cynically evident; in Oldfield's Whole World days, this Charleston would have been a satirical Charleston of suitable dash and verve, but here it was a hollow gesture; it seems that Oldfield performs it as a piece of comical levity, a token input expected of him, a paragraph in a master-plan. Side two's 'Woodhenge', which brightly substitutes tuned percussion for synthesizers for phraseless *legato* effects, is proof that Oldfield's inspiration was alive and well but simply too often captive to contractual and artistic fiat. 'Punkadiddle' is a somewhat patronizing satire on the New Wave which Oldfield high-handedly despised in interviews (although he was quick enough to play keyboards on a Skids track). The interspersal of an Irish jig with Members-type suburban stomp hits the spot, as do Oldfield's strangled yells of 'Oi!' and the ironic adumbrations of football-crowd adulation echoed in and out of the music.

If Oldfield's role as court composer to the coffee table set needed an extra boost, it came with his acceptance of the commission to rewrite the theme tune to the BBC children's programme *Blue Peter*. Its nautical jollity is leeched out, a lassitude revisited on 1980's *QE2*, a record of milestone-making flatness despised even by many Oldfield diehards.

Oldfield, as Tom Newman says above, was jolted by New Wave, and furious at Virgin Records' decision to offer newer artists more favourable terms. He flirted with songs, then rejected them, then took them up again, then rejected them. The result was a series of extremely uneven albums. The obsession with side-long instrumental rambles persisted well into the 1980s, through *Five Miles Out* (1982) and *Crises* (1983), by which time his tetchy rift with Branson's Virgin had degenerated into outright hostility.

Again it's the subsidiary pieces which frustrate; 'Taurus II' (1982) is a riffy shambles which unaccountably lasts for nearly twenty-five minutes, a theme with variations of stultifying dullness – save for a demure, distant variation with fiddle, synthesizer, chimes and pipes. It's the nursery piece 'Orabidoo' from *Five Miles Out* which lets you know (just in case you'd forgotten) that Oldfield has a heart. 'Orabidoo' treats its textural palette with exquisite sensitivity, even if the melodic material is paltry. It's too long, but the modulations and developments show an urbane acquaintance with technique and the contrast of nursery-rhyme melodic contours with harsh percussion and ornamental cascades with stately *legato* is delightful. While long, compared to 1980s Yes (from whom it most obviously derives its textural language), it's a winner.

That Oldfield had become content to play a role was already self-evident by the time he revamped *Tubular Bells* for no very good reason in 1992. Certainly nothing else than ontological self-doubt (remember Robert Wyatt's words about Oldfield being unsure of how to be himself?) could have led to such a piffling retread of a fine album. Like the shinily hand-tooled household ornaments his music began to resemble in the 1970s, he seemed intent on forever polishing the surface. This was on the one hand predictable; latterly an evangelical thunderer against all things post-1977, he had told the *NME* in 1989 'take the drums away from 90 per cent of modern music and what have you got? Total shit.'[8] Nevertheless, his 1990 *Amarok* and 1991's *Heaven's Open* do suggest an unclouding of vision. He may have undertaken one of rock's more pathetic prima-donna gestures, camping out in a tent in the grounds of his enormous mansion as a protest against 'the over-commercialization, mechanization and mass production of modern music'[9] but there were signs that Oldfield, despite this zealous act of faith in Progressive ideology, was making his peace with newer forms. Janet Brown's deconstructive Thatcher-voiced commentary through the music of the piece 'Amarok' and the minimal synthesizer loops, inserted found sounds and trespassing jazz in *Heaven's Open* paint a more complex picture of Oldfield; Moraghan draws a neat comparison with *Ommadawn* (even to the extent of the Anglicized Gaelic of the title) with Hammond organ, uilleann pipes and African drums.[10]

The problem with much of this music is what one might call second-hand predictability. This is not fundamentally a criticism of its melody or harmony, but simply of the way it has become ubiquitous. Too much of its sounds like travelogue, or commissions for wildlife documentaries. And that intimist, pictorial genre had, since the 1970s, been dependent almost entirely upon slavish adherence to the methods of Oldfield's integration of a range of musical linguistic discourses into a pretty and immediate Western tonal idiom. Tills began ringing, and soon TV was full of Oldfieldish evocations of picturesque otherness (library music, as Anthony Phillips has informed us, took off in the 1980s), Northumbrian Mini Moogs, Saharan sleigh-bells, all within range of a transcription for any average amateur musician or any half-open set of ears (which makes the retreat from the likes of *Ommadawn* and the steely spirals opening *Incantations* all the more regrettable).

Oldfield's later work simply sounded like his imitators, referential only to a school of music now utterly bereft of its originality. As if this wasn't postmodern enough, though, Oldfield went the whole hog and imitated other people imitating himself, rerecording and reworking *Tubular Bells*. Had the album not been accompanied by publicity more appropriate to a small war, its status as mere lip-service to his own sellability might have been obviated. To be fair, though, Oldfield does try, through judicious use of samplers, to breathe some life, to donate some flexibility to what had been seen as a sacred Rosetta stone of Progressive mores; in other words, to meddle with its iconic artistic status. True, it is just as polite, its syntax as jejune and bourgeois as before, morally rather than intellectually improving. But given the issues that Oldfield's music always threw up in terms of postmodernity – the uncertainty of stylistic provenance, artistic centre, the origin of his texts and their relation to time and place – this was another knot in the attempt to explain Oldfield. Additionally, the saturation of everyday life with music – not least music often derivative of his own – meant that Oldfield's output had fewer concrete referents than ever.

But, finally, wasn't its unrelentingly breezy diatonicism, its narcotic inevitability, damnable and utterly alien to 'progressive' or 'Progressive' ideals and concepts? Possibly – but given the trajectory of music in the late 1980s and early 1990s, and the rise of passive listening and easy listening to rank alongside the rockist ethic of active, disturbing, heart-and-soul listening and appreciation, it occupied an even more precarious position. Could Oldfield's schoolmarmish harmonies be said to be any less valid than others? Could Progressive's? Could the 'insipidity' automatically attributed to them both now actually place them closer than ever to any actual cutting-edge of subversion modern popular music might pretend to possess?

10 IMAGINARY SOUNDTRACKS
(PROGRESSIVE IN THE 1990S)

DREAMS THEMED AND STREAMED

The splintering of taste which followed the triple-pronged assault of Live Aid, MTV and digital technology (both in recording and reproduction technology) initially perturbed rock critics. A further bourgeoisification of rock was seen as inevitable. Music, many cried, was becoming merely another lifestyle accessory in a decade obsessed with them. The revulsion found its target in New Age, a hydrogenated, undemanding music which percolated during the mid-1980s down from entrepreneurialized West Coast hippy culture.

From believing that music could alter collective consciousness, musical America now believed it could alter individual consciousness. The residual anti-urban, anti-modern, environmentally attuned precepts of hippy thought no longer inspired rock riffs for mass consumption but music for essentially private use: healing, lulling, amniotic, an adventure for oneself by oneself. It was no surprise that this music, as practised by the likes of Shadowfax and Kitaro, almost always derived from musical outgrowths of hippydom; Pink Floyd, the Mahavishnu Orchestra, Tangerine Dream, but expertly refined, sieved free of all impurities. Small wonder one critic dubbed New Age 'music for Yuppie mating rituals'.[1]

Much New Age employed notably Progressive sympathies; much was made of explorations of inner and outer space. Critics misread messages from surface similarities; New Age and Progressive (such as it then was) became symbiotically linked as middle-class artefacts, barely deserving of the term 'music' at all. But the slow reappraisal of rock's historiography in the wake of Live Aid and the admission by many contemporary artists of adolescent rockist loyalties of continuing importance – many of which concerned Progressive – often didn't help dismantle this lazy critical dogma.

Dave Mustaine of Heavy Metallers Megadeth refers to Pink Floyd's *Wish You Were Here* as 'great for unwinding to after sex or after a show. Or after a sex show. Preferably all three.'[2]

But is Progressive and easy listening's undeniable cousinhood all it seems? Or have critics overlooked details?

In England the proponents of the new genre, which took root with alarming speed, listed, as their chief inspirations, erstwhile Progsters Rod Argent (who had turned to making a handsome living selling electronic keyboards), a grateful and born-again Rick Wakeman and, by association, Progressive instrumentalists Anthony Phillips and Mike Oldfield.

Progressive thereby took another knock; once again, as with Punk, the aesthetic agenda of mainstream criticism swamped alternative standpoints. That stance instinctively equated 'good' music with 'direct listening', music to be consumed actively, not passively, music that cajoled and challenged – itself a throwback to 1960s rockism, even when filtered through the agency of postmodern pop criticism, just as prescriptive in its way as anything written in *IT* by the likes of Mick Farren.

The possibility that an alternative view could be held was never entered into. One could, like Joseph Lanza in his splendid history of muzak and associated genres, hold up Satie's inheritance of Matisse's 'non-obtrusive art' as a defence. An ardent advocate of music that diverged from the totalities of Wagnerism (popular in early twentieth-century France), Satie composed music for Peladan's Parisian salon exhibitions that could be listened to or ignored, and Lanza and others have read this as a bravely subversive gesture. Progressive's link with easy listening could, therefore, be read as cultural viability, particularly when Lanza delves into the cultural referents of his subject.

Lanza's case for critical revaluation of music that is passively or semi-passively consumed is masterly. He points up manifold other similarities between mood music and Progressive rock. 'Light' and 'mood' music was obsessed, like counter-cultural music, with travel, distance, whether to Hawaii or outer space, but, crucially, with home always in mind. In fact these were nominally metaphorical travels, conducted from the comfort of an armchair, much as Cinerama took one around the world while seated in the fleapit. Lanza's researches also reveal the high degree of technological determinism in the evolution of the genre's aesthetic; he writes of pioneering studio techniques in performance and production in the evocation of the sellably sublime, of violins processed through transducers and potentiometers in the manufacture of suitably transcendent sounds in the recording of what he charmingly terms 'space-age bachelor-pad music'.[3] And Lanza gleefully reminds us of mood music's artistic pretensions − classically bourgeois − the sleeve note to Melachrino's *Music to Help You Sleep* (shades of New Age) avidly quoted Proust, Shakespeare, Nietzsche and Ovid on the art of dreaming. Dalì designed the cover-art to Jackie Gleason's *Lonesome Echo*; '[the] first effect is that of anguish, of space, and of solitude. Secondly, the fragility of the wings of a butterfly, projecting long shadows of late afternoon, reverberates in the landscape like an echo.'[4] Postmodernism at work already, purloining highbrow language to borrowed lowbrow notions of the highbrow.

It is postmodern irony writ large that the very stylistic postures by which the counter-culture sought to escape bourgeois artistic mores were Ur-bourgeois in themselves. But in any case contrary to its publicity, Progressive had not always been consumed as Olympian address. Often it was listened to in a state of advanced intoxication. It was and is consumed both as clarion-call and shag-soundtrack. As Lanza points out, passive listening *does not undermine the artistic or social value of music as symbol or agent of change and innovation.* Brian Eno's embrace of ambient, background music-making techniques prove that such music need not be automatically emotionally neutral, his *Music for Airports*, used experimentally at Pittsburgh Airport in 1982, brought a barrage of complaints from passengers that its uncertain tones made them feel uneasy, and there was a unanimous demand for the original background music to be restored.[5]

This is particularly relevant in the light of a postmodern revisitation of easy-listening and MOR music and also the advent of Rave in the 1990s; although superficially unrelated to Progressive, both musics, dance in particular, can be viewed as being spiritual cousins of Progressive, and can help us understand its current cultural position better.

RAVERS FROM THE GRAVE

But how? Dance music is surely active music, physical music, the ultimate statement of the dominion of rhythm over melody, of body over mind, unimpeachably democratic, open-textual, whereby the only function of sound is representation of nothing but subjective physical *jouissance*. The Art of Noise's *Ambient Collection* (1990) apostrophized 'everything good about the hard and uncompromising trance-dance of house and the surrealism of ambient instrumentalism ... an unfocused daydream with no background or foreground. A sense of not being yourself, of being apart from what you're listening to.'[6] There is lack in dance music – lack of relief, lack of detail, of differentiation. How could it possibly find common ground with Progressive rock?

For starters, the need for chill-out culture alongside dance culture, where physical limits on dancefloor dissolution begged a gentler otherworldliness to restore a raver's metabolic balance, steered the course of popular music right back into the environmental sculpturing of Eno, the healing tones of New Age and, ultimately, to the transcendentalism of hippyism.

Secondly, Progressive's genesis and gestation in psychedelia and noise and drones fed a liaison with a new counter-culture and a filial aestheticism, a new emphasis on the visual and the dissolute as cultural brethren. Progressive's liaison with such minimalist musical concerns began with the faddish 1960s cult of Terry Riley's *In C* and *A Rainbow in Curved Air* as mantric talismans for hippy-dippery (these and other pieces, such as those of Philip Glass, were strongly influenced by the drone effects of Indian classical music, another cred-emblem for the epoch). But some musicians sought deeper resonance in the repetition and Robert Fripp and Brian Eno's historic *No Pussyfooting* (1973) brought the disciplines of minimalism, the rhythmically dictated elision of melody and harmony, to bear on contemporary rock. The harmonic variation of music determined by rhythm would prove increasingly persuasive in the concert hall through the devotional compositions of John Tavener, the monkish raptures of the Estonian Arvo Pärt and the Georgian Giya Kancheli and the latterday music of the lapsed Serialist Henryk Górecki (also commercially exploited in the late 1990s by ex-Soft Machine man Karl Jenkins's esoteric pot-pourri of ethnic chant, systems music and MOR, *Adiemus*). The diminished speed of sequences between chords did not intrinsically undermine their complexity of construction or progress.

But as music writer Mike Kidson rightly indicated in an article on Progressive and dance for *Facelift* magazine, the drone aspects of Indian music had also been taken on board by Gong's Daevid Allen and Steve Hillage, whose 'glissando' guitar effects originated in the tape-looping scrims of sound to which Allen would recite his surrealist poetry in the 1960s.[7] This would offer another locus for dance and Progressive mores in the 1990s.

Whether dance music had arisen in the late 1980s or not, it is unlikely that Gong and its various satellites would have ceased their Flying Dutchman-like progress through the bohemian backwaters of the globe. But by 1988 their wanderings centred increasingly on the UK, by now in the grip of the 'second summer of love' dance phenomenon. Gong merely walked in and joined the party.

True, the dichotomy between Gong's surreal lyrics and 3/4 acoustic-guitar ballads posited a formal, through-composed element, but the droning element of Gong had never gone away (was this Fohat singing?), and even in 1988 poetry and invocations spanned two decades as though nothing had passed between.

'The new dispensation of the Gong vibration,' as Allen put it, 'would include a "house" rhythm section';[8] a tabla player had been there for some time, and Allen's logic seemed impeccable. The result? Gong Maison (literally 'Gong House'), a version of which would release 1990's *Shapeshifter* album under the Gong name. The amalgam of trance-beats, crude sampling (dog samples for 'Dog-o-matic' *et al.*) and rowdy guitar splurges was among the most complete reintegration of Progressive ideology and cutting-edge contemporary music since the 1960s.

Gong's engagement with alternative lifestyles not only chimed with the hedonism of dance but also its universalist concerns of inner and outer environmental appreciation, an ambient culture which, to quote Simon Reynolds's brilliant summary of psychedelia, 'valorizes the notion of the imaginary soundtrack'[9] much as the Glastonbury disciples of 1971 had done. To this end they once again knitted happily into the itinerant, counter-cultural lifestyles of Rave and Traveller culture, and recruited guitarist Steffy Sharpstrings from venerable spacerocking shamblers and crusty-convoy concert-party Here and Now.

Parallel to Allen's Gong activities were those of his ex-partner Gilli Smyth's Mother Gong, whose lineups had experimented with mantric and invocational rhythms of their own, such as reggae and funk. By 1988, Mother Gong had 'gone the whole way and programmed all the effects, and the mixer and all the cues for the microphone, and actually this has made it into a very ... technologically advanced show that [required] a dedicated sound team ... but between these programmes we also have areas which are free, random events'.[10]

Gong performances, as always, were not 'events' in the standardized concert tradition; their emphasis on vibe as opposed to music reduced the need for precision, expertise and technology.

Younger Turks lurked, liver wires than the pensionable Allen, and with beat in their bones. Alex Paterson, late of dance pioneers the KLF, formed the Orb in 1988, and patented the womblike ether of ambient to a mass UK audience. He also coaxed ex-Gong guitarist Steve Hillage from his production-console exile into performance once again, adding Hillage's solar-powered sustain and feedback to enhance the depth of his soundscaping.

Hillage's post-Gong career barely got airborne before Punk ethics shot it down. His blending of blues guitar with sonic experimentalism – notably with extreme use of pedals and reverberation – attracted scoffing accusations of an anaemic Hendrix; his heritage of compositional exploration, harmonic worldliness and textural opulence also attracted flak. As if that wasn't enough, Hillage's occult obsessions, fuelled by Gong, erupted in his solo work to an almost hectoring extent. Few pieces were not either inspired by, or did not contain paeans to, the solar mythology to which Hillage had become enslaved.

Hillage mingled edgy riffing, melodies and episodically playschool complex Progressive epigonism. Texturally he was a little more individual and innovative, contrasting passages of melting tenderness with rugged, raucous ensemble; Lindsay Cooper's delicate, bubbling bassoon notes over a gliding idyll of organ chords forming the centrepiece of 'Salmon Song' from Hillage's debut album, *Fish Rising* (1975) is one of the genre's most charming inspirations; never ultra-refined, but idiosyncratically sensual. But it was perhaps Hillage's most spiritually saturated work, 1979's *Rainbow Dome Musick*, which ensured his place in rock history some ten years after the event.

Commissioned for performance at that year's Mind-Body-Spirit Festival at Kensington Olympia (a kind of Ideal Pyramid Exhibition devoted to marketizing the New Age of higher consciousness – perhaps the ultimate Head Shop–Body Shop crossover), its celestial, looping synthesizers and glissando guitar provided as hypnotic and mesmerizing a multi-track experience as any heard in Progressive, or indeed in rock at that point.

The cyclical character of Hillage's (albeit highly colouristic, representational and contrasted) atmospheric vision wasn't lost on the likes of Alex Paterson's Orb. The lengthy workouts of that outfit's *Adventures Beyond the Ultraworld* debut mixed sheets of sound spirited from the music of *Rainbow Dome*, billowing acres of simple chordal repetitions and drizzling electronics, all dutifully bearing suitably cosmicized titles. By 1991's *UFOrb*, however, Technoid thuds had given ground to dub basslines, noticeably more periodic interpolations of light and shade, and virtuosically adept sampling which humbled Gong's (e.g. the sample of comedian and writer Victor Lewis Smith's spoof phone call on 'Towers of Dub'). Add more Hillage (remarkably fluent) and it was little wonder that before long head stalls trading in Fabulous Furry Freak Bros. merchandise could be seen at Orb concerts.

Hillage set up his own shop in the E-and-whizz souk with System 7, inspired by and grateful for Paterson's intense interest in and rediscovery of his once critically reviled music. Hillage preferred uncomplicated Techno grooves, and his honest directness results at times in a dullardly literalism (i.e. the rigid dualizing on the 1994 'Fire' and 'Water' mixes of his *Point Three* album, which signify (but of course) hardcore and chill-out takes on similar material). But Hillage's occasional visionary refinement lives in the likes of the seascape 'Sirenes', the twee Orientalism of 'Dr Livingstone I Presume'. 'Batukau''s guitar solos show that the years have imposed restraint on Hillage – this could almost be MOR guitar were it not for the inimitable range and resourcefulness.

Whereas, in Kidson's words, the Orb mixed approaches 'broadly concerned with sonic novelty rather than cultural compatibility, bunging a dance beat together with an "ambient" lapidary construction', Ultramarine represented a step further in the reconciliation of Progressive and Techno/ambient mores in a more through-composed, organic fashion closer to traditional Progressive sequentiality than that of Dance. Ultramarine's 1993 album, *United Kingdoms*, followed up an EP entitled 'Wyndham

Lewis' and, for *Wire*'s Louise Gray, was 'a mesh of acoustics, electronics and wide-open spaces'.[11] King Arthur, Guinevere and Merlin appeared on the sleeve, and Robert Wyatt, who contributed vocals to the album, dressed up as Merlin for the promotional videotape. One track featured, 'Song of the Lower Classes', entailed a visit to Cecil Sharp House, altar of folk traditionalism and scholarship, to establish the material's provenance (thereby not quite giving rise to the resonant generic term 'Cecil Sharp House Music'). Caravan's wind player Jimmy Hastings was seen accompanying the band at sundry gigs; once again the fifths and thirds of classic Progressive rock swirled in easy, oozing motion; the band then reprocessed Kevin Ayers's track 'Hymn' with remixes by u-ziq and Mouse on Mars; this, however, like their version of Matching Mole's 'Instant Kitten', was essentially constituted in non-ambient fashion, 'based ... on harmonizations of a linear melody'.[12] But, as Kidson points out, such treatment begged the question as to how far the couplings could go; many Progressive melodic profiles were simply too extended to bear repeated exposition in Techno style. And didn't the vertical complexity of their harmonies often induce diversity and variation in linear/horizontal development?

'The difficulty,' suggests Paul Schütze, 'lies in the fact that virtually everyone is using identical methodologies based around certain popular pieces of sequencing software. All software has subtle biases within its architecture, making it easier to do one thing rather than another. It is easiest to make modular rhythmic music with a 4/4 time-signature. To develop and edit something more complex is much harder, so of course everyone makes music in 4/4. This results in minimal horizantal development and a very diagrammatic type of music.'[13]

Another hosannaed dance act, Eat Static, concentrated on even lusher textures, if without the chordal differentiation and developmental complexity of Godfrey. They were moonlighters from a more conventional Progressive band, the tireless Ozric Tentacles. Christened after a fictitious cereal, stalwarts of convoy and campus, the Ozrics, as their cult following rapidly (and somewhat inevitably) dubbed them, retrod the old straight tracks laid down by their direct musical forebears, Hawkwind and Here and Now. Six albums appeared on privately released cassette tapes before the band bowed to public demand and signed to independent Demi Monde (then, in the wake of distribution difficulties, effortlessly setting up their own Dovetail Records enterprise) for the manufacture of CDs and vinyl. Here was Progressive revivalism on the rampage, replete with knowingly hermetic and cultic imagery and vocabulary (early works contain titles like 'Sploosh!', 'Erpriff' and 'Wreltch'). When the Dovetail records began to appear, their covers sported a mascot-like elfin figure (of suspicious visual similarity to the pothead-pixie personnel of Gong's cosmology) as the still, smirking centre of a psychedelic paint-factory explosion.

The band had taken shape a year after encountering keyboardist Joie Hinton at the 1983 Stonehenge Free Festival (neither the first nor the last of innumerable such gigs for this crusty-friendly outfit); Hinton's samples of Asian and Middle Eastern folk music began to enrich his employers' material both in terms of compositional ambition and textural variety. This was at the time a sprawling melange of appropriations, the most evident being from Hawkwind, Hillage and Gong, uneasily allying timbral roughness with sonic enquiry and lavishly harmonized riffs.

The band's odd combination of squalid rawness and exoticism both Western and Eastern was further complicated by a schizophrenic performance mentality, oscillating between barnstorming brutalities of feedback and studio refinements of formidable technical discipline and application – even on early recordings (1987's *There is Nothing*). The advent of flautist John Egan that same year indicated a greater sense of adventure than ever.

The music then, as now, was of a principally rhythmic inspiration, but this is not to underestimate the Ozrics: their later music revels in a polyglot rhythmic zip far from the one-paced mastodon trudge of Pink Floyd, and exhibits both intense instrumental virtuosity but also a discerning ear for emotional sophistication.

By *Arborescence* (1994), the guitar solos of Ed Wynne boasted enthralling elan, but transgressed workaday blues voicings and stresses just enough to hold the listener's interest. Duality between up-tempo and slower numbers (usually of black-hearted, sweat-streaked dub) may be somewhat overdone, but the ingenuity of reworking ambient linearity in the likes of the wondrously light-textured spirals and curlicues of 'There's a Planet Here' (1994) and increasing use of drop-beats serves notice of a serious challenge to the time-honoured critical lie of Progressive elaboration's fundamental incompatibility with (at least imagined) qualities of 'guts', expressivity and spontaneity.

The upshot of this hippy resurgence was a vigorous reclamation of the notion of the legitimacy of music as cipher of a higher reality. It would pave the way for the slow but steady rebuilding of a singularly contemporary Progressive aesthetic some thirty years after the original occurrence. It would, by necessity, be different from hitherto. The identity of its proponents was the principal difference. They were younger, of different origin, emerging from different tutelages. How, in the circumstances of the early 1990s, could the Progressive personnel of the late 1960s – particularly in the light of the history outlined above – hope to participate?

FROM STADIUM TO SHED – THE PRACTICE OF PROGRESSIVE TODAY

Pink Floyd became a three-piece some time in the early 1980s. The stresses of the *Wall* project and its consequent presentation on stage and in the cinema had exploded into hostility between Roger Waters and the other three members. The story has been told too often to bear repetition here (especially good on the topic is Schaffner's *A Saucerful of Secrets*). Summarily, Waters, whose glandular nihilism had soured yet more on 1983's *The Final Cut*, had first effectively sacked keyboardist Rick Wright and then verbally squared up to guitarist Gilmour (one critic wrote that Waters '[had] such a chip on his shoulder it's a wonder his arm doesn't drop off').[14] Waters quit, the other three reassembled under the Floyd name, and Waters promptly sued.

The intervening recordings – Pink Floyd's *A Momentary Lapse of Reason* (1987) and *The Division Bell* (1994) and Waters's *The Pros and Cons of Hitchhiking* (1984), *Radio KAOS* (1987) and *Amused to Death* (1992) – merely render the proceedings irrelevant in the context of this book. The music is almost without exception like a needle stuck in a groove from *The Wall*, the sleepwalking chords and arrangements leavened only by an abiding interest in formal informality, in structural contrariness. Waters's own work continued to plough an ever-deepening abyss of gloom; metres and harmonies were moribund, the solo work often redundant, but Waters managed to retain a sense of textual commitment and literary facility throughout, attacking feminism (*Hitchhiking*) and mass media (*KAOS* and, more trenchantly and at times penetratingly, *Amused to Death*). His soundtrack for Raymond Briggs's animated nuclear tragicomedy *When the Wind Blows* (1987) was an exception: tasteful, restless and surprisingly intimate. It merely highlighted the folly of Waters's concept albums; therein, it seemed, he was utterly captive to the rockist reality of 'the album', unwilling or unable to resist the clichés of the 'rock song'. As on his underrated 1970 experimental film soundtrack collaboration with Ron Geesin, *The Body*, Waters's capacities became infuriatingly apparent, and the eye-glazed nature of his album work became all the more reprehensible, given the ability he still displayed with lyrical input. Like Pink, the self-pitying and cynical anti-hero of Waters's *The Wall*, Waters seemed to have fulfilled his own prophecy and allowed his creation to become mummified by the aesthetics of rock mainstream.

Waters, in a phrase of a pithiness often lacking from his songs, described one sceptical journalist as being 'one taco short of a Mexican meal' (for the record, this was the *Guardian*'s Adam Sweeting).[15] Sweeting's disdain for Waters was possibly based on the pensionable and wrongheaded equation of Progressive with bourgeois sentiment (in journalese, what the fuck did a rock grandee such as Waters think he was doing, singing about media manipulation?) While Waters still had his conceits, he at least didn't exhibit the same shameless indulgence as his erstwhile Floyd chums; Mason and Gilmour's well-publicized motor-sport obsession resulted in a video and album based on their participation in the Carrera Panamericana, a continent-bestriding motor race from Mexico to the USA. Gilmour: 'Lots of overgrown schoolboys getting together and having heaps of fun driving fast cars around Mexico. What more could you want?'[16] Some interesting music, maybe?

But when musicians were driven to this kind of opulence by the rewards of their pasts, what motivations could the present offer?

Money, for a kick-off. The Yes saga had descended into a writ-split-and-quit farrago of mutual dislike and corporate pillow-fighting as rival tribes of erstwhile members fought for custody of the Yes marque. In 1989, a collaboration between Anderson, Wakeman, Bruford and Howe had to be called precisely that for legal reasons, despite the fact that the band were Yes in all but name.

Says Bruford,

Anderson–Wakeman–Bruford–Howe was first and foremost a business thing. I still wasn't crazy about the music, but there were some interesting bits; every now and again Rick would play something fabulous, like Elgar, and I'd have a chance to stretch out and do something with it – if we could have developed the group over a very long period of time instead of, say, over five minutes, I believe that band could have been very interesting, but that wasn't the way Arista [AWBH's label] wanted it. I did it because I knew it could pay for Earthworks [Bruford's experimental jazz outfit].[17]

The album was calculated to appeal to diehards; sweeping orchestral bridges, episodic songs, multitudinous solos. But this, as did the *90125* project, lacks momentum, the emotional syntax of the music is still boringly rock-based; the orchestration, once pearly and luminous, sounds merely stodgy, and technology remains under-utilized; even Horn's primitive samplings of 1983 are absent here. These three qualities, which the old Yes did so much to explore, remain dormant. But the come-on of this apparent nostalgism – Roger Dean was the author of the (gatefold) sleeve – packed the planet's sports arenas to the rafters, and suddenly the Yes stalemate was miraculously resolved, although not without unreported (and, by popular consent, unreportable) tantrums, arm-twistings and litigation. The solution was an eight-man lineup comprising almost every former band member for a 1991 album entitled *Union*. Bruford unreservedly described the follow-up tour as

> ludicrous, really. For some of us, it was a very lucrative bit of fun, others needed it desperately. Like Jon, who was so up to his neck in debt it wasn't true. He'd spent years trying to get everything he could out of the system, and it bit back. So he has to go on singing, like a canary in a mineshaft.[18]

The octet encountered receptions of homecoming ecstasy, in the US particularly, but unsurprisingly disintegrated; the music of *Union*, an unhappy testament to hubris, conceit and corporate expediency, unintentionally embodies all the crimes that had been (often mistakenly) laid at the band's door hitherto. It's overdone, overwrought and overproduced, with fast-buck West Coast consonance winning out over refinement (how could eight musicians spend a realistic period putting together such an album anyway and expect musical subtlety to triumph over war-wounded egos?) and textural ingenuity.

This horror made the re-formation of ELP in 1992 seem a model of modesty by comparison. Emerson had made a living scoring unremarkable films during the 1980s (*Nighthawks* and, more promisingly, Dario Argento's *Inferno*, among others). There had been interludes, perhaps best forgotten; the attempt to revive the band in 1986 with drummer Cozy Powell in Palmer's stead looked, in Phil Sutcliffe's words, 'too much like the outcome of a want ad asking for "heavy drummer, surname must begin with P"'.[19] No mercy was shown to the ill-fated *Three* project of 1988, which teamed Palmer and Emerson with bespoke AOR songwriter Robert Berry, also a guiding light behind GTR a woebegone band which, in 1986, had combined the guitar talents of Steve Howe and Steve Hackett and had managed to make two of the most distinctive guitarists in rock sound like autopiloted sessioneers at a Foreigner recording.

ELP's *Black Moon* (1992) did at least aspire to interest and *excite* the listener, and it would be a churlish mind that overlooked a vigour in the playing which had formerly been notable by its absence. The material, though, suffered from the Yes malaise: cynicism and over-exposure to the wallet-fattening blandishments of easy-out FM mores, intervals and developmental procedures had blunted edges and dulled nerve-endings both of players and listeners. Whereas before musicians like Emerson might have spent that extra hour or so polishing a transition or adding a line to heighten emotional impact, now the joins showed; the illusion was merely a shoddy excuse.

But ELP's crusty insistence on revisiting their past and not trying hopelessly to remake it, actually sounded more in tune, more spirited and fresher in the early 1990s than Yes's multiple-personality disorder.

Postmodernity was now a fact of life, not just an appealing novelty, as it had been in the 1980s; then, Marillion could get away with aping Genesis, but by the 1990s, kitsch and nostalgia had become such hot properties, cultural entities of such currency that outright imitation became a statement; to the ranks of good-time lookalike bands (Björn Again, Fake That *et al.*) came Re: Genesis, an outfit devoted to recycling Gabriel-era stage sets and songs, period performance taken to its acme (for fans of post-Gabriel Genesis, there is And Then There were Five). Described by even the hardest-core Progressive acolytes as 'a good laugh', is this what the super-serious Progressive project had come to? Or was it ever so serious? Was it ever as has been imagined and then recorded? Have we simply lost the plot as regards Progressive's place in rock history?

Progressive survives today in much the same way artisanal crafts or endangered wildfowl survive: through the selfless, financially unremunerative toil of devotees which may range from humping Mellotrons halfway around a continent to setting up a website for Caravan fans in Iceland. Microcosmal it may seem in this era of multi-media rock juggernautism, but its modesty is more than matched by the dedication of its admirers. Disc production and distribution are entrusted to similarly small but zealous cells.

Progressive is, at least, receiving occasional, tokenist acknowledgement. The shadowy dance outfit organization KLF announced: 'The live half of [Pink Floyd's] *Ummagumma* is essential to both of us. "Set the Controls for the Heart of the Sun" is the centrepiece for the whole of the Floyd's career.'[20] US Techno guru Marshall Jefferson expostulated: 'Man, I love rock'n'roll! I started off with rock and roll: Pink Floyd, Led Zeppelin ... Procol Harum – sheeyut! When I do my rock'n'roll group it's gonna be a double album and there's gonna be soloing that'll knock your head off.'[21] Bernard Butler of Britpop student idols Suede said: 'Now that I've discovered the Floyd, I can't understand why people listen to the Orb.'[22] Vernon Reid, guitarist and musical helmsman of US black HMers Living Color, has cited similar influences (even the politically suspect Rush) as have the Pixies. 'There's this weird attitude towards Progressive and who it might or might not actually influence,' says Paul Schütze. 'Like Fishbone. You listen to the introductions on the tracks to his album. Immense. Phenomenally bombastic music-making.'[23]

Times are tough, however. On an advertisement for the revivalist Canterbury band, Richard Sinclair's Caravan of Dreams, there can be seen the (only just) tongue-in-cheek plea, 'help musicians survive'.[24] Robert Godfrey is more sanguine. 'I don't know,' he says pensively of his band The Enid. 'We can't do anything. People often don't want to know, so it's a struggle.'[25]

Godfrey has problems of his own, fighting for legal recognition of his composing credits for the fledgling Barclay James Harvest. 'I won the case in the end. But I didn't get any money because, according to the legal profession, I'd just left it too long to file a case. These were the people who for years had been telling me not to bother. The legal system has effectively denied me a pension,' he fumes. 'I get credits on BJH albums now, but that's about it.'[26] Robert Fripp, while this book was being written, sent the author a 200-page dossier detailing his acrimonious ongoing legal proceedings against EG Records, his erstwhile owners, aptly titled 'Endless Grief'.

Despite atomizations of taste, crossovers and the whole postmodern anarchy, relativism has not yet extended to a rediscovery of Progressive rock or its ideology, even in its necessarily reshaped 1990s, postmodern form. The wind blows colder; people are having to shape up or ship out.

'In the early days,' observes Mike Stobbie, 'whenever acts like this met up, everyone hated each other, because we all thought there was such a small market. But now in the 1990s everyone is helping each other and we may be able to stick around longer.'[27]

Progressive in its original form not only does not exist any longer, it *cannot* do so. Its vocabulary – the hybrid vocabulary, purloined from the vocabularies it mixed and matched in the 1970s – has itself become ever more elaborate; but just because the material has changed, this does not mean that Progressive *ideology* cannot continue to work with it. Progressive's popular signifiers – imagery, musicianship, dynamic contrasts – should themselves have become a part of the past to be pirated, just as Bach fugues and Coltrane solos were themselves plundered by Progressive.

The semantic dichotomy opened in the 1980s between mainstream 'Progressive' and 'progression' – when 'Progressive' no longer meant what it said – yawns wider. A review of an album by neo-Progressive band Moria Falls in the fanzine *Organ* reported: 'The last thing you want a Progressive band to do is progress' (a view heartily and unself-consciously echoed by the band themselves).[28] Bands openly using the techniques of 1977 Genesis or 1971 King Crimson cannot be said to 'progress' in any recognizable sense of the word. That does not exclude them from Progressive ideology, which refers to kind, not degree, to a specific aesthetic. But what then, even when postmodernism has supposedly banished universals like 'progression', can be said to constitute Progressive rock that progresses?

Let us examine extant Progressive acts. From the deliberate imitation of Re: Genesis and the pastiche of Pallas, IQ, Jadis *et al.*, we proceed tentatively to radical post-ambient sonic pioneers and compositional engineers like Paul Schütze as well as pilgrims of real-time improvisation and performance as well as studio craft such as Tim Hodgkinson and the rest of the post-Henry Cow constellation, and we must maintain that they are the true inheritors of Progressive ideology.

There are others who seem to engage warily with aspects of Progressive ideology, with producing music, beautiful, unusual or refined sounds, for the sake of it. The acidic guitar-led études of the Durutti Column, billed as post-Punk experimentalists in 1980, are now located in a much more impressionist pigeon-hole in a changed musical landscape. Sundry offshoots of early-1980s designer popsters Japan, notably the work of Richard Barbieri, Mick Karn and Steve Jansen, have generated haunting, mannered, Parnassian pop (Rain Tree Crow etc.). David Sylvian's teaming up with Robert Fripp seemed absurdly obvious, given his increasingly esoteric work in aestheticizing pop music into languorous soundscapes; his *Damage* live LP with Fripp (1994) is a wonder of elegiac splendour. Norfolk's No-Man (also Fripp collaboratees) took the premise of the various projects which arose out of early-1980s pop band Japan (Karn and Barbieri, Rain Tree Crow etc.) and extended it, using the linear developments of electronic and ambient pop and elaborating their vertical structures, with exquisite instrumental additions, best seen perhaps in the act's 1996 album, *Heaven's Taste*. Bill Nelson, who had cut his teeth by proposing intimate, baroque ballads in the early 1970s in opposition to Progressive's searching ambition, discovered electronics in the 1970s and by 1995 was producing extraordinary miniature Progressive masterpieces by combining classic pop chords and developments, gymnastic guitar solos, resonant, pithy sampling and clattering'n'chattering drum'n'bass rhythms. This is how Yes could (and should) have sounded in the mid-1980s.

The inextinguishable Canterbury constellation blazes on, albeit with lightbulb intensity. Even though the harmonic and melodic contours may not have changed much, the work of the likes of Hopper, Miller etc. cannot escape the postmodern; indeed, they pre-empted it, having established already that it was a melting-pot of influences to the point whereby its rock provenance could be disputed its chief component. Furthermore jazz, had itself been inseminated by musical influences such as avant-garde classical and funk, and this further muddied the waters. Voiceprint Records, set up in County Durham by the tireless Robin Ayling in November 1990, is a label not only devoted to rescuing the recorded heritage of this prodigious collective of musicians but also, with its Resurgence and Blueprint labels, gives a home to some of the more interesting players in the Progressive field today – No-Man, Bill Nelson, Anthony Phillips.

The US, particularly under the aegis of the Massachusetts-based Cuneiform Records, hosts manifold acts whose Progressive credentials feature contemporary classical, jazz and non-Western influences – a little tardy after the 1960s example set by Frank Zappa's Mothers of Invention, but in the interim those constituent influences themselves had changed in any case. Jazz, however, was still preferred as a model for free improvisation rather than as a chordal springboard.

U Totem, Dr Nerve and Tortoise 'produced music that was simultaneously low-key and electrifying, transfiguring the hands-on, real-time group interaction of rock via the virtual chambers of the studio',[29] in the pioneering vanguard of veteran English studio experimenters This Heat. Shared characteristics also included a prodigious variety of instrumental colour; the band Sabalon Glitz, for example, have hoarded fifteen keyboards as well as dulcimer and stylophone.

This indicated less a leaning to lushness than a timbral exploration; in Simon Reynolds's formulation of the new US 'post-rock' soundworld, 'the guitar,' he says, '[is] no longer kinetic (a riff machine) but atmospheric (a texture and timbre generator)'.[30] A retreat to 'raw' analogue in the stead of 'sterile' digital is a matter of economics – while the cheapness of instruments in the States may explain the profligacy of instrumentation, post-rock is still a penurious concern, but additionally the distancing of white musical norms from black has (perhaps ironically) led to the elevation of 'live performance over studio trickery'.[31]

Paul Schütze, an Australian émigré living and recording in

London, perhaps best represents the contemporary manifestation of Progressive ideology mediated through postmodernism.

Site Anubis (1996), a concept scenario of urban catastrophe radiating from an 800-foot statue of the Egyptian god Anubis, is humblingly complicated and methodical, but in temporal terms, the music's narrative remains largely static; texture is where Schütze scores, detonating a nebula of ornaments and adjuncts to his unanchored and often vaguely tonal explorations. Schütze recorded *Anubis* as a Chinese-whispering fusion, a cumulative approach requiring selected musicians to apply their own accompaniments to backing tracks without ever meeting up; bassist Bill Laswell in New York played over Schütze's electronics, and passed on the results to drummer Dirk Waechtelaer in Brussels who contributed his parts before handing the music over to the next performer, and so on.

'It's got a lot to do with film,' Schütze reports of his compositional process. 'If I make a piece, the piece defines a space ... I want depth. I imagine a space and then position things at certain points in that picture.'[32] It is, as Rob Young writes, 'increasingly sensual ... as full of tiny details as a tropical jungle'.[33] Schütze's albums concern lyrical narratives of millennial dysfunction, discussing the relative mythic qualities of urban and rural spaces, exploring the relationship between the organic and the mechanical in an askew reprise of the Progressive ideological dichotomy between Marshall amplifiers and Grantchester Meadows.

Schütze is non-committal when offered the Progressive affinities of his music. 'None of it [*Site Anubis*] was written – it was all improvised. They're all extremely good players but none of them are virtuosi in the accepted sense of the word. They're not signature players, which is what a lot of Progressive musicians were.'[34] Schütze contends: 'In the space of a few bars, you'd know it was Carl Palmer playing or Alan White playing. Signatures. That's what Progressive was all about. Individuality.'[35]

Schütze is a convinced admirer of 1970s Progressive rock, but nevertheless states: 'I don't feel the *need* to hear, now, the Progressive rock that I liked in the 1970s. What I think I need to hear, I think, is a combination of all those elements brought up to date.'[36]

His arguments for the effective loss of Progressive's centrality to the popular music-making of his time is compelling and ingenious; technology has simply rendered it obsolete (although not irrelevant):

> I could write an impossible, unplayable drum part and set a sequencer up and it could perform it live, but what's the point? The point was to see Prog bands achieving – or falling short of these goals – a bit like sport, like athletics. Most bands don't need players of that calibre. The music, commensurately, is not about that. Seeing things live now is more about the quality of sound and the atmosphere than about performance, musicianship *per se*. The craft is in a more abstract realm.
>
> Sampling has fundamentally changed the way we relate – all of us – to sound. And as for MIDI – well, most of the music that you hear most of the time would not be possible without MIDI. MIDI is so fundamental to what most people do that musicians don't even register it as being important any more – almost like electricity. It's dispensed – to a certain degree – with the need for the type of playing that was important in Progressive rock, i.e. extremely accurate, accomplished, precise playing. It doesn't dispense with the type of playing essential to jazz, which is incredibly subjective – emotional, raw, feeling, that stuff. A lot of Progressive tricks can be reproduced now by non-musicians – the feeling can't.[37]

He does at least distance himself from Ambient, believing his music to inhabit a realm of complexity which demands attention. 'Ambient,' he says, 'is narrative-free.' Schütze is, however, an eager opponent of post-structuralist thought pertaining to music, believing in ideals, in the universal nature of musical qualities. He also contends that narrative, overarching concept forms of continuous musical narrative – in addition to an emphasis on craftsmanship – is returning in new guises, citing albums by Tricky and Portishead ('concept albums in all but name'). As with his own work, Schütze suggests that cinema is the dominant narrative form for the composers of these albums. 'Filmic narratives,' he continues, 'which are indelibly linked to romantic nineteenth-century classical programme music, which in turn is linked to Progressive rock.'[38]

POSTSCRIPT: TO BE OVER ... OR NOT TO BE OVER?

Paul Schütze declares that the mid-1990s is one of the most exciting periods of music for years. His ideals of strict anti-commercialism, of music as sovereign realm of communication, of artistry and craftsmanship, contain haunting echoes of the aspirations of Progressive musicians of yore. His music also suggests older affinities: it is multi-layered, complexly conceived and performed with searching intensity, devoted to exploration not only of vertical and horizontal possibilities but in the organization, the hierarchy of sound in a rock context. Schütze's music, even in its most forbidding, trenchant shades of darkness, is recognizably of rock provenance – just. Or rather it would not have been possible without rock, specifically Progressive.

Perhaps the only trace of Progressive still residing in rock culture is its bourgeois sense of ambition and artistry, skewed but sustained by the diversity of new styles and technologies available to musicians. The cultural terms are naturally different. The excision of the blues is still possible, but not in the context of 1970, as pop and blues forms have become so prevalent in the background noise of the modern world, thanks to MTV and dance culture.

There are other factors that ideally should shape our perception of Progressive, but rarely do so, simply because it is so marginalized from rock discourse. Take any number of modern-day events in popular music; U2's *Zoo TV* tour was a cyclopean *son-et-lumière* expression of monstrous vanity that outdid anything perpetrated even by Pink Floyd or ELP.

Yet the analogies with Progressive are never drawn. Test Department, whose staggering choreography of ritualism, industrial decay and heavy engineering to accompany their titanic barrages of percussion and sampling, continue to extend the ambition of their live shows; recent recordings, such as *Totality* (1996) display a symphonic sense of orchestration no longer concerned *only* with the arrangements of toneless noise but recognizable tonal components: notes, chords, scales, intervals as well.

Other Progressive provinces are being recolonized. Hipster mixmeister to the stars and dance guru, Howie B, declared his 1995 *Music for Babies* to be a 'concept' work about the birth of his daughter Chilli. Containing such titles as 'Allergy' (about a milk allergy) and 'Here Comes the Tooth' (about teething), it is a kind of housey *symphonia domestica* and of a programmatic feyness which might have proved too saccharine even for the likes of Jon Anderson.

Elsewhere, the rulebook has been completely torn up. In 1980s Japan, Progressive hit hard. While often imitative in the strict musical sense – after the fashion of many Japanese cultural assimilations from the West – there was also a commensurate imagistic hiccup in translation and, by way of compensation, indigenous originality in upending generic stereotypes. First, the imagery of Japanese 1980s Progressive rock borrowed heavily from that of its Western forebear, centring on graphically airbrushed fantasyscapes, but it also took the romantic/impressionist *raison d'être* of the graphics to new lengths, simply reusing images of sumptuous decadence from the likes of Burne-Jones and Delville for record sleeves (the albums of Gerard being a specific example).

But the Romanticism informing Japanese Progressive, while predictably expressed in music of an indigestibly rich symphonic stamp after the van of Yes and Genesis, saw double-take blurrings of other Progressive aesthetic stances. The wardrobes employed by bands such as Teru's Symphonia and Scheherazade, and by players such as guitarist Terutsugu Hirayama (of the two last-named bands) and keyboardist Toshio Egawa (Gerard, Scheherazade) flouted accepted notions of Western rock-heroic sexuality. The act of performing a cultural text presumably read as being essentially 'feminine' led to the application of caked cosmetics and the wearing of diaphanous flowing gowns and pre-Raphaelite hairstyles. The intrusion of the feminine into a masculine form was taken to extremes by the trio Ars Nova, nothing less than an all-female analogue of that ultimate embodiment of Progressive expertise and swaggering masculine stamina, ELP.

One of the recurrent themes most frequently encountered in writing this book is the absence of the comfortable, middle-class attitudinalizing that was attached to Progressive and its proponents in the 1970s. Progressive musicians, it seems, have never been any more or less refined than any other rock players.

The music journalist Mike Barnes recounted an evening spent with mid-1980s neo-Progressive band Twelfth Night:

> I was listening to Genesis and smoking grass with one of the guys. And then the rest of the band march in and start singing 'Drugs and Genesis, drugs and Genesis, go together like cunts and penises ...' to the tune of 'Love and Marriage'. That's when I knew Progressive rockers could live at the bottom of the pile too.[39]

Progressive rock's claims to elevation and exclusivity cannot be taken too seriously; its origins were the same as those of all popular music. Just because it sought to escape them, it cannot hope to be judged by standards different from those by which we judge the rest of popular music. Critics assume that because it pretended to inhabit higher ground, it should always be judged on those terms – thereby, even in abusing Progressive, falling into the trap of believing its pretence. Progressive is not art music, and cannot be judged, good or bad, as such.

In spite of analyses, made in the 1970s, whose pomposity and puerility outranked their penetration, Progressive rock was *not* the new classical music. In 1971 Francis Monkman told *Sounds*: 'In terms of quality, music that is being written now is always more important just because it is being written now.'[40] Oh well, Ludwig, that's told you. But Ian Anderson, a year before, had suggested that rock was not even yet a craft, let alone an art.[41]

Robert Wyatt adds: 'I remember a classical reviewer doing a review of a rock concert which sounded just like a Yes fan reviewing a concert by Mud. In fact it was a classical reviewer reviewing a concert by Yes.'[42]

Can we properly clarify the relationship between Progressive and art music? Allan Moore's prognosis on the subject foregrounds the difficult concepts of 'extensionality' and 'intensionality'. Briefly, 'intensional' music is harmonically and structurally rigid, but affords expressive interpretation within its structure. 'Extensional' music, conversely, constructs music from 'basic musical atoms' with rigorous formal discipline and requires strict fidelity to the composer's instructions. The traditional musicological approach equates popular music forms with the iniflectional liberties of 'intensional' music and classical performance practice with sobriety and the bourgeois obsession with textual fidelity.

This, as Moore points out, is highly debatable; the interpretative liberties taken in classical music by a Bernstein or a Brendel seem fatally to undermine the theory. Critical approaches to Progressive have accused it of aspiration to a similar 'extensional' severity and rigour to classical music, thereby negating its legitimacy as rock music through a rejection of 'spontaneity' and 'feel' in favour of cold intellectualism.[43] Not only does this completely ignore the ability of musicians to apply interpretation to the most compositionally strict music, it imagines that rock players have the technical mastery to adhere to 'extensional' disciplines in the first place. Few can. Tamm is one of the few commentators on Progressive even to raise the question of the tussle between art music's expressive powers and the exigencies of the printed score.[44] But Moore (after Tagg) then states that this discrediting of the intensional/extensional debate dissolves any recognizable barriers between musics.[45]

I would only partly agree; this overlooks the role played by the relationship between rock music and rock consumers, the meanings derived by listeners from Progressive (or any) rock through a multitude of intervening signs and images (record sleeves etc.) which they reciprocally read into the notes and which shapes their listening habits and their responses to music. This is a quintessentially rock-pop culture, which creates its own dynamic between fans, players and the industry that exerts a small but significant influence on the direction of musical composition. During Dick Hebdige's pioneering studies of youth subculture in the 1970s, both the original texts and those of Hebdige's slavish apostles in the 'rock comics' (to use Allan Jones's memorable phrase),[46] dazzled by the surfaces of Punk's creation of its own individual identities for its fans, overlooked those of Progressive. In rock, where musical discourse and image and text are so intertwined, it is hard to support all of Moore's (and Tagg's) theses that attempts to demarcate musics cannot *strictly* be made.[47] Musicologically yes; but when the influence of audience habits, mediated through the industry, has inevitably to shape compositional technique, one cannot write the social and economic conditions of the music's production entirely out of the equation.

Moore also mentions the importance of 'learned competence' in the assimilation and appreciation of any musical style.[48] Can one learn competence in any rock style without the mediation of visual and other sensory data?

The question of surfaces brings us neatly to one final vexed question in the Progressive debate: its (previously unexplored) relationship to postmodernity.

Rick Wakeman once said of his introduction to Yes:'I thought, "they can't arrange everything." But you can. And they did.'[49] None the less, the honest Wakeman honourably denies that Yes ever set out to be clever;'It often stems from how it feels. Oftener than not, we'll record it down, and then somebody will go, "What bloody time-signature is that?".'[50] The extensional/intensional dualism writ large – moptop *vs.* maestro. But to Bill Bruford goes the last, most telling word: 'If Yes had designed a building, it would have been the most extraordinary kind of horrific Gothic/Edwardian/Modern/Medieval/pseudo-pastiche. But we weren't. We were designing music.'[51]

This elides neatly with Charles Jencks's sketch of postmodern architecture, with its inherent 'double-coding' (employing techniques and conventions of modernist architecture combined with archaic or regional or local adjuncts).

On the one hand, the music of most Progressive bands (e.g. of Yes), can be described first and foremost in terms of a *modernist* project. That is, dignifying continual progress, rationality, discipline; artistically, it deals in universals, in truth, justice and beauty. The hostility its cognoscenti showed towards forms such as Punk and Disco, whose essentially metropolitan aspect seemed to embody the dehumanizing, disposable nature of late capitalism is a case in point. In the face of these phenomena, Progressive pitched 1960s revolutionary romanticism. But too many critics have taken this latter stance at face value – even those who dutifully followed Barthes' lead and declared authorial volitions as irrelevant. There is little doubt that the bourgeois modernist aspect of the music was paramount in the minds of its creators; the desire to create 'good' music which would 'last' and 'rise above' the vagaries of fashion is too recurrent a theme in Progressive discourse to deny that. But Progressive is none the less a symptom of postmodernity, the same as Punk, Disco, Techno, whatever. And despite its proponents' best intentions, just how much of a coherent musical centre did much Progressive have? By its own admission, it was mongrel, half-breed, then and now – indeed its cross-border raiding helps define it perhaps better than anything.

Listen to 'Albion Fair' by The Enid (1979) – a 'silly piece' in composer Godfrey's words,[52] an eccentric hymn to England and English inspiration switching from Gershwinian to Rachmaninovian piano writing within a few bars. Steve Howe's electric flamenco guitar solo on 'Sound Chaser' from Yes's *Relayer* (1974) is another sliding floor.

Most of Progressive, it's true, seeks a serious, *earnest* musical performance and practice free of disruption, a homogeneity of expression within a particular Western mindset of musical continuity. Musical jokes are usually fenced off (like ELP's music-hall pastiches) from the 'real' music. Listeners, for example, could never imagine that a fairground organ could suddenly start playing 'Popeye the Sailor Man' in the middle of Yes's *Tales from Topographic Oceans* (more's the pity – side two needs something to liven it up) or that a chorus of trainee Alpine yodellers will be drafted in to attack Phil Collins with ocarinas during Genesis's 'Supper's Ready'. Mike Oldfield, for all the insipidity of his composition, was at least brave enough to spice his homebrews with some banjo or bodhran now and again – although once again it was all in the service of preserving, rather than deconstructing, some higher musical 'whole'.

For Fripp, rock was intelligent and exciting music because of its formal malleability. Bernard Benoliel emphasized the special emotional syntax lent by rock playing in musical developmental techniques in his analysis of Mike Oldfield. Allan Moore sees in rock the potential for endless textural play.

All these are valid points. For me, additionally, the methodical organization of sound which characterized Progressive can also lead to immense and indelible musical *jouissance*, due to the structural ambition that mastery of the recording studio can bestow upon recording artists. The intervallic developments and crashing climaxes of Genesis's 'Firth of Fifth', for example, use a harmonic language not that much more advanced than most mainstream pop music. Yet for me it is as goose-pimplingly thrilling as any Gladys Knight or Jimi Hendrix performance, for the simple reason that the application of new structural techniques to the placing and deployment of emotional triggers in the music – diminished seventh chords, cycles of fifths, etc. – in a quasi-classical format, and the organization of the orchestral-style soundstage upon which these are subjected to timbral manipulation to enhance emotional effect, is a result of studio exactitude and perseverance as well as the adrenalizing jolt of creative ecstasy. Studio mastery did not begin and end with Progressive – but its centrality to the way Progressive used its own quirky language is unique in rock and pop history.

Chris Cutler's attitude to the compositional attitude is challenging and interesting; about plunderphonics and sampling, about the melange of musical styles, he denied a postmodern intention, and told Andrew Jones: 'The fact that this music brings together elements from different musical genres is based on some overriding sense of music as a whole.'[53] He could equally have been describing Progressive's heyday.

Yes's own music, like that of Pink Floyd, Henry Cow, Mike Oldfield, This Heat and others, warp-drove the development of studio technology in the 1970s. The mind-boggling multi-layering and editing obsession that created the likes of *Close to the Edge*, *Ummagumma*, *Unrest*, *Tubular Bells* and *This Heat* were responsible for enormous advances in musical reproduction. The comparative failure of Yes to match their live 'Gates of Delirium' to the studio version arises from the sheer specialization of the piece's soundworld in the studio. In an era when differentiation, when individuality was a badge of honour, the studio came in handy. It led to accusations of detachment, of frigid calculation; accusations not levelled at Pierre Boulez, some of whose compositions (such as *Rèpons*) are wedded to the massive mainframe computers they were composed on and can be played outside their home environment but rarely.

But Yes, Pink Floyd *et al.*, actually bucked, rather than upheld a traditional rockist emphasis on spontaneity and immediacy by this act of supreme aesthetic detachment. Again such qualities could not be identified by contemporary media; by the time the media could suss this one out, detachment was a dirty word. By the time it wasn't, in the 1980s, so much mud had stuck to Progressive it didn't seem worth cutting through it all. Were not ZTT, the brainchild of eminent anti-Progressive theoretician Paul Morley, responsible for similarly auteurist experiments in the 1980s?

Cutler believes that the most fruitful areas for musical development lie in the recording studio, in the development of 'the medium in which the music is played'.[54] Cutler points out that without studio facilities, rock, and particularly musically ambitious rock, would not exist. 'Even groups who don't use these facilities nevertheless possess an aesthetic, a judgement about what kind of sounds are interesting, that comes from this medium ... without cutting tapes, without editing you would never have ... perfection.' Cutler cites the music of Romanian electro-acoustician Iancu Dumitrescu as an example:

You can't tell what it is that's making that sound. Which comes not from manipulation ... basically it's played on real instruments by real people, but the aesthetic comes from electronics, concrete sound. These things enter the imagination ... the decision-making process, which is ultimately what the aesthetic process is, and there's no going back. Studio and electricity are the *sine qua non* of this stuff ... you don't need fifty violins to make the violin line audible. You [just] need the volume.'[55]

For Cutler, studio manipulation doesn't diminish the vitality of performance, it simply frees it from temporal considerations; 'the actuality of performance is not lost, but is freed from time; it can be taken apart'.[56]

To this end, to fill out the sonic distinctiveness of 'The Gates of Delirium', keyboardist Patrick Moraz beat up bedsteads and lumps of old iron, and processed them through the studio, to achieve emotional effects in the battle sequence. 'By the time he was doing his solo album [*The Story of i*], in 1976,' recalls Paul Schütze, 'Moraz was producing, with the help of all these keyboards you'd never heard of and the studio, sounds that not even really advanced electro-acoustic composers had come up with.'[57]

Robert Wyatt records his view of Hendrix's solution to the problem:

I noticed that Hendrix was playing the studio and not the guitar. For example, there was a lot of worry at the time as to whether you could reproduce what you did on record on stage because outside pop music rock records were adverts for stage performances rather than the other way round. If you couldn't play it, it was wrong to record it. But Hendrix was using things like backwards tapes, changing speeds – a lot of speed changes – reverb, all kinds of stuff. Loud and quiet things in microphones give quite different textures, which are changed again when you diminish or increase the volume.

Interestingly, Wyatt adds: 'He had a very disarming response to people who told him he couldn't play it live. He said: "Once you've heard it, you can play it." '[58]

Hugh Hopper has argued: 'A lot of my early stuff was in fact sampling. Technology has caught up – a lot of stuff can now be done live.'[59] A call for a reappraisal of attitudes to Progressive, surely? We can only hope.

Progressive musicians did not have that technology at their disposal. What they did was use available kit to build an aesthetic of their own, essentially hybridizing many other aesthetics. Their aim was often canonical, in so far as they used Western bourgeois sacred/symphonic models, but avant-garde and jazz techniques were also popular. Progressive shouldn't be condemned for its use of canonical material when the tricks it played with that canonical material were so interesting and produced music which – while it might have tried to imagine otherwise – represented high-class pop music for the heart while also exciting the mind.

It is simply unfair merely to aim the epithet of 'bourgeoisification of rock' at it. I have heard comparisons made between Progressive and the civilizing obsessions of Victorian artists; did it not take the insights and visions of a Romantic vanguard and turn them into middle-class artefacts, much as Tennyson had rendered Swinburne's and Blake's wildfire romanticism (and Landseer and Alma-Tadema had emasculated Romantic painting) for the drawing-room consumption of prosperous Victorians?

Not at all. The aforementioned epigoni did little or nothing to advance the form or content of their medium; this is a charge that cannot be laid against Progressive, even by the most ferocious opponent.

But didn't Progressive inculcate absurdly bourgeois discourse into rock music? Chord progressions of cheesy romanticism that were less Liszt than Liberace?

Again, this presupposes the canonical, ever-repeated nature of the rockist ethic in pop music. Even the likes of Ian Penman and Paul Morley, the NME's Gog and Magog of anti-Progressive criticism, returned tediously to the themes of passivity and sentiment. But in the pop universe, can anything be said to take subversive primacy over any other form?

Punk, which helped sanctify the ethos of adolescent, hormone-driven 'feeling' in rock discourse, was, in Paul Schütze's words,

A very important social movement within Britain. But taken without the social dimension (which did not travel well except as a look) it was, musically, a huge non-event. Most of the important musical developments subsequent to Punk would have happened regardless and lay roots in far older traditions. Techno and Electronica, for example, have their roots in Disco and Krautrock. Chances are they were delayed by Punk. Certainly any music which had a vocabulary encompassing anything more than dumb rage was regarded with a quite fascistic hostility for some time after this most non-musical of 'revolutions'. Bands like This Heat and the Art Bears managed to emerge in this period, I imagine, only by existing in some fertile parallel universe. As for the rest, hardly a trace has been transmitted or developed beyond mere nostalgia.[60]

Is the music all that matters to Progressive and its descendants? When Punk – whose identity has now almost been defined as much by what it reviled (Progressive) as by its own discourse – did what it had to do and said what it had to say, something was left out. Progressive rockers were only *a part* of the rock hierarchy that Punk (at least in the UK) called to account. Rod Stewart, Elton John, the Who and Led Zeppelin played bigger venues and lived the rock lifestyle to the hilt more emphatically than most Progressive artists. Which surely means that Punk's beef, and the beef of all rock critiques since, is with the music of Progressive. Musical factors *were* the ultimate definition of Progressive's identity.

Only when musical factors are placed first and foremost can Progressive's re-evaluation in critical discourse and in the minds of rock consumers properly begin, its relative values be assessed and its intrinsic values recognized.

REFERENCES

INTRODUCTION

1 Logan, N. and Woffinden, B., *The New Musical Express Encyclopedia of Rock*, Salamander, London, 1982, p. 207
2 Quoted in Moore, Allan F., *Rock: The Primary Text*, OUP, Milton Keynes, 1993, p. 16
3 Ibid., pp. 12-16 passim
4 Quoted in Ibid., p. 16
5 Ibid., pp. 12-16 passim

CHAPTER 1

1 *Guardian*, 2 November 1991
2 Frith, S. and Horne, H., *Art into Pop*, Methuen, London, 1987, p. 81
3 Green, J., *Days in the Life: Voices from the English Underground 1961–1971*, Heinemann, London, 1988, p. 62
4 Quoted in Palmer, T., *All You Need Is Love*, Futura, London, 1976, p. 230
5 McInnes, C., *Absolute Beginners*, McGibbon & Kee, London, 1959, p. 49

6 Frith and Horne, op. cit., p. 75
7 Quoted in Frith and Horne, p. 76
8 Green, op. cit., p. 7
9 Quoted in ibid. p. 10
10 Interview with Robert Wyatt
11 King, M., *Wrong Movements*, SAF, London, 1995 (no page nos)
12 Ibid.
13 Ibid.
14 Interview with Robert Wyatt
15 King, op. cit.
16 Ibid.
17 Quoted in Frith and Horne, op. cit., p. 94
18 Quoted in Green, op. cit., p. 47
19 Schaffner N., *A Saucerful of Secrets: The Pink Floyd Odyssey*, Sidgwick & Jackson, London, 1991, p. 1
20. Quoted in Green, op. cit., p. 105
21 Ibid., p. 104
22 Quoted Schaffner, op. cit., p. 15
23 Quoted in King, op. cit.
24 Green, op. cit., p. 275
25 Schaffner, op. cit., p. 49
26 Quoted in King, op. cit.

27 Interview with Robert Wyatt
28 Quoted in Green, op. cit., p. 105
29 Unpublished interview with Joe
    Boyd by Barry Miles, 1976,
    reproduced in Schaffner, op. cit.,
    p. 73
30 Quoted in Green, op. cit., p. 138
31 Alexander Scriabin (1872–1915),
    Russian composer, whose
    mystical and synaesthetic obses-
    sions with music and light led
    him to compose a part for a
    'colour organ', diffusing multi-
    hued lights during his orchestral
    work 'Prometheus: Poem of Fire'
    (1910). Scriabin's hyper-sensual,
    proto-expressionist style and
    preoccupations with Eastern
    mysticism brought him a belated
    vogue in the late 1960s and early
    1970s.
32 Interview with John Peel
33 Frith and Horne, op. cit., p. 90
34 Schaffner, op. cit., p. 57
35 Quoted in ibid., p. 80
36 Quoted in Zigzag magazine, July,
    1973; reproduced in Schaffner,
    op. cit., p. 80
37 Ibid., p. 64
38 Ibid.
39 Ibid.
40 Ibid.
41 Interview with Chris Cutler
42 Ibid.
43 Moore, op. cit., p. 99
44 Ibid., p.78
45 Quoted in Schaffner, op. cit., p. 84
46 Quoted in Green, op. cit., p. 222
47 Quoted in ibid., p. 88
48 Quoted in ibid., p. 206
49 Quoted in ibid., p. 259
50 Quoted in ibid., p. 175
51 Quoted in ibid., p. 245
52 Quoted in ibid., p. 259

CHAPTER 2
1   Moore, op. cit., p. 84
2   Rolling Stone, 4 February 1971
3   Quoted in Frith, S., Sound Effects:
    Youth, Leisure, and the Politics of
    Rock'n'Roll, Constable, London,
    1983, p. 69
4   Nuttall, J., Bomb Culture, Paladin,
    London 1972, p. 190
5   Quoted in Goodwin, J., (ed),
    Music, Mysticism & Magic, Arkana,
    London, pp. 286–7
6   Interview with Bill Bruford
7   Interview with Pete Sinfield
8   Interview with Bill Bruford
9   Ibid.
10 Ibid.
11 Interview with Anthony Phillips
12 Interview with Bill Bruford
13 Interview with Pete Sinfield
14 Ibid.
15 Logan and Woffinden, op. cit.,
    p. 128
16 Tamm, E., Robert Fripp: From
    King Crimson to Guitar Craft,
    Faber & Faber, London, 1991,
    p. 102
17 Ibid., p. 46
18 Q Magazine, July, 1992
19 Quoted in Chambers, op. cit.,
    p. 105
20 Quoted in Green, op. cit., p. 318
21 Chambers, I., Urban Rhythms –
    Pop Music and Popular Culture,
    Macmillan, London, 1985, p. 107
22 Quoted in Schaffner, op. cit.,
    p. 75
23 Gallo, A., Genesis: I Know What I
    Like, DIY Press, Los Angeles,
    1980, p. 14
24 Chambers, op. cit., p. 104
25 Frith and Horne, op. cit.
26 Moore, op. cit., p. 96
27 Quoted in ibid., p. 96

28 Interview with Chris Cutler
29 Interview with Glen Sweeney
3() Schaffner, op. cit., p. 124
31 Ibid., p. 128
32 McDonald, B. (ed.), *Pink Floyd: Through the Eyes of ...*, pp. 262-3
33 Dallas, K., *Bricks in the Wall*, Baton Books, London, 1987
34 *New Musical Express*, 11 January 1975
35 Ibid.
36 McDonald, op. cit., p. 271
37 Ibid., p. 263
38 Ibid., p. 273
39 *Melody Maker*, 19 May 1973
40 Ibid.
41 Quoted in Chambers, op. cit., p. 117
42 Schaffner, op. cit., p. 83
43 Green, op. cit., p. 61

CHAPTER 3

1 Eisen, Jonathan, *The Age of Rock*, Viking, New York, 1969
2 Scaffner, op. cit., p. 79
3 Gallo, op. cit., p. 20
4 Interview with John Peel
5 Wakeman, R., *Say Yes! An Auto-biography*, Hodder & Stoughton, London, 1994, pp. 95–6
6 Interview with Bill Bruford
7 Interview with Glenn Sweeney
8 Interview with Tom Newman
9 Green, op. cit., p. 277
10 Gallo, op. cit., p. 32
11 Hedges, D., *Yes: The Authorised Biography*, Sidgwick & Jackson, London, 1981, p. 35
12 Ibid., pp. 35–6
13 Interview with Tom Newman
14 Interview with John Peel
15 Quoted in Frith, *Sound Effects:* p. 78

16 Interview with John Peel
17 Interview with Dave Stewart
18 LP Sleevenote, *Egg* (Egg), Deram Nova, Decca Records 1970
19 Interview with Roger Dean
20 Quoted in Joynson, V., *The Tapestry of Delights: The Comprehensive Guide to British Music of the Beat, R'n'B, Psychedelic and Progressive Eras 1963–1976*, Borderline, London, 1995
21 Mully, M., *Rolling Stone*, New York, 1 October 1970
22 *Melody Maker*, 9 May 1970
23 Interview with John Peel
24 Interview with Anthony Phillips
25 Quoted in Palmer, op. cit., p. 260
26 Lubin, D., *Rolling Stone*, 2 December 1970
27 Interview with John Peel
28 Cromelin, R., *Rolling Stone*, 18 June 1972
29 *Melody Maker*, 4 July 1970
30 Quoted in *Facelift* magazine No. 1, pp. 2 / 3
31 Ibid.
32 Quoted in McDonald, B., op. cit.
33 Ibid.
34 Ibid.
35 *Facelift* magazine No. 2, p. 4
36 Interview with Bill Bruford
37 Green, op. cit., p. 23
38 Interview with John Peel
39 Interview with Robert Wyatt
40 Interview with John Peel
41 Frith., op. cit., p. 206
42 Ibid., p. 207
43 Interview with Roger Dean
44 Ibid.
45 Interview with John Peel
46 Interview with Roger Dean
47 Ibid.

48 Ibid
49 Interview with John Peel
50 *Melody Maker*, 10 November 1973
51 *Zigzag* magazine, April 1975
52 Sleevenote *Acquiring the Taste*, Vertigo, 1971
53 *Proclamation* magazine No. 3, p. 42
54 Fallowell, D., *Records and Recording* magazine, March 1973
55 Fallowell, D., *Records and Recording* magazine, January 1975
56 Moore, op. cit., p. 80
57 Interview with Bill Bruford
58 Ibid.
59 Hedges, op. cit., p. 60
60 Morse, T., *Yesstories: Yes in Their Own Words*, St Martin's Press, New York, 1996, p. 140
61 Interview with Bill Bruford
62 Quoted in Morse, op. cit., p. 139
63 Ibid., p. 12
64 Cromelin, R., *Rolling Stone* magazine, 9 November 1972
65 Interview with Bill Bruford
66 Joynson, op. cit., p. 488
67 Cutler, C., *File Under Popular*, ReR Megacorp, London, 1991, p. 122
68 Quoted in Green, op. cit., p. 341
69 Quoted in Hedges, op. cit., p. 63

CHAPTER 4
1 Interview with John Peel
2 Ibid.
3 Ibid.
4 *Rolling Stone*, 14 May 1972
5 *Melody Maker*, 17 October 1970
6 Quoted in Joynson, op., cit., p. 528
7 Quoted in Green, op. cit., p. 328
8 *Melody Maker*, 5 September 1970

9 Ibid.
10 Quoted in Green, op. cit., p. 309
11 Ibid, p. 313
12 Interview with John Peel
13 Quoted in Green, op. cit.. p. 129
14 Quoted in McDonald, op. cit., p. 9
15 Interview with Tom Newman
16 Interview with Robert Wyatt
17 Quoted in King, op. cit.
18 Interview with Robert Wyatt
19 Wright, P., *Guardian*, 11 November 1995
20 Interview with Robert Wyatt
21 Interview with John Peel
22 Interview with Robert Wyatt
23 *Facelift* magazine No. 5
24 *Facelift* magazine No. 7, p. 8
25 Interview with Dave Stewart
26 Ibid.
27 Ibid.
28 Ibid.
29 *Melody Maker*, 26 September 1970
30 Quoted in Green, op. cit., p. 403
31 Interview with John Peel
32 Moraghan, S., *Mike Oldfield: The Man and His Music*, Britannia Press, London, 1994, p. 19
33 Interview with Alfreda
34 *Wire* No. 134, February 1995
35 Palmer, op. cit., p. 276
36 Interview with Pete Sinfield
37 Ibid.
38 Interview with Tony Herrington
39 Interview with Robert Wyatt
40 Interview with John Peel
41 Interview with Robert Wyatt
42 Interview with Pete Sinfield
43 Interview with Bill Bruford
44 *Wire*, February 1995
45 Interview with Robert Wyatt
46 Interview with Chris Cutler

47 Quoted in Wright, op. cit.
48 Interview with Robert Wyatt
49 *Wire*, March 1996.
50 *New Musical Express*, 23 February, 1974
51 Lambert, C., *Music Ho!*, Dent, London, 1966
52 *Sounds*, 29 January, 1972
53 Interview with Tom Newman
54 Quoted in Moraghan, op. cit., p. 24
55 Ibid.
56 Palmer, op. cit., p. 271
57 Quoted in Moraghan, op. cit., p. 77
58 Interview with Robert Wyatt

CHAPTER 5
1 Moore, op. cit., p. 86
2 Schaffner, op. cit., p. 171
3 Quoted in McDonald, op. cit., p. 278
4 Quoted in Schaffner, op. cit., p. 175
5 Ibid., p. 164
6 McDonald, op. cit., p. 245
7 Interview with Bill Bruford
8 Hedges, op. cit., p. 86
9 Holden, S., *Rolling Stone*, 30 August 1973
10 Quoted in Morse, op. cit., p. 124
11 Ibid., p. 45
12 Ibid., p. 115
13 Ibid., p. 45
14 Holden, S., *Rolling Stone*, 30 August 1973
15 Josephson, N., 'Progressive Rock', *Musical Quarterly*, London, April 1992
16 *Proclamation* magazine, No. 3, p. 42
17 Hedges, op. cit., p. 90
18 Holden, S., *Rolling Stone*, 30 August 1973
19 Interview with Pete Sinfield

20 Sleevenotes, *Brain Salad Surgery*, CD remaster, Victory Records, 1996 – the author thanks Pete Sinfield for a preview of this useful source.
21. Ibid.
22. *Melody Maker*, 29 August 1970
23 *New Musical Express*, 15 October 1977
24 Interview with Pete Sinfield
25. Ibid.
26 *Melody Maker*, 17 July 1971
27 *Brain Salad Surgery* sleevenotes
28. Interview with Anthony Phillips
29 I am grateful to Allan F. Moore for this observation
30 Josephson, op. cit., p. 85
31 Quoted in Gallo, op. cit., p. 24
32 Fallowell, D., *Records and Recording* magazine, December 1973
33 Quoted in Palmer, op. cit., p. 263
34 Josephson, op. cit., p. 85.
35 Quoted in Gallo, op. cit., p. 40
36 Quoted in Palmer, op. cit., p. 263
37 Quoted in Bowler, D. and Dray B., *Genesis: A Biography*, Sidgwick & Jackson, London, 1992, p. 88
38 Fripp, R., sleevenotes, *The Great Deceiver* CD, Discipline Global Mobile Records 1992, p. 62
39 Quoted in Hedges, op. cit., p. 69
40 Quoted in Gallo, op. cit., p. 148
41 Fripp, op. cit., p. 2
42 Ibid., p. 33
43 I am grateful to Allan Moore for this insight
44 Interview with Bill Bruford

CHAPTER 6
1 Frith, op. cit., p. 83
2 *New Musical Express*, 30 September 1975
3 Logan N. and Woffinden, B., op.

cit., p. 182

4 Josephson, op. cit., pp. 86–9

5 Morse, op. cit., p. 37.

6 Interview with Paul Schütze

7 Burchill, J. and Parsons, T., *The Boy Looked at Johnny*, Pluto, London, 1978, p. 32

8 Quoted in Hedges, op. cit., p. 193

9 *Melody Maker*, 17 July 1971

10 *Melody Maker*, 10 November 1973

11 *Rolling Stone*, 21 December 1972

12 Schaffner, op. cit., p. 212

13 Quoted in Hedges, op. cit., p. 108

14 Quoted in McDonald, op. cit. pp. 196–7

15 *New Musical Express*, 11 January 1975

16 Quoted in Dallas, op. cit.

17 Gifford, C., *The Script: Marillion, An Illustrated Biography*, Omnibus Press, London, p. 59. The drummer in question is Ian Mosley of Marillion, ex-Curved Air, Trace and The Steve Hackett Band

18 Interview with Tom Newman

19 Comment from Mike Barnes

20 Interview with Mike Stobbie

21 Interview with Roger Dean

22 Laing, D., *One Chord Wonders*, OUP, Milton Keynes, 1985, p. 3

23 Frith, op. cit., p. 147

24 Palmer, op. cit., p. 287

25 Quoted in Schaffner, op. cit., p. 182

26 Quoted in McDonald, op. cit., p. 91

27 Interview with Bill Bruford

28 Ibid.

29 Quoted in Gallo, op. cit., p. 149

30 Ibid., p. 161

31 Interview with Bill Bruford

32 *New Musical Express*, 5 February 1977

33 *New Musical Express*, 15 October 1977

34 *New Musical Express*, 28 April 1979

35 Moore, op. cit., p. 93

36 Ibid., p. 93

37 Moore, op. cit., pp. 93–4

38 *New Musical Express*, 20 May 1978

39 *Melody Maker*, 9 July 1977

40 *New Musical Express*, 9 July 1977

41 *New Musical Express*, 4 November 1978

42 Quoted in Hedges, op. cit., p. 119

43 Quoted ibid.

44 *Melody Maker*, 12 March 1977

45 Interview with Pete Sinfield

46 Ibid.

47 Ibid.

48 *New Musical Express*, 25 November 1978

49 Interview with Pete Sinfield

50 Quoted in Bowler, D. and Dray, B., op. cit., p. 132

51 *Wire*, December 1995

52 Interview with Bill Bruford

53 Interview with Dave Stewart

54 I am grateful to Allan Moore for pointing this out.

55 Interview with Dave Stewart

56 Quoted in Wright, op. cit.

57 Ibid.

58 Ibid.

59 Ibid.

60 *Audion* magazine, February 1995

61 Quoted in Wright, op. cit.

62 Ibid.

63 Ibid.

64 Interview with John Peel

65 Sniffin' Glue magazine

66 Gallo, op. cit., p. 156

67 Quoted in Bright, S., *Peter Gabriel, An Authorised Biography*, Sidgwick & Jackson, London, 1988, p. 90

68 Ibid., p. 89
69 *New Musical Express*, 10 June 1978
70 Interview with John Peel
71 Interview with Bill Bruford
72 Quoted in Tamm, op. cit., p. 29
73 *New Musical Express*, 11 November 1978
74 *Brain Salad Surgery* sleevenotes
75 Ibid.
76 Interview with Tom Newman
77 Quoted in Schaffner, op. cit., p. 196
78 *Proclamation* magazine No. 4, p. 45
79 Interview with Dave Stewart

CHAPTER 7

1   *Melody Maker*, 14 April 1979
2   *Melody Maker*, 4 August 1979
3   Interview with Pete Sinfield
4   Quoted in Green, J., (ed.), *The Book of Rock Quotes*, Omnibus, London, 1977, p. 100
5   *New Musical Express*, 7 May 1977
6   Jones, A., *Plunderphonics, Pataphysics and Pop Mechanics*, SAF, London, p. 22
7   Quoted in ibid.
8   Interview with Robert Godfrey
9   Ibid.
10 Ibid.
11 Ibid.
12 Ibid.
13 Ibid.
14 *New Musical Express*, 11 September 1976
15 Interview with Robert Godfrey
16 Ibid.
17 *Progressive Forum* magazine No. 2.
18 Comment from Mike Barnes
19 Bowler, D. and Dray, B., op. cit. p. 240
20 Interview with Dave Stewart
21 Interview with Bill Bruford
22 Quoted in *Melody Maker*, 30 June 1979
23 *New Musical Express*, 1 December 1979
24 *Melody Maker*, 1 December 1979
25 Dallas, K., op. cit.
26 Ibid.
27 *New Musical Express*, 19 March 1983
28 *Melody Maker*, 28 March 1980
29 Hedges, op. cit., p. 13
30 Ibid., p. 136
31 Gill J., *Sounds*, 26 August 1980
32 Quoted in Hedges, op. cit., p. 138
33 Ibid. p. 137
34 Frith, op. cit., p. 151
35 Interview with Tom Newman
36 Comment from Mick Fish
37 Interview with Dave Stewart
38 Quoted in Morse, op. cit., p. 137
39 Interview with Dave Stewart
40 Interview with Robert Godfrey
41 Ibid.
42 Interview with Tom Newman
43 Frith, op. cit., p. 164
44 Interview with Chris Cutler

CHAPTER 8

1   Moore, op. cit., p. 150
2   Ibid., p. 151
3   Bright, op. cit., p. 136
4   Tamm, op. cit., p. 132
5   Interview with Bill Bruford
6   Sleevenote, *Frame by Frame: The Essential King Crimson*, Virgin Records, 1991
7   Interview with Bill Bruford
8   Tamm, op. cit.
9   Ibid., p. 144
10 Quoted in ibid., p. 136
11 Interview with Bill Bruford
12 Quoted in Bright, op. cit.
13 Ibid.
14 Quoted in Gifford, C., op. cit., p. 18

15 Ibid., p. 16
16 Interview with Mike Stobbie
17 Ibid.
18 Ibid.
19 Quoted in Clerk, C., *Marillion in Words and Pictures*, Bobcat, London, 1985, p. 5
20 Interview with Robert Godfrey
21 Ibid.
22 Morse, op. cit., p. 76
23 Ibid., p. 77
24 Interview with Paul Schütze
25 Ibid.
26 Ibid.
27 Ibid.

CHAPTER 9

Peter Hammill:
1 Quoted by Alan Terrill, *Record Collector* magazine, July 1986
2 CD sleevenote, *I Prophesy Disaster*, Virgin Records, 1993
3 Hammill P., CD sleevenote, *Maida Vale*, Band of Joy Records, 1994
4 *Wire*, September 1995

Robert Fripp:
1 Fripp R., CD sleevenote, *1999 – Soundscapes Live in Argentina*, Discipline Global Mobile Records, 1995
2 Ibid.
3 Tamm, op. cit.
4 Ibid., p. 115
5 *Melody Maker*, 5 October 1974
6 Tamm, op. cit., p. 134
7 Ibid.
8 Ibid., p. 153
9 Ibid., p. 89
10 Ibid., p. 162
11 Ibid., pp. 125–9
12 Ibid., p. 128

13 Ibid., p. 200
14 *Rolling Stone*, 6 December 1973
15 Ibid., p. 154
16 Ibid., p. 88

Anthony Phillips:
1 Gallo, op. cit., p. 27
2 Interview with Anthony Phillips
3 Ibid.
4 Ibid.
5 Ibid. Morris Pert is a percussion virtuoso and respected avant-garde composer. His playing can be heard on many Progressive albums of the mid- to late 1970s and early 1980s. He led his own band, Suntreader, from 1973 and collaborated extensively with Brand X.
6 Interview with Anthony Phillips
7 Ibid.
8 Ibid.
9 Ibid.
10 Ibid.
11 Phillips, A., LP sleevenote, *Private Parts and Pieces Vol 2 – Back to the Pavilion*, Passport Records, 1980
12 Interview with Anthony Phillips
13 Ibid.
14 Ibid.
15 Ibid.
16 Ibid.
17 Ibid.

Mike Oldfield:
1 Palmer, op. cit., pp. 271–5
2 Quoted in Moraghan, op. cit., p. 77
3 Ibid., p. 81
4 *Melody Maker*, 14 April 1979
5 *New Musical Express*, 25 November 1978
6 *Melody Maker*, 14 April 1979

7   Ibid.
8   *New Musical Express*, 5 August 1989
9   Moraghan, op. cit., p. 154
10 Ibid., p. 156

CHAPTER 10

1   Quoted in Lanza, J., *Elevator Music*, Quartet, London, 1994, p. 186
2   Quoted in McDonald, op. cit., p. 287
3   Lanza, op. cit., pp. 119–25
4   Quoted in ibid., p. 76
5   Ibid., p. 198
6   Ibid., pp. 211–12
7   Kidson, M., *Facelift* magazine No. 12, pp. 34–9
8   *Facelift* magazine No. 6
9   *Wire*, January 1996
10 *Facelift* magazine No. 7
11 *Wire*, September 1993
12 Kidson, op. cit.
13 Interview with Paul Schütze
14 Q magazine, November 1992
15 Ibid.
16 McDonald, op. cit., p. 235
17 Interview with Bill Bruford
18 Ibid.
19 Q magazine, July 1992
20 Quoted in McDonald, op. cit., p. 263
21 Quoted in ibid., p. 275
22 Quoted in ibid., p. 198
23 Interview with Paul Schütze
24 Ibid.
25 Interview with Robert Godfrey
26 Ibid.
27 Interview with Mike Stobbie
28 Interview with Moria Falls
29 *Wire*, March 1996
30 Ibid.
31 Ibid., p. 29
32 Interview with Paul Schütze
33 *Wire*, July 1996
34 Interview with Paul Schütze
35 Ibid.
36 Ibid.
37 Ibid.
38 Ibid.
39 Comment from Mike Barnes
40 *Sounds*, 13 November 1971
41 *Rolling Stone*, 10 December 1970
42 Interview with Robert Wyatt
43 Moore, pp. 12–16
44 Tamm, op. cit., p. 27
45 Moore, pp. 12–16
46 *Melody Maker*, 14 April 1979
47 Moore, pp. 12–16
48 Ibid.
49 Quoted in Hedges, op. cit., p. 61
50 Quoted in Morse, op. cit., p. 121
51 Quoted in Hedges, p. 61
52 Interview with Robert Godfrey
53 Quoted in Jones, op. cit., p. 25
54 Quoted in ibid.
55 Quoted in ibid.
56 Cutler, C., op. cit., p. 35
57 Interview with Paul Schütze
58 Interview with Robert Wyatt
59 *Facelift* magazine No. 5
60 Interview with Paul Schütze

BIBLIOGRAPHY

Amis, Martin: *Dead Babies*, Penguin, Harmondsworth, 1975

Berman, Marshall: *All That is Solid Melts into Air*, Verso, London, 1985

Bowler, Dave and Dray, Brian: *Genesis: A Biography*, Sidgwick and Jackson, London, 1992

Bright, Spencer: *Peter Gabriel: An Authorised Biography*, Sidgwick and Jackson, London, 1988

Burchill, Julie and Parsons, Tony: *The Boy Looked at Johnny*, Pluto Press, London, 1978

Chambers, Iain: *Urban Rhythms: Pop Music and Popular Culture*, Macmillan, London, 1985

Clerk, Carol: *Marillion: Their Story in Words and Pictures*, Bobcat Books, London, 1985

Cutler, Chris: *File Under Popular*, ReR Megacorp, London, 1991

Dallas, Karl: *Bricks in the Wall*, Baton Books, London, 1987

Dean, Roger: *Views*, Dragon's Dream/Big O, London, 1975

Dean, Roger and Howells, David: *Album Cover Album*, Paper Tiger, Limpsfield, 1982

Duxbury, J.R.: *Rockin' the Classics and Classicizin' the Rock*, Greenwood Press, New York, 1991

Fielder, Hugh: *The Book of Genesis*, Omnibus Press, London, 1984

Frame, Pete: *Rock Family Trees*, Omnibus Press, London, 1986
—   *Rock Family Trees 2*, Omnibus Press, London, 1992
Frith, Simon: *Sound Effects:Youth, Leisure and the Politics of Rock'n'Roll*, Constable,
           London, 1983
—   *Music for Pleasure*, Polity, London, 1987
Frith, Simon and Horne, Howard: *Art into Pop*, Methuen, London, 1987
Gallo, Armando: *Genesis: I Know What I Like*, DIY Press, Los Angeles, 1980
Gambaccini, Paul *et al.* (eds): *The Guinness Book of British Hit Albums*, Guinness
           Publishing, London, various dates
Gambaccini, Paul *et al.* (eds): *The Guinness Book of British Hit Singles*, Guinness
           Publishing, London, various dates
Gifford, Clive: *The Script:A Marillion Biography*, Omnibus Press, London, 1986
Gonzalez, Didier: *Histoire Mondiale du Rock Progressif: L'Ecole Anglais Tomes 1–3*,
           Bordeaux, France, 1991–95
Goodwin, J. (ed.): *Music, Mysticism & Magic*, Arkana, London, 1987
Green, Jonathon: *Days in the Life:Voices from the English Underground 1961–1971*,
           Heinemann, London, 1988
—   (ed.): *The Book of Rock Quotes*, Omnibus, London, 1977
Harvey, David: *The Condition of Postmodernity*, Blackwell, London, 1990
Hedges, Dan: *Yes:The Authorised Biography*, Sidgwick and Jackson, London, 1981
Jones, Andrew: *Plunderphonics, Pataphysics and Pop Mechanics*, SAFA, London, 1995
Joynson, Vernon: *The Tapestry of Delights: A Comprehensive Guide to British Music
           of the Beat, R'n'B, Psychedelic and Progressive Eras*, Borderline, London,
           1995
King, Mike: *Wrong Movements: A Robert Wyatt History*, SAF, London, 1994
Laing, Dave: *Three Chord Wonders*, OUP, Milton Keynes, 1985
Lanza, Joseph: *Elevator Music:A Surreal History of Muzak, Easy-Listening and other
           Moodsong*, Quartet, London, 1994
Larkin, Colin (ed.): *The Guinness Encyclopedia of Popular Music (Vols. 1–6)*,
           Guinness, London, 1992
Logan, Nick and Woffinden, Bob: *NME Encyclopedia of Rock*, Salamander,
           London, 1982
McDonald, Bruno (ed.): *Pink Floyd: Through the Eyes of ...*, Sidgwick and
           Jackson, London, 1995
McDonald, Ian: *Revolution in the Head; The Beatles' Records and the Sixties*,
           Random House, London, 1994
McInnes, Colin: *Absolute Beginners*, McGibbon and Lee, London, 1959
Moore, Allan F.: *Rock:The Primary Text*, OUP, Milton Keynes, 1992
Moraghan, Sean: *Mike Oldfield: the Man and His Music*, Britannia Press, London,
           1994
Morse, Tim: *Yesstories:Yes in Their Own Words*, St Martin's Press, New York, 1996
Murray, Charles Shaar: *Shots from the Hip*, Penguin, Harmondsworth, 1990
Nuttall, Jeff: *Bomb Culture*, Paladin, London, 1972
Palmer, Tony: *All You Need is Love*, Futura, London, 1976

Robinson, Dave: *The British Progressive Rock Directory Vol. 1*, Leicester, 1993
—   *The British Progressive Rock Directory Vol. 2*, Leicester, 1995
Savage, Jon: *England's Dreaming*, Faber and Faber, London, 1991
Schaffner, Nicholas: *A Saucerful of Secrets: The Pink Floyd Odyssey*, Sidgwick and Jackson, London, 1991
Shaw-Parker, David: *The Lemming Chronicles: A Critical Appreciation of the Music of Peter Hammill and Van der Graaf Generator*, Pandoras Box, London, 1993
Stewart, Dave: *Introducing the Dots*, Blandford Press, Poole, 1981
Tamm, Eric: *Brian Eno: His Music and the Vertical Colour of Sound*, Faber and Faber, London, 1989
—   *Robert Fripp: From King Crimson to Guitar Craft*, Faber and Faber, London, 1991
Theroux, Paul: *The Family Arsenal*, Penguin, Harmondsworth, 1977
Thorgerson, Storm: *Walk Away Renee*, Paper Tiger, Limpsfield, 1975
Wakeman, Rick: *Say Yes! An Autobiography*, Hodder and Stoughton, London, 1995
Walser, Robert: *Running with the Devil: Power, Gender and Madness in Heavy Metal Music*, Wesleyan University Press, Hanover (NH), 1993
Whiteley, Sheila: *The Space Between The Notes*, Routledge, London, 1992

DISCOGRAPHY (SELECTIVE)

Jon Anderson *Olias of Sunhillow* (1976) *Angels Embrace* (1995)

Art Bears *Hopes and Fears* (1978) *Winter Songs* (1979) *The World as It is Today* (1980)

David Bedford *Nurses' Song with Elephants* (1971) *Star's End* (1974) *The Rime of the Ancient Mariner* (1975) *Odyssey* (1976) *Instructions for Angels* (1977) *Song of the White Horse* (1984)

Beggar's Opera *Waters of Change* (1971)

Brand X *Unorthodox Behaviour* (1976) *Livestock* (1977) *Masques* (1978)

Bill Bruford *Feels Good to Me* (1978) *One of a Kind* (1978) *The Bruford Tapes* (*Live*) (1980) *Gradually Going Tornado* (1980)

Bruford/Moraz *Music for Piano and Drums* (1983) *Flags* (1984)

Kate Bush *The Dreaming* (1982)

Colosseum *Valentyne Suite* (1969) (CD with first album, *Those Who are About to Die Salute You*, 1969)

Comus *First Utterance* (1971) *To Keep from Crying* (1974)

Cressida *Cressida* (1970)

David Cross *Low Flying Aircraft* (1986) *Memo from Purgatory* (1987) *Testing to Destruction* (1993)

Curved Air *Air Conditioning* (1970) *2nd* (1971)

Eat Static *Abduction* (1993)

Egg *Egg* (1970) *The Polite Force* (1971) *Civil Surface* (1974) *Compilation: Egg Featuring Dave Stewart* (CD 1992)

Emerson Lake and Palmer *Emerson Lake and Palmer* (1970) *Tarkus* (1971) *Pictures at an Exhibition* (1972) *Trilogy* (1972) *Brain Salad Surgery* (1973) *Welcome*

Back My Friends to the Show That Never Ends (*Live*) (3LP 1974) *Works Vol. 1* (2LP 1977) *Works Vol. 2* (1977) *Love Beach* (1978) *Black Moon* (1993) *Return of the Manticore* (4CD 1993)

The Enid *In the Region of Summer Stars* (1976) *Aerie Faerie Nonsense* (1977) *Touch Me* (1979) *Six Pieces* (1979) *Something Wicked This Way Comes* (1983) *The Spell* (1984) *The Seed and the Sower* (1987) *Tripping the Light Fantastic* (1994)

Ropert Fripp *Exposure* (1978) *I Advanced Masked* (w. Andy Summers) (1983) *Bewitched* (1984) *The Bridge Between* (1994) *Soundscapes Live in Argentina* (1994) *A Blessing of Tears* (1995)

Fred Frith *Guitar Solos* (1974) *Gravity* (1980) *Live Improvizations* (w. Tim Hodgkinson) (1990) *Compilation: Step Across the Border* (1993)

Peter Gabriel *1* (1977) *2* (1978) *3* (1980) *4* (1982)

Genesis *From Genesis to Revelation* (1969) *Trespass* (1970) *Nursery Cryme* (1971) *Foxtrot* (1972) *Genesis Live* (1973) *Selling England by the Pound* (1973) *The Lamb Dies Down on Broadway* (2LP/CD 1974) *A Trick of the Tail* (1976) *Wind and Wuthering* (1976) *Seconds Out* (*Live*) (2LP/CD 1977) *And Then There were Three* (1978) *Duke* (1980) *Abacab* (1981) *Three Sides Live* (1976–81) (2LP/CD 1982)

Gentle Giant *Gentle Giant* (1970) *Acquiring the Taste* (1971) *Octopus* (1973) *The Power and the Glory* (1974) *Free Hand* (1975) *Playing the Fool* (*Live*) (1977)

Gilgamesh *Gilgamesh* (1975) *Another Fine Tune You've Got Me Into* (1978)

Godley and Creme *Consequences* (3LP/2CD 1977)

Gong *Continental Circus* (1971) *The Flying Teapot* (1973) *Angel's Egg* (1973) *You* (1974) *Shapeshifter* (1993)

Gong Maison *Gong Maison* (1990)

Gracious! *Gracious!* (1970)

Gryphon *Gryphon* (1973) *Midnight Mushrumps* (1974) *Rain Dance* (1975)

Steve Hackett *Voyage of the Acolyte* (1975) *Spectral Mornings* (1979) *Defector* (1980)

Peter Hammill *Chameleon in the Shadow of the Night* (1973) *The Silent Corner and the Empty Stage* (1974) *In Camera* (1975) *Nadir's Big Chance* (1976) *Over* (1977) *The Future Now* (1978) *Ph7* (1979) *A Black Box* (1980) *As Close as This* (1985) *In a Foreign Town* (1987) *Fireships* (1992)

Hatfield and the North *Hatfield and the North* (1974) *The Rotters' Club* (1975) *Afters* (1979)

Hawkwind *In Search of Space* (1971) *Warrior on the Edge of Time* (1975)

Henry Cow *Legend* (1973) *Unrest* (1974) *In Praise of Learning* (w. Slapp Happy) (1975) *Concerts* (1976) *Western Culture* (1978)

Steve Hillage *Fish Rising* (1975) *L* (1976) *Green* (1978) *Rainbow Dome Musick* (1979)

Tim Hodgkinson *Each in Our own Thoughts* (1990)

Hugh Hopper *1984* (1973) *Hoppertunity Box* (1977) *Meccano Pelorus* (1991)

Incredible String Band *The 5000*

Spirits or the Layers of the Onion
(1967) *The Hangman's Beautiful
Daughter* (1968) *Wee Tam, and the
Big Huge* (2LP/CD 1969)
IQ *Tales from the Lush Attic* (1983)
Isotope *Illusion* (1974)
It Bites *The Big Lad in the Windmill*
(1986) *Once Around the World*
(1988)
Jethro Tull *Stand Up* (1969) *Benefit*
(1970) *Aqualung* (1971) *Thick as a
Brick* (1972) *A Passion Play* (1973)
Minstrel in the Gallery (1975) *Songs
from the Wood* (1977) *Heavy Horses*
(1978) *Bursting Out* (Live)
(2LP/CD 1978) *Stormwatch* (1979)
Crest of a Knave (1986) *Compilation:
20 Years of Jethro Tull* (5LP 1988)
King Crimson *In the Court of the
Crimson King* (1969) *In the Wake of
Poseidon* (1970) *Lizard* (1970)
Islands (1971) *Larks' Tongues in
Aspic* (1973) *Starless and Bible Black*
(1974) *Red* (1974) *Discipline* (1981)
Beat (1982) *Three of a Perfect Pair*
(1984) *Vrooom* (mini CD 1994)
Thrak (CD 1995) *B'boom* (Live)
(CD 1994) *Thrakattack* (Live)
(2CD 1996) *Compilations: Frame by
Frame* (4CD 1993) *The Great
Deceiver* (Live) (1973–4) (4CD
1994)
Marillion *Script for a Jester's Tear*
(1983) *Fugazi* (1984) *Misplaced
Childhood* (1985)
Matching Mole *Matching Mole*
(1972) *Little Red Record* (1973)
National Health *National Health*
(1977) *Of Queues and Cures* (1978)
D.S. Al Coda (1981) *Complation:
The Complete National Health* (2
CD 1990)
The Nice *The Thoughts of Emerlist*

Davjack (1967) *Ars Longa Vita
Brevis* (1968) *The Nice* (1969) *Five
Bridges* (1970)
No Man *Flowermix* (1995)
Mike Oldfield *Tubular Bells* (1973)
Hergest Ridge (1974) *Ommadawn*
(1975) *Boxed* (4LP/2CD 1976)
Incantations (2LP/CD 1978) *Songs
of Distant Earth* (CD 1994)
Orb *Adventures Beyond the Ultraworld*
(1989) *UFOrb* (1992)
Ozric Tentacles *Erpsongs* (1984)
Tantric Obstacles (1985) *Live
Ethereal Cereal* (1986) *Erpland*
(2CD 1990) *Jurassic Shift* (1993)
Arborescence (1994)
Pallas *Arrive Alive* (1983) *The
Sentinel* (1984)
Anthony Phillips *The Geese and the
Ghost* (1977) *Private Parts and Pieces
Vol. 1* (1980) *Private Parts and Pieces
Vol. 2 Back to the Pavilion* (1980)
1984 (1981) *Private Parts and Pieces
Vol. 5 Twelve* (1986) *Private Parts
and Pieces Vol. 6 Ivory Moon* (1987)
Tarka (1988) *Slowdance* (1990)
Pink Floyd *The Piper at the Gates of
Dawn* (1967) *A Saucerful of Secrets*
(1968) *More* (1969) *Ummagumma*
(2LP/CD 1969) *Atom Heart
Mother* (1970) *Dark Side of the
Moon* (1973) *Wish You Were Here*
(1975) *Animals* (1977) *The Wall*
(2LP/CD 1979)
Porcupine Tree *Moonloop* EP (1993)
The Sky Moves Sideways (1994)
Procul Harum *Shine on Brightly*
(1968) *A Salty Dog* (1969) *Live
with the Edmonton Symphony
Orchestra* (1972) *Grand Hotel*
(1973)
Propaganda *Secret Wish* (1986)
Quintessence *Dive Deep* (1970)

Rameses *Space Hymns* (1970)
Mike Rutherford *Smallcreep's Day* (1980)
Paul Schütze *New Maps of Hell* (1994) *Rapture of Metals* (1995) *Site Anubis* (1996)
Second Hand *Death May be Your Santa Claus* (1971)
Slapp Happy *Desperate Straights* (1974)
Soft Machine *Soft Machine* (1968) *Volume 2* (1969) *Third* (1970) *Sixth* (2LP 1973) *Bundles* (1975) *Live at the Proms* (1970/1993) *Spaced* (1969/1996)
Spring *Spring* (1971)
Steamhammer *Steamhammer* (1968)
Strawbs *From the Witchwood* (1971)
System 7 *777* (1993) *Point 3; The Fire Album/The Water Album* (1994)
T2 *It'll All Work Out in Boomland* (1970)
This Heat *This Heat* (1976)
Trees *The Garden of Jane Delawney* (1970)
Twelfth Night *Live at the Target* (1981)
UK *UK* (1978) *Danger Money* (1979)
Ultramarine *United Kingdoms* (1993)
Van der Graaf Generator *The Least We Can Do is Wave to Each Other* (1970) *H to He, Who am the Only One* (1971) *Pawn Hearts* (1971) *Godbluff* (1975) *Still Life* (1976)
Rick Wakeman *The Six Wives of Henry VIII* (1973) *The Myths and Legends of King Arthur and the Knights of the Round Table* (1975) *No Earthly Connection* (1976)
Robert Wyatt *End of an Ear* (1970) *Rock Bottom* (1974) *Ruth is Stranger than Richard* (1975) *Compilation: Going Back a Little Bit* (2CD 1994)
Yes *Yes* (1969) *Time and a Word* (1970)

The Yes Album (1970) *Fragile* (1971) *Close to the Edge* (1972) *Yessongs* (Live) (3LP/CD 1973) *Tales from Topographic Oceans* (2LP/CD 1973) *Relayer* (1974) *Going for the One* (1977) *Tormato* (1978) *Drama* (1980) *90125* (1983) *Compilation: Yesyears* (4CD 1991)

USEFUL ADDRESSES

Art Bears, Kevin Ayers, David Bedford, Bill Bruford, Caravan, David Cross, Eat Static, Egg, Fred Frith, Gilgamesh, Gong, Hatfield and the North, Henry Cow, Steve Hillage, Hugh Hopper, Isotope, Matching Mole, National Health, Orb, Ozric Tentacles, Porcupine Tree, Dave Stewart, Robert Wyatt, all 'Canterbury': *Facelift* (fanzine), c/o Phil Howitt, 39 Nicolas Road, Manchester M21 9LG

Also: Voiceprint Records, PO Box 5, Derwentside, Co. Durham, UK DH9 7HR

Also: Richard Sinclair's Caravan of Dreams, c/o Heather Kinnear, 24 Roper Road, Canterbury, Kent, UK CT2 7EG

Also: Chris Cutler, Henry Cow, Art Bears etc.: RéR Megacorp, 79 Beulah Road, Thornton Heath, Surrey, UK DR7 8JG

Also: Dave Stewart/Barbara Gaskin Mont Campbell: Broken Records, PO Box 4416, London SW19 8XR

Also: Gong Appreciation Society (GAS), PO Box 871, Glastonbury, Somerset, UK BA6 9FE

Barclay James Harvest Fan Club (UK): 35 Wood End Green Road, Hayes, Middlesex, UK UB3 2SB

Gentle Giant: *Proclamation, The Occasional Gentle Giant Magazine*, c/o Pete Gray, 2 Coniston Close, Stukeley Meadows, Huntingdon, Cambridgeshire, UK PE18 6UD

Peter Hammill/Van der Graaf Generator: *Pilgrims, The Peter Hammill/VDGG Fanzine*: c/o Fred Tomsett, PO Box 86, Sheffield, South Yorkshire, UK S11 8XN

IQ: PO Box 24, Bishops' Waltham, Southampton, Hampshire, SO32 1XJ

Jethro Tull: *A New Day* (fanzine), 75 Wren Way, Farnborough, Hampshire, UK GU14 8TA

King Crimson/Robert Fripp: c/o Discipline Global Mobile, PO Box 1533, Salisbury, Wiltshire SP5 5ER

No-Man: PO Box 628, Hemel Hempstead, Hertfordshire, HP1 1PF

Pallas: Flat 3, 2 Pepper Street, Isle of Dogs, London E14 9RB

Anthony Phillips: c/o Alan Hewitt, 174 Salisbury Road, Everton, Liverpool IL5 6RQ

Pink Floyd: *The Amazing Pudding* (fanzine), c/o Bruno McDonald, 64 Cleveland Road, South Woodford, London E18 2A1

Yes: Yes Music Circle, 44 Oswald Close, Leatherhead, Surrey, UK KT22 9UG

General:

Audion magazine, 1 Conduit Street, Leicester, Leicestershire, UK LE2 0JN

The British Progressive Rock Directory: David Robinson, 8

Mortimer Way, Loughborough, Leicestershire, UK LE11 0EY

Classic Rock Appreciation Society, c/o Martin Hudson, 47 Brecks Lane, Brecks, Rotherham, South Yorkshire, UK S65 3JQ

Musea Records, 68 La Tinchotte, 57117 Retonfey, France

The Organ (fanzine), PO Box 790, London, UK E17 5RF

Progression (fanzine), c/o John Collinge, PO Box 7164, Lowell, MA01852, USA

Wayside Music/Cuneiform Records, PO Box 8427, Silver Spring, MD20907-8427, USA

INDEX